P9-DCN-704

SARMATIA

SCYTHIA ANTIQUA

CHERRONSS
TAURIC POOL

PONTUS EUXINUS

ASIA MINOR

Taurus M.

Cyprus

SEA

ARMENIA

Artaxata

Niphates

Abus M. Araxes R.

ATROPATIA

Masius M.

Amanus M.

Antioch

Nisibis

MESOPOT

Nineveh

Tigris R.

ARENE

ASSYRIA

Euphrates

Seleucia

Ctesiphon

Babylon R.

Balsara

Teredon

Kishon
Dan
Lake of Genesaret
Bethel
Jericho
JERUSALEM
Bethlehem
PALESTINE

Memphis

EGYPT

Nile River

Syene

RED SEA

Meroe

ARABIA

The Arabian Drouth or Desert

Persian Gulph or Bay
Balsaras haven

R. Gozan

Habor

Ecbatana

Susa

Chaspes R.

Caucasus

Hecatompylos

HYRCANIA

Parthia

MARGIANA

Ariana

MEDIA

PERSIA

Susiana

Persepolis

SEA or LAKE

LAKE ARAL

Sogd

A

Calm of Mind

John S. Diekhoff

CALM OF MIND

TERCENTENARY ESSAYS ON
Paradise Regained
AND
Samson Agonistes
IN HONOR OF
JOHN S. DIEKHOFF

Edited by Joseph Anthony Wittreich, Jr.

THE PRESS OF
CASE WESTERN RESERVE UNIVERSITY
CLEVELAND & LONDON
1971

PR
3565
C3.

Copyright © 1971 by The Press of Case Western Reserve University
Cleveland, Ohio 44106. All rights reserved.
Printed in the United States of America.
International Standard Book Number: 0–8295–0214–9.
Library of Congress Catalogue Card Number: 79–148728.

Preface

Edward Gibbon once said that only two kinds of tributes can bring honor to a man whose name is fixed to a book: one arises from "literary esteem," the other from "personal affection." For me—and for those who have joined with me in presenting this volume of essays—there is a double propriety in fixing the name of John S. Diekhoff to this book. He has distinguished himself as an eminent Miltonist, and to many of us he has been a generous friend. He has also contributed—unwittingly—the plan for this collection.

Toward the end of a semester, some years back, John Diekhoff was besieged with students who, having determined early in the semester that they were going to contribute originally to the mountain of scholarship on *Paradise Lost*, discovered that what they had to say had been said many times before. His advice was to turn to *Paradise Regained* and *Samson Agonistes*, where major critical work was yet to be done. This is the counsel that I passed on to the contributors to this volume. They have responded with a series of essays that provide fresh and sometimes interlocking perspectives on the poems that Milton published last, whatever their date of composition.

In recent years both Milton's brief epic and his tragedy have received a fair share of critical commentary, which has generated many of the nagging problems that the essays in this volume confront. While Professor Hughes' essay moves mightily over Milton's career as polemicist and poet, the other essays, intentionally narrower in compass, consider a wide range of critical issues, many of them interrelated, that *Paradise Regained* and *Samson Agonistes* individually pose. The continuity between essays is considerable, and on occasion that continuity

v

ALUMNI MEMORIAL LIBRARY

Creighton University

Omaha, Nebraska 68131

345937

is calculated. My own essay, for example, provides a context for Professor Curran's. Points in my essay that might otherwise have figured prominently in Curran's were deliberately avoided, thereby enabling him to focus more completely on the Romantic epic and also to strike off in directions that he might not otherwise have taken. Aware of many of the issues represented in the essays on *Samson Agonistes*, Professor Shawcross gathered them together in his own essay, which, besides commenting importantly and originally on Milton's tragedy, serves as an epilogue to the volume.

Although this volume fastens attention to *Paradise Regained* and *Samson Agonistes*, it does not shun the perception that Milton's poetry, from the very early lyrics to the late epics, must be taken finally as a canon—that Milton's poems together, in the words of Northrop Frye, make up "a single poetic testament." In this regard, an observation Wordsworth made on his own poetry may shed some light on Milton's. By way of defining the relationship between *The Excursion* and *The Prelude*, Wordsworth remarked that "the two works have the same kind of relation to each other . . . as the ante-chapel has to the body of a Gothic church." And the minor pieces, he says, "will be found to have such a connection with the main work as may give them claim to be likened to the little cells, oratories, and sepulchral recesses, ordinarily included in those edifices." If Milton had been moved to define so explicitly the connection between his various poems, he would probably have embraced Wordsworth's analogies, and he would certainly have seen his poems similarly entangled with one another: Milton's poems are part of a unified scheme; they share a permanent, if sometimes shifting, structure of ideas. If the canons of some poets are made up of unrelated poems, Milton's canon, like that of Blake, of Wordsworth, and to a lesser extent of Shelley, is composed of a series of poems (and, one might add, prose works) that form a grand and harmonious vision without a loss of integrity in any individual work. The essays in this volume, involved for the most part with only two of the many poems Milton wrote, illuminate one significant aspect of Milton's total vision. Until the publication of *Paradise Regained* and *Samson Agonistes* three hundred years ago, Milton's poetical statement remained open-ended; with their publication that statement was given final form.

I am proud, of course, that John Diekhoff has asked me to contribute an essay to this volume and prouder still that he allowed me to invite the other contributions. Many have joined with me in this tribute to a dedicated scholar and teacher, and it is to those many that I owe

my largest debt. Without their contributions, this volume would have
been impossible; without their wise counsel, it would have been less
adequate.

Very special thanks go to the Syndics of the Fitzwilliam Museum,
Cambridge, for permission to reproduce Blake's twelve illustrations to
Paradise Regained. The map of place names in Milton's brief epic, used
as endpapers to this volume, is reproduced from Charles Dunster's edition of the poem (1800).

J. A. W.

Madison, Wisconsin
January, 1971

Contents

The Achievement of John S. Diekhoff

When John Diekhoff received his Ph.D. from Western Reserve University in 1937, he was more than a promising apprentice; he had published his first article on Milton three years previously, in 1934, and by 1937 five more articles on Milton had appeared. In his tenure as a doctoral candidate at Western Reserve University—years during which he held the rank of instructor of English at Oberlin College—John Diekhoff was fortunate to be a student at an institution where Milton studies were represented by a scholar of international reputation. In 1966 student honored teacher with an edition of essays entitled *James Holly Hanford: John Milton, Poet and Humanist* (The Press of Western Reserve University). In that same tradition, John Diekhoff is honored by the essays in this volume dedicated to him by his students and friends.

Since Professor Hanford's influence generally pervades most Milton studies, one would expect all the more that John Diekhoff's work—early and later—would reveal something of the critical attitudes and historical awareness of his dissertation director. As one would expect, Hanford's student was cautioned to attend to the text, "that which before us lies," and to "speak of things at hand," as he trained himself for projects more ambitious. His dissertation was a textual study entitled "Milton's Craftsmanship as Revealed by the Revisions to the Poems of the Trinity College Manuscript"; from his early research, he began publishing results almost immediately. His first essay, "Rhyme in *Paradise Lost*," is as ambitious a topic as any for a young scholar. In this poem "without Rime . . . the Invention of a barbarous Age, to set off wretched matter and lame Meter," Diekhoff notices, discusses, and evaluates the many instances of obviously deliberate rhyme in the epic: "seventeen actual couplets in *Paradise Lost*" and "forty-five instances in *Paradise Lost* of rhymes separated but by a single line." In addition there are various other rhyme possibilities and potentialities noticed and catalogued in this modest essay of five pages which is concerned with presenting significant statistical data. "The rhymes in *Paradise Lost* are not mere accident," the essay concludes, and Milton scholars are provided with an accurate statistical report upon which to base their subsequent assumptions and arguments over the effects of rhyme in Milton's epic. Other articles may supersede this one in their interpretive analysis, but no one can ignore the data presented; the essay remains a starting point for any investigation of rhyme in *Paradise Lost*.

Prosodic studies based upon the Trinity Manuscript revisions continued to appear as John Diekhoff progressed on his dissertation. From rhyme he turned to the matter of terminal pause in Milton's verse, a subject which involved a detailed consideration of Milton's spelling of pronouns in emphatic positions. The study, again five pages in length, ranges over *Paradise Lost* and *Comus*. The third essay from this predoctoral period, "The Punctuation of *Comus*," was under way simultaneously with its predecessor: the earlier article reveals that its author was busy with the whole matter of punctuation in the masque. He had already discovered that "in *Comus*, for example, in the manuscript there is almost literally no punctuation at the end of lines—not even at the ends of sentences and speeches. In the 1023 lines of the Trinity Manuscript *Comus* there are only thirty terminal punctuation marks; in the 1645 edition there are thirty in the first sixty lines. Twenty-one of the thirty terminal punctuation marks in the manuscript are periods. There are twenty-one terminal periods in 212 lines of the printed text." Again focusing upon a textual matter—this time, however, the 1645 text of *Comus* is compared with the version which appears in the Trinity Manuscript—the article argues a distinction between rhetorical and prosodic punctuation and contends that Milton's punctuation "must be studied as springing from a double or triple principle of grammar, verse, and rhetoric. . . ." The intention of this article was to shed light on Milton's "versification (especially upon his use of the caesura and the verse paragraph) and upon his use of the sentence, [to] help sometimes with the interpretation of obscure passages, and [to] . . . be useful in the study of other seventeenth-century literary figures."

This early interest in *Comus* led to a subsequent and definitive article on the text of the various versions of the masque: the Trinity and the Bridgewater manuscripts, and the 1637, 1645, and 1673 printed editions. "The Text of *Comus*: 1634–1645" is a standard essay on a complicated problem; students will continue to turn to the lucid presentation of the relationships noted among versions there. Some thirty years later the essay was included in a critical anthology on *Comus* edited by John Diekhoff, a collection to which he contributed an entirely new article on the contemporary performance of the masque. His scholarly apprenticeship, however, was surely concluded with the publication of that essay on the text of *Comus*, and it is only a coincidence that his Ph.D. was awarded in the same year.

Several events bear a causal relationship to the genesis of *Milton on Himself* (Oxford University Press, 1939; rpt. Humanities Press, 1965)—an important collection recognizing the warning Milton himself uttered in the *Defensio Prima*: "We must not regard the poet's words as his own, but consider who it is who speaks." While this quotation is not (surprisingly) included in the volume, Diekhoff obviously had it in mind when he wrote that "to let Satan or Christ speak for Milton is comparable, almost, to letting Iago or Othello speak for Shakespeare." While the volume prints its extracts under twelve subject divisions (with a chronological arrangement within divisions and with extensive cross-references)—"A Plan of Life," "1608–1654," "Personal Appearance," "Love," "Friendship," "Morality," "Blindness," "Poetic Aspirations and Achievements," "Inspiration," "Prose," "The Secretaryship," "Miscellaneous"—it scrupulously avoids assuming that a poetic speaker voices Milton's own specific concerns. Thus the book presents a point of view about Miltonic autobiography opposed to that characteristic of an important predecessor, E. M. W. Tillyard's *The Miltonic Setting: Past and Present* (Cambridge University Press, 1939). There Tillyard assumes that Milton is speaking in an authentic autobiographical voice in the "Vacation Exercise" when he weighs "in his mind two kinds of 'epic.'" And he claims that *Elegia Sexta* is Milton's "personal self-dedication" to the poet's vocation. One recalls further that Professor Hanford, whose *Milton Handbook* contained a long chapter of autobiographical excerpts from the prose of Milton accompanied by additional selections from the major biographies, also seconded Tillyard's assumptions that frequently there was no distinction between Milton himself and his persona. *Milton on Himself* was early conceived and begun as an inclusive collection to which Miltonists could turn when they found themselves tempted but not satisfied by Hanford's necessarily restricted selections in the *Handbook*. We can imagine Hanford working on the third edition of the *Handbook*, published in 1939, while his former student compiled his selections for *Milton on Himself*. While the book's immediate predecessor, then, was the first chapter of the old *Handbook*, and while it had its predecessors in Hiram Corson's *An Introduction to the Prose and Poetical Works* (Macmillan, 1899) and James G. Graham's *Autobiography of Milton, or Milton's Life in His Own Words* (London, 1872), none of these predecessors had the advantage of the Columbia Milton from which Diekhoff's book quotes. S. B. Liljegren's charges against Milton are answered as comprehensively as possible by quoting a text which was the most trustworthy to date.

The same year as *Milton on Himself* appeared, so did an article more ambitious than its predecessor on the text of *Comus* and one which had its genesis in Diekhoff's thesis: "Milton's Prosody in the Poems of the Trinity Manuscript." Working with the contentions of the third edition (Oxford University Press, 1921) of Robert Bridges' *Milton's Prosody*, Diekhoff's article attempts to determine how Milton scanned his verses and concludes that through a series of "fictions" (chief of which was elision) Milton "regarded his verses [*i.e.*, the blank verse] as regularly iambic and decasyllabic." Careful, detailed reading (especially according to the principal rules of elision as they are inferred from practice in *Comus*) of the Trinity Manuscript poems corroborates the general truth of Bridges' assumptions about Miltonic elision: "In *Comus*, then, as in *Paradise Lost*, we find Milton writing syllabic verse, verse which he kept decasyllabic by means of certain for the most part clearly defined liberties. In *Comus*, however, regular as it is, there still remain a considerable number of verses in which we find extra-metrical syllables. These Milton allows himself in *Comus* (as Verity observes) at the end of the line, in the middle after some pause, or in both places."

The extremely detailed analysis of prosody concludes with a general suggestion that may have influenced John Shawcross' subsequent article ("Establishment of a Text of Milton's Poems Through a Study of *Lycidas*," *Papers of the Bibliographical Society of America*, LVI [1962], 317–331) on the importance of a study of *Lycidas* in order to establish criteria for a plausible text of all Milton's work. *Lycidas* is, Diekhoff claims, "in many ways the most interesting of Milton's poems, from the standpoint of prosody, and is certainly the most interesting in the Trinity Manuscript." While he cites Saintsbury's *History of English Prosody* as his major source for the discussion, still the latter part of this paper is one of the more lucid arguments on the effect of rhyme and cadence in *Lycidas*. Again, as with the article on *Comus*, this work remains a standard reference for all students of Milton, and, again, it is not difficult to see in it something of the significance of Diekhoff's doctoral research and no little of the influence of his supervisor.

In 1940 John Diekhoff left Oberlin, where he had taught for eleven years, to accept a post at Queens College as assistant professor of English. In that year before the war and a few years before his own military service was to begin, he had been working on and published a detailed Miltonic *exempla* of T. S. Eliot's general thesis in "The Function of Criticism." In that essay Eliot had remarked that "the larger part of the labour of an author in composing his work is critical labour; the labour of sifting, combining, constructing, expunging, testing: this frightful toil is as much critical as creative." Diekhoff's article, "Critical Activity of the Poetic Mind: John Milton," represents (with the possible exception of a short note to follow, "A Note on *Comus*, Lines 75–77") the last fruits of his substantial research into the revisions of the Trinity Manuscript poems published before he completed work on his full-length study of *Paradise Lost*. That study was substantially completed before 1943 and before his various duties in the office of the Director of Military Training from 1943 to 1946. Proof of its progress is apparent in a 1942 article on "The Function of the Prologues in *Paradise Lost*." There Diekhoff argues that each of the "prologues" in *Paradise Lost* has a narrative as well as a rhetorical function, for in each the "speaker" marks a stage in the argument and furnishes proof of his own special abilities to conduct such an "argument." This interest in the speaker as rhetorician and the poem as rhetorical argument was part of that major study published after the war—*Milton's Paradise Lost: A Commentary on the Argument* (Columbia University Press, 1946; rpt. Humanities Press, 1958). C. S. Lewis' *A Preface to Paradise Lost* (Oxford University Press, 1941) and Douglas Bush's *Paradise Lost in Our Time: Some Comments* (Cornell University Press, 1945) were the two important predecessors of Diekhoff's book in that decade. Diekhoff's book was completed before Lewis' was published, but unfortunately a severe paper shortage in America delayed its publication. Unlike those of his contemporaries, however, Diekhoff's book is not a "defense" of *Paradise Lost*; rather it is a careful explication of the Miltonic argument, a delineation of "what Milton's conception of virtuous action is, what the problem and what the obligation of the human individual is, what the reward for perseverance and what the penalty for failure." The book was important enough to be reviewed by, among

others, E. M. W. Tillyard, Allan H. Gilbert, A. S. P. Woodhouse, French
R. Fogle, and Elizabeth Marie Pope. In the *Review of English Studies*,
XXXIII (1947), Tillyard commented that Diekhoff's presentation of
Milton's argument was done "with care, subtle perception, good sense,
and in the briefest space compatible with clarity. . . . Diekhoff's solution
of the *felix culpa* problems," he concluded, "or whether Paradise was
or was not well lost, is masterly. . . . As a whole, Diekhoff's is the best
exposition of Milton's argument there is." Diekhoff's short study, along
with those by Bush and Lewis, will remain a model of precision, skill,
and economy for many a modern scholar. Each of these important
books delivered its argument and designed its strategies in considerably
under two hundred pages.

    Although his interest in Milton remained strong in the decades
after the publication of his book on *Paradise Lost*, John Diekhoff turned
his energies and abilities more and more to larger issues in education,
leaving Queens College for the post of director for the Center of Liberal
Education for Adults at the University of Chicago in 1950. He relin-
quished that post in 1952 to return to New York—this time to Hunter
College, where he held the title of Professor of Education and Director
of the Office of Institutional Research (1953–1956). Soon his interest
in adult education was to attract the attention of Western Reserve University, whose Cleveland College had long been an established urban
education center with its separate faculty and staff entirely devoted to
the adult full- and part-time undergraduate. For a period of seven
years, from 1956 to 1963, he served as Dean of Cleveland College, and
his versatility is revealed by the fact that his appointment carried with
it the title of Professor of Education in the College of Arts and Sciences.
Unfortunately, his duties as Dean left him less time for Milton research,
as his time was spent administering a large academic program. Except
for a two-year appointment as Professor of Higher Education at the
University of Michigan from 1963 to 1965 the latter part of Diekhoff's
career was spent in Cleveland at Western Reserve University.

    While one might not expect Milton essays during this period, one
might still expect that some publications would result from this wealth
of administrative experience. There was an important book on *The
Domain of the Faculty* (Harper, 1965) and an impressive report on
the whole matter of NDEA and the modern foreign languages (1965).
This latter report, commissioned by the Modern Language Association,
gave Diekhoff frequent occasion to cite the work of another Miltonist
equally interested in the position of foreign languages and foreign-
language study in America: William Riley Parker. There was also an

article about Milton's education—"The General Education of a Poet: John Milton"—which was a discussion of the poet from the viewpoint of Diekhoff's new interests. In 1965, his Michigan appointment over, he returned to Western Reserve as Associate Dean of Faculty and Professor of English. After little more than a decade, he would have the opportunity to teach Milton again, but not before he was also asked to serve, "occasionally," as Acting Dean of the Graduate School and then as Chairman of the English Department, and "regularly" as Vice Provost of the newly federated Case Western Reserve University. He continued to serve on the Commission on Colleges and Universities of the North Central Association, and on the editorial board of the Yale Milton; he has only recently co-authored a report on the influence of the private sector upon public education in the state of Tennessee. The profession remains fortunate to have a man of Diekhoff's capabilities, interests, enthusiasm, and energy.

Return to Western Reserve meant Diekhoff's reacquaintance with "academic" Milton, his resumption of teaching and graduate supervision, and the revival of his scholarly publication in Milton studies. In 1966 his edition of seminal essays by Holly Hanford was published. In each of those essays one finds lucid and succinct formulations of many of the attitudes toward Milton that we continue to acknowledge as "correct." These are essays which changed the course of Milton scholarship in the twentieth century and which still remain models for method and inquiry.

Diekhoff's return to Cleveland also meant that we would soon be acquainted, for I had joined the English Department the year before. But most importantly for him it meant additional time to study, to teach, and to write. John Diekhoff immediately assembled another book of essays—this time important works on *Comus*—which included a new essay of his own, "A Maske at Ludlow" (his earlier piece on the text makes up part of the volume also). His essay urbanely covers matters of casting and staging, mentions the matter of "cuts," and places special emphasis on the topical center of the courtly entertainment: its "glozing words" of courtesy and flattery. These eleven essays are accompanied by a text of the Bridgewater *Comus*. Diekhoff knew that the textual inclusion was the *sine qua non* of his work. Along with it, students now had the advantage of a rich selection of critical materials to facilitate their own work with Milton's poem.

The essays presented here are part of a double tribute being paid to John Diekhoff by his colleagues. At the annual Christmas meeting of the Milton Society of America, a group which he served as President for the year 1957–1958, he was honored as Scholar of the Year, and as part of the tribute paid to him the forthcoming publication of *Calm of Mind* was announced. I am pleased to participate in the dedication of these essays on *Paradise Regained* and *Samson Agonistes* to my colleague and friend.

JAMES G. TAAFFE

Case Western Reserve University
Cleveland, Ohio
January, 1971

John S. Diekhoff: A Bibliography

Entries under individual headings are chronologically arranged.

BOOKS AND MONOGRAPHS

Milton on Himself. Oxford University Press, 1939; rpt. Humanities Press, 1965.

Milton's Paradise Lost: A Commentary on the Argument. Columbia University Press, 1946; rpt. Humanities Press, 1958.

Democracy's College. Harper & Brothers, 1950.

The Domain of the Faculty. Harper & Brothers, 1956.

Prologue to Teaching (with Marjorie B. Smiley). Oxford University Press, 1959.

Tomorrow's Professors. Fund for the Advancement of Education, 1959.

NDEA and Modern Foreign Languages. Modern Foreign Language Association of America, 1965.

A Maske at Ludlow. The Press of Case Western Reserve University, 1968.

Private Higher Education in Tennessee (with Ida Long Rogers). Tennessee Council of Private Colleges, 1970.

ARTICLES ON ENGLISH LITERATURE

"Rhyme in *Paradise Lost*." *PMLA*, XLIX (1934), 539–543.

"Terminal Pause in Milton's Verse." *Studies in Philology*, XXXII (1935), 235–239.

"The Happy Ending of *Adam Bede*." *ELH*, III (1936), 221–227.

"The Punctuation of *Comus*." *PMLA*, LI (1936), 757–768.

"*Lycidas*, Line 10." *Philological Quarterly*, XVI (1937), 408–410.

"The Milder Shades of Purgatory." *Modern Language Notes*, LII (1937), 409–410.

"The Text of *Comus*, 1634–1635." *PMLA*, LII (1937), 705–727. Reprinted in *A Maske at Ludlow*. The Press of Case Western Reserve University, 1968.

"Milton's Prosody in the Trinity MS." *PMLA*, LIV (1939), 153–183.

"Critical Activity of the Poetic Mind: John Milton." *PMLA*, LV (1940), 748–772.

"A Note on *Comus*, ll. 75–77." *Philological Quarterly*, XX (1941), 603–604.

"The Function of the Prologues in *Paradise Lost*." *PMLA*, LVII (1942), 697–704.

"Eve, the Devil, and *Areopagitica*." *Modern Language Quarterly*, V (1944), 429–434.

"The Trinity Manuscript and the Dictation of *Paradise Lost*." *Philological Quarterly*, XXVIII (1949), 44–52.

"The General Education of a Poet: John Milton." *Journal of General Education*, XIV (1962), 10–21.

"Foreword" to James Holly Hanford, *John Milton: Poet and Humanist*. The Press of Western Reserve University, 1960. Pp. v–viii.

"Eve's Dream and the Paradox of Fallible Perfection." *Milton Quarterly*, IV (1970), 5–7.

ARTICLES ON EDUCATION

"A Finger-Post for Colleges." *Education*, LIV (1934), 559–561.

"The Mission and the Method of Army Language Teaching." *Bulletin of the American Association of University Professors*, XXXI (1945), 606–620.

"Staffing the Colleges." *The Journal of Higher Education*, XX (1949), 445–456, 490.

"Freedom or Equality: Federal Aid for Schools and Colleges." *The Educational Forum*, XIV (1950), 469–476.

"General Education in Wartime: A Lesson from World War II." *School and Society*, XXXVI (1950), 241–245.

"Responsibility for the Training of College Teachers." *Journal of General Education*, III (1951), 224–231.

"A Cooperative Experiment in Adult Education." *School and Society*, XXXVIII (1952), 167–169.

"An Experiment in Adult Education." *School and Society*, XXXVIII (1952), 113–118.

"Keeping Pace with Youth." *National Parent-Teacher*, XLVII (1952), 16–18.

"Let Mr. Chips Fall Where He May." *The American Scholar*, XXI (1952), 275–282.

"Time Off for Good Behavior." *Journal of General Education*, IV (1952), 41–47.

"No Place for Privilege." *The Educational Forum*, XVII (1953), 169–175.

"And Haply May Remember." *The Educational Forum*, XVIII (1954), 482–485.

"Father and Son." *The CEA Critic*, XVI (1955), 1, 3.

"From the Cradle to the Grave," in "The University's Role in Adult Education—A Symposium." *The Journal of Higher Education*, XXVI (1955), 10–12.

"A Program of Faculty In-Service Training," with Ruth G. Weintraub. *The Journal of Higher Education*, XXVI (1955), 343–350.

"Schooling for Maturity." *Notes and Essays on Education for Adults*, No. 13, Center for the Study of Liberal Education for Adults, May, 1955, pp. 1–19.

"Who Teaches Teachers What?" *The Educational Forum*, XX (1956), 229–238.

"The Alumni University." *The Journal of Higher Education*, XXVIII (1957), 353–361.

"The Alumnus and His Alma Mater." *Association of American Colleges Bulletin*, XLIII (1957), 557–562.

"Population and Higher Education." *The Educational Forum*, XXII (1958), 203–208.

"Learning—Perpetual Adventure." *The National Parent-Teacher*, LIV (1959), 16–18.

"The School Conspiracy." *Educational Research Bulletin*, XXXVIII (1959), 197–202, 224.

"Family Preparation for College." *The National Parent-Teacher*, LV (1960), 8–10.

"Memorandum for the Central Planning Committee." *Clearing House Publication*, Center for the Study of Liberal Education for Adults, November, 1960, pp. 1–49.

"The Passing Buck Stops Here." *Educational Research Bulletin*, XXXIX (1960), 1–10.

"Residential Education: No Place Like Home." *Adult Education*, X (1960), 238–246.

"The Teacher of Adults," in *On Teaching Adults*, ed. Marilyn V. Miller. Center for the Study of Liberal Education for Adults, Chicago, 1960, pp. 77–91.

"Untaught Teachers." *Saturday Review*, XLIII (1960), 90, 103.

"Many Opinions." *Papers on Adult Education and Related Subjects*, No. 20, June, 1961. University College of Syracuse University, Syracuse, New York. Pp. 1–11.

"Teacher Go Home." *Saturday Review*, XLIV (1961), 52–54.

". . . The Ability of the Individuals Comprising It. . . ." *The N.U.E.A. Spectator*, National University Extension Association, October-November, 1962. Pp. 14–15.

"The Last Encyclopedists." *Saturday Review*, XLV (1962), 62–63; recorded for the blind, *Choice Magazine Listening*, December, 1962.

"The Academic Freedom of the Student." *North Central News Bulletin*, October, 1963, pp. 4–21.

"Higher Education," in *Becoming an Educator*, ed. Van Cleve Morris. Houghton Mifflin, 1963. Pp. 251–288.

"How to Select a College for Your Youngster." *The PTA Magazine*, LVIII (1963), 2–4.

"How to Visit a College." *The PTA Magazine*, LVIII (1963), 20–22.

"Some Important Research Gaps in the Teaching of College English," in *Needed Research in the Teaching of English*, ed. Erwin R. Steinberg. U.S. Dept. of Health, Education, and Welfare, Office of Education, 1963. Pp. 21–25.

"We Need a Philosophy." *Occasional Papers*, No. 6, Center for the Study of Liberal Education for Adults, Chicago, 1963. Pp. 1–8.

"The General Education of the College English Teacher," in *The Education of Teachers of English*, ed. Alfred H. Grommon. Appleton-Century-Crofts, 1963. Pp. 516–521.

"Growing Time," in *Proceedings of the Seminar on Leadership in University Adult Education.* Michigan State University, 1963. Pp. 3–12.

"Adam, Automation, and the American College. *Journal of General Education,* XVI (1964), 215–225.

"The College Graduate as a Lifetime Reader." *ALA Bulletin,* LVIII (1964), 995–997, 1000–1002.

"The Mind Is Its Own Place." *The PTA Magazine,* LVIII (1964), 12–14.

"The University as Leader and Laggard." *The Journal of Higher Education,* XXXV (1964), 181–188.

"Priorities in Language Education." *PMLA,* LXXX (1965), 24–28.

"The Professional School in the University." *Journal of Education for Librarianship,* VI (1965), 103–110.

"Algo Henderson." *Newsletter of the Center for the Study of Higher Education,* University of Michigan, August, 1966. Pp. 3–6.

"Keep Questions Open." *International Journal of American Linguistics,* XXXII (1966), 1–11.

"The Learning Man." *Outlook,* Western Reserve University, Winter, 1966. Pp. 10–12.

"The Administrator and His Faculty Colleagues." *Proceedings of the 48th Annual Meeting of the Tennessee College Association,* Nashville, Tennessee, March 27, 1969, XLIX, 16–25.

"My Fair Ludlow." *Educational Reform,* XXXIII (1969), 281–288.

REVIEWS

Wolfe, Don M. *Milton in the Puritan Revolution.* New York, 1941.
In *Sewanee Review,* XLIX (1941), 426–428.

Kelley, Maurice. *This Great Argument.* Princeton, 1941.
In *Sewanee Review,* L (1942), 266–267.

Parker, William Riley. *Milton's Contemporary Reputation.* Columbus, 1940.
In *Modern Language Notes,* LVII (1942), 403–404.

Cornford, F. M. *Microcosmographia Academica, Being a Guide for the Young Academic Politician.* Chicago, 1945.
In *Saturday Review of Literature,* XXIX (1946), 69–70.

Koos, Leonard V. *Integrating High School and College.* New York, 1946.

Stiles, Dan. *High Schools for Tomorrow.* New York, 1946.
In *Saturday Review of Literature,* XXIX (1946), 28.

Gilbert, Allan H. *On the Composition of "Paradise Lost": A Study of the Ordering and Insertion of Material.* Chapel Hill, 1947.
In *Modern Language Notes,* LXIV (1949), 129–130.

Rudy, S. Willis. *The College of the City of New York: A History, 1847-1947.* New York, 1949.
In *Journal of Higher Education,* XXII (1951), 222.

Perspectives on a Troubled Decade: Science, Philosophy, and Religion, 1939–1949. Ed. Lyman Bryson, Louis Finkelstein, and R. M. MacIver. New York, 1950.
In *Journal of Higher Education,* XXII (1951), 450–451.

Tillyard, E.M.W. *Studies in Milton.* New York, 1951.
In *Saturday Review of Literature,* XXXV (1952), 14.

Essert, Paul L. *Creative Leadership of Adult Education.* New York, 1951.
In *Journal of Higher Education,* XXIII (1952), 226.

General Education. Ed. Nelson B. Henry. Chicago, 1952.
In *Journal of Higher Education,* XXIV (1953), 101–102.

Jones, Howard Mumford. *One Great Society: Humane Learning in the United States.* New York, 1959. Review Article.
In *Journal of Higher Education,* XXXI (1960), 167–170.

JANE CERNY
CASE WESTERN RESERVE UNIVERSITY

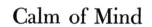

Calm of Mind

Milton's *Eikon Basilike*

MERRITT Y. HUGHES
1893–1971

At various times Milton worked on four royal images: one human, one diabolic, and two divine. On the first he worked as an iconoclast. On the second he worked as an ironist. On the two last he worked as a poet, an iconoplast or creative shaper of images. Without any poetic purpose to give form or depth to his tract, he wrote *Eikonoklastes* to shatter the image of the "martyr king," Charles I, which John Gauden, later bishop of Exeter and Worcester, had patched together and published anonymously under the title *Eikon Basilike*. It need detain us no longer than is necessary to observe its contrast with his equally severe ironic portrait of Satan in *Paradise Lost*.

The experience of writing *Eikonoklastes* could contribute but little to the creation of Milton's Satanic *eikon basilike*. Unlike Gauden's image of King Charles, Satan must be a figure of distinct intelligence— sagacious in every way except in his misprision for wisdom. Milton's main quarrel with Charles had been with his limited intelligence, the "serious" but far from "industrious mind" which for C. V. Wedgwood explains his lack of interest in administration, his ignorance of the public concerns which should have been diplomatic bridges between him and Parliament.[1] Blow by blow, as he considers Charles' negotiations with the leaders of Parliament, Milton constantly wonders at the king's characteristic readiness to call "his obstinacy, Reason, and other mens reason, Faction."[2] Milton is amazed at the king's professed adoration for Reason, which he calls "the '*Divinest power,*' thereby to intimate as if at reasoning, as at his own weapon, no man were so able as himself. Might we be so happy as to know where these monuments of his Reason may be seen, for in his actions & his writing they appear as thinly as could

1

be expected from the meanest parts."[3] The writing of *Eikonoklastes* was irksome to Milton because he had no respect for the mind that was mirrored in *Eikon Basilike*. It had nothing in his eyes to relate it to divine reason, participation in which stamped men as made in the image of God, and which was God's prime attribute as ruler of the universe.

THE COUNTERFEIT *EIKON BASILIKE*—SATAN

In writing *Paradise Lost* Milton was delighted to have as a character a highly intelligent aspirant to kingship, even though the image to be drawn must—in the words of Abdiel—be mad enough to be to himself "enthrall'd" (VI.181). He must rebel against Wisdom itself and finally have to acknowledge the fact in the famous soliloquy ending in a farewell to hope, fear, and remorse: "Evil be thou my Good" (IV.110). Behind Satan are the scenes in Hell which are most dreadful because the inhabitants fail to improve their situation even by achieving technical mastery over its mineral resources to build *"Pandaemonium,* the high Capital / Of Satan and his Peers" (I.756–757). There they will promptly commit themselves to a military state to be forever dominated by hunger for *Lebensraum.* Their finest hour in Hell has come and gone with the display of the "Imperial Ensign" (I.536) and the blasts of the trumpets heard when

> through the gloom were seen
> Ten thousand Banners rise into the Air
> With Orient Colours waving: with them rose
> A Forrest huge of Spears: and thronging Helms
> Appear'd, and serried Shields in thick array
> Of depth immeasurable. (I.544–549)

Satan's object in constructing Pandaemonium has been to create a setting for an imperial conspiracy, not for the establishment of a civil government. In Hell he must become a figure no less commanding than when in Heaven he first led his hosts into battle, sitting in his "Sunbright Chariot," "exalted as a God," and "Idol of Majestie Divine" (VI. 99–101). The trappings are those of a human idol, "a person that is the object of excessive or supreme devotion or that usurps the place of God in human affections."[4] The devils' idolatry suggests the ecstatic welcome of Napoleon's supporters when he returned from exile in Elba, or the surrender of masses of civilians to the charisma of Hitler in Berlin and

Vienna. Satan's great Capital is serving its purpose; in reviving his military glory as a field marshal in the celestial battle, Milton is transforming the great Capital into a royal image, an established *eikon basilike*. Hence the pageantry of the opening scene in Book II:

> High on a Throne of Royal State, which far
> Outshon the wealth of *Ormus* and of *Ind,*
> Or where the gorgeous East with richest hand
> Showrs on her Kings *Barbaric* Pearl and Gold,
> Satan exalted sat . . . (ll. 1–5)

For a moment the pageant dazzles, but to sophisticated readers the allusions to the splendors of the sultans of the East would suggest tyranny. "Turkish Tyranny"[5] was a European scandal which Milton regarded in *Eikonoklastes* as comparable to the kind of royal absolutism at which Charles I had aimed. Elsewhere he had recalled a widely believed story of a conspiracy in the entourage of Catherine de Médicis to follow the massacre of St. Bartholomew by the establishment of "a plain Turkish Tyranny . . . in *France.*"[6] Satan's oriental aura marks him as a tyrant. Later, in *Paradise Regained,* his cohorts acknowledge him as such by unanimously hailing him as "their Great Dictator" (I.113). But in *Paradise Lost* his followers have no sense of being slaves. As E. E. Stoll observed, "Amid their pastimes [in Hell], Satan's cohorts are demigods, though dethroned"; in public debate they speak boldly, like peers of the realm.[7] And with Stoll we must give the devil his due as a political strategist in Pandaemonium no less than as a seducer in Eden. We have to side with A. J. A. Waldock[8] against C. S. Lewis about his first harangue from the throne as betraying signs of weakening intelligence. His audience is not too discouraged by military defeat to feel anything but satisfaction in his claim to have "Establish't . . . a safe unenvied Throne" (II.23) for himself as their recognized protector. Now he hopes to consolidate his position by a diplomatic conquest of new territory. He actually secures himself by undertaking to discover that territory without any help from his subordinates. The debate ends with his rhetorical question:

>   Wherefore do I assume
> These Royalties, and not refuse to Reign,
> Refusing to accept as great a share
> Of hazard as of honour, due alike
> To him who Reigns, and so much to him due

        Of hazard more, as he above the rest
        High honourd sits? (II.450–456)

    The rhetoric is Homeric. It echoes Sarpedon's appeal to Glaucus
to justify their royal glory as kings of the Lycians by leading a last Tro-
jan attack on the Greek ships (*Iliad* XII.310–328). But recent study of
Satan's rhetoric has exposed his arts as familiar to schoolboys, who were
commonly introduced to the "gracefull and ornate Rhetorick taught out
of the rule of Plato, Aristotle, Phalereus, Cicero, Hermogenes, Logi-
nus," as Milton assumed in *Of Education* that they should be.[9] He also
assumed that they would be immunized against imposture by learning
of Aristotle's distinction between the rhetoric of true orators, whose
vocation is simply to give the people the truth with confidence that it will
prevail, and that of dissembling sophists, who are masters of such "dear
Wit and gay Rhetorick" (*A Mask*, l. 789) as Comus displayed to the
undeceivable Lady. Inculcation of a sensitive revulsion against sophistry
was—as J. M. Major shows in "Milton's View of Rhetoric"[10]—an accepted
duty of the epic poet, though Milton took pleasure in practicing it when
he put specious words into Belial's mouth in the demonic council in
Pandaemonium and into Satan's mouth in all his addresses to his victims in both Hell and Eden.
    The basis of such false oratory is analyzed by J. M. Steadman in
"*Ethos* and *Dianoia*: Character and Rhetoric in *Paradise Lost*."[11] An
ordinarily good education should prepare men to recognize such
"feigned oratory" by penetrating the character and motivation of a
speaker. The "dual character and dual orientation" of Satan should deceive no one, for they are obviously addressed to the discerning judgment of readers as much as they are to their imaginary audiences.
Overtly the speeches are attempts to deceive the audiences. Covertly
they are designed to exercise the perspicacity of the readers. They betray the ethos of the speakers to watchful readers not only by the falsity
of their reasoning but also by their success with their gullible audiences.
    But what if the readers are swept along with the imaginary audi-
ences as many audiences of *Julius Caesar* have been seduced along
with the Roman mob by Mark Antony's incendiary speech? To protect
his readers a poet may intervene with a warning as a playwright cannot. In the epic tradition the poet's intervention was a recognized part
of his creation of personalities. Modern recognition of it was signalized
by J. H. Summers in *The Muse's Method*,[12] and definite appreciation of
Milton's sustaining epic voice was achieved when Anne Davidson Ferry

made us sensitive to its multiform presence.[13] L. L. Martz, defending Milton's emergences in *Paradise Lost* against Waldock's objection to them, welcomed the poet's "individual voice . . . everywhere in the poem, advising, exhorting, warning, praising, denouncing, lamenting. . . ."[14] In *Surprised by Sin* Stanley Fish vindicated the intrusion of Milton's warning voice as an irritant essential to the function of serious epic.[15] In a study of Milton's decorum Thomas Kranidas extended our perception of Milton's editorial manipulation of detail and tone in Satan's speeches as a main device in shaping his image.[16]

Two years before the publication of Waldock's challenging book B. Rajan exposed the patent perversions of fact which often escape notice in Satan's speeches—perversions which should "amuse, rather than perplex, those who were brought up to think of him as the first liar."[17] Recently J. S. Lawry has explored the "labyrinth of unreason" which explains the "Athenian rhetoric" of Satan's temptation speeches to his followers in Heaven and to Eve in Eden.[18] He implies that Milton's aptest image of Satan may be that of "Some Orator renown'd / In Athens or free Rome" (*PL* IX.670–671), who is rising to betray the first obligation of an orator, which is to truth. Satan's addresses are all betrayals of the character of the true orator; almost all offer opportunities for the sophisticated Christian reader to recognize what J. M. Steadman calls his "mastery of sophistical argument and ethical and pathetic proof, his skilful use of 'Idolisms' and fallacies, and his ability to dissemble his real motives and assume the character most likely to win his audience's favor and belief."[19]

The outward form and the character of the aspirant to "the Throne and Monarchy of God" (I.42) have declined from their princely nature in Heaven to that of an exposed and exiled pretender. He is coming to resemble what C. S. Lewis called "more a Lie than a Liar, a personified self-contradiction."[20] What is happening, says Rajan, is the "recoil" of his passions and their attendant sophistries upon "the intelligence which released them."[21] He himself has become a mere image and idol, the false *eikon basilike* misruling a horde of adventurers living on illusions to which he and they are slaves.

THE SON—A ROYAL IMAGE REFLECTED

Among many surviving French representations of the Trinity we have two which show the royally robed Father and Son who sit facing each other while a dove hovers close above them. In one case the faces and figures seem to be nearly identical. In the other the faces differ slightly, but without suggesting any imparity. If a dramatic dialogue could be imagined as taking place between them, it could not possibly take the tone of filial wisdom prevailing over paternal rigidity; the Son's vindication of mercy as no less applicable than justice to the treatment of fallen man would be inconceivable. The outcome of the dialogue would have to be the same sympathetic filial compliance with the paternal hope for mankind which ends the dramatic dialogue in Heaven. At its end Milton has the listening angels wonder that the Son's

> meek aspect
> Silent yet spake, and breath'd immortal love
> To mortal men, above which only shon
> Filial obedience: as a sacrifice
> Glad to be offer'd, he attends the will
> Of his great Father. (*PL* III.266–271)

Again in the incarnate Son of *Paradise Regained* the angels see obedience as the essence of the

> True Image of the Father whether thron'd
> In the bosom of bliss, and light of light
> Conceiving, or remote from Heaven, enshrin'd
> In fleshly Tabernacle, and human form . . . (IV.596–599)

And filial obedience is the first consideration to enter his mind as he awakens from exhaustion after his first temptation by Satan. From the sting of famine he says that he fears

> no harm,
> Nor mind it, fed with better thoughts that feed
> Mee hungring more to do my Fathers will. (II.257–259)

And in the opening lines of the poem the essence of his assured victory over Satan in the impending temptations is declared to be his "firm obedience" to that will, in contrast with the disobedience which lost Eden for mankind.

But in itself obedience is not necessarily a virtue and need not imply sympathy between master and servant, father and son. In a political setting it may be mere compliance with custom or surrender to tyranny. In *Paradise Lost* the angels who praise obedience are aware that it must be rooted in love and wisdom. It is hard to think that the kind of honor for parents which is imposed upon children in the Fifth Commandment was respected by Milton himself on the basis of its promised reward of long life (Exod. 20:5, 12) or its involvement in the threatened sanctions of a "jealous God" to secure obedience to the entire Decalogue. There is no better evidence of Milton's approval of Jesus' assertion of the primacy of the First Commandment—"Thou shalt love the Lord thy God with all thy heart, and with all thy soul, and with all thy mind" (Matt. 22:37)—than its mark on Raphael's explanation of loyal angelic obedience to God—"freely we serve, / Because we freely love" (V.538–539). More explicit is his departing advice to Adam:

> Be strong, live happie, and love, but first of all
> Him whom to love is to obey . . . (VIII.633–634)

More striking, though less conspicuous in the text, are Michael's observations to Adam about the Savior's satisfaction of God's law and about the role of love in the history of the Church. In the Savior's career on earth Michael foresees that he will fulfill the law of God

> Both by obedience and by love, though love
> Alone fulfill the Law. (XII.403–404)

Here love is directed toward both God and mankind; divine justice is satisfied and humanity is redeemed by the Savior's love, the "charitie so deare" (III.216) to which the Father had appealed with seeming doubt whether so precious a virtue could be found in all Heaven. Finally, when Michael renews the promise of the "Paradise within" for Adam and for humanity, and names the virtues essential to it, he omits obedience. In renewing the promise the archangel deprecates mere knowledge of it as something far short of the attainment. His final admonition to Adam is,

>   . . . add
> Deeds to thy knowledge answerable, add Faith,
> Add vertue, Patience, Temperance, add Love,
> By name to come call'd Charitie, the soul
> Of all the rest: then wilt thou not be loath
> To leave this Paradise, but shalt possess
> A paradise within thee happier farr. (XII.581–587)

Besides being man's divinely commanded first duty to God, love or loyalty was a feudal obligation to kings, sworn by both noblemen and knights. Taking an unromantic view of it in "The Chivalric Cast of Milton's Epic Hero," J. E. Seaman views the character of the Son of God in both *Paradise Lost* and *Paradise Regained* as resting upon "the basic heroic principles . . . [of] obedience to God and the charity which is inseparable from it."[22] The link with chivalric romance has been noticed by Barbara Kiefer Lewalski as a fleeting analogy between the Savior and "those later Adam-Christ figures, the knights-errant":[23]

> Knights of *Logres*, or of *Lyones*,
> *Lancelot* or *Pelleas*, or *Pellenore*. (*PR* II.360–361)

Seaman sees the tradition of the questing knight as rooted in St. Paul's expanding metaphor exhorting the Ephesians to "put on the whole armour of God . . . having your loins girt about with truth, and having the breastplate of righteousness . . . the shield of faith . . . the helmet of salvation, and the sword of the Spirit, which is the word of God" (Eph. 6:13–17). The panoply is not a dress uniform. It answers to the young Savior's vision of his future:

> . . . that my way must lie
> Through many a hard assay even to the death,
> E're I the promis'd Kingdom can attain. (*PR* I.263–265)

In the developing dialogue with Satan, the Savior will speak of the Father as "Truth" itself. Satan tries to corrupt his loyalty to truth with an image of himself as the easily potential lord of Parthia and Rome. His reply is a question (referring to his Father):

> What if he hath decreed that I shall first
> Be try'd in humble state, and things adverse,
> By tribulations, injuries, insults,
> Contempts, and scorns, and snares, and violence,
> Suffering, abstaining, quietly expecting
> Without distrust or doubt . . . (*PR* III.188–193)

Betraying no lust or sense of royal power of his own, the Savior calls himself simply "the Son of God." His attitude to Satan's offers of worldly power is the steady conviction that to lay down a kingdom is

> Far more magnanimous, then to assume. (*PR* II.483)

Unable to comprehend such magnanimity, Satan thinks he can understand the components of the "large heart" of the Son of God. Flatter-

ing him with an appraisal of his "God-like Vertues," Satan says that his
heart

> Contains of good, wise, just, the perfect shape. (*PR* III.11)

What he means by "good" and "just" the devil does not explain, but
his use of "wise" makes it clear that he understands political shrewdness.
Advertisement of his talents would make the Savior the universally consulted oracle of policy. He is unhappy at the thought of such prestige
and its fringes of vulgar glory; but he is committed to glory of the kind
which is

> attain'd
> Without ambition, war, or violence;
> By deeds of peace, by wisdom eminent,
> By patience, temperance. (*PR* III.89–92)

And the virtue by which he most distinctly hopes to fulfill his mission is
wisdom in combination with all others.

For the disciples who, unlike Satan, are genuinely eager for the
fulfilment of the prophecy that

> The Kingdom shall to *Israel* be restor'd (*PR* II.36)

the Savior's wisdom is full of "grace and truth." Today grace and truth
are corruptible. In a modern public figure grace may take the form of
a kind of charisma which is dangerous to both men and society. And
truth, which should make men free, has too often contributed to their
enslavement by compromising with "proud Tyrannick pow'r" (*PR*
I.219). The liberation of truth and the restoration of equity figured considerably in the young Savior's meditations. He reveres truth as divine,
but there is a risk of overconfidence when certainty of truth as individually possessed becomes articulate in taunts even to manifest char-
latans. Charlatanry in the ancient world had been shameless and sacro-
sanct in the oracles "at *Delphos* or elsewhere" (*PR* I.458) which the
Savior reminds Satan have lately fallen silent, while

> God hath now sent his living Oracle
> Into the World, to teach his final will,
> And sends his Spirit of Truth henceforth to dwell
> In pious Hearts, an inward Oracle
> To all truth requisite for men to know. (*PR* I.460-464)

Does the Savior's taunt betray a flaw in the thinking of the author of *Areopagitica*? In the Messiah's annunciation of an overruling "inward Oracle" is there an unconscious concession to the craving of even the most enlightened human establishments for some degree of control over public information and debate? In the Messiah's words there seems to be a deliberate echo of Jesus' promise to his disciples that "the spirit of Truth" will come to "guide you into all truth" (John 16:13). Milton was aware that all around him in the churches and in Parliament that promise was the refuge of the authors of the law against which he protested in *Areopagitica*.

In an unpublished dissertation J. S. Moag regards the Savior's statement that truth is an "inward Oracle" as "a singularly occult announcement of the nature of his kingship."[24] And there is difficulty in relating the Savior's oracular spirit of truth to the two different motives which since the time of Daniel's prophecy had been uneasily balanced in the Jewish Messianic idea. Joseph Klausner has recognized them as (1) "politico-national salvation" (the reestablishment of the Kingdom of Israel with its temple rebuilt in Jerusalem), and (2) "religio-spiritual redemption" by an all-wise Messiah, an international "political and spiritual hero." His image "was paradoxically kingly because his kingdom was not of this world."[25]

In the warning of Milton's Messiah that of his "reign Prophetic Writ hath told,/ That it shall never end" (*PR* III.184–185), we may see a projection of the ambivalent Jewish conceptions of the promised Messiah. These conceptions survived among Christians and came to have a considerable influence on Milton's own thinking, which in the eyes of twentieth-century scholars is governed by the most representative philosophical movements of the Renaissance. The prevailing view was set in 1917 by Edwin Greenlaw's essay "A Better Teacher than Aquinas."[26] Rightly, I believe, its main thesis still prevails in spite of A. J. A. Waldock's condemnation of Greenlaw as "bemused by Plato, Aristotle, and Spenser," and blinded by his theory of the "central philosophy" of *Paradise Lost* as coming "from Greece, not from Genesis."[27] Waldock did not appreciate even the philosophical elements in Scripture which the Neoplatonists united with their tradition—especially the element of reverence for wisdom in its mysterious scriptural senses. He did not understand the importance of truth in the Messianic tradition whenever it faced the "idolisms of the gentiles," or its importance as the illuminating power of the Neoplatonists. Did Milton also think of truth as philosophically embattled against Bacon's idols of the cave, the tribe, the marketplace, and the theater? Certainly his conception was colored by the thinking which William Haller has described as coming to him "by way of Italian and English renaissance poetry, the idea that truth is the transcendent reality of which reason in man is the dynamic reflection and that reason is the faculty which enables the elect to distinguish that reality from the illusions by which it is beclouded in the apprehension of men in consequence of the original fall."[28]

Haller's stress is upon truth and knowledge as an imaginative concept working critically and creatively in both personal experience and public life. The range of his essay differs from Arnold Stein's elaborate analysis of *Paradise Regained* as "a dramatic definition of heroic knowledge."[29] But Haller's essay results in a conception which is not irreconcilable with Stein's revelation of "intuitive knowledge" ripened by "proved intellectual and moral discipline" as emergent from the Savior's dramatic dialogue with Satan. In Stein's discussion "heroic knowledge" is not alien to the wisdom of which the Savior's disciples speak as "full of grace and truth." The Savior's wisdom is both intellectual and moral. Glimpses of it are to be found even in Renaissance works of the kind represented by Erasmus' *Education of a Christian Prince*. The virtues which they taught were among those comprised in the Father's representation of the Son to the angels as possessing the "consummate vertue" which we should see in the "perfect Man," his incarnate Son, who is

To earn Salvation for the Sons of men. (*PR* I.167)

To catalogue those virtues and hierarchize them would weaken their impact. Their force should be felt as Satan feels it when he tells his worried diabolic council that the Messiah displays

All vertue, grace and wisdom to atchieve
Things highest, greatest . . . (*PR* I.68–69)

In these and all the other virtues which Satan later recognizes in the Savior's

Majestick brow
Seated as on the top of Vertues hill (*PR* II.216–217)

Satan is aware of no divine epiphany. For Satan, the Savior's virtues are abstractions remote from any life known to him. For Milton all virtues were most vital parts of life. Of that the substance and style of his prose are evidence. In looking at the concrete effects of the efforts of the preaching of Christ's coming kingdom in England, however, Milton was as unhappy as Michael Fixler recalls in *Milton and the Kingdoms of God*[30] that Ralph Cudworth was when he reminded the House of Commons in a sermon that "although the millennial Kingdom of God had not yet come, it was 'more than a *Platonicall Idea*,' and that their business until that time was to establish justice and righteousness. Christ . . . did not come into the world to preach up abstractions, but to change and perfect men."[31] Cudworth had no formula for perfecting human imperfection, but he defined his object as the restoration in individual men of the image of God in which man had first been created. His object was the same as the "end of learning" which Milton said in *Of Education* was "to repair the ruines of our first Parents by regaining to know God aright, and out of that knowledge to love him, to imitate him, to be like him, as we may the neerest by possessing our souls of true vertue, which being united to the heavenly grace of faith makes up the highest perfection."[32]

At high moments Milton expected all creative experience to yield visions like his own ravishment by "the very visible shape and image of vertue, whereby she is not only seene in the regular gestures and motions of her heavenly paces as she walkes, but also makes the harmony of her voice audible to mortall eares."[33] Such was the vision which he attributed to the Lady in *A Mask* when she sees the "unblemish't form of Chastity" (ll. 214–215). In *Paradise Lost* Satan comes as close as a fiend can come to such an epiphany when he is surprised in Eden by a guardian cherub who, to his "youthful beautie added grace/ Invincible":

> . . . abasht the Devil stood,
> And felt how awful goodness is, and saw
> Vertue in her shape how lovly . . . (IV.846–848)

Again, at a critical point in his temptation of the Savior, Satan at least pretends to see "the perfect shape" of goodness, wisdom, justice in the Savior's heart (PR III.10–11).

Milton has been faulted for giving the Lady an epiphany of chastity rather than of charity.[34] In reply Sears Jayne observes that interchange of *castitas* for *caritas* "was a commonplace of the period," resting on the Neoplatonic integration of chastity with the charity which is love of heavenly beauty.[35] With Milton we should remember that in the Platonic background there was Socrates' doctrine of our souls' prenatal visions of the virtues, and of the terrible love which wisdom and the other lovely realities would arouse in us if we could regain sight of them (*Phaedrus* 250D). In a favorite Ciceronian passage (*De Officiis* I.v.15) Renaissance Neoplatonists found the doctrine revived in an eloquent summation of all the virtues intrinsic in the Roman conception of righteousness (*honestum*), a glimpse of which, if it could be physically seen, would arouse such love as Plato says that wisdom (*sapientia*) would arouse if eyes could see it.

In Italy the Platonic doctrine bore fruit in the theory and practice of the visual arts. Tracing that development in his introduction to *Icones Symbolicae*, E. H. Gombrich surveys its full florescence at the peak of baroque ecclesiastical painting in the great Roman churches, where Milton may have seen some examples.[36] In some of the large murals figures distinctly intended to represent various virtues in lovely human shapes would reveal their Platonically celestial nature by mingling with angels. Sustained contemplation of them might give a pious onlooker a sense of the Platonic shapes so lovely. With their epiphanies of the virtues the paintings could be regarded as examples of the coalescence of Christian and Platonic revelation which Marsilio Ficino tried to establish in his *Theologia Platonica*. Gombrich quotes him as believing that the symbolic images of the painters could reflect the living essences of the virtues as they exist in the divine mind, and could impart a trace of their celestial power to the onlookers.

Since Milton never mentioned Ficino or any of his works, it is not safe to assume a direct link between his references to virtues in their lovely forms and the speculations of Ficino and his followers. But for a clear echo of the thought in the *Phaedrus* Milton needed to go no further than Bacon's remark in *The Advancement of Learning* on Plato's having "said elegantly, 'That vertue, if she could be seen, would move great love and affection.'"[37] By cumulative proof scattered on many pages of *Plato and Milton* Irene Samuel establishes Milton's passionate interest in the Platonic dialogues from which Bacon ultimately got the idea which he quoted, knowing that it had become almost a commonplace.[38] So it is hard to tell whether Milton drew the doctrine of love most consciously from the Platonic sources in the *Phaedrus* and *Symposium* as he knew them at first hand, or from various writers in the Neoplatonic tradition as it was represented by its many transmitters in Rome, Florence, and England down to the Cambridge Platonists.

If we return now to the large heart of the Savior which Satan said contained "of good, wise, just, the perfect shape," magnanimity emerges as perhaps the most inclusive (if not the most essential) of the virtues of which he is the supreme epiphany. Milton strove to endue the composite image with both historic and metaphysical reality. He was aware of its development from Aristotle's portrayal of it in the *Nicomachean Ethics* (IV.iii) to its later classical association by Cicero with all that is reputable (*omnis honestas*) in his treatise *On Moral Goodness* (*De Officiis* I.xliii.152). Milton was also aware of the assimilation of magnanimity as knightly or courtly or Christian heroic virtue by writers like Tasso, Leonardo Bruni, and Castiglione, who seem to Mrs. Lewalski to have regarded it essentially as "renunciation of the world in order to pursue perfection and the contemplative life."[39] Definition of it in such terms has been illuminatingly studied by J. M. Steadman in his article "*Paradise Regained*: Moral Dialectic and the Pattern of Rejection"[40] and in his critique of magnanimity in *Milton and the Renaissance Hero*,[41] where he finds the virtue passing finally into humility as the Son of God stoops from his glory to suffer the shame of the Cross.

Steadman does not draw any comparison between the humility of Christ and the human version of the virtue which Dostoevski attempted in his portrayal of Prince Myshkin in *The Idiot*. We may suspect that Milton was as well aware as Dostoevski was that Europe had failed to create a convincing portrait of perfect human virtue. It is easy to agree with J. B. Broadbent that in Satan Milton created "a grave satire on corruption of the condition [he] valued above all others, rational sovereignty of the soul."[42] That sovereignty Milton certainly intended to portray in "*Israel's* true King" (*PR* III.441), whose fitness for that title was the paradox of his refusal of it on any mundane terms. It is only as the "True Image of the Father" (IV.596) that the angels see him after his final triumph over Satan. The conqueror of the rebel angels in Heaven has confirmed his claim to be his Father's true image by defeating all Satan's wiles on earth. He has confirmed it by mastering all human virtues up to humility. Whether that ultimate virtue is also a part of the invisible Father's nature is a question yet to be broached.

THE DIVINE ROYAL IMAGE

It is paradoxical that the Son, whose glory it is to be the true image of the Father, should be honored by many critics of *Paradise Lost* as the Father's moral superior. For the angels who see him the Son is first of all the Father's

> Divine Similitude,
> In whose conspicuous count'nance, without cloud
> Made visible, th'Almighty Father shines. (*PL* III.384–386)

The Son himself, accepting the Father's commission to rid Heaven of the rebel angels, declares that at need he is ready to put on either the "terrors" or the "mildness" of his Father, and to be his Father's "Image in all things." The rebels' conspiracy finds him in immediate sympathy with his Father's instant resolve on their prompt expulsion from Heaven. To hate his Father's enemies "with perfect hatred" (Pss. 139:22) is one thing, for the Father's hatred of them, though dispassionate, is outspoken. Sympathy with it requires no close rapport between him and his Son. But after the rout of the rebels, in the dramatic dialogue in Book III (ll. 80–216), the Son must penetrate the Father's concealed, fundamental concern for man's welfare. It is at least not obviously easy to see the Father's providential concern for man as overriding his determination to administer justice to those who have joined with Satan. But the onlooking angels have seen "the strife / Of Mercy and Justice" (III.406–407) in the Father's face as reflected by the Son. They have seen that strife end in mercy's victory when the Father and the Son agree with perfect joy upon his chivalrous redemption of the offenders. Filial love fulfils itself in an act of archetypal philanthropy.

Forgetting that the Son is his Father's image, we attribute all his virtues to him as if they corresponded to nothing in the Father's nature. With G. W. Knight we see the Father as "an oriental despot" and the Son as "an incarnation of that royalty blending justice and mercy defined once and for all by Portia's speech in *The Merchant of Venice*."[43] Or with John Peter we see the Father as wrathful and self-aggrandizing throughout the dialogue while the Son is so naïvely "compassionate that he can adjust himself even to the abrupt unexplained demand for a sacrifice."[44] Peter sees the Son as "unimpeachable" in his diplomatic condescension to an arteriosclerotic despot who is at home only in the "totalitarian state" which Sir Herbert Grierson saw in Milton's Heaven.[45] Many analysts of Milton's God and of Milton's own character find it easy to agree with Broadbent that especially in "the preliminary speeches in Heaven," they are compelled to submit "to the intolerable fact that God should universally exercise both the monarchic absolutism Milton rebelled against on earth, and the omnipotence, freedom and incontrovertible rightness that he aspired to."[46]

In her unpublished doctoral dissertation, "Milton's Ways with God,"[47] Sister Hilda Bonham quotes a score of recent critics whose objections to Milton's God justify Marjorie Nicolson's sympathy for him as the target of "batteries of both heavy and light artillery . . . turned upon Him by such commentators as F. R. Leavis, A. J. A. Waldock, John Peter, [and] William Empson."[48] But Sister Bonham calls a roll of his defenders, though several of them agree with Joseph Frank that the divine explanation of theology in Book III is "the least poetic and least convincing section of *Paradise Lost*."[49] Whether to regard the absence of the poetic in this passage as a defect is a question which the best analysts decline to discuss. An enlightened minority agree with Arnold Stein that the plan of the epic made it "necessary that God be present and speak."[50] To Frank Kermode the "bold" location of his statement of the theological rules of the poem as "coming straight from God Himself" at his first appearance is unquestionably tactful. Kermode sees that the controversial matter is "not at the heart of the work, [yet] had to be in it."[51] Denis Saurat put it more boldly when he wrote: "Ces idées [of God] sont l'armature même du poème qui ne serait, sans elles, que la répetition d'une légende absurde et choquante aux bons sens."[52]

The theological rules must be accepted for what they are, the accepted doctrine of Christ's sacrifice to redeem mankind from the death penalty of the mortal sin original in Eden. As a self-explanatory term for it C. A. Patrides proposes the "penal-substitutionary theory of the Atonement."[53] Its statement cannot avoid being legalistic, and the voice declaring it must be that of God conceived as absolute in a metaphysical sense, and as absolutely responsible for human destiny. The subject and the nature of the speaker both impose the "flat" style of the speech, the lapse into prose as Pope felt it to be when he wrote the half-forgotten couplet:

> Milton's strong pinion now not Heav'n can bound,
> Now serpent-like, in prose he sweeps the ground,

to lead up to the immortal line:

> And God the Father turns a School-divine.
>   (*Imitations of Horace* II.i.99–100, 102)

But when Stein illuminates the succinct rhythms of God's prose—so strikingly different from the elaborately long rhythms of Milton's tracts—

they emerge as inevitably right for the voice coming from the omniscience sitting "High Thron'd above all highth" (III.58). Abstracted from the universe of action, Milton's God reveals himself in terms that He himself has chosen.

Reflections akin to these on the tone of God's speech from the throne become an explanation and a perfect defense for the lack of poetic quality when D. C. Allen observes that "metaphor and simile are useless to him for he knows what he has created and needs no comparatives."[54] The remark spots a clue to Milton's avoidance of metaphor here and often elsewhere in the poem. The danger for the reader is that he may be left with the impression that Milton regarded the omniscient speaker as no less abstract than the "Truth" with which the Savior identifies him in *Paradise Regained* (III.183), or the personified Truth that is called "strong next to the Almighty" in *Areopagitica*.[55]

In the two opening books of *Paradise Lost* Satan's rhetoric is a dramatic foil for the divine voice, which Jon Lawry calls "cold and difficult." Its function, he says, is to "oppose Satan by presenting an argument for severe justice, from which the Son will come to understand the need and the way of redemptive love."[56] In the court of opinion where Milton's God is now judged, it should be remembered that in the imaginary council in Heaven he is an advocate in his own cause. He must speak impersonally; he must speak like Truth itself. Not surprisingly his "drab legalities" are, as B. Rajan declared, "too curt and chill to be poetically successful."[57] In listening to them we should imagine ourselves listening to a judge's instructions to a jury. We should think twice before sharing F. E. Hutchinson's regret that "Milton makes the Almighty argue like a lawyer."[58] Since the judge is also a master metaphysician, we may also listen for cosmic overtones in what he says. For, as Irene Samuel points out, the speaker is "Total Being, *the* Primal Energy, *the* Voice of Reason, *the* Moral Law that makes possible a moral cosmos as surely as the laws of physics make possible a physical cosmos."[59] The speaker is the true God, whose first attribute Milton declares in *De Doctrina Christiana* to be Truth.[60]

The oldest symbol of truth is light, the physical light of the sun which Adam calls "of this great World both Eye and Soule" (V.171). But by a metaphor of which we are hardly conscious it can be understood as the "Celestial light" which Milton prayed might

> Shine inward, and the mind through all her powers
> Irradiate. (*PL* III.52–53)

Two millennia of meditation on light lay behind his prayer. They had extended the spectrum of its meaning to include the invisible, life-creating, physical nature and the visible effects on the eye, which in human experience extend to the mind and all its visions, imaginative, scientific, and philosophical. D. C. Allen reminds us that Milton's readers might think of light as a "graduated divine impulsion, 'descendens a Patre luminum,' who was himself symbolized by essential light."[61] To the initiated Milton might seem to wrap up a complete theology and cosmology when he declared that

> God is light,
> And never but in unapproached light
> Dwelt from Eternitie . . . (*PL* III.3–5)

From the invocation Milton moves directly into the celestial council where God's justice is firmly defended, though by the Son's sacrifice mercy for man is secured. For confirmation that God's mercy is dominant in Milton's thinking about Providence we may turn to a significant final act at the end of the account of the Creation in Book VII. When the Son has shaped the universe out of Chaos and is returning to Heaven with his invisible Father and the angelic hosts accompanying him, he passes through its open gates and deliberately leaves them open:

> for God will deigne
> To visit oft the dwellings of just Men
> Delighted, and with frequent intercourse
> Thither will send his winged Messengers
> On errands of supernal Grace. (*PL* VII.569–573)

Gracious traffic between Heaven and Earth is the purpose of Creation. In telling Adam about it Raphael is exemplifying it by his own presence in Eden. Later in their conversation Adam tells Raphael about an earlier celestial visitor, a "Presence Divine" (VIII.324) which appeared in his first moments of consciousness, brought the beasts to him to be named, and finally at his request created Eve. The Presence has called itself simply his "Guide" (VIII.298), but in the course of their dialogue nobler names suggest themselves to Adam: Author of the Universe, Maker, th'Almighty, and Creator bounteous and benign. At one point Adam's fast-developing theology flowers with the name of Universal Lord for the Presence which he is coming to regard as uniquely supreme above all his creatures. Though Adam is not aware of the fact or of its meaning, it should be clear now that the mysterious Presence is the Son, the Creator of the world, speaking as God's representative there, as he will do as God's judge of man in Book X, lines 95–228. Adam cannot recognize the Presence as readers can; but better than any theologian has ever been able to do, he should be able to understand his visitor's assurance that, by virtue of his free spirit, he is made in God's image.

In all his readers' memories Milton assumed a clear recollection of God's words in Genesis 1:26: "Let us make man in our own image, after our likeness." The accepted interpretation was like the gloss in the Geneva Bible: "The image . . . of God in man is expounded (Eph. 4:24): 'The man was created after God in righteousness & true holiness, power, &c.' " In *De Doctrina Christiana* Milton drew the same conclusion from the same text, but in the same chapter he spoke of man's likeness to God as mainly, but by implication not entirely, spiritual. In paraphrasing the biblical account of the Creation he remembered Ovid's brief account of man's creation in *Metamorphoses* (I.76–86) and drew on the symbolic overtones of the Ovidian description of the first man as resembling the gods who rule all things. For Ovid the newly created man was honorable as other creatures are not, and was gifted with powers corresponding to his uplifted countenance.

It is interesting to find Sir Walter Raleigh's chapter "Of Man's Estate in His First Creation" in *The History of the World* quoting the verse from Genesis, following it with some of Ovid's lines, but devoting most of his chapter to proving—with the help of St. Augustine and Cicero, but against Zanchius and some other theologians—that no physical likeness is intended in Genesis, for man's resemblance to God is solely in man's mind.[62] Little by little, Raleigh has moved away from man's innocence and righteousness as the ground of his resemblance to his Maker to put the greater stress on the mind. Like Milton, he felt that the mind, or Right Reason, was God's great gift to man, and that it was man's best means of preserving righteousness. As God governed the world, man's mind should rule his passions. Where man

> permits
> Within himself unworthie Powers to reign
> Over free Reason, God in Judgement just
> Subjects him from without to violent Lords;
> Who oft as undeservedly enthrall
> His outward freedom . . . (*PL* XII.90–95)

As long as the stress was on the ascendancy of the mind over the body, piety might be uncorrupted and government might be sound.

But history showed that there had always been a danger, even among
Christians, that undue admiration of man's physical glory would end
by making God into the image of man or inventing pantheons of an-
thropomorphic deities. "Surely," Raleigh wrote, "Cicero, who was but a
Heathen, had yet a more divine understanding than these gross Here-
ticks: 'the vertue which is in man (saith he) came neerer the similitude
of God, than the figure.' For God is a spirituall substance, invisible,
most simple; God is a just God: God is mercifull: God is Charity it self,
and (in a word) Goodness it self, and none else simply good." The
Christian corollary to this doctrine is fervently asserted to Satan by the
Savior in *Paradise Regained* when he declares that God's motive in creation had not been

> for glory as prime end,
> But to shew forth his goodness, and impart
> His good communicable to every soul
> Freely. (III.123–126)

Rule over all creatures had been God's first gift to man. In Genesis
1:26 the statement of God's purpose to make man in the divine image is
immediately followed by the gift of "dominion over the fish of the sea,
and over the fowl of the air, and over the cattle, and over all the earth.
. . ." From those words Raleigh drew the usual interpretation that "man
was after the image of God in respect of rule and power." In them God's
primacy needed no acknowledgement. Nor could the fact be neglected
in the imagery of a poem which was grounded on divine omnipotence
and on divine providence controlling every step of the narrative from the
exaltation of the Son to the fulfilment of the last prophecy revealed to
Adam by Michael in the visions of Book XII.

If the defense of Providence is the purpose of *Paradise Lost*, it is
most distinctly achieved by the self-sacrifice of the Son for man's salvation. The Son's humiliation is an instrument of Providence. Its lesser
instruments are the Son's services to Adam and Eve when he twice descends from Heaven to talk with them. And we should include the services of the angels who come to talk with them or to protect them
(though unsuccessfully) against Satan's approaches in the Garden.
These condescensions are the best vindication of God's glory as ruler of
the universe. But God, whose Son is the "radiant image of his Glory"
(*PL* III.63), does and says nothing suggesting that in the original of
that image there is anything corresponding to the Son's humility. When
revolt threatens Heaven, the Father commits his scepter and power to

the Son as any head of state might commit military authority to a prince and heir apparent. But the Son, while accepting the command, refuses the inheritance:

> Scepter and Power, thy giving, I assume,
> And gladlier shall resign, when in the end
> Thou shalt be All in All, and I in thee
> For ever, and in mee all whom thou lov'st.
> (*PL* VI.730–733)

We remember that later, in the council in Book III, when in an apocalyptic passage God foretells the destruction of the world by fire and the emergence of a new world after the Son's judgment upon "Bad Men and Angels," he says, speaking directly to the Son:

> Then thou thy regal Scepter shalt lay by,
> For regal Scepter then no more shall need,
> God shall be All in All. (*PL* III.339–341)

In *Milton's God* William Empson observes that only a few lines earlier God has given the Son "all power" to "reign forever."[63] Empson regards the paradox as clearly "deliberate." But it is not clear that Milton felt a contradiction (as distinct from the paradox) when he made God repeat the words from 1 Corinthians which Empson notes that he quoted in *De Doctrina Christiana* I.xv:[64]

> Then cometh the end, when he shall have delivered up the kingdom to God, even the Father. . . . For he hath put all things under his feet. But when he saith all things are put under him, it is manifest that he is excepted, which did put all things under him. And when all things shall be subdued unto him, then shall the Son also himself be subject unto him that put all things under him, that God may be all in all. (15:24–28)

Empson gives Milton credit for a sincere belief in a "mystical" congruity between God's final words and the earlier bestowal of all power on the Son. He exonerates Milton of any sympathy with the "literal autocracy" which St. Paul "presumably had in mind." To avoid that political heresy Empson suggests that Milton "contrives to make the text imply pantheism." If that is so, we may hopefully read pantheism into Ralph Cudworth's conclusion of his great argument against atheism in all its forms, of which he regarded pantheism as one of the most insidious. In *The True Intellectual System of the Universe*[65] he quotes the saying of the poet Linus, the fabled son of Apollo: "Man must hope for all things since nothing is beyond hope. All things end in God, nor is anything to be despaired of." Rather than look for hidden heresies in Milton's concept of God as All in All, it would be more helpful to consider the extent to which the ancient formula was related to the later Neoplatonic tradition which P. O. Kristeller describes as being committed to "the thought of God" as "the efficient cause, end, and exemplar of the world."[66]

In the last of the celestial dialogues in *Paradise Lost* the Son reminds the Father of his promise that after the end of the world all his redeemed are to dwell with him:

Made one with me as I with thee am one. (XI.44)

If Milton had chosen to develop this promised eternity of "joy and bliss," he might have felt it necessary to describe the glorified bodies of the blessed in terms of their "agility, subtlety, impassibility, and clarity or brightness," which C. A. Patrides mentions as representative of contemporary Protestant rhapsodies on heaven.[67] Or Milton might have attempted more profound meditations akin to John Donne's thinking in an Easter sermon which he might have heard preached in St. Paul's in 1628. Quoting St. Jerome, Donne explained: "Here God does all in all; but here he does all by Instruments; even in the infusing of faith, he works by the Ministery of the Gospel: but there he shall be all in all, doe all in all, immediately by himself; for, Christ shall deliver up the Kingdome to God, even the Father."[68]

In these eschatological speculations God's image is still royal—still an *eikon basilike*. Here a strong impulsion upon all religious thinking was at work. Quoting R. G. Collingwood in *The Idea of Nature*, Dame Helen Gardner sums it up with the observation that any thinking about God as providentially concerned in human affairs is hardly possible unless it brings the entire historical process "back into unity with Himself."[69]

The thought of divine involvement in human affairs implies a royal image, omnipotent but also omnipatient—a suffering image. Providence cannot be indifferent to human struggle and humiliation, and it cannot understand them without something like sympathy. Or, in the philosophical terms of C. M. Coffin, we may think of God, who is " 'All,' as suffering the tensions generated by that other 'All' which is the 'plenitude of creation,' the multiplicity of particulars other than Himself which are at the same time *of* Himself. At the end of time the two Alls merge to become 'All in All.' "[70]

By virtue of his participation in the sufferings of his creatures God is righteous, and he is also royal in the most refined sense of the doctrine that the king can do no wrong. In a metaphysical sense the divine image was absolute and superhuman, but Milton and most of his readers have shared Raleigh's view that imitation of the righteousness of that image was a human obligation which gave more than metaphorical force to the biblical statement that man was made in the image of God.

NOTES

This paper is a revised and expanded version of one read before the Milton Society of America at its meeting in Denver, Colorado, on December 27, 1969.

1. *The Kings' Peace* (London, 1955), p. 152.
2. *The Works of John Milton*, ed. Frank Allen Patterson et al. (18 vols.; New York, 1931–1938), V, 79 (hereafter cited as *Works*).
3. *Works*, V, 257.
4. *Oxford English Dictionary*.
5. *Works*, V, 170.
6. *Observations on the Articles of Peace*, *Works*, VI, 253.
7. *Poets and Playwrights* (Minneapolis, 1930), p. 255.
8. *Paradise Lost and Its Critics* (Cambridge, 1947), pp. 68–70.
9. *Works*, IV, 286.
10. *Studies in Philology*, LXIV (1967), 685–711.
11. In *Language and Style in Milton: A Symposium in Honor of the Tercentenary of Paradise Lost*, ed. R. D. Emma and John Shawcross (New York, 1967), pp. 193–232.
12. (Cambridge, Mass., 1962), passim.
13. *Milton's Epic Voice* (Cambridge, Mass., 1963), passim.
14. *The Paradise Within* (New Haven, 1964), passim.
15. *Surprised by Sin: The Reader in Paradise Lost* (London, 1967), passim.
16. *The Fierce Equation* (The Hague, 1965), passim.
17. *Paradise Lost and the Seventeenth-Century Reader* (London, 1947), p. 96.
18. *The Shadow of Heaven* (Ithaca, 1968), pp. 237, 309.
19. "*Ethos and Dianoia*," p. 221. See n. 11 above.
20. *A Preface to Paradise Lost* (London, 1942), p. 95.
21. *Paradise Lost and the Seventeenth-Century Reader*, p. 101.
22. *English Studies*, XLIX (1968), 102–103.
23. *Milton's Brief Epic: The Genre, Meaning, and Art of Paradise Regained* (Providence, 1966), pp. 224–226.
24. "Traditional Patterns of Dialogue and Debate in Milton's Poetry" (Northwestern University, 1964), passim.
25. *The Messianic Idea in Israel* (London, 1956), p. 392.
26. *Studies in Philology*, XIV (1917), 196–217.

27. *Paradise Lost and Its Critics*, pp. 60, 58.
28. "Milton and the Protestant Ethic," *The Journal of British Studies*, I (1963), 53.
29. *Heroic Knowledge* (Minneapolis, 1957), p. 17.
30. (London, 1964), p. 85.
31. *A Sermon Preached* was delivered March 31, 1647.
32. *Works*, IV, 277.
33. *The Reason of Church-Government, Works*, III, i, 185.
34. Malcolm M. Ross, *Poetry and Dogma* (New Brunswick, N. J., 1959), p. 196.
35. *A Maske at Ludlow: Essays on Milton's Comus*, ed. John S. Diekhoff (Cleveland, 1968), p. 168n.
36. "Icones Symbolicae: The Visual Image in Neo-Platonic Thought," *Journal of the Warburg and Courtauld Institute*, XI (1948), 163–192.
37. *The Works of Francis Bacon*, ed. James Spedding (15 vols.; New York, 1869), VI, 289.
38. (Ithaca, 1947), passim.
39. *Milton's Brief Epic*, p. 244.
40. *University of Toronto Quarterly*, XXXI (1962), 416–430.
41. (Oxford, 1967), pp. 137–160.
42. *Some Graver Subject* (London, 1960), p. 78.
43. *Chariot of Wrath* (London, 1942), p. 150.
44. *A Critique of Paradise Lost*, p. 14.
45. *Milton and Wordsworth* (New York, 1937), p. 117.
46. *Some Graver Subject*, p. 148.
47. (Northwestern University, 1964), passim.
48. *John Milton: A Reader's Guide to His Poetry* (New York, 1963), p. 223.
49. "Milton's Movement Towards Deism," *Journal of British Studies*, I (1968), 44.
50. *Answerable Style* (Minneapolis, 1953), p. 128.
51. *The Living Milton*, ed. Frank Kermode (London, 1960), p. 91.
52. *Milton et le matérialisme chrétien en Angleterre* (Paris, 1928).
53. "Milton and the Protestant Theory of Atonement," *PMLA*, LXXIV (1959), 9.
54. *The Harmonious Vision* (Baltimore, 1954), p. xi.
55. *Works*, IV, 348.
56. *The Shadow of Heaven*, p. 148.
57. *Paradise Lost and the Seventeenth-Century Reader*, p. 96.
58. *Milton and the English Mind* (London, 1949), p. 124.
59. "The Dialogue in Heaven," *PMLA*, LXXII (1957), 602.
60. *Works*, XIV, 40.
61. *The Harmonious Vision*, p. 101.
62. *The History of the World*, 9th ed. (London, 1652), pp. 19–21.
63. 2nd ed. (London, 1965), p. 133.
64. *Works*, XV, 370.
65. 1st ed. (1678), p. 890.
66. *The Philosophy of Marsilio Ficino* (New York, 1943), p. 123.
67. *Milton and the Christian Tradition* (Oxford, 1966), pp. 283–284.
68. *The Sermons of John Donne*, ed. G. R. Potter and Evelyn Simpson (Berkeley and Los Angeles, 1953–1962), VIII, 233.
69. *A Reading of Paradise Lost* (Oxford, 1965), pp. 23–24.
70. "Creation and the Self in *Paradise Lost*," *ELH*, XXIX (1962), 3.

Inaction and Silence: The Reader in *Paradise Regained*

UNIVERSITY OF CALIFORNIA, BERKELEY

I

Recently Russell Fraser has prosecuted an old charge with new vigor and a commendable precision.[1] Milton's Platonism, he contends, led him to de-emphasize and deliberately to eschew those very qualities of language that are the lifeblood of poetry—concreteness and specificity. In his effort to "dispense with the limiting or particular instance and to announce the general law that informs it" (p. 174), he produced an art in which the surface of things is obliterated (p. 177), adjectives generalize rather than specify, metaphor shades into tautology, personality becomes anonymous, dialogue is "far removed from living speech" (p. 188), and the life-giving nutriment of detail is rejected in favor of deadening abstractions.

What makes Fraser's thesis more than a revival of Leavisian objections is his insight into the source of Milton's poetic "deficiencies." The Platonic impulse, which is also the rationalistic impulse, is grounded in "a hatred of surfaces" (p. 174) and a corresponding desire "to exalt the naked truth"; and in human terms, the category of "surfaces" includes *everything*, the works of Memphian kings, the fretted dome of St. Peter's, the endeavor of the artist, the clothing of "painted" language, even the act of reasoning itself—includes, in a phrase, "all mortal things," which, as Fraser explains, "are not simply to be set aside as naught, but inveighed against as the miscreating labor of Mammon . . . whose kingdom embraces all the world and its business" (pp. 195–196). It is not surprising then, although a cause for regret, that an aesthetic committed to the devaluing of earthly things would result in poetry whose "human interest" was minimal, and therefore in a poetry which has little claim to our serious attention. "For the rationalist, as he asserts the proposition that all but the One is inanimate fantasy, withholds from the mind its proper nutriment, that feeding on particulars which is essential to its vigor and health" (p. 196).

To this last Milton might reply, "It depends on what you conceive the health of the mind to be"; for the particulars which Fraser approves as the "proper nutriment" of the mind would be regarded by one of the Platonic party as manifestations of that from which the mind must be freed if it is to become truly healthy. I assert nothing more (or less) than the familiar Platonic doctrine that the business of the mind is to disengage itself from the confining pressure of sensibles and rise to the perception of, and therefore to the possession by, Reality or the "Naked Truth." If this is accepted not only as an article of Milton's belief, but as the basis of an aesthetic *strategy*, those characteristics of his poetry which lead Fraser (implicitly) to lament its failure may be viewed as evidence of its success.

To put the matter simply: Fraser assumes that Milton loses sight of a great truth about the way poetry works, but it is Milton's *insight* into what the working of poetry means, that is, of what it is a symptom, which underlies his aesthetic and dictates his strategy. A response to the kind of poetry Fraser would approve (the moving, quick, vital poetry of particulars) is a response which confirms the mind's natural (but perverse) tendency to equate its horizons with the horizons of reality. The appeal of the poetry of particulars is an appeal to something in us that Milton would have us transcend; his poetry, by working against its own best interests (in a narrow sense), works against that something and so becomes a vehicle for the raising of the reader's mind to the point where reality discloses itself. "Sloughing off the world of sensory experience and coming directly at the naked truth" (p. 172) is not only Milton's "desire"; it is the gift he would bestow on his readers.

Thus when Fraser asserts that Milton "yearns to be delivered from poetry" (p. 174), he does not go far enough, and indeed his own observations encourage us to go farther. What Milton yearns to be delivered from, and what he would deliver us from, is the frame of reference from which poetry (and all language) issues, the *merely* human frame of reference that is tied to specific times and places and to the limited perception of the isolated individual. Poetry is merely an inevitable casualty of this deliverance, because like all earthly forms—physical, linguistic, perceptual—it falls away when the aspiring mind embraces, and so becomes indistinguishable from, the object of its search. To be free of poetry is to be free of the self, of its uniqueness and therefore of its partiality, and this, I would argue, is the impulse behind Milton's art—to lose the self in a union with God, to exchange our (human) values for his, so that it can be truly said, "In him we live and move and have our being."

In some sense I am merely reaffirming what is already a critical commonplace: the central issue in Milton's poetry is the relationship between man and God. What I would add is the observation that the definition of that relationship (both in the text and in the mind of the reader) is a *refining* or purging process, which because its direction is away from everything we naturally value, including the value of our thoughts and their expression, is linguistically self-destructive. And this accounts, I believe, for the presence in much of Milton's poetry of two plots or actions, one narrative or dramatic and the other verbal. On the dramatic level the definition of the relationship between man and God takes the form of a progressive narrowing of the area in which the self is preeminent or even, in a causal sense, active. On the verbal level there is a progressive diminishing, first of the complexity of language and then of its volubility, until finally, as the relationship between the self and God is specified, there is only silence. In other words, there is a perfect and inevitable correspondence between the conceptual thrust of the poem and the progress (or anti-progress) of its language. Milton's heroes characteristically perform actions or make decisions which in context affirm the claims of God at the expense of the self until that self exists only in terms of its reliance on God. And when that happens the voice of the individual is heard no more. The unfolding of these patterns, in turn, puts enormous pressure on the reader, who if he is to be answerable to the poem's movement must learn how to value inaction or the abdication of action and respond to silence. What is required of the reader is an aesthetic reversal, which, insofar as it involves the putting away of earthly standards of (verbal) beauty, signals the putting away of the self and the exchanging of an egocentric point of view for one that finds everything in God.

Some of my readers will recognize this as the argument of *Surprised by Sin* and will suspect that I am about to extend its interpretation of *Paradise Lost* to *Paradise Regained*, but the two poems are very different, and they engage their readers in very different ways. In

Paradise Lost, the reader is given the task of discovering the principles of faith and action which will enable him to resist the Satanic appeal; in *Paradise Regained*, those principles are available from the very beginning, and the problem is to apply them in specific situations. As it turns out, this is more of a problem for the reader than for the hero, and the relationship between them is another basis for distinguishing the two epics: in the one, the reader and the characters are joined by a common weakness (although there is a difference of degree) and to some extent they undergo their trials together; in the other, only the reader acknowledges the pressure of the temptations, and he is left to come to terms not with Satan (who is a noticeably less compelling figure than he was in the earlier poem), but with a protagonist whose actions are inexplicable, especially in the light of the values he espouses and (supposedly) embodies. All of this is reflected in the basic pattern of reader response. In *Paradise Lost*, that pattern, as I have described it, is one of mistake-correction-instruction; but the pattern in *Paradise Regained* is one of expectation (on the basis of what one takes to be the principles of Christian action)-disappointment-perplexity. These two patterns in turn generate two different kinds of activity, one arduous and dynamic, involving the achieving and abandoning of successive stages of insight, the other intellectual and reflective, involving the refining and extending of an insight that is never superseded.

I am aware that one could move from the noting of these differences to an evaluation of the two epics, but evaluation seems to me to be less interesting and less useful than description. In both poems, the issues and the reader's stake in the issues are the same. What is different is the quality and shape of his involvement with them. *Paradise Lost* and *Paradise Regained* are complementary explorations of the set of paradigmatic relationships—between man and God, morality and aesthetics, language and self, hero and audience—which underlies Milton's poetry. It will be my contention that in the later poem their working out results in as coherent and satisfying an experience as that provided by its more celebrated predecessor.

II

More than any other major poet Milton has been the beneficiary of his detractors. It is the objections to his verse that have finally generated the most useful insights, largely, I think, because the anti-Miltonists are usually pointing to something that is there and therefore to something which his admirers can not afford to ignore. In the case of *Paradise Regained* the chief objections can be reduced to Fraser's criticism of "At a Solemn Music": "Nothing happens" (p. 189).

This is of course not wholly accurate. Satan is conspicuously busy most of the time, but his busyness is the busyness of a stage manager. He is constantly setting up scenes and arranging what he hopes will be confrontations, but his activity only serves to accentuate the anticlimactic nature of what happens when the scenes are played out and the confrontations actually occur. That is, the pattern of temptation-rejection which constitutes the whole of the poem's plot is itself patterned in such a way as to defuse the dramatic thrust it potentially embodies. Again and again Satan cranks up a huge amount of machinery which in turn generates an enormous pressure of anticipation—what will the Son do? how will he get out of this one? what would I have done in his place— only to be met (as we are met too) by an evasive and (in terms of the expectations the verse has encouraged) inadequate response: "No, thank you"; "I'd rather not"; "With my hunger what hast thou to do?"; "Think not but that I know these things; or think I know them not."

This stepping back from a situation, *after* the pressures it exerts have been acknowledged, is characteristic not only of the Son but of the unambiguously human characters who hang around the edges of the central drama. At the beginning of Book II, we come upon the apostles (speaking chorus-like with one voice) and Mary, as they struggle to come to terms with the disconcerting fact of the Son's disappearance, and in the course of their soliloquies they display the pattern of inaction that is writ larger in the more extended temptation scenes. This is a pattern based on the disappointment of expectation, and it unfolds in two stages: (1) the establishment of a set of circumstances and the attendant felt need for an "appropriate" response, and (2) the subsequent withholding of that response. In this case the circumstances are established in the context of a formal complaint:

> Alas, from what high hope to what relapse
> Unlook'd for are we fall'n! Our eyes beheld
> Messiah certainly now come, so long
> Expected of our Fathers; we have heard
> His words, his wisdom full of grace and truth;
> Now, now, for sure, deliverance is at hand,
> The Kingdom shall to *Israel* be restor'd:
> Thus we rejoic'd, but soon our joy is turn'd
> Into perplexity and new amaze:

> For whither is he gone, what accident
> Hath rapt him from us? will he now retire
> After appearance, and again prolong
> Our expectation? God of *Israel*,
> Send thy Messiah forth, the time is come;
> Behold the Kings of th'Earth how they oppress
> Thy chosen, to what height thir pow'r unjust
> They have exalted, and behind them cast
> All fear of thee; arise and vindicate
> Thy Glory, free thy people from thir yoke!
> *But let us wait* . . . (II.30–49, emphasis mine)

In this passage the disappointment of expectation occurs on two levels: it is what the apostles are reacting to, and it is what we react to in the reaction of the apostles. They have been encouraged by the baptism of Jesus to believe that the deliverance of their nation "so long expected" is at hand; and just when the fulfillment of the scriptural promise seems imminent, it is apparently withdrawn. Understandably they react with perplexity and impatience, but, less understandably, that impatience leads neither to anger nor to disillusionment but to a renewal of patience—"But let us wait." To the extent that we find their resignation surprising (perplexing), it presents us with the same problem that the disappearance of Jesus presents to them. It is not on its face sufficient to the occasion; and our experience of its insufficiency is very much like our experience of the Son's conduct in the temptation scenes.

Significantly, the desire of the apostles for a dramatic and imminent redress of their many grievances (a desire we come to share) is the basis of the appeals and arguments with which Satan attempts to provoke the Son to action: "Thy years are ripe and over-ripe" (III.31); "Zeal and duty are not slow, / But on Occasion's forelock watchful wait" (III.172–173); "each act is rightliest done, / Not when it must, but when it may be best" (IV.475–476). In short, "the time is come" and if you seize it not, the deliverance of Israel will not be effected and the kings of the earth will continue to oppress God's people: "*Judaea* now and all the promis'd land / Reduc't a Province under Roman yoke" (III.157–158); "Zeal of thy Father's house, Duty to free / Thy Country from her Heathen servitude" (III.175–176); "Might'st thou expel this monster from his Throne / Now made a sty, and in his place ascending / A victor people free from servile yoke" (IV.100–102). In every instance Jesus stubbornly reaffirms the resolution the apostles make here in Book II—to do nothing at all:

But let us wait. (II.49)

> I shall first
> Be tried in humble state . . .
> Suffering, abstaining, quietly expecting. (III.188–189, 192)

> My time I told thee . . .
> . . . is not yet come. (III.396–397)

> To his due time and providence I leave them. (III.440)

Waiting is the only action (or non-action) the characters in *Paradise Regained* ever take, and this includes Mary, whose moving expression of a mother's anxieties is preliminary to a similar declaration of passivity:

> O what avails me now that honor high
> To have conceiv'd of God, or that salute,
> Hail highly favor'd, among women blest!
> While I to sorrows am no less advanc't,
> And fears as eminent, above the lot
> Of other women, by the birth I bore,
> In such a season born when scarce a Shed
> Could be obtain'd to shelter him or me
> From the bleak air; a Stable was our warmth,
> A Manger his; yet soon enforc't to fly
> Thence into *Egypt*, till the Murd'rous King
> Were dead, who sought his life, and missing fill'd
> With Infant blood the streets of *Bethlehem*.
> From *Egypt* home return'd, in *Nazareth*
> Hath been our dwelling many years, his life
> Private, unactive, calm, contemplative,
> Little suspicious to any King; but now
> Full grown to Man, acknowledg'd, as I hear,
> By *John* the Baptist, and in public shown,
> Son own'd from Heaven by his Father's voice;
> I look't for some great change; to Honor? no,
> But trouble, as old *Simon* plain foretold,
> That to the fall and rising he should be
> Of many in *Israel*, and to a sign
> Spoken against, that through my very Soul
> A sword shall pierce; this is my favor'd lot,
> My Exaltation to Afflictions high;
> Afflicted I may be, it seems, and blest;
> I will not argue that, nor will repine.

But where delays he now? some great intent
Conceals him; when twelve years he scarce had seen,
I lost him, but so found, as well I saw
He could not lose himself; but went about
His Father's business; what he meant I mus'd,
Since understand; much more his absence now
Thus long to some great purpose he obscures.
But I to wait with patience am inur'd. (II.67–102, emphasis mine)

Again, by omitting any transition between the anguished voicing
of genuine needs and the unexpectedly sudden gesture of resignation,
the poet calls attention to the perversity (in human terms) of his characters' non-response. For in neither soliloquy is Milton concerned to portray a mind whose processes correspond to our idea of a "normal"
psychology; in both cases the conclusion—"But let us wait"; "But I to
wait with patience am inur'd"—is felt to be wholly discontinuous with
the strong sense of urgency communicated by the lines that precede it.
The result is a reading experience that can fairly be characterized as
frustrating.

And, indeed, frustration is characteristic of much of our experience
of *Paradise Regained*. Again and again the verse creates in us a need for
resolution, in the form of some action or event, and again and again it
declines to fulfill the need it has itself created. When the apostles search
for the absent Christ, the roll call of places they visit exerts a pressure
for his discovery, not only in Judea but in the verse: "in *Jericho* / The
City of Palms, *Aenon*, and *Salem* Old, / *Machaerus* and each Town or
City wall'd / On this side the broad lake *Genezaret*, / Or in *Peraea*"
(II.20–24); but the search and the forward movement of the poetry end
alike in an anticlimax and in the disappointment of the expectations of
both the apostles and the reader:

but return'd in vain. (II.24)

In the account of his early life the Son recalls, and recreates in his language, the attraction he felt, and now makes us feel, for decisive action:

yet this not all
To which my Spirit aspir'd; victorious deeds
Flam'd in my heart, heroic acts; one while
To rescue *Israel* from the *Roman* yoke,
Then to subdue and quell o'er all the earth

> Brute violence and proud Tyrannic pow'r,
> Till truth were freed, and equity restor'd. (I.214–220)

The rhetoric is martial, but Jesus declines its urgings (even though they are his own) and refuses to deliver the response he himself has called for: "Yet held it more humane, more heavenly, first / By winning words to conquer willing hearts, / And make persuasion do the work of fear" (I.221–223). The point is of course an orthodox one, but in the context established so forcefully by the verse—"To rescue *Israel* from the *Roman* yoke," "to subdue . . . Brute violence and proud Tyrranic power"—it seems less than what is required, and we are left with the disappointment of an issue unresolved, and a confrontation avoided.

These are small moments, and one would hesitate to make much of the pattern they embody were it not also the pattern of the temptation scenes, which are constructed in such a way as to make us feel the pressures of the issues they involve. The first temptation draws us in immediately, and Arnold Stein's comments are very much to the point:[2] "After the long introduction, which has prepared us for a long contest, the sudden brush, abrupt and possibly final, catches the reader unprepared; in the immediate heightening of his sense of the dangerous excitement potential in the contest, he is, by the most physical of dramatic means, made to identify with the protagonist" (pp. 42–43). The question I would ask is, "Which protagonist?," for Satan's trap is baited in such a way as to make it impossible for the reader to dismiss its appeal as easily as Jesus seems to:

> But if thou be the Son of God, Command
> That out of these hard stones be made thee bread;
> So shalt thou save thyself and us relieve
> With food, whereof we wretched seldom taste. (I.342–345)

"So shalt thou save thyself and us relieve." The subtlety of this suggestion, at least insofar as it works upon the reader, is to be located in its tail-like second half, "and us relieve." This is the first appearance in the poem of what Stein finely calls "the bait of charity" (p. 91). The "us" in question are of course the men of the desert, born, as Satan says, to "much misery and hardship"; and the reality of their suffering is not diminished simply because the tempter is discerned to be other than he "seem'st." That is to say, while Satan surely lies when he represents himself as one of the "wretched," this does not mean that there are none who live under the conditions he describes. All of the temptations in *Para-*

dise Regained are real, in the sense that they are posed with reference to real problems, and all of them, as Stein's summary statement indicates, are baited with charity: "The stones turned to bread would provide food for self and the 'wretched'; the acceptance of the banquet would relieve nature and her 'gentle Ministers' of their troubled shame over the hunger of the lord of nature; the affectation of 'private life' was depriving 'All Earth her wonder at thy acts'; the acceptance of Parthia would deliver the ten tribes, as their fathers were delivered from the land of Egypt" (p. 91).[3] But if the concerns to which Satan's arguments speak are acknowledged and validated by the moral reader, they are either ignored or scorned by the responses of the Son:

> He ended, and the Son of God replied.
> "Think'st thou such force in Bread? is it not written
> (For I discern thee other than thou seem'st)
> Man lives not by Bread only, but each Word
> Proceeding from the mouth of God, who fed
> Our fathers here with Manna? In the Mount
> *Moses* was forty days, nor eat nor drank,
> And forty days *Eliah* without food
> Wander'd this barren waste; the same I now:
> Why dost thou then suggest to me distrust." (I.346–355)

Rather than deal with the issues Satan's challenge raises, Jesus seizes on what is almost a literary quibble to make his very special point. He takes "save thyself" in its spiritual significance and proceeds as if hunger were not a reality but a metaphor. As a result the dialogue becomes a vehicle of *non*-communication; we hear two voices supposedly addressing each other, but they issue from wholly different points of reference. The temptation is proffered in the context of a perceived human need, but the response is made in terms of the way in which Satan's request—turn these stones into bread—reflects on the Son's relationship to God. "Why dost thou then suggest to me distrust?" is the line that pinpoints *his* concern. "If I were to do as you ask, it would imply that God cannot sustain his servants without natural means. The examples of Moses and Elijah—who trusted—suggest otherwise and it is in their tradition that I would enroll myself." On one level, of course, this is a perfect and orthodox response; but on another level (of which we cannot help but be aware) it is profoundly unsatisfactory if only because the immediate problem (and this continues to be true in every instance) is

left behind, not even dismissed but simply unattended to, except perhaps by the reader who in later scenes is himself one of those whom
Jesus declines to help.

The parallel to the soliloquies of Mary and the apostles is, I trust,
obvious. There is the same felt disparity between the presentation of the
problem and the egregious passivity of the (non) response. Just at that
moment when we expect an issue to be met head on, the speaker wraps
himself in a piety and says in effect, "Let God worry about it." Later it
will be: let God worry about the Roman populace groaning under the
yoke of an aged and sybaritic emperor; let God bring about the deliverance of the ten lost tribes; let God's word do the work some would as-
sign to human eloquence.

III

This, of course, is a critique from a Satanic point of view, but it is
the Satanic point of view that we share, at least during the early stages
of the poem. That is to say, the poem's basic pattern—of pressure in the
direction of action followed by a deliberate refusal to act—is as exasper-
ating for us as it is for Satan. The difference, finally, is what is made of
that exasperation. Satan is trapped by it, unable to deviate from his
planned course of action even after it has repeatedly proved unsuccess-
ful. Modern clinicians would call his behavior compulsive. Milton's
diagnosis takes the form of a series of powerful and related images:

> But as a man who had been matchless held
> In cunning, overreach't where least he thought,
> To salve his credit, and for very spite
> Still will be tempting him who foils him still,
> And never cease, though to his shame the more;
> Or as a swarm of flies in vintage time,
> About the wine-press where sweet must is pour'd,
> Beat off, returns as oft with humming sound;
> Or surging waves against a solid rock,
> Though all to shivers dash't, th'assault renew,
> Vain batt'ry, and in froth or bubbles end;
> So Satan, whom repulse upon repulse
> Met ever, and to shameful silence brought,
> Yet gives not o'er though desperate of success,
> And his vain importunity pursues. (IV.10–24)

No amount of "bad success" will provoke Satan to reconsider his strategy and the assumptions behind it. He learns nothing from experience and is thus a perfect example of one who is " 'morally' so indisposed toward truth that nothing would suffice to make him see,"[4] a mind so complacent in its own limitations as to be unteachable, even by the searchingly irenic method of dialectic.

The reader, however, is in a different position, and the problem the Son's conduct poses for him is correspondingly different. Satan wants to know who Jesus is and is frustrated by his inability to force him out into the open. The reader knows from the first who Jesus is, and if he is frustrated, it is because evasiveness and passivity are not part of what he knows. Satan's interest in the Son's statements is limited to the indication they give of the success or failure of his strategy, while the reader's interest is a function of his predisposition to regard the Son as an exemplary figure. What is a challenge for one is a puzzle for the other. What does this mean? Why is the Savior responding in this curious way? In what sense am I to imitate *these* (non) actions?[5] Thus while Satan's question, "What does thou in this world?" is rhetorical in the sense that he neither expects nor desires an answer, the reader, whose stake in the whole matter is very much greater, asks the question seriously: "What dost thou in this world?"

The answer of course is right there on the surface, where important answers usually are, and it is given innumerable times, although Satan never understands it and the reader's understanding is something he must work for. Not surprisingly, the Son himself provides the most precisely direct explanation of what he is doing:

Mee hung'ring more to do my Father's will. (II.259)

Every time the Son declines the opportunity to redress a wrong or meet a need, he refuses to claim for himself an efficacy apart from God. No matter what form Satan's temptations take, their thrust is always to get Jesus to substitute his will for God's, to respond to his own sense of crisis, to rely only on remedies which are at hand and in his own control. The temptation, then, whatever issues Satan attempts to attach to it, is preeminently a temptation to self-assertion—"save thyself" (I.344); "If at great things thou wouldst arrive" (II.426); "These Godlike virtues wherefore dost thou hide?" (III.21); "Aim therefore at no less than all the world" (IV.105); "So let extend thy mind o'er all the world" (IV.223) —and in relation to it, not doing anything is the most positive of actions.

That is, doing the Father's will requires the relinquishing of one's own, the most difficult of all acts, although its visible manifestations are necessarily unimpressive. "What dost thou in this world?" I do my Father's will, and therefore *I* do nothing.

Obviously, the choice of a hero whose main business is the immolation of his own will presents certain difficulties (which are actually difficulties in the nature of the audience). All of the strengths, poetic and dramatic, are on the other side. Milton is as aware of this as anyone, but his strategy is not, as one might expect, to minimize the attractiveness of self-assertion or (somehow) to make passivity dramatically appealing. Rather, he chooses to regard our natural affinity for language and actions that are concrete and immediately satisfying as a symptom of a radical defect, which, if it is to be extirpated, must first be acknowledged. Accordingly, he deliberately provokes what will, in the context of the reader's predisposed sympathies, be recognized as the *wrong* response or at least a response that is problematic, and therefore a response we will feel obliged to think about. That is to say, the reader who is discomforted by the Son's behavior will be moved to ask a question—what can this mean?—and to the extent that he becomes able to answer the question, the source of his discomfort will be removed.

This suggests a pattern of (possible) progress in the reader's career—from impatience to understanding to approval—which constitutes a subplot in the poem's action. The main plot works itself out in terms of the Son's response to Satan, the reader's plot in terms of his response to the Son's response to Satan. The Son declines to act on the basis of the motives Satan nominates, caring only to do his Father's will; but these are motives which are at least superficially appealing, and it is disconcerting when they are not only scorned, but dismissed, as if the issues of hunger and poverty and tyranny were fictions. It is not that we want the Son to do what Satan asks, but that we want him to do *something*, even if it is only to explain himself more fully. What he does, however, is move on, leaving us to do the explaining (it is the task the poem sets us) and to come to terms with the inappropriateness of his response. If we succeed, and the critical history of the poem indicates that success is by no means assured, it is because our idea of what is "appropriate," and therefore *our* response to him, has changed.

This change of response, if it occurs, is an action parallel to the action the Son performs in the narrative, the subordination of the self. In the act of understanding the poem, or trying to, we become less self-centered, for to the extent that understanding involves approval of what the Son does, it involves also the discarding of the values in which the dignity of the self inheres—wealth, power, fame, charity, statesmanship, language, literature, philosophy, mind—and the substituting for them of the single and all-inclusive value of obedience to God. In terms of the choice the poem poses for us, a choice of responses, obedience to God is a function of our relationship to its hero. A successful reading of the poem then will be marked by a *re*valuing of the Son's passivity, which implies of course a *de*valuing of assertive action and self-expression. The experience of the poem is for the reader as well as for the Son a denying of the claims of the individual will—each stage of it imposes a further restriction on the operation of that will—and for both the end of that experience is nothing less than the putting away of the self.

IV

It is not surprising, then, that the pattern of action in the poem—the progressive narrowing (to nothing) of the area in which the self is allowed to operate—should be paralleled by a pattern of language in the course of which the individual voice is more and more circumscribed until in the end it falls silent. Speech no less than action (it *is* an action) is the potential vehicle of pride; the more one approaches the state of perfect obedience, the less distinctive and identifiable will be his accents.

It is a commonplace of criticism to observe that *Paradise Regained* is a contest not only of wills but of styles.[6] Satan's language, especially when it becomes the vehicle of temptation, is full, luxuriant, rhythmically satisfying and rhetorically dazzling, while the Son's replies display a rather narrow range from terseness ("What hast thou to do with my hunger?") to obfuscation ("Think not but that I know these things or think I know them not") to what is perhaps the worst line in English poetry: "Mee worse than wet thou find'st not." These styles reflect the stances and attitudes of the two speakers, on the one hand an imagination in love with its own fanciful creations, on the other, in Louis Martz' words, "a mind engaged in an immense effort at self-control . . . poised, tense, alert, watching any tendency toward elaboration, luxury, self-indulgence."[7] "*Self*-indulgence" is exactly right, for the Son's language, in its restraint and anonymity, is further evidence of his determination to give the least possible scope to the self. It is the verbal equivalent of standing and waiting, of doing nothing, and the judgment it makes on more personal styles is perfectly predictable:

> Remove their swelling Epithet thick laid
> As varnish on a Harlot's cheek, the rest,
> Thin sown with aught of profit or delight,
> Will be found unworthy . . . (IV.343–346)

This famously disturbing statement has caused Milton's admirers much embarrassment. Even Martz feels obliged to account for a judgment "so much more drastic and more violent than that made by the rest of the poem." The "whole poem," he explains, "qualifies and moderates this fierce renunciation."[8] I would say rather that the whole poem prepares us for this renunciation which is as inevitable as it is sweeping. The increasingly marked contrast between the two styles coincides with the reader's increasing awareness of what it is that the Son is refusing to do —declare his independence of God. As a result, language becomes identified not only with the false values (wealth, power, earthly kingship) that are the basis of Satan's appeal but also with the overruling temptation they always represent, the temptation to value (and therefore to assert) the self.

It is for this reason that the drama of the temptation scenes is counterpointed by a sustained attack on "talk." The first epithet the Son applies to Satan suggests that the fiend's substance is largely verbal: "compos'd of lies" (I.407). Lying, the Son continues, is "thy sustenance, thy food," a food Satan offers to "the Nations" in the form of verbal "Delusions" (I.443). When the kingdom of Heaven is established, Satan will fall silent ("they shall find thee mute"), and mankind will be nourished not by words but by the living Word which dwells in "pious hearts":

> God hath now sent his living Oracle
> Into the World to teach his final will,
> And sends his Spirit of Truth henceforth to dwell
> In pious Hearts, an inward Oracle
> To all truth requisite for men to know. (I.460–464)

There is in these lines an implied equation (later to be made explicit) between illumination and silence, an equation that quite probably has its source in Augustine: "For God speaks with a man not by means of some bodily creature making sound in bodily ears . . . rather he speaks by the truth itself, if one is worthy of listening with the mind instead of with the body."[9] The man whose heart is the dwelling place of God's truth will find bodily sounds superfluous and distracting. This distinction

between an inner and an outer word is one that Satan never understands, although in his volubility he continues to reinforce it. The ways
of Truth, he complains, are "hard . . . and rough to walk" (I.478) but
they are "smooth on the tongue." I may be unable to follow them, but
"permit me / To hear thee . . . / And talk at least" (I.483–485). Satan
talks and talks and talks, and at every opportunity the Son displays his
scorn for the productions of the tongue. You say that my years are over-
ripe and I have not yet had my share of glory? "What is glory but the
blaze of fame, / The people's praise . . . / And what delight to be by such
extoll'd, / To live upon thir tongues and be thir talk" (III.47–48, 54–55).
For one who would live upon the Manna of the Word, there could be
nothing more truly inglorious. Even celebrated heroes like Scipio gain
a reward that is "but verbal" (III.104).

All the while Satan's honeyed speeches grow longer and longer,
until, in the description of Rome, the "rich, sensuous coloring and high
rhetoric of the world" is carried "to its absolute and appropriate limit."[10]
Characteristically the Son remains "unmov'd," and responds with a
parody of the Satanic style:

> . . . thou should'st add to tell
> Thir sumptuous gluttonies, and gorgeous feasts
> On *Citron* tables or *Atlantic* stone,
> (For I have also heard, perhaps have read)
> Their wines of *Setia*, *Cales*, and *Falerne*,
> *Chios* and *Crete*, and how they quaff in Gold,
> Crystals and Murrhine cups emboss'd with Gems
> And studs of Pearl, to me should'st tell who thirst
> And hunger still. (IV.113–121)

So secure is the Son that he offers his tempter a literary critique and even
suggests additions that would make his presentation more effective. He
also demonstrates how easy it would be for him to contend with Satan
on his own rhetorical terms, were they not so contemptible. The anticipatory judgment of "sumptuous gluttonies" falls as much on the language as on the content of the succeeding six lines. By this point, the
Son is less angry than bored; it is, he complains, "but tedious waste of
time to sit and hear / So many hollow compliments and lies / Outlandish
flatteries . . . *talk*" (IV.123–125, emphasis mine). When Satan obliges
with a more direct statement of his terms—"The Kingdoms of the world
to thee I give; / . . . if thou wilt fall down"—his offer, *and* his "talk," are
rejected with "disdain":

> I never lik'd thy talk, thy offers less,
> Now both abhor, since thou hast dar'd to utter
> Th'abominable terms. (IV.171–173)

Satan's "talk" and the kingdoms over which he claims to rule are allied
in their inferiority to an inner word and an inward kingdom. For a
moment, the fiend himself seems to acknowledge this—"let pass, as they
are transitory, / The Kingdoms of this world"—and in their place he
offers, of all things, the ability to talk. The substance of the temptation
has been the kingdoms of the world, the vehicle a language reflecting
the values of those kingdoms. Having rejected the substance, the Son
is now offered the vehicle:

> . . . as thy Empire must extend,
> So let extend thy mind o'er all the world
> In knowledge, all things in it comprehend.
> All knowledge is not couch't in *Moses'* Law,
> The *Pentateuch* or what the Prophets wrote;
> The *Gentiles* also know, and write, and teach
> To admiration, led by Nature's light;
> And with the *Gentiles* much thou must converse,
> Ruling them by persuasion as thou mean'st,
> Without thir learning how wilt thou with them,
> Or they with thee hold conversation meet? (IV.222–232)

It is in these lines that the true status of language in relation to the central issue of the poem is revealed. It is not merely that talk is valueless,
but that Satan's invitation to value talk is an invitation to value the self.
This is clearly what is meant when the Son is urged to "let extend thy
mind o'er all the world." Satan is here an apostle of the creative imagination, of the poet as maker and self-acknowledged legislator of the
world. The "thick-laid varnish" of secular literature is the overlay of
man's brain (what Herbert calls his "sparkling notions") on the clarity
of God's word. Its superfluousness is the superfluousness of the individual mind to the validation of truth, and when the Son rejects the arts of
language he does what he has been doing all along: he refuses to play
God.

The dismissal of pagan learning, then, is not a gesture discontinuous with what we have seen previously; rather, it follows inevitably
from the hero's attempt to find a mode of action which embodies the
least recognition of the self, and to the extent that we have come to

understand his other attempts in this direction, we will understand this one too. For if the experience of the poem effects a change in our response to Christ's actions, it effects a corresponding change in our response to his language. The reversal of values, away from the self and toward God, is also an aesthetic reversal. Selflessness and stylelessness are one.

V

To this point, our investigation of *Paradise Regained* has yielded a description of its movement which accords perfectly with the outline put forward earlier in this essay: it is a poem concerned to work out the relationship between man and God, and it proceeds on two levels; on the narrative level, there is a progressive narrowing of the area in which the self is preeminent or even active, and on the verbal level there is a corresponding diminishing, first of the complexity of language, and then of its volubility; and the two diminishings put pressure on the reader to reverse his initial response to the stances of the protagonists. It remains only to point out that these patterns complete themselves at the poem's climactic moment, when inaction is raised to the level of disappearance and terseness of speech finds its apex in silence. I refer of course to the moment when Satan places the Son on the pinnacle, expecting him either to fall down and so prove himself no adversary or cast himself down and so tempt God's providence. He does neither. He does nothing. *He disappears:*

> To whom thus Jesus. Also it is written,
> Tempt not the Lord thy God; he said and stood. (IV.560–561)

Line 561 is, as Barbara Lewalski observes, "notably ambiguous."[11] Does Jesus here say (as he has said before), "If I were to do as you suggest I would be tempting God's providence," or does he say, "You ought not to tempt your God, who I am." This ambiguity has been resolved by Woodhouse, who declares for both meanings: "This is Christ's supreme act of obedience and trust, and it is also the long awaited demonstration of divinity. The poem's two themes are finally and securely united; and 'Tempt not the Lord thy God' carries a double meaning, for, in addition to its immediate application, it is Christ's first claim to participate in the Godhead. In an instant, and by the same event, Satan receives his answer and Christ achieves full knowledge of himself."[12] To this interpretation Arnold Stein opposes a vigorous and compelling dissent:

What has happened? Surely not that Christ is directly replying to Satan's challenge by finally declaring himself, by saying: thou shalt not tempt *me*, the Lord thy God! That would be to violate the whole discipline, so perfectly sustained, of Christ's moral and intellectual example: the witness of whence he is by the seeking of glory not for himself but for Him who sent him, the hungering to do the Father's will.

To see this as Christ's "claim" . . . is to abandon much of the force of the disciplined demonstration—as well as to abandon Milton's own passionate religious and moral belief, and his own disciplined unwillingness to pry into God's maintained mysteries.

(pp. 128, 224–225)

Stein's objection can be met and yet maintained if we specify the nature of the "claim" being made. The assertion that the figure on the pinnacle is the Lord God is anything but prideful, for Christ's "claim" to that identity rests on his demonstrated willingness to lose his own. He is God to the extent that *he*, as a consciousness distinguishable from God, is no more. The "supreme act of obedience" is also the supreme act of resignation, a letting go of the self so final that no trace of it remains. "Tempt not the Lord thy God, he said." Who said? The Son, of course, since the sounds issue from his mouth, but the words are not his ("Also it is written") except in the sense that he has identified himself with their speaker. It is not that he appropriates the words, but that they, and their source, appropriate him. This is what Augustine means when he declares that "the word of God is not another's to those who obey it."[13] The man who wraps himself in the Scriptures, as Christ does here, becomes an adjunct of them and ceases to have an independent existence. This is not an extra-literary point, but one made by the reading experience itself, when we are unable to separate out the responsibility for this line. The voice we hear is not the voice we have come to know, but the impersonal voice suggested by the "it" in "it is written." Christ does nothing less here than find a way to assert selflessness. It is a linguistic miracle in which language, the primary sign of personality, becomes the means by which personality is extinguished. The Son performs the impossible feat of saying silence and makes himself disappear.

In his place, of course, is a new and stronger self, the amalgam I-thou to whose presence the force of the ambiguity bears witness. The only response we can give to these lines is, as Stein remarks, a "gasp," in recognition of the tremendous power that has been released by the Son's voluntary laying down of his identity. What is demonstrated here is not divinity, but the reward which awaits anyone (including the

reader) who subordinates his will to that of the Father. Every man can
be God if he answers Satan's question—"Who are you?"—as Christ does:
"I am what the Father will make of me." To say "I am nothing" is to be
(with God) everything. George Herbert spoke of this strength through
weakness, gain through loss, power through inaction, as "imping my
wing on thine." As usual, however, the Scriptures themselves have the
last word, even in literary criticism: "All things are more ours by their
being his." In this case that truth is dramatically validated by what
happens to the Son when he succeeds (exactly the wrong word) in
emptying himself of all but his hunger to do his Father's will. Everything
he has renounced in his own name is restored to him tenfold. The angels
whose presence he refused to command in the wilderness now bring to
him the fruit of life in place of the deadly fruit he had rejected: the victory he had scorned when the means and the time were specified by
Satan is now his in the moment of Satan's defeat ("But Satan smitten
with amazement fell"), and his earlier prophecy—"Who advance his
glory, not thir own, / Them he himself to glory will advance"—is spec-
tacularly fulfilled as his triumph is celebrated not by the tongues of a
miscellaneous rabble, but by "Angelic Choirs" and "Heavenly Anthems."
Even language and the arts of literature are returned to him (and to the
reader) in the form of the magnificent Antaeus simile, pagan still, but
now new washed and baptized in the name of the Lord. But of all the
things restored to the Son, the most important is surely the opportunity,
so many times offered and so many times refused, to save. Whatever dismay the reader may at times have felt at the Son's evasiveness and passivity is now more than redeemed by the intensely personal reassur-
ance tendered him in the poem's quietly powerful closing:

Now enter, and begin to save mankind. (IV.635)

Or, in other words, "Now begin to act." Action, which has before
been the vehicle of temptation, is now not only allowed, but enjoined.
This is no paradox, but a final recognition of the distinction to which the
Son has been faithful in the course of his trials, a distinction that is
finely drawn by Northrop Frye: "The Christian must learn to will to re-
lax the will, to perform real acts in God's time and not pseudo acts in his
own."[14] In order to perform real acts, that is, acts in accordance with the
will of God, one must first refrain from performing pseudo acts, acts
which reflect and assert the will of the individual; so that the prerequisite for real action is the disposition to withhold action even in the face

of situations which seem to call for it. It is this disposition that has
informed the Son's behavior and presented so much of a puzzle to Satan
and, for a time, to the reader:

> Suffering, abstaining, quietly expecting
> Without distrust or doubt, that he may know
> What I can suffer, how obey; who best
> Can suffer, best can do; best reign, who first
> Well hath obey'd. (III.192–196)

This ordering of obligations is mirrored perfectly in the form of the
narrative and in the relationship between its events and the response of
the reader. The Son suffers and obeys, and the subordination of his will
to the will of the Father is reflected in his passivity. That passivity, in
turn, acts as a constraint on the response of the reader, who would like
to be able to applaud some decisive action. When the Son's triumph over
himself is complete, his active powers (no longer his) are released; and
this releases and authorizes the response of the reader. Moreover, the
action he now applauds, the multiple defeats of Satan (past, present,
future), includes or makes possible all the actions which he would have
liked the Son to perform when they were urged by Satan—the feeding
of the hungry, the restoration of David's throne, the quelling of tyrannic
power, and the freeing of the people from their (inner) yoke. In short,
action and response are purified together; one has its proper direction
(provided by God) and the other its proper object (the doing of God's
will), and what was disallowed to both hero and reader when the circumstances and the conditions were nominated by Satan (in the name
of the self) is now authorized and approved when the circumstances and
the conditions are nominated by God. What the poem asks that we give
up it returns in exactly the measure of our compliance with its request.

Yet even here, when the frustrations large and small of the verse
and the narrative are swept away in a prolonged moment of action and
response, it is a moment of anticipation and a response to events that
do not occur within the confines of the poem. *Paradise Regained* remains
true to its own self-imposed limitations, which are the limitations it has
imposed on its hero and its reader, and ends with another of the with-
drawals from drama that have been the basis of its dialectic:

> Thus they the Son of God our Savior meek
> Sung Victor, and from Heavenly Feast refresht
> Brought on his way with joy; hee unobserv'd
> Home to his Mother's house private return'd. (IV.636–639)[15]

NOTES

1. "On Milton's Poetry," *Yale Review*, LVI (1967), 172–196.
2. *Heroic Knowledge* (Minneapolis, 1957).
3. One might add that there is a need also for the powerful eloquence which a knowledge of Greek and Latin rhetoric would presumably generate.
4. The words are Robert Cushman's in *Therapeia* (Chapel Hill, 1957), p. 216. Cushman is discussing Plato's belief that some minds are hopelessly indisposed toward revelation. The relevant text is the *Seventh Epistle* (344a): "Neither receptivity nor memory will ever produce knowledge in him who has no affinity with the object, since it does not germinate to start with in alien minds."
5. The reader will ask these questions in part because other, more natural, questions have been precluded by the opening scenes (see especially I.131–181) where he learns what will *not* happen. The Son will not fall to Satan's temptations, he will not even waver; and in the absence of narrative suspense, the center of the reader's interest is not the fact but the manner of the hero's victory.
6. See, e.g., Louis Martz, *The Paradise Within* (New Haven, 1964), p. 183.
7. Ibid.
8. Ibid., p. 197.
9. *City of God* XI.2.
10. Martz, pp. 186, 194.
11. *Milton's Brief Epic* (Providence, 1966), p. 316.
12. "Theme and Pattern in *Paradise Regained*," *University of Toronto Quarterly*, XXV (1955–1956), 181.
13. *On Christian Doctrine*, trans. D. W. Robertson (New York, 1958), p. 167.
14. "The Typology of *Paradise Regained*," in *Milton: Modern Essays in Criticism*, ed. Arthur E. Barker (New York, 1965), pp. 440–441.
15. Since this essay was written I have read Lawrence Hyman's fine article, "The Reader's Attitude in *Paradise Regained*," *PMLA*, LXXXV (1970), 496–503. Mr. Hyman argues that "throughout the entire poem Christ progressively rejects those human values and human feelings that prevent him from realizing his divine nature" and that this action brings him into conflict with "the human values of the reader" (p. 500). He believes, however, that the distance between the reader and Christ increases as the poem unfolds, whereas I believe that the effect of the poem is to bring them together. Mr. Hyman overemphasizes, I think, the "inhuman" aspects of Christ's behavior. In the poem, the emphasis falls on the ability of every human to imitate that behavior. This point is made very clearly by the many references to Job, Alexander, Scipio, and Socrates, and by Satan himself in lines 531–540 of Book IV:

> And opportunity I here have had
> To try thee, sift thee, and confess have found thee
> Proof against all temptation as a rock
> Of Adamant, and as a Center, firm;
> To th'utmost of mere man both wise and good,
> Not more; for Honors, Riches, Kingdoms, Glory
> Have been before contemn'd, and may again:
> Therefore to know what more thou art than man,
> Worth naming Son of God by voice from Heav'n,
> Another method I must now begin.

I would also like to call the attention of the reader to the interpretations offered recently by B. Rajan and Jon Lawry. In a beautifully written essay (in *The Lofty*

Rhyme [London, 1970], pp. 113–127) Mr. Rajan emphasizes the "special kind of alertness" (p. 122) required of the reader in *Paradise Regained*: "As the duel of the mind evolves in its stripped clarity we are meant to measure each movement of the combatants with an intentness not inferior to that of the writing itself . . . the act of reading thus becomes a specific foundation for growth in the reader's mind" (pp. 121–122). And Mr. Lawry is especially good in *The Shadow of Heaven* (Cornell, 1968) on the relationship between the temptation of the Son and the analogous temptation of the reader: "The literary temptation for the audience, rather like the theological temptation for the Son, is to fill a necessary vacuum by means of some decisive, traditional, fallen action. . . . For both the Son and the audience, human error would allow the glamorous Satanic desire called impatience . . . to best Christian patience in the desert Field" (pp. 299–300). "In *Paradise Regained*, we must acknowledge our taste for 'fallen' literary and intellectual heroics like those of Satan rather than like those of the Son's choice and Milton's brief epic" (p. 299).

Sin in *Paradise Regained*: The Biblical Background

MOTHER MARY CHRISTOPHER PECHEUX, O.S.U.

COLLEGE OF NEW ROCHELLE

The temptations in *Paradise Regained* have been studied from many points of view, each of which yields its own illumination. To complement the analytical studies which discuss the various kinds of sin involved in the threefold temptation,[1] it may be helpful to consider the essential nature of sin itself, that enemy which it is the mission of the Son of God to subdue.[2] Since the Bible would naturally be the chief source for Milton's concept of sin, this essay proposes to examine the principal biblical themes of sin as they relate to the action of *Paradise Regained*.[3]

Although the Old Testament uses a variety of terms which can be and have been translated by the word "sin," it is possible to isolate those which occur most frequently. Biblical scholars agree that the words used most often stem from the root *ht'*,[4] the basic meaning of which is "to miss the mark, to fail, to deviate." The original secular context and literal meaning later took on religious and metaphorical overtones. To miss the mark can imply being led astray in a broader sense; hence, to lack some element in attaining a desired end, or to be deceived. The root appears in its literal sense in Judges 20:16: "Every one could sling stones at an hair breadth, and not miss." Psalm 25:8 hovers between the literal and the metaphorical: "Good and upright is the Lord: therefore will he teach sinners in the way," while in such verses as Joshua 7:20 the abstract concept has superseded the concrete image: "Indeed I have sinned against the Lord God of Israel, and thus and thus have I done."

The semantic subtleties of the Hebrew idioms would not have been lost on the scholar-poet who, even in his blindness, had his secretary read to him every morning from the Hebrew Bible;[5] but the important point for this study is that the notion of sin as a misstep or error, besides being close to the Greek concept of *hamartia*[6]—the kind of failure which is caused less by a revolt of the will than by a deviation of the mind— has strong biblical roots. It forms an important part of the ethical frame- work of *Paradise Lost*, expressed clearly, for example, in Adam's expla- nation to Eve:

> But God left free the Will, for what obeys
> Reason, is free, and Reason he made right,
> But bid her well beware, and still erect,
> Lest by some fair appearing good surpris'd
> She dictate false, and misinform the Will
> To do what God expressly hath forbid. (IX.351–356)[7]

Adam's description is all too clear a prophecy of what in fact occurs as Eve listens to the serpent's glozing words.

   Milton had a lifelong interest in this deceptive aspect of sin and in the moral importance of distinguishing good from evil. An early entry in the *Commonplace Book* remarks that "in moral evil much good can be mixed and that with remarkable cunning." A quotation from Tertullian follows: "So the devil steeps whatever deadly dish he prepares in God's dearest . . . benefits."[8] The morally upright man must be alert in order not to be deceived. It is certainly not surprising to find Milton using this concept in *Paradise Regained*; Christ, the sinless man, must show intellectual acumen in a moral context. What is noteworthy, however, is that a very large number of the occurrences are in the first book, where they are pervasive, while the few references in the later books are massed together in summarizing passages. Such a distribution invites investigation.

   The narrator stresses the idea of deception in the first lines of the poem: the Tempter is to be "foil'd / In all his wiles"; Christ is to be proved the "undoubted" Son of God. After the council of the devils, he reiterates that Satan is going to try Christ with "all guile" in order to "subvert" him. Satan boasts that he has deceived Eve; he recognizes that "well couch't fraud, well woven snares" are the means he must now em- ploy; and he admits that he has glibbed the tongues of the false prophets with lies. The Father speaks ironically of Satan's "utmost subtlety" and great cunning; he says that Christ will be able to resist his solicitations, winning what the first man had lost, "by fallacy surpris'd." The angels, in their short hymn of nine lines, declare that Christ is to vanquish hellish wiles by wisdom, proof against whatever may seduce him, and that he will frustrate the stratagems of hell. Christ himself recognizes his mission to "teach the erring Soul / Not wilfully misdoing, but unware / Misled." He affirms that Satan is composed of lies and that lying is his sustenance. In the long passage on the oracles he stresses the evil of the half-truths with which Satan has deluded mankind; lines 430 to 444 are little more than a tissue of repetitions of this idea (I have italicized the significant words):

> Yet thou *pretend'st* to truth; all Oracles
> By thee are giv'n, and what confest more true
> Among the Nations? That hath been thy *craft*,
> By mixing somewhat true to *vent more lies*.
> But what have been thy answers, what but *dark*,
> *Ambiguous* and with *double sense deluding*,
> Which they who ask'd have *seldom understood*,
> And *not well understood*, as good not known?
> Who ever by consulting at thy shrine
> Return'd the wiser, or the more instruct
> To fly or follow what concern'd him most,
> And run not sooner to his *fatal snare*?
> For God hath justly giv'n the Nations up
> To thy *Delusions*.

Contrasted with all this is the simple assertion of the truth which Christ has come to reveal, a truth not recondite or complicated but simple and open to all:

> God hath now sent his living Oracle
> Into the World to teach his final will,
> And sends his Spirit of Truth henceforth to dwell
> In pious hearts, an inward Oracle
> To all truth requisite for men to know. (I.460–464)

Christ's clear vision immediately penetrates Satan's disguise: "For I discern thee other than thou seem'st" (l. 348).

Even the metaphors in this book fit the theme of deception: the infernal consistory is held "within thick Clouds and dark tenfold involv'd" (l. 41); Satan's steps are "girded with snaky wiles" (l. 120); the desert in which Christ wanders is pathless and dark, double-shaded with Night's sullen wing. There may even be a play on the literal and metaphorical meanings of error when Satan says, "Hard are the ways of truth, and rough to walk" (l. 478). The book ends as he bows low "his gray dissimulation."

In Book II the disciples experience perplexity and amazement; Belial speaks about hearts tangled in amorous nets and about credulous desire; the narrator characterizes Satan as "sly," and "subtle," and remarks that the spirits chosen to assist the Tempter (presumably in the banquet scene) are likest to him in guile; Christ, finally, recognizes the pompous delicacies of the banquet as "no gifts but guiles" (l. 391) and characterizes riches as "the wise man's cumbrance if not snare" (l. 454). Near the end of the book he explains the true function of kingship:

> . . . to guide Nations in the way of truth
> By saving Doctrine, and from error lead
> To know, and knowing worship God aright. (ll. 473–475)

In his soliloquy he remarks that he has spent forty days "wand'ring this woody maze" (l. 246)—a metaphorical equivalent of the kind of temptation he is meeting.

Omitting the metaphorical occurrences, I have counted twenty-six separate references in Book I to the idea of deception and error, and they are scattered throughout the book. In Book II there are only seven, but again they appear throughout (in lines 38, 115, 163, 166, 237, 391, and 454). There is a rather startling change in Book III: only in two passages, one at the beginning and one at the end of the book, do such references occur. At the beginning:

> So spake the Son of God, and Satan stood
> A while as mute confounded what to say,
> What to reply, confuted and convinc't
> Of his weak arguing and *fallacious* drift;
> At length collecting all his *Serpent wiles.* (ll. 1–5; italics mine)

And at the end:

> So spake *Israel's* true King, and to the Fiend
> Made answer meet, that made void all his *wiles.*
> So fares it when with truth *falsehood* contends.
>   (ll. 441–443; last two italics mine)

The lines suggest that this part of the campaign is now ended, and the opening of Book IV confirms the impression:

> Perplex'd and troubl'd at his bad success
> The Tempter stood, nor had what to reply,
> Discover'd in his fraud, thrown from his hope,
> So oft, and the persuasive Rhetoric
> That sleek't his tongue, and won so much on *Eve*,
> So little here, nay lost; but *Eve* was *Eve*,
> This far his over-match, who self-deceiv'd . . . (ll. 1–7)

References to the idea in other parts of the book are few but interesting. Satan himself, looking back over his vain attempts, admits that they have brought him no advantage: "missing what I aim'd" (l. 208), an ironic inversion of the biblical metaphor for sin; while Christ, just before the final confrontation, contemns the false portents of the night of storms and says scornfully, "Desist, thou art discern'd" (l. 497). Once in the temptation of learning and three times in the climactic and summarizing song of the angels does the idea occur again, in both places closely interwoven with the second main biblical theme; hence the discussion of these passages will be postponed.

Before examining the second common aspect of the idea of sin in the Bible it is important to recognize that the first is not a question of mere ignorance but involves some formal element of guilt. It is true that the Bible (particularly the Book of Leviticus, for example in chapters 4 and 5) offers examples of sins which can be considered mere violations of taboos. Even here, however, a distinction is made between the external violation of a regulation and the internal attitude which prompted the act; the former must be expiated, but the expiation itself is external, as was the transgression: "Ye shall have one law for him that sinneth through ignorance. . . . But the soul that doeth ought presumptuously . . . the same reproacheth the Lord; and that soul shall be cut off from among his people" (Num. 15:29–30). No doubt the implications of disobedience to the Law became more refined throughout the years of Israel's history, and if the wisdom literature of the late pre-Christian period often seems to equate folly and sin, it is not simple ignorance which is condemned, but a culpable failure to remain close to God. Error, folly, blindness, and wrongdoing are closely allied; the man who is deceived has in most cases failed to keep his reason alert and hence is guilty if he falls.

It is scarcely necessary to observe that in Milton's thinking there could be no element of any primitive concept which might hold a man guilty for an act performed in complete and blameless ignorance. On the other hand, Milton's penchant for completeness suggests the pos-

sibility that he might have wanted to include in the poem at least indirectly (as he included Belial's suggestion about women) every type
of sin. The taboo type of law infraction is not worthy of serious consideration by Christ, but it might be used by Satan. It may be that one purpose, though not the chief one, of the banquet scene is to cover the more
primitive biblical concept. Satan apparently is deliberately lying when
he says that the foods served in the banquet are not forbidden by the
Mosaic law; if Christ had accepted them, he might have been accused
of having technically violated a divine command.[9]

At any rate, in its more subtle forms the temptation to sin through
a mistake in judgment is not to be lightly dismissed; as Adam warns Eve,
she should not contemn the possible stratagems of one who was wise
and subtle enough to seduce angels (PL IX.306–308). Moreover, another prominent biblical theme is that of blindness as a punishment for
sin; in such a case, the apparently excusable error is really the result of a
previous act, or series of acts, of willful choices of evil. "His own iniq-
uities shall take the wicked himself, and he shall be holden with the
cords of his sins. He shall die without instruction; and in the greatness of
his folly he shall go astray" (Prov. 5:22–23); "lest any of you be hardened
through the deceitfulness of sin" (Heb. 3:13). Milton expounds this in
his De Doctrina Christiana, showing that hardness of heart is a punishment for obdurate sin,[10] and Christ refers to it in the passage on the
oracles: "For God hath justly giv'n the Nations up / To thy Delusions;
justly, since they fell / Idolatrous" (I.442–444).

In most mistaken choices, Milton seems to believe, there is involved
some culpable blindness, some lack of adjustment of our vision to God's.
This stern but logical doctrine explains the severity of a passage that
might otherwise seem out of character. Christ's words are harsh:

> And what the people but a herd confus'd,
> A miscellaneous rabble, who extol
> Things vulgar, and well weigh'd, scarce worth the praise?
> They praise and they admire they know not what;
> And know not whom, but as one leads the other. (PR III.49–53)

The Christ of Paradise Regained is not (or at least not only, or not at this
point) the compassionate shepherd of a flock; he cannot exonerate those
who remain in ignorance of the truth because they fail to bestir themselves sufficiently, who are passively led into evil ways without inquiring into the credentials of their leaders.

This is the point which Christ seems to be making when he recognizes his mission to "teach the erring Soul / Not wilfully misdoing, but unware / Misled" (I.224–226). There can be degrees of culpability in the materially sinful action, ranging from the complete formal innocence of one who "sins" through a lack of knowledge to a willful self-deception practically indistinguishable from explicit defiance of God. The phrase just quoted from Book I seems to point directly to the kind of action discussed thus far; Milton would have expected the reader to see the literal meaning behind the metaphorical "erring" and perhaps to recall the biblical metaphor. "Unware" suggests a lack of alertness and therefore some fault, but the emphasis is on "misled," which is placed in a position very prominent grammatically by its inversion and metrically by its initial position in the line. At the same time this aspect of sin is contrasted with a more serious kind—"wilfully misdoing."

Although the distinction is both logical and important, the second meaning is a natural outgrowth of the first. For in all of Hebrew thought the failure, the misstep, the error has as its term a person: sin is a failing toward someone, a violation of a bond, a rejection of a covenant with God. Even if there is another human party who is injured by the breach, fundamentally the sin is against God—a refusal to respond to his initiative and love. Hence the second characteristic feature of sin in the Bible appears in words derived from the root *psh'*, meaning "to rebel." Sin is a consciously willed offense against God. No longer is it a question of deception, even self-deception, but of deliberate defiance of the Supreme Being, the breaking of the relation of loyalty and peace. It was inevitable that this more refined concept should receive emphasis as the conscience of Israel developed. Though it is not confined to the prophetical books, some of its most striking expressions occur there, as in Isaiah: "Hear, O heavens, and give ear, O earth: for the Lord hath spoken, I have nourished and brought up children, and they have rebelled against me" (1:2) and in Ezekiel: "Son of man, I send thee to the children of Israel, to a rebellious nation that hath rebelled against me; they and their fathers have transgressed against me, even unto this very day" (2:3).

Milton's treatment of sin in *De Doctrina Christiana*, as well as the tenor of all his works, demonstrates his conviction that sin is essentially this deliberate rebellion against God.[11] Whatever the attendant circumstances, it is the inner attitude that matters: the will to obey God's law or the will to disobey it. The familiar line from *Paradise Lost* is a terse summary: "Against his better knowledge, not deceiv'd" (IX.998). Christ therefore must be tested in the fundamental straightness of his will with

that of God. It is not enough that he has resisted all the appeals to make
the wrong choices, to think that earthly power or glory are the means
by which he is to win a kingdom; succumbing to these temptations
would have implied some guilt, some selfish or imperfect motivation,
but the yielding would not have been on a par with Adam's open-eyed
rejection of God.

The earlier books of *Paradise Regained* have been devoted to the
first phase of the campaign; now the second, more crucial, part must
begin. The structure of the poem reveals a close correspondence with
both the logic of the concept of sin and its historical manifestations in
the Bible: it makes a definite distinction between error and rebellion,
while at the same time it shows that one is not wholly disconnected from
the other.[12] At one point Satan seems to be making both the distinction
and the connection: "My error was my error, and my crime / My
crime," he laments (III.212–213), perhaps echoing Job 34:37: "For he addeth
rebellion unto his sin" (literally, he adds *pesha'* to his *ḥaṭṭa'th*). As has
been seen, sin as error received very strong emphasis in the first book,
somewhat less in the second, very little in the third and fourth. On the
other hand, the temptation to open rebellion against God does not appear at all in the first two books, but it begins to emerge in the third and
becomes prominent in the fourth. This chiasmic arrangement is well
calculated to bring out both aspects of sin. There is some overlapping,
in keeping with the notion that both involve a deviation from God's
law, but the dramatic development of the poem reveals the greater complexity of the second type.

Most of the references in Book III to the idea of rebelling against
God occur in the dialogue concerning glory. Satan's first assay is still
tinged with a faint hope of succeeding in some sort of deception, as he
merely insinuates that Christ should not hide his "Godlike Virtues."
Christ picks up the hint but develops it in the opposite direction: glory
comes not from exalting oneself to a level closer to God but from receiving his approbation. He gives Satan a lesson in history by showing that
the great conquerors have ultimately tried to displace God; they

> . . . swell with pride, and must be titl'd Gods,
> Great Benefactors of mankind, Deliverers,
> Worship't with Temple, Priest and Sacrifice. (ll. 81–83)

Christ, on the contrary, effaces himself: "I seek not mine, but his / Who
sent me, and thereby witness whence I am" (ll. 106–107). Still more

clearly he describes man's basic sin, the willful breaking of the bond uniting him to God:

> Who for so many benefits receiv'd
> Turn'd recreant to God, ingrate and false,
> And so of all true good himself despoil'd,
> Yet, sacrilegious, to himself would take
> That which to God alone of right belongs. (ll. 137–141)

This is the basic sin not only of man but also of Satan, as he himself recognizes: he is "struck with guilt of his own sin." Christ explains that not rebellion against God but humble obedience is the way marked out for man; those can best reign who have first obeyed (l. 195); to anticipate the time marked out by God's providence is not the way of the just man (ll. 396, 440).

In Book III, then, Satan has, though still with a certain amount of subtlety, tempted Christ to more or less open rebellion against God. In Book IV the subtlety is dropped entirely and the temptation appears in its naked ugliness. The great vision of Rome concludes with Satan's assertion of his own supremacy: "To me the power / Is given, and by that right I give it thee" (ll. 103–104), and with the advice: "Aim therefore at no less than all the world, / Aim at the highest" (ll. 105–106). The assertion is repeated as the Tempter plays his last card:

> The Kingdoms of the world to thee I give;
> For giv'n to me, I give to whom I please,
> No trifle; yet with this reserve, not else,
> On this condition, if thou wilt fall down,
> And worship me as thy superior Lord. (ll. 163–167)

It is a temptation to idolatry, and Christ excoriates the blasphemy:

> I never lik'd thy talk, thy offers less,
> Now both abhor, since thou hast dar'd to utter
> Th'abominable terms, impious condition. (ll. 171–173)

Subterfuge and evasion are here ruled out; the explicit offer has been made, and the choice can be only between a total yes and a total no.

At this point in the narrative the essence of the Old Testament idea of sin is linked closely with some of the developments in the New Testament. Particularly in St. John's Gospel it is clear that the coming of

Christ creates a crisis; men must decide for him or against him, and to turn knowingly away from him is to sin unto death: "I am come a light unto the world, that whosoever believeth on me should not abide in darkness. . . . He that rejecteth me, and receiveth not my words, hath one that judgeth him: the word that I have spoken, the same shall judge him in the last day" (John 12:46, 48). The Synoptics, too, see the unpardonable sin as resisting the work of Jesus in spite of the conviction that it is the work of the Holy Spirit. There comes a time in each man's life when (always supposing that he has sufficient enlightenment) he must either accept or reject Jesus and his message. Because Milton chose to keep his narrative within the confines of the account of Christ's own temptation, he could not present this conflict directly (although it may be suggested in the choice of fidelity made by Mary and the disciples). But, whether embodied in the person of one who is the accredited agent of God or seen as a direct confrontation with God himself, there is always a choice for or against the truth; a submission to a higher being, or a rebellion against him.

Because the Christ of *Paradise Regained* recognizes the decisive nature of the offer, his tone changes. The words he uses (ll. 170–194) are harsh, uncompromising, disdainful: "abhor," "abominable," "dar'st thou," "accurst," "blasphemous." The "abhorred pact, / That I fall down and worship thee as God" is rejected as vigorously as it has been presented:

> Get thee behind me; plain thou now appear'st
> That Evil one, Satan for ever damn'd. (ll. 193–194)

There follows the lengthy "temptation to learning" and Christ's equally lengthy reply. The passage has been sufficiently attacked and, I think, more than sufficiently defended. An analysis of its relation to the concepts of sin which I have been considering may indicate from one additional viewpoint its consistency with the rest of the poem.

From many viewpoints, the temptation seems anticlimactic. Satan has uttered the ultimate blasphemy—fall down and worship me—and Christ has unequivocally rejected the offer. The well-couched fraud of the first three books has failed; so too has the direct invitation, the undisguised Faustian bargain. Is there any other device the Tempter can employ? He has failed to induce Christ to use the wrong means to attain his kingdom; he has failed to incite him to a direct revolt against God; but his wily mind conceives one more faint hope. If the act of idolatry itself can somehow be disguised, made to seem something other than it is, the Adversary may still prevail.

The core of this temptation occurs in lines 221 to 224:

> Be famous then
> By wisdom; as thy Empire must extend
> So let extend thy mind o'er all the world,
> In knowledge, all things in it comprehend.

It is not a temptation to pursue as an end what should only be a means, as some of the earlier temptations were; it is a temptation to usurp a prerogative that belongs only to God. There is an ominous ring in the repetition of the word "all." It is an absolute, beyond restriction, reminding us of another invitation to disregard a restriction: "Yea, hath God said, Ye shall not eat of every tree of the garden? . . . For God doth know that in the day ye eat thereof, then your eyes shall be opened, and ye shall be as gods, knowing good and evil" (Gen. 3:1, 5). Milton must have been aware that one meaning of the Hebrew idiom "to know good and evil" is to know all things, to know them in their essence, as God knows them. "So let extend thy mind o'er all the world" is an echo of the words which had sounded in Eden: "Ye shall be as gods, knowing good and evil." Limitation is removed, and the second Adam is invited to assume infinity.

But the second Adam is not dazzled, and he can cut through the mass of verbiage to the central issue. It is no wonder that his tones are harsh, as they were when the more undisguised temptation to idolatry was presented to him. Does not the Stoic philosopher yield to this very temptation of removing all limitations from the human condition?

> The Stoic last in Philosophic pride,
> By him call'd virtue; and his virtuous man,
> Wise, perfect in himself, and all possessing
> Equal to God . . . (ll. 300–304)

The Perfect Man can understand what it is to which Satan is tempting him, and he can reject it with the clearsighted forcefulness which has never abandoned him. But he knows that for lesser men the issue may not be so clear-cut. For them, Satan may again resort to his tactics of deception, and Christ foresees the probable effects on the ignorant multitude. He is not rejecting Greek learning or Greek poetry. As far as he is concerned, he is saying that he will not, as man, aspire to a knowledge

of all things; as far as others are concerned, he laments only that im-
proper use will be made of things good in themselves, which will be
expected to give something they can not give. And here the metaphor
of deception reappears. The Greek teachers deal in "subtle shifts";
"Alas! what can they teach, and not mislead" (IV.308–309):

> Who therefore seeks in these
> True wisdom, finds her not, or by delusion
> Far worse, her false resemblance only meets,
> An empty cloud. (ll. 318–321)

It seems possible to see the Greek temptation under this double aspect. For Christ, it is a temptation to exalt himself to a level with God;
for lesser men, an incentive to make a misguided choice. In the narrative context, however, the former aspect is more important, and the fundamental issue in the temptation, as I read it, is the aspiration to "be
as God" by knowing all things. It remains, though in a more subtle form,
the equivalent of that rebellion against the will and the law of God
which in its most extreme form leads to idolatry.

To this notion of rebellion there is a corollary with which Milton
was preoccupied throughout his literary career. Both the etymology of
the biblical words meaning "to rebel" and the general seventeenth-century framework of thought involved the doctrine of hierarchy. When
man disobeys God, part of his condign punishment lies in the subsequent
rebellion of his lower faculties against his higher, so that in a true sense
he is not his own master. Statements of this belief are frequent in *Paradise Lost*; one of the most familiar passages describes the result of the
first sin in these terms:

> For Understanding rul'd not, and the Will
> Heard not her lore, both in subjection now
> To sensual Appetite, who from beneath
> Usurping over sovran Reason claim'd
> Superior sway. (IX.1127–1131)

Christ declared that "whosoever committeth sin is the servant of sin"
(John 8:34), and St. Paul describes the inner conflict "bringing me into
captivity to the law of sin which is in my members" (Rom. 7:23).

Reflections of this concept are found throughout *Paradise Regained*.
In Book I, Christ tells Satan that as a result of his original revolt he is
a "poor miserable captive thrall" (l. 411). In Book II he contrasts the
freedom of the virtuous man with the anarchy reigning in the wicked:

Yet he who reigns within himself, and rules
Passions, Desires, and Fears, is more a King;
Which every wise and virtuous man attains:
And who attains not, ill aspires to rule
Cities of men, or headstrong Multitudes.
Subject himself to Anarchy within,
Or lawless passions in him, which he serves. (ll. 466–472)

There are times, moreover, when the punishment of servitude is inflicted on a whole nation. The historical books of the Old Testament are filled with the idea,[13] and for Milton, as for many others of his generation, the history of the Jews was being repeated in their own England.[14] The outward slavery becomes a metaphor for the inward slavery which has preceded it. Thus, in Book III of *Paradise Regained*, the ten captive tribes are said to have wrought their own captivity (l. 415). The idea is elaborated in Book IV, when the Roman people are described: "That people victor once, now vile and base, / Deservedly made vassal" (ll. 132–133).

What wise and valiant man would seek to free
These thus degenerate, by themselves enslav'd,
Or could of inward slaves make outward free? (ll. 143–145)

More important for Christian thought, however, than the individual's state of slavery to sin or outward servitude as punishment for the sins of a nation was a third stage of development: the fact, demonstrated again and again in the history of the world, that slavery to sin is a universal phenomenon. St. Paul, especially in the Epistle to the Romans, stresses the solidarity of the human race in this state of slavery: "for we have before proved both Jews and Gentiles, that they are all under sin"; "for all have sinned, and come short of the glory of God"; "and so death passed upon all men, for that all have sinned" (3:9, 23; 5:12). The sad fact was, and Reformation theology emphasized the point, that sin and man's servitude to it were universal.[15] But another fact, one of the most central in Christianity, is that Christ delivered man from this slavery by himself becoming sin's conqueror: "And ye know that he was manifested to take away our sins; and in him is no sin. Whosoever abideth in him sinneth not" (1 John 3:5–6); "But now being made free from sin, and become servants to God, ye have your fruit unto holiness, and the end everlasting life" (Rom. 6:22).

The release of man from the slavery of sin through the victory of Christ is celebrated in *Paradise Regained*. What Christ proclaimed in the Gospels was the deliverance of man and the possibility of salvation, both individual and communal, through repentance. Yet this deliverance is not wrought through any magical formula; it requires man's cooperation, his own efforts to serve the true God. The moving passage on the ten tribes, at the end of Book III, shows the refusal of God to deliver those who deliberately turn away from him: "No, let them serve / Thir enemies, who serve idols with God" (ll. 431–432). But this does not mean that God has abandoned them; at some time known only to him they will be moved by some "wond'rous call" to sincere repentance and will once more enter with joy the promised land.

For those who serve idols (and, Milton might add, for the people of England) that time is in the future; but for the individual Christian, that time can be now. When Christ stands erect upon the pinnacle, Satan the deceiver realizes that he has himself been deceived, while Satan the rebellious aspirer to God's throne is cast down: "But Satan smitten with amazement fell" (IV.562). Each of the two epic similes inserted at this climax helps to emphasize one of the key ideas. In the Hercules image we see Antaeus, who here represents Satan, repeatedly rising in his pride, only to be finally throttled and felled, while in the Sphinx simile, as Merritt Hughes well puts it, Christ "destroys the monster whose riddles threaten all human life."[16]

The song of the angels at the end of the poem is filled with references to the victory of the Perfect Man over both types of sin, that of the intellect and that of the will; Satan's deceptiveness, his rebelliousness, and the superior power of Christ all appear at times in a single line or phrase.

> True Image of the Father, whether thron'd
> In the bosom of bliss, and light of light
> Conceiving, or remote from Heaven, enshrin'd
> In fleshly Tabernacle, and human form,
> Wand'ring the Wilderness, whatever place,
> Habit, or state, or motion, still expressing
> The Son of God, with Godlike force endu'd
> Against th' Attempter of thy Father's Throne,
> And Thief of Paradise; him long of old
> Thou didst debel, and down from Heav'n cast
> With all his Army; now thou hast aveng'd
> Supplanted *Adam*, and by vanquishing
> Temptation, hast regain'd lost Paradise,
> And frustrated the conquest fraudulent:

He never more henceforth will dare set foot
In Paradise to tempt; his snares are broke. (IV.596–611)

Christ has not yielded to the supreme temptation of idolatry, so he deserves to be addressed as "True Image of the Father" (for all other images are idols). Satan is both the "Attempter of thy Father's Throne" (therefore a rebel) and the "Thief of Paradise" (therefore a crafty deceiver). These epithets are balanced by the actions ascribed to Christ in the lines immediately following: the warlike image is countered by "debel" (referring to a victory in the past) and "vanquishing" (the present triumph); while the phrase "hast regain'd lost Paradise" suggests the restoration of what the thief had filched. The next line beautifully combines the ideas of revolt and of deception: "And frustrated the conquest fraudulent." Even more succinctly, two lines later: "His snares are broke."

In *The Reason of Church-Government* Milton had affirmed his conviction that truth sets free from the thralldom of sin;[17] now, near the end of his life, he was showing the concrete demonstration of that abstract statement. His belief in it had never wavered, though perhaps his expectations of its application had changed. In the Son of God he saw Truth itself overcoming the darkness of moral error personified in Satan, casting off the chains which kept man captive to sin.

In the second part of the hymn, following the pattern set in the poem as a whole, the emphasis is on the defeat of open rebellion. From line 618 to line 634 there is not a single line which does not contain some relevant word or phrase; I have italicized these (the proper name *Abaddon* is the only word italicized in the text):

> But thou, Infernal Serpent, *shalt not long*
> *Rule* in the Clouds; like an Autumnal Star
> Or Lightning *thou shalt fall* from Heav'n *trod down*
> *Under his feet*: for proof, ere this thou *feel'st*
> *Thy wound*, yet not thy last and *deadliest wound*
> By this *repulse* receiv'd, and hold'st in Hell
> *No triumph*; in all her gates *Abaddon* rues
> *Thy bold attempt*; hereafter learn *with awe*
> To *dread* the Son of God: hee all unarm'd
> Shall *chase* thee with the *terror* of his voice
> *From thy Demoniac holds*, possession foul,
> Thee and thy Legions; *yelling* they shall *fly*,
> And *beg to hide them* in a herd of Swine,
> Lest he command them *down into the deep*,

Bound, and to torment sent before thir time.
Hail Son of the most High, heir of both worlds,
Queller of Satan, on thy glorious work
Now enter, and begin to save mankind.

It may not be without significance that in the quiet closing of the
poem the "Savior meek" is "sung Victor" and is "brought on his way";
for it is clear now that there will be no misstep or error on the path
which will lead the humble Savior and loyal Son of the Father to the
completion of his destined work.

The foregoing examination of *Paradise Regained* in the light of
some important biblical themes of sin offers not a new reading but possible clues to the full meaning of some of its puzzling features. One
basis of the division of the poem into books, for example, may be the
distinction between error and rebellion, since the first type of sin is dealt
with in the first two books, the second in the last two. The former concept may have had some influence on the banquet scene; and a related
theme (blindness of heart as a punishment for sin) makes more intelli-
gible Christ's sternness toward the ignorant multitude. The second concept—deliberate rebellion—helps to explain the position in the poem of
the temptation to learning, showing it as a culmination, not an anticlimax, and associating it closely with the fall of the first Adam. Finally,
the theme of man's slavery to sin and Christ's victory over it, both prominent in the New Testament, are emphasized at the conclusion of the
poem.

NOTES

1. See especially Elizabeth M. Pope, *Paradise Regained: The Tradition and the
Poem* (Baltimore, 1947), and Barbara Lewalski, *Milton's Brief Epic: The Genre,
Meaning, and Art of Paradise Regained* (Providence, 1966).
2. *De Doctrina Christiana* I.xv, in *The Works of John Milton,* Columbia edition
(1931–1938), XV, 301; hereafter cited as *Works.*
3. By isolating the influence of the Bible I do not, of course, imply that this was
an exclusive source; but since it would be impossible for Milton to deal with temptation and sin apart from the biblical background, an examination of key ideas in the
Bible may prove helpful in interpreting the poem.
4. The following standard reference books discuss sin in the Bible: *Bible Key
Words* [from Gerhard Kittel's *Theologisches Wörterbuch zum Neuen Testament,*
trans. and ed. J. R. Coates; this one-volume edition includes the section "Sin"] (New
York, 1951); *Dictionary of the Bible,* ed. John L. McKenzie (Milwaukee, 1965);

Dictionnaire de la Bible, ed. F. Vigoureux (Paris, 1912); *Encyclopedic Dictionary of the Bible,* ed. Louis F. Hartmann [a translation and adaptation of A. van den Born's *Bijbels Woordenboek*] (New York, 1963); *Jewish Encyclopedia,* ed. Cyrus Adler, Isidore Singer et al. (New York, 1925); *Lexicon für Theologie und Kirche,* ed. M. Buchberger (Freiburg, 1957–1967); *The Interpreter's Dictionary of the Bible,* ed. G. A. Buttrick et al. (New York, 1962).

5.   *Mr. John Milton: Minutes by John Aubrey,* in *The Early Lives of Milton,* ed. Helen Darbishire (New York, 1965), p. 6.   Milton's decided preference for the Hebrew text of the Old Testament is demonstrated by Harris Francis Fletcher, *The Use of the Bible in Milton's Prose* (Urbana, 1929), passim; see also the same author's *The Intellectual Background of John Milton* (Urbana, 1961), II, 104.

Milton reflects the concept embodied in *ht'* when he observes the *De Doctrina Christiana* I.xi (*Works,* XV, 199) that every act is good in itself: "it is only the irregularity, or deviation from the line of right, which, properly speaking, is evil." Another common word for sin, *'awon,* also suggests a deviation or distortion, with emphasis on the effect of the sin on the sinner.

6.   The Septuagint uses this term most frequently as a translation of *ht'* (*Bible Key Words,* p. 1).

7.   *John Milton: Complete Poems and Major Prose,* ed. Merritt Y. Hughes (New York, 1957); citations from Milton's poetry in my text are to this edition.

8.   *Complete Prose Works of John Milton,* Yale edition (1953–), I, 362. The note by Ruth Mohl, editor of the *Commonplace Book,* dates the entry before 1638.

9.   For a different viewpoint, see Michael Fixler, "The Unclean Meats of the Mosaic Law and the Banquet Scene in *Paradise Regained,*" *Modern Language Notes,* LXX (1955), 573–577, and the same author's *Milton and the Kingdoms of God* (Evanston, 1964), pp. 255–257. Fixler thinks that Satan is lying but that he does not expect to be believed.

10.   I.iv (*Works,* XIV, 165 ff.).

11.   English translations of the Bible use "transgression" regularly as an equivalent of the Hebrew word meaning rebellion, and Milton, citing 1 John 3:4, uses this term: "Sin, as defined by the apostle, is ἀνομία, or 'the transgression of the law' " (*De Doctrina Christiana* I.xi [*Works,* XV, 179]).

12.   The distinction I am making between the two kinds of sin is not, of course, novel, but it has not hitherto been seen as an important structural element in the poem or as a key to its meaning. Dick Taylor, however, from a somewhat different viewpoint, stresses the importance of seeing the temptations under a twofold aspect: man works toward salvation through both moral strength and intellectual perception ("Grace as a Means of Poetry: Milton's Pattern for Salvation," *Tulane Studies in English,* IV [1954], 57).

13.   The motif runs through the historical books: e.g., Josh. 7:11–12; Judg. 2:14, 4:2; 6:1; 1 Sam. 12:9.

14.   Milton discusses the punishment of whole nations in *De Doctrina Christiana* I.xi (*Works,* XV, 185 ff.).

15.   For Milton's comments, see ibid., pp. 179 ff.

16.   *Complete Poems,* p. 477; see also Northrop Frye, "The Typology of *Paradise Regained,*" *Modern Philology,* LIII (1956), 237.

17.   *Works,* III, 272.

The Obedience of Christ in
Paradise Regained

WILLIAM B. HUNTER, JR.
UNIVERSITY OF NEW HAMPSHIRE

There is little question that Milton wished his readers to understand *Paradise Regained* as being in some sense a companion poem to *Paradise Lost*—a relationship which does not obtain in any comparable way, for instance, between either work and *Samson Agonistes*.[1] In addition to their parallel titles, the opening lines of *Paradise Regained* expressly suggest comparison with *Paradise Lost*: the author who had sung of the loss of Paradise "By one man's disobedience" will now sing of its recovery "By one man's firm obedience fully tried / Through all temptation." The invocation which follows prays for assistance from the same Spirit that had inspired him in the earlier poem. At this point, however, the works ostensibly diverge, both in subject and in tone, to be related to each other only in the fact that each has temptation as a central subject. Adam and Eve unsuccessfully withstand the blandishments of Satan, and Christ triumphantly wards them off.

Without necessarily believing the story of the Fall of Man in its literal narration in Genesis, most modern readers can accept the account of the loss of Paradise as Milton depicts it. God arbitrarily forbade man to eat the fruit of the Tree of Knowledge. Man did so and accordingly suffered punishment for being disobedient. Whether God's arbitrary command was just or not is somewhat beside the point; at issue is disobedience of any divine law. Accordingly, Adam does not question at the end of the poem either the fact that he has sinned or the correctness of his punishment. Paradise has been lost for him and, presumably, for the reader.

Evaluation of *Paradise Regained*, however, is quite different. Anyone who possesses even the slightest familiarity with Christian tradition
but who has not read the poem would probably imagine that in it Paradise is regained by Christ's suffering and death. It turns out otherwise,
of course, in that Milton instead depicts Satan's temptation of Jesus in
the wilderness, just after his baptism by John and just before he began
his ministry. It is true that only in this episode does Christ confront Satan
in the open according to the Gospel accounts, as Eve had confronted
him in Genesis; but even so many readers have been surprised and
somewhat disappointed by this choice of subject, an attitude extending
back at least to Thyer, who in the eighteenth century confessed that
"it may seem a little odd at first, that Milton should impute the recovery
of Paradise to this short scene of our Saviour's life upon earth, and not
rather extend it to his agony, crucifixion, etc." He goes on to surmise
that Milton chose this subject because it paralleled the temptations of
Paradise Lost or because its author was too old to tackle another long
work. Warburton repeated these speculations, suggested that the choice
of subject lay in Milton's "wrong notions in divinity," and concluded
that in any case "the plan is a very unhappy one, and defective even in
that narrow view of a sequel, for it affords the poet no opportunity of
driving the Devil back again to Hell from his new conquests in the air.
In the mean time nothing was easier than to have invented a good one,
which should end with the resurrection."[2] Such critical attitudes are
still difficult to answer, despite efforts to place the poem in the context
of the short epic and to explain the significance of the various temptations.[3] Most readers, as Thyer observed, tend to accept the subject of
Paradise Regained only because of parallels between its temptations
and those of *Paradise Lost*. The loss of Paradise to mankind through
Adam's disobedience is perfectly clear. But how and in what sense is it
now regained?

As a matter of fact, *Paradise Regained* is based upon a very important dogmatic distinction regarding Christ's obedience to God's will in
his life and death. When he became incarnate as the God-Man, the Son
of God emptied himself of his divinity or concealed it so that the human
being Jesus could grow and develop just like anybody else. Unlike anybody else, however, he led a perfectly good life—good not only in every
Christian sense but also good in the sense in which a Jew of his day
would understand the word. In particular, he and he alone was able
throughout his life to keep the laws of God as they had been revealed in
the Old Testament (particularly in the books of Exodus through Deu-

teronomy). According to Christian dogma expressly developed in the Reformed tradition of which Milton was a part, this was understood as Christ's *active* obedience to the will of God.[4] His death on the cross was, in contrast, known as his *passive* obedience. Obviously, active and passive obedience cannot be clearly separated from one another, but in the hands of Reformed writers they were considered to support two different though related goals of Christ for the benefit of mankind: recovery of eternal life (by means of his active obedience) and release from punishment for sin (by means of his passive obedience).

To understand the theological background of the concept of obedience, one should begin with consideration of the major biblical texts which underlie the theory. In Deuteronomy 27:26 (repeated by Paul in Galatians 3:10), anyone is cursed who "confirmeth not all the words of this law to do them." The curse, assumed to be death, thus lies upon anyone who does not keep the Mosaic laws. On the other hand, according to Leviticus 18:5 (repeated in Luke 10:28, Romans 10:5, and Galatians 3:12), anyone who does manage to keep the Lord's statutes and judgments "shall live in them." From these and similar passages derive Jewish legalism, the attempt to practice in every detail the precepts of the Old Testament. To keep them is life, in some sense of the word; to break them is death.

Adam broke the law—not, however, the law of Moses but the single command of Genesis 2:17: "of the tree of the knowledge of good and evil, thou shalt not eat." Because he did not violate Mosaic law, Adam has no particular significance for the orthodox Jew as originator of sin; rather, he is important as Father of the Race. But in the New Testament it was necessary to interpret the meaning of Christ's passion so as to show in what way he could be said to have died for mankind. Because his death must have occurred in response to some need, Paul developed the idea of the inherently sinful nature of all mankind, tracing it back to the original sin of Adam. "All," he writes, "have sinned" (Rom. 3:23); or "In Adam's fall we sinned all," as the *New England Primer* put it. Thus Christ's life and death were understood as atoning for the sinfulness which the entire human race had inherited.[5]

Paul then explicitly compares the actions of Adam and Christ: "as by one man's disobedience many were made sinners, so by the obedience of one shall many be made righteous" (Rom. 5:19), a text which Milton must have had in mind as he developed *Paradise Regained* as in some sense a companion poem to *Paradise Lost*. Paul did not view obedience to the law, however, merely as abstention from eating of the

Tree of Knowledge; rather, obedience was due to the elaborate structure of Mosaic law which as its first demand upon any man required
that he be circumcised shortly after birth. Accordingly, Christ begins
his obedience to the law by undergoing circumcision on the eighth day
of his life (Luke 2:21), a fact which is the central idea of Milton's poem
upon the subject:

> we by rightful doom remediless
> Were lost in death, till he that dwelt above
> High-thron'd in secret bliss, for us frail dust
> Emptied his glory, ev'n to nakedness;
> And that great Cov'nant which we still transgress
> Entirely satisfi'd,
> And the full wrath beside
> Of vengeful Justice bore for our excess,
> And seals obedience first with wounding smart
> This day. (ll. 17–26)

That is, mankind still transgresses the covenant between God and man
expressed in the Old Testament laws, but Jesus "entirely satisfied" them,
beginning his obedience to them by the pain and bloodshed of the circumcision which in its accomplishment requires both active and passive
obedience.

The concept of obedience was essential to the Reformed tradition,
with its emphasis upon original sin. According to Calvin, Christ acquired
righteousness for fallen mankind "by the whole course of his obedience," the authority being "the testimonie of *Paul*." He proceeds to assert that the redemption of mankind began with the Incarnation itself,
not with the later passion: "From the time that he tooke upon him the
person of a servant, he began to pay the ransome to redeeme us."[6] It
will be observed that Calvin makes no clear-cut division between active and passive obedience; indeed, the terms are not employed. The
recognition of the importance of Christ's life as well as his death for the
salvation of mankind is, however, emphasized. It remained for later
Reformed dogmatists to amplify the distinction.

Alsted continued the tradition into the next century. "The satisfaction provided by Christ," he holds, "is not to be looked for only in
the death of the Cross,"[7] but he does not expatiate upon Christ's obedience to the law. The position was fully stated in the Reformed tradition by Johannes Wollebius, whose *Christianae Theologiae Compen-*

dium (Basel, 1626, or later editions) Milton had certainly read with some
care. Wolleb may have come to his extensive discussion of active obedience as a corrective to the opinions of Reformed writers like Piscator,[8]
who had argued that the efficacy of Christ's active obedience was limited
to the salvation of only his own human nature. According to this view,
mankind at large was saved by the passive obedience of the Passion
alone. In opposition to this interpretation Wolleb argued that Christ
satisfied divine justice for mankind in both ways. "The satisfaction of
Christ," he writes, "consists, therefore, both of the bearing of punishment
and of perfect righteousness. In the first, passive obedience is especially seen; in the second, active obedience."[9] He goes on to explain that
those two kinds of obedience cannot be sharply distinguished; nevertheless, they do constitute the two different kinds of satisfaction which
Christ offered: passive obedience to atone for the punishment which
mankind underwent as a result of Adam's sin, and active obedience to
gain for mankind eternal life.[10] True righteousness, he writes, "consists
of actual obedience," and Christ "fulfilled this actual obedience . . . in our
place." Thus Christ's obedience to the law is a necessary part of man's
salvation: "actual obedience is not only a necessary condition of the
Christ as priest, but also a part of his satisfaction and merit." And then,
in a fine conclusion which contrasts the roles of Adam and Christ: "If
the actual disobedience of Adam is a cause of meriting damnation, why
is not the actual obedience of the second Adam a cause of meriting salvation? The conclusion that we reject would only be possible if we were
willing to say that the first Adam is more important for our damnation
than is the second for our salvation." Indeed, the law to which Christ
was subject is the same law prescribed for us, including everything to
which that law bound us.[11] In sum, the law bound man to obedience to
it and to punishment for infraction of it. Christ's active obedience satisfied this law; his passive obedience satisfied the punishment which mankind had incurred through Adam's sin.

In his *De Doctrina Christiana* Milton makes this same division,
though he does not employ the terms "active" and "passive." Christ's
satisfaction, he writes, is "the complete reparation" which he made "by
the fulfilment of the law [that is, by active obedience], and payment of
the required price for all mankind [by passive obedience]."[12] After quoting a few proof texts, he adds that Christ was obedient to the Father
"in all things." The same dogma is reflected in the statement about
Christ's mission which Michael gives Adam in Book XII of *Paradise*

Lost: the Savior will not destroy Satan but will instead destroy "his works" in mankind, an achievement accomplished only

> by fulfilling that which thou [Adam] didst want,
> Obedience to the Law of God, impos'd
> On penalty of death. (ll. 396–398)

He will accomplish this "Both by obedience and by love, though love / Alone fulfil the law."[13] Then through his death he will void the punishment inherent in man's sinful state. His (twofold) obedience is imputed to mankind through faith (XII.390–410).

When he chose the temptation of Christ in the wilderness as the episode upon which to base *Paradise Regained*, Milton must have also been consciously accepting as his ostensible subject the concept of active obedience, for Christ responds to each of Satan's offers with a quotation from Old Testament law: the first, the change of stones into bread, by Deuteronomy 8:3; the second, the offer of all of the kingdoms of the world, by Deuteronomy 6:13; and the third, his preservation upon the pinnacle of the temple, by Deuteronomy 6:16. The importance of obedience to the law as a means of countering Satan's guile goes as far back as Irenaeus, who observed that when Satan tempted him Christ "did not draw the means of confounding him from any other source than from the words of the law, and made use of the Father's commandment as a help towards the destruction and confusion of the apostate angel." Irenaeus proceeded to analyze the three temptations in just these terms, observing in conclusion that Christ "spurned him from Him finally as being conquered out of the law; and there was done away with that infringement of God's commandment which had occurred in Adam, by means of the precept of the law, which the Son of man observed, who did not transgress the commandment of God."[14]

According to Reformed dogma, it will be remembered, in practicing this active obedience to the law Christ was recovering eternal life for mankind. The "Paradise" which is being regained in the poem must accordingly refer especially to man's eternal life with God. As the angels sing at the conclusion of Book IV, Christ has "regained lost Paradise" which, rather than the Garden of Eden, is "A fairer Paradise" where mankind "shall dwell secure, when time shall be" (ll. 606–616). In view of the parallelism of its title, it seems probable that the "Paradise" of *Paradise Lost* also means more than the Garden and implies man's eternal life with God. As Raphael observes,

> one Almighty is, from whom
> All things proceed, and up to him return,
> If not deprav'd from good. (V.469–471)

If by his considered choice of the temptation episode as the subject of his poem Milton placed active obedience to the law in the foreground of *Paradise Regained*, one may inquire how he understood its obverse, Christ's passive obedience. The earliest statement of the subject is the youthful and abortive poem, "The Passion," which does not move along in its subject far enough to introduce the concept of obedience. The idea does appear, however, as I have argued in another article,[15] in a powerful metaphorical statement at the center of *Paradise Lost*, where the War in Heaven carries beneath its surface meaning the depiction of Christ's passion, followed by his resurrection and concomitant exaltation.

Within the surface narrative of *Paradise Regained*, which, as has been shown, rests upon the concept of obedience to the law, Milton seems deliberately to have introduced nonbiblical materials which also expressly represent Christ's passive obedience. As has been observed, the two forms of obedience do not differ from one another absolutely. Nor may one find the application of passive obedience only at the time of the Passion. As Wolleb remarked, "Both extend from the beginning of the incarnation to his [Christ's] death." As a result, he views the "innumerable sufferings which Christ underwent" as not separable from the final passion but as a preparation for it and "an integral part of his satisfaction."[16] As Christ tells Satan in *Paradise Regained*, "Who best / Can suffer, best can do" (III.194–195). Accordingly, it is not surprising to find Milton adding to the surface narrative of obedience to the law the details of Christ's extreme hunger, augmented by the banquet which Satan placed before him (II.337 ff.), and especially of his passive endurance of the storm (IV.409 ff.). It is perhaps no accident that in this poem the only quotations from the law are those which appear in the Gospel accounts as the responses to the three temptations named there. For the other temptations, which Milton himself invented, the answers are not couched in any such legal quotations, a fact which suggests that Milton conceives of Christ as moving within a range of obedience which goes quite beyond the scope of the law, as indeed did the Passion itself. Finally, in his depiction of the third temptation Milton seems to be combining the two forms of obedience: Christ passively submits to being carried to the pinnacle of the temple, details upon which the biblical text is silent. Then, exemplifying his active role, he responds to Satan's poser, accompanied by quotations from the Psalms, with his own final quotation of Deuteronomic law.

Within these complementary concepts of obedience one may thus see further into the relationships between Milton's two great poems about Paradise. The longer one ostensibly centers upon one man's disobedience of the law, the second upon another man's obedience to it. But both works also include the passive nature of Christ's life as he suffered for mankind and imply, in very different ways, his "obedience unto death." Together the poems suggest the whole of Christ's mission, the one on a larger, the other on a smaller scale.

NOTES

1. Just how close this relationship is has been questioned by W. B. C. Watkins, who considers *Paradise Regained* "more a postscript to *Paradise Lost* than a sequel" (*An Anatomy of Milton's Verse* [Baton Rouge, 1955], p. 104); and by Don Cameron Allen, who thinks that if we turn to *Paradise Lost* for an understanding of details of *Paradise Regained*, "we confuse our judgment of the short epic and distort, if we do not destroy, the central issues of the second poem" (*The Harmonious Vision* [Baltimore, 1954], p. 110).

2. These quotations are conveniently available in the notes to *Paradise Regained* in the editions of Thomas Newton, I, 3. I have used the second edition (London, 1753).

3. See the book-length studies by Elizabeth Pope (Baltimore, 1947) and Barbara Lewalski (Providence, 1966), and especially the fine evaluation of recent scholarship by Howard Schultz, "A Fairer Paradise?" *ELH*, XXXII (1965), 275–302.

4. As will be shown, the idea is extensively developed by writers in the tradition of Calvin, but it also has a cognate place among other groups, e.g., the Lutherans. See Heinrich Schmid, *Doctrinal Theology of the Evangelical Lutheran Church* (rpt. Minneapolis, 1961), pp. 355 ff.

5. See especially C. A. Patrides, "Milton and the Protestant Theory of Atonement," *PMLA*, LXXIV (1959), 7–13, and his further statement in *Milton and the Christian Tradition* (Oxford, 1966), pp. 131 ff.

6. *Institution of Christian Religion* II.xvi.5. I have quoted from Thomas Norton's translation (London, 1599).

7. Johannes Alstedius, *Theologia Scholastica Didactica* (Hanover, 1618), p. 715, as translated in Heinrich Heppe, *Reformed Dogmatics* (London, 1950), p. 459.

8. Johannes Piscator, *Aphorismi Doctrinae Christianae* (Herborn, 1592).

9. Translated by John W. Beardslee in *Reformed Dogmatics* (New York, 1965), p. 99.

10. Ibid., p. 106.

11. Ibid., p. 107.

12. *The Works of John Milton* (New York, 1931–1938), XV, 315–317. Cf. *Westminster Confession of Faith* VIII.4: Jesus "was made under the law, and did perfectly fulfil it."

13. "Love," according to Paul (Rom. 13:10), "is the fulfilling of the law." Satan, on the other hand, is obedient only through fear (*PR* I.422).

14. *Against Heresies* V.xxi.2, in *The Ante-Nicene Fathers* (rpt. Grand Rapids, 1967), I, 549–550.

15. "Milton on the Exaltation of the Son," *ELH*, XXXVI (1969), 215–231.

16. Beardslee, *Reformed Dogmatics*, pp. 99–100.

The Private Mythology of *Paradise Regained*

J. B. BROADBENT

UNIVERSITY OF EAST ANGLIA, NORWICH

STRUCTURE

The narrative is arbitrary. Mary, the apostles, and Belial appear early and no more. Commentators, struggling to justify the order of the temptations, and to determine which appetite is being tempted, relapse into treating the poem as a newspaper report from which we may guess real motives:

> Lewalski . . . makes the point that, since Christ first feels hunger at this juncture [II.245], he was not hungry during the stones-into-bread temptation.[1]

We should do better to assume that the order of events is not skeletal to the events themselves, or to the language. Neither is the division into books. Books III and IV split a conversation; IV is too full. What does it mean when a poem's body is at odds with its bones? (a) That the poet's chest is still so obstructed with the troublesome stuff that he cannot shape it—i.e., inadequate projection. Or (b) that the poet does not really want to expose his material, yet he has half done so—i.e., conflicting motives.

"REAL OR ALLEGORIC I DISCERN NOT" (IV.390)

The structural weakness is overlaid with a general air of dreaminess. We do not know what genre the poem belongs to. "Brief epic" is not a

definition but an excuse: the poem lurches from the obsolescent brief
heroics of the scene in hell to the modernistic vague domestication of
"the quest of some stray ewe, / Or withered sticks to gather" (I.315–
316).² Tillyard, whose account of the poem is still the most perceptive,
wrote: "*Paradise Regained* is indeed unusually compounded of twi-
light, trancelike descriptions, conversations remote from the marketplace or senate-house or inn yet suggesting delicately the cadences of
real talk, and brilliant visions."³ Characters pop up unintroduced (e.g.,
Mary at II.60), or come on only to disappear. There are abrupt transi-
tions between scenes. There are uncertain shifts between actual and apparent, waking and dreaming. The most complete example is Book II.
Here are Christ's experiences before the banquet temptation:

l. 242   real hunger in the desert
l. 260   goes to sleep
l. 264   Elijah and the ravens
l. 270   Elijah in the desert
l. 278   Daniel "at his pulse" (one line)
l. 279   dawn
l. 282   wakes "and found all was but a dream"
l. 285   climbs hill
l. 291   descends into grove
l. 294   grove as "a woody scene," i.e., stage set
l. 296   grove as "haunt / Of wood-gods and wood-nymphs"
         (who don't appear)
l. 298   sudden appearance of "a man" who is, but is
         not stated to be, Satan in his second disguise

The impressive distantness, the silence (even during scenes of war),
the dreamlike confusion sometimes, are manifested in the great visions;
at III.310, for example, annotators are baffled about what campaign is
being fought and which side is winning; IV.40 and IV.57–59 present
Rome, for all its solid detail of "pillars and roofs / Carved work," as almost a trick of "what strange parallax . . . / Of vision multiplied through
air" and of the "airy microscope"—so much so that commentators (not
Svendsen) have wondered if Milton understood the nature of the in-
strument.⁴

We are repeatedly reminded of the air. Milton thought of it as the
medium of sight; it was also the realm of Satan, and a favorite word of
Milton's.⁵ But it is mainly sinister in this poem, not only as Satan's realm
and the medium of illusion but as thin (I.499), bleak (II.74), thick (II.
117), and breathtaking—the "airy jaunt" of IV.402. Of course this illusori-

ness was an old concern of Milton's; it has relevance to the action, as the world's false glitter. But it still seems to me odd that the general ambience for a treatment of the Gospels' very concrete story, and for Christ's recovery of Paradise, should be so doubtful. For it is not just the temptations which seem illusory: the entire poem, including the triumphs of Christ, reads like a series of dreams.

Satan raises the issue at IV.372. Christ has rejected Athens in terms of "false . . . dreams, Conjectures, fancies . . . fabling . . . doubted . . . vain boast, / Or subtle shifts . . . evade . . . mislead . . . ignorant . . . awry . . . delusion . . . false resemblance . . . An empty cloud . . . Uncertain and unsettled . . . shallow . . . intoxicate . . . trifles . . . sponge" (IV.291–329). In short, he has not only reduced the world linguistically to a dream, but has reduced it with such emphasis that dream itself is his obsession. Satan asks, "What dost thou in this world?" There are theological answers (though Christ does not offer them); but in the poem all that rejection-as-dream is surely itself part of the general dreamwork. It continues even in the supposedly objective ending of that conversation and transition to narrative: Satan

> to the wilderness
> Brought back the Son of God, and left him there,
> Feigning to disappear. (IV.395–397)

Feigning to disappear! That is to say, producing the illusion of an illusion. And this he does so as to disturb Christ's sleep with actual "ugly dreams."

Perhaps Milton was moving toward a sophisticated theory of temptation-inquisition-brainwashing: the paradox that the worst torment is dream. It is not what the rats will do to me but what I fantasy they will do; not what I did to her but my remorse for what I think I did; not (as we are told) that we have committed incest but that we dreamed of it. At the same time, the most effective defense may be to insist that the world is an illusion and the only reality is one's own spiritual identity. So temptation, punishment, and survival are all at worst and best thin air. Certainly the "gray dissimulation" is a Kafkaesque figure; certainly Milton's construction of an ambience which is itself the temptation, because it is a fantasy, is subtler than the cockroaches and arseholes of St. Anthony paintings. However, I cannot myself reconcile that treatment with the poem's historical or mythical basis: that is, the initiation of a divine hero at a point in time within the Roman empire. If it is myth, what's all this about Parthia? Kafka did not concern himself with politics at that level. If it is not myth, why so dreamy?

IDENTITY, PARENTAGE, BIRTH, BAPTISM, SONSHIP

It is in the area of this heading that the actuality of Christ is most obvious. Milton does not see through to the mythic base, the puberty rites; he merely rehearses, with insistent repetitiveness, the problems of birth and sonship—that is, of identity as proved by love and power. The theme is repeated in hell in Book I, in heaven, and on earth—and in Satan's penultimate speech in Book IV (see I.86, 122, 134–166, 186, 198–209, 227–238; IV.500–520).

The motif of birth and sonship is tied naturally, but with unnatural insistence, to the baptism. The baptism occurs at I.18–32, with verbatim repetition at I.70–86. It recurs again at the beginning of Book II. There are also strong references at I.327–330 and elsewhere. I suggest that all this is not merely clumsiness, but an inadequately depersonalized expression of one of Milton's central anxieties: Does my life justify sonship? It is similar to the lost-child motifs of Shakespeare's last plays, but those plays *work it out*; Milton seems merely to hammer it. The anxiety is apparent in the early finicking about his age; in the Latin poems to his father; in the constant choice of filial heroes; and in the train of poems about the use of talent, from "How soon hath Time" and *Lycidas* and "When I consider" to *Samson*:

> Why was my breeding ordered and prescribed
> As of a person separate to God,
> Designed for great exploits; if I must die
> Betrayed, captived, and both my eyes put out (ll. 30–33)

—having also betrayed my nation, and my father, with a woman?

MILTON AND HIS MOTHER

In considering Milton's own sonship we are apt to forget his mother: he does not encourage us to remember her. Yet some kind of unresolved love in that direction must be postulated as ground for marrying so late and virginally, yet so often, and with polygamous thoughts even oftener; and for all that rage of purity and sensuality and contempt, the superb erotic ideals, in prose and verse; and for all the dramatized sonships of his work. It is as if she were being perpetually pursued and never reached. Along with that, one could put the guilty hatred of the father which is the concomitant of the filial themes; perhaps Satan and Samson as cult-figures; and some strange gentleness such as Satan's love for Christ—"Though to that gentle brow" (*PR* III.215).

The classic text for Milton's mother, and the one most relevant to *Paradise Regained*, is "Methought I saw my late espoused Saint":

Methought I saw my late espoused saint
    Brought to me like Alcestis from the grave,
    Whom Jove's great son to her glad husband gave,
    Rescued from death by force, though pale and faint.
Mine, as whom washed from spot of child-bed taint
    Purification in the old Law did save,
    And such as yet once more I trust to have
    Full sight of her in heaven without restraint,
Came vested all in white, pure as her mind.
    Her face was veiled, yet to my fancied sight
    Love, sweetness, goodness in her person shined
So clear as in no face with more delight.
    But O as to embrace me she inclined,
    I waked, she fled, and day brought back my night.

The date of composition is unknown. Editors disagree on which wife the sonnet refers to. Mary died very shortly after giving birth, well within the Levitical period of uncleanness after labor; Katherine died after the time of purification. Some think it is Katherine, veiled because Milton married her after going blind. Some think "whom" in line 5 is the Virgin because of a text in Luke 2:22: "And when the days of her purification according to the law of Moses were accomplished, they brought him to Jerusalem, to present him to the Lord." Indeed the whole chapter of the Gospel links the poem to *Paradise Regained*. It contains the complete Nativity story, the circumcision, and then, after the verse quoted, Simeon pronounces the Nunc Dimittis; there is the prophecy of Anna, and the teaching in the temple at twelve—all the materials for Mary's musings in the poem.

I don't doubt that Milton had one of his wives in mind when he composed the sonnet; but it refers to her in terms which are profoundly maternal. There is nothing surprising in this except the density of evidence in this small case. She is dead; she has borne a child; she is pure, veiled, loving, sweet, good—all her qualities are those of ideal woman, not necessarily wife. Then she leans over him as mothers when they first imprint us lean over the crib.

At a more sophisticated level, admitting the Oedipal implications, we notice the confused ambiguities of the first two lines. The sonnet starts, apparently, with a merging or a denial of familial roles. The emphasis falls off "Milton" onto the filial but mighty Hercules, "Jove's great son," who actually takes the wifely Alcestis in his arms: he applies "force," she is "pale and faint." Then the emphasis falls off both Milton and Hercules onto the "glad husband" of Alcestis—that is, the roles of rescuing son and receiving husband are fused.

However (and this is the second Oedipal point) she is veiled, white, pure; and she flees. The possession of the mother must not be realized, we must not see whose face it is we really love (a popular nineteenth-century mass-produced bust in white stone called *The Bride* is of a girl's face sheathed in and blinded by an apparently windblown and ribbed veil of lawn). But (and thirdly) there is hope that if we purify her sufficiently of "child-bed taint" (that is, take away the taboo) then we may "have / Full sight of her in heaven without restraint"—a restraint evident in the contorted syntax of lines 5–8.[6]

Reverting to *Paradise Regained*, we note that it contains the Virgin as a character. This is quite unnecessary, and uncharacteristic of Milton. The lines in which she refers to the Nativity are especially unlike Milton's ornate accounts in the *Ode* and at *PL* XII.360:

> above the lot
> Of other women, by the birth I bore,
> In such a season born when scarce a shed
> Could be obtained to shelter him or me
> From the bleak air; a stable was our warmth,
> A manger his . . . (II.70–75)

This is a real mother talking.

INTERPRETIVE PROPOSALS

We approach the middle of the knot. Before we get lost in it, here are the proposals I have to make:

(a)   Milton uses Mary as an image of his own usually disregarded (or wife-identified) mother.

(b)   He uses Christ as the medium through which he can relate to Mary (hence the son-birth-parentage theme).

(c) This relationship is innocent because Mary and Christ are by definition immaculate.

(d) At the same time the temptations objectify sexual interests.

(e) But, Milton having created them, Christ rejects them.

(f) This rejection allays the taboo anxiety.

(g) It preserves Christ and Mary in a private conspiracy against the world.

(h) It proves the son's potency in face of the worldly father-figure Satan (a feeble but aged man in Book I, a strong and and powerful one in Book II).

(i) Finally Satan is defeated by falling off the phallus which the Son now occupies.

(j) Christ is rewarded at the end with food and returns to Mary. These proposals hardly need enlargement; but I shall try to relate some of them to literary features of the poem.

PRIVACY, PLAINNESS, DOMESTICITY

The Nativity lines above exemplify the unusually idiomatic plainness to be found everywhere in *Paradise Regained*: "At first it may be" (I.399), "I mean" (II.6), "just in time" (III.298), "Me worse than wet thou find'st not" (IV.486); the low similes of flies, bees, children gathering pebbles, sneezes; the comforting pastoral details—"Fowls in their clay nests were couched" (I.501), "dried the wet / From drooping plant, or dropping tree" (IV.433–434), "Him walking on a sunny hill he found, / Backed on the north and west by a thick wood" (IV.447–448). This I admit is already apparent in *Paradise Lost*, Books XI–XII; but we do not find there the insistence also on actual privacy, as in the fishermen "Close in a cottage low together got" (*PR* II.28), in contrast to the obvious glories of Greece and Rome, the devil's airy visions and mobility and so on. The poem echoes with the words "private," "remote," "retired," "home"; and that is where it ends.

If we see the poem as partly about the protection of a maternal privacy from various forms of what is public, we have some explanation of its unworldly dreaminess. The public forces are guilt-laden versions of the private desires for what the mother gives (food), and for what he wants to give the mother (power). They are also threats to the private. The banquets, luxury, elephants and archers and shining towers, are versions of the erotic, frightening in their perverse grandeur—"So that's what I want!" So rejected. The totally public, all-seeing, time-and-space-piercing visions of great capitals of law and intellect are essentially alternatives to love. They represent also perhaps the world that condemns the private; and the passions that have to be controlled—the "dizzy multitude" (II.420), "headstrong multitudes" (II.470), "miscellaneous rabble" (III.50), the "headlong" apostates (III.430): why so much dizziness? We note then that Satan's offerings are usually rejected as intrusive, or monstrous: "Why shouldst thou then obtrude this diligence?" (II.387); "That cumbersome / Luggage of war" (III.400–401); "Outlandish flatteries" (IV.125); "their swelling epithets thick-laid / As varnish on a harlot's cheek" (IV.343–344).

INTERIORITY

The temptations do not excite desire. They do elicit disdain. They are "pompous delicacies" (II.390), "ostentation vain" (III.387), "tedious" and "wearisome" (IV.307, 322)—especially compared with Christ's "private hours" (IV.331; and perhaps, for us, compared with Milton's more private style). For Christ's instinct is introspective. As to some extent in *Samson*, it is Christ's *thoughts* which are emphasized. Of course there are traditional and theological grounds for "heroic knowledge"; but it is not so much what he thinks or what he knows that matters as the fact that he introspects: "Musing and much revolving . . . deep thoughts . . . converse / With solitude . . . Thought following thought [a quotation from Petrarch] . . . O what a multitude of thoughts." Those phrases occur within twelve lines (I.185–196). Mary in Book II is presented in terms of "troubled thoughts . . . pondering oft . . . with thoughts / Meekly composed"; and her soliloquy shifts swiftly back into her son's mind:

> The while her son tracing the desert wild,
> Sole but with holiest meditations fed,
> Into himself descended . . . (II.109–111)

There is, then, a privacy of theme, and an internality of characters. The narration itself is also internalized. This is difficult to demonstrate, but here are some suggestions. From the beginning of the poem we must admit muting as a characteristic—muting especially of the traditional heroic elements such as the invocation and the council in hell. For my own part, the poem seems inaudible, and its scene invisible, until I.294, when we enter the desert. When Book II opens with ostensibly public business—the baptism, Andrew and Simon—we find that it reads as notes or quotations or long-remembered bits from the Bible, not now freshly displayed but conglomerated, as if still inside another's head. Christ's speech beginning at line 439 is a conglomeration of quotations from the Old Testament, historians such as Josephus, the maxims of the sort one puts in a commonplace book (though at line 458 Milton switches for eight lines to Shakespeare on kingship). Of course there are passages of objectification, notably Satan and the temptations; but these, as we have seen, are illusory.

Sometimes the interiority of the narrative flows into the characters. Christ is subject to the obsessional repetitions of inner thought: "Where will this end? Four times ten days I have passed / Wandering this woody maze" (II.245–246). In his speech at II.432 he just piles up exempla to oppose Satan's exempla knock-for-knock. His replies, like Eve's before the Fall, sometimes circle in intellectual despair:

> But what have been thy answers, what but dark
> Ambiguous and with double sense deluding,
> Which they who asked have seldom understood,
> And not well understood as good not known? (I.434–437)

This is a stirring of the same pool as Satan's at, say, II.324–329:

> Hast thou not right to all created things,
> Owe not all creatures by just right to thee
> Duty and service, nor to stay till bid,
> But tender all their power? Nor mention I
> Meats by the law unclean, or offered first
> To idols, those young Daniel could refuse . . .

How obviously the case of Daniel comes not from any dramatic need but from the arguing and text-stored mind of the author of *De Doctrina Christiana*.

MILTON AND CHRIST

The interiority of style supports the assumption that Milton here identifies with Christ. Other evidence for this rather obvious point is Christ's first speech at I.196 ff. It circles round identity ("self" is the key word at first, then "son-sire"); and it recounts Christ's childhood in the quite uncarpentering terms of Milton's:

> When I was yet a child, no childish play
> To me was pleasing, all my mind was set
> Serious to learn and know . . . (I.201–203)

At II.443 Christ claims exactly the sort of knowledge Milton had—"for throughout the world / To me is not unknown what hath been done / Worthy of memorial." He goes on to cite heroic Romans of the third century B.C. Augustine had also cited them as examples of pagan virtue competing with Christian. It seems to me that Augustine's focus is correct, validated by his actual relationship with Rome, while there is something about Milton's Christ's allusion which is vulgar. At the beginning of Book III Satan seems, I'm afraid, to flatter Christ with just those qualities that Milton believed himself to have—indeed that we all believe ourselves to have; but it is a ridiculous mistake to show Christ bearing our sins when one is trying to show him exemplifying our virtues!

SUMMARY SO FAR: PRIVACY, DREAM, INTERIORITY; INCEST TABOO

The privacy, the remote wilderness of the temptations, may be said to represent the taboo on incest (private = secret), and the dreadful passion of it ("wild beasts came forth the woods to roam," I.502). The interiority, the uncertain shifting between real and allegoric, represents the ultimately phantastic nature of the incestuous desire. Together, the dreaminess, the privacy, the interiority—"It's all happening in the head"—seem to represent that element of "incest" (or that version of the metaphor we call incest) which is a withdrawal from the world back to the womb: a rejection of the adult male's scepter (II.486) for the child's "bosom of bliss" (IV.597).

THE BANQUET

The center is the banquet temptation. The sequence of events is odd:

II.60–108	Mary ponders.
109–114	Brief reference to Christ in the desert.
115–148	Satan explains Christ in terms of his mother, and Adam and Eve.

149–171 Belial, following Satan's hint that "Adam by his wives' allurement fell," says, "Set women in his eyes."

172–234 Satan, in spite of his own hint, rejects Belial's proposal as *not manly enough* (l. 225); but, in spite of that rejection, rehearses what a Belial-type temptation would be like for twenty lines (Jove's rapes, etc.). Then, in outlining manlier temptations such as wealth and glory, he refers to the "sitting queen" and Jove's love for the zone of Venus; but male power pushes that temptation away, "her female pride deject, / Or turn to reverent awe." Finally, Satan slides back from honor, fame, and so on, to the more sensuous area: "And now I know he hungers where no food / Is to be found."

235–244 Transition to wilderness.

245–259 Christ's speech on hunger, obsessively repetitive and rhyming:

		passed
		food
tasted	appetite	fast
		part
	nature	need not
	nature	repast
needing		endure
	hunger	declares
nature	need asks	
	need	
	hunger remain	remain
	this body's wasting	
	famine	
	fed	feed
hung'ring		my Father's will

Commentators are puzzled:

> M[ilton]'s introduction of this banqueting scene finds no support either in Scripture or in the tradition. Pope . . . regards it as an attempt to preserve the equation between the temptations of Adam and Eve and those of Christ.[7]

Obviously the confusion is Milton's, and begins much earlier than the actual banquet. Belial and Satan cannot decide between the sexual, which is delicious but "effeminate," and the public power, which is "manlier" but not so interesting. Christ is unable to arrive at a definition of hunger. These difficulties resolve when we agree that the sexual and the public temptations are versions of each other; and that hunger may be emotional as well as physical. This conflation would not be easy for Milton because it involves the equation of the manly with the effeminate. Satan, however, more or less effects it with his banquet.

After Christ's speech on hunger we have the dream sequence analyzed above, about Elijah and the ravens. This too is crammed with eating words, naturally enough; but what the dream sequence mainly does is to reintroduce the Belial theme. It is night; Christ dreams, "as appetite is wont to dream, / Of meats and drinks" (II.264–265). Appetite in this poem is always associated with temptation from outside rather than need from within: "For no allurement yields to appetite," Satan complains at II.409. Eve's dream in Book V of *Paradise Lost* shows that Milton knew what dreams may be about, and associated them with temptation. Clearly Christ's dream of Elijah is at least a commentary upon temptation, if not a temptation itself: the ravens bring food "with their horny beaks," complemented ninety lines later with the cornucopia, "Amalthea's horn"; but they are "taught to abstain."

As we have seen, there is next a confused transition. It includes the ambivalence of the "woody scene," a place which is both nature and art, and which is inhabited by both Christ and pagan gods and nymphs. Satan appears. There is talk of food, manna, providing angels, hunger; and then the banquet itself, presented as a masque spectacle—that is, as an illusion of ornate solidity.

Editors say we should compare Tasso. But Armida's banquet is a fairy picnic of shiny cups and plates and virgins. The danger lies anyway not in the food but in the witch's magic wand, which drives men to jump into the water and turn into fish. It is, then, simple, openly fantastic, and openly sexual. Milton's is complicated, heavily concrete, and most elaborately and ambivalently sexual.

The banquet temptation in *Paradise Regained* is an extraordinary affair. It starts with the conventional table-breast of sixteenth-century poetry:

> Was it a dream or did I see it plain,
> A goodly table of pure ivory
> All spread with juncates, fit to entertain
> The greatest prince with pompous royalty
>
> · · · · · · · · · · · · · · · ·

> Her breast that table was so richly spread,
> My thoughts the guests which would thereon have fed.
>
> (*Amoretti* 77)

Then it moves into buffoonery, a rejection-description of all this food as cumbersome luggage—"In pastry built" (*PR* II.343). Then we shift again, via Eve, to sex:

> Alas how simple, to these cates compared,
> Was that crude apple that diverted Eve! (*PR* II.348–349)

But the power of the apple is admitted in "diverted": it means amused, and seduced, as well as turned astray. And then we have at the sideboard the lovely boys whom Milton had celebrated in *Elegia VII*, and those alluring nymphs of Ovid and romance who appear in the *Nativity Ode* and in *Paradise Lost* now and then (e.g., I.448, XI.582) to be rejected, here half-held in a series of *f* sounds—"fruits and flowers . . . Fairer than feigned . . . fabled . . . faëry . . . forest."

It is diverting, yet seems not to cohere as a temptation. If anything, I should say we have a genuine mocking of gluttony, as clumsy, as bad art, like the varnished epithets in Book IV; and a genuine desire for the sexuality of the stripling youths and the nymphs—though they too are presented in terms of art, of obsolete art, and eventually disappear into a romantic incantation, the whispering of music "and Flora's earliest smells"; that is, sex and art sink back into nature and memory.

What remains is the effect of hunger-as-desire or food-as-sex. This theme is repeated, in a devious way. At IV.110, Christ says he is not moved by the offer of military control of the Middle East,

> though thou should'st add to tell
> Their sumptuous gluttonies, and gorgeous feasts
> On citron tables or Atlantic stone

—and so on. Commentators labor over this intrusion of the apparently wrong temptation:

> Pope . . . remarks that the emphasis on luxury and physical pleasure in these lines is in keeping with the treatment of the temptations by Protestant theologians . . . who, as they regarded the first temptation as one not of gluttony but of distrust in God, were obliged to interpret the kingdoms-of-the-world temptation as an attempt to excite bodily appetite.[8]

I don't regard this as more rational than my proposal—that is, that all
these temptations are versions of hunger for a love which is ultimately
maternal (it feeds), and for a power which is incestuous (it takes the
father's empire); and that the confusion is caused by Milton's ambivalence, and perhaps our own, about this subject.

SATAN'S FALL

This hunger is at other times faintly sharpened (the gratuitous line
"The fairest of her sex Angelica" at III.341), blunted ("abate her edge"
at II.455), and rewarded (the hooded Dawn who lays the storm and the
bad dreams and dries nature's tears at IV.426). It is triumphant with
the fall of Satan. He carries Christ up onto a pinnacle which has also
worried interpreters: "The nature of the 'pinnacle' (the word is used in
Matt. 4:5 and *Luke* 4:9) was, as Pope . . . explains, much debated.
Some commentators . . . held that it was merely a flat roof. . . . Others
made it a balustrade or a peaked gable or a spire."[9] Others, more modern, have seen it as an antetype of the cross. William Golding, I suppose,
would vote for the spire. Its phallic nature, though, is hardly remarkable;
what is remarkable is the liturgical complex of placement, traduction,
and antistrophe on the word "fell" that follows. The word and its deriva-
tives ring seven times in lines 562–571. The passage is, that is to say,
not a description but a celebration, a hymn of victory. It is largely a
sexual victory, as in the song of Deborah:

> He asked water, and she gave him milk; she brought forth butter
> in a lordly dish. She put her hand to the nail, and her right hand
> to the workmen's hammer; and with the hammer she smote Sisera,
> she smote off his head, when she had pierced and stricken through
> his temples. At her feet he bowed, he fell, he lay down; at her feet
> he bowed, he fell; where he bowed, there he fell down dead.
> (Judg. 5:25–27)

It is then hardly a surprise to find Satan's fall given two similes about
parentage and identity. He falls first "As when Earth's son Antaeus . . .
strove with Jove's" grandson, Hercules;

>   and oft foiled still rose,
>   Receiving from his mother Earth new strength,
>   Fresh from his fall, and fiercer grapple joined,
>   Throttled at length in the air, expired and fell . . .
>   (IV.565–568)

The typology Hercules : Antaeus :: Christ : Satan :: sky : earth :: spirit : flesh was available. But in Milton's simile it is strangely confused. I don't think it is going too far to say that what comes over is the notion of a mother's son fighting a father's; but which wins we're not sure.

The second simile is about Oedipus himself:

And as that Theban monster that proposed
Her riddle, and him, who solved it not, devoured;
That once found out and solved, for grief and spite
Cast herself headlong from the Ismenian steep,
So struck with dread and anguish fell the Fiend. (IV.572–576)

The Sphinx jumped from the acropolis of Thebes into the river Ismenus when Oedipus answered its riddle, What goes on four legs, two legs, and three legs, and is weakest with most legs? The answer is, A man. It was as his reward from the Thebans for ridding their country of the Sphinx that Oedipus was unknowingly given his mother as wife, and made king of that land. On the face of it, the allusion could hardly be less appropriate to its location in *Paradise Regained*; or, at the level of personal myth, hardly more.

GRATIFICATION

Christ is then, like Oedipus, given his maternal and regal rewards. Here is the maternal imagery of boudoir, food, and fundamental drink: angels "on their plumy vans received him soft" and carried him "As on a floating couch":

Then in a flowery valley set him down
On a green bank, and set before him spread
A table of celestial food, divine,
Ambrosial, fruits fetched from the tree of life,
And from the fount of life ambrosial drink . . . (IV.586–590)

Then they hymn him as "True image of the Father"; but while they sing, "he unobserved / Home to his mother's house private returned."

Adam/Eve and Cain/Abel are then seen to be variants of a theme which can also occur in other forms, as in the well-known myth of Oedipus. The actual symbolism in these two cases is nearly identical. . . . In the Oedipus story, in place of Eve's Serpent we have Jocasta's Sphinx. Like Jocasta the Sphinx is female, like Jocasta the Sphinx com-

mits suicide, like the Serpent the Sphinx leads men to their doom by verbal cunning, like the Serpent the Sphinx is an anomalous monster. Eve listens to the Serpent's words and betrays Adam into incest; Oedipus solves the Sphinx riddle and is led into incest.[10]

NOTES

1. *The Poems of John Milton*, ed. John Carey and Alastair Fowler (London, 1968), p. 1105. All quotations of Milton's poetry are from this edition, hereafter referred to as Carey and Fowler.

2. J. B. Broadbent, "Milton and Arnold," *Essays in Criticism*, VI (1956), 404–417.

3. *Milton*, British Council Pamphlet (London, 1952), p. 40.

4. Kester Svendsen, "Milton's 'Aerie Microscope,' " *Modern Language Notes*, LXIV (1949), 525-527.

5. Josephine Miles, *Eras and Modes in English Poetry*, 2nd ed. (Berkeley and Los Angeles, 1964), p. 268.

6. What can we make of the myth as a whole? Its other elements are: (a) as a daughter, Alcestis refused to cut up her father at Medea's suggestion; her sisters were less pious; (b) as a bride, Alcestis appeared to Admetus as a knot of serpents in the bed because he had forgotten to sacrifice to Artemis and was drunk; (c) the parents of Admetus refused to die in his stead.

7. Carey and Fowler, p. 1109.

8. Ibid., pp. 1140–1141.

9. Ibid., p. 1161.

10. Edmund Leach, *Genesis as Myth and Other Essays* (Cambridge, 1969), p. 18.

William Blake: Illustrator-Interpreter of *Paradise Regained*

JOSEPH ANTHONY WITTREICH, JR.

UNIVERSITY OF WISCONSIN

> Illustration . . . has become unfortunately a synonym for superficiality. It is, I fear, too late to reclaim the word, so I have elsewhere been content to use it in its derogatory sense. When, however, one speaks of a man illustrating a poem, one must surely mean that he has done more than paint a pretty picture to accompany it. He has presumably succeeded in translating something of that poem into his own plastic medium.[1]

One of the many ironies of twentieth-century criticism is that for all it has taught us about Blake as a poet-painter it has done little, until very recently, to enhance our understanding and appreciation of Blake as an illustrator-critic.[2] No one is going to deny that the modern critical movement has contributed incalculably to our understanding of both poetry and criticism. But one must recognize, too, that the modern age of criticism has fostered formalization and regimentation, which together have tended to push criticism of our antecedent centuries beyond our categories of analysis. After E. J. Ellis, William Butler Yeats, and George Saintsbury, Blake the critic is rolled into the distance, because the kind of criticism he wrote *or painted* is no longer recognized as criticism.[3] The immediate problem that faces us, then, is one of classification and definition. If we wish to ascertain what works make up Blake's canon of literary criticism, we must consider, first, the nature of literary criticism; and as we do that it is perhaps better to acquire a sense of how criticism was categorized and defined in the late eighteenth and

93

early nineteenth centuries than to detail and elaborate what it means today. In the process, we are likely to discover that Blake pushes us beyond "the cultured gardens of conventional criticism" and "demands that we surrender much of our usual operational gear."[4]

Ralph Cohen has probed so deeply into eighteenth-century applications of the term *criticism* that a summary of his discussion may suffice to provide a background to my own.[5] The eighteenth century distinguished three types of criticism: (1) process or philosophical criticism, (2) product or historical criticism, and (3) by-product or corrective criticism. Concerned with the activity of the poet in composition, the first sort derives largely from letters and manuscripts. The second involves the formal discipline of evaluating and theorizing about literary works and finds its chief vehicle in essays, lectures, and books. The last type appears as explanation and interpretation and takes the form, at least in the eighteenth century, of parodic and imitative poems as well as illustration. The illustrations Blake painted for poems that he himself composed suggest that he understood the interpretive function of illustration, and his own assertion that "Imitation is Criticism"[6] indicates his adherence to the idea of the imitative or parodic poem as interpretation and elucidation of the work it assumes as context. The point for us to keep in mind is that neither attitude is eccentric in an age that regarded imitation and illustration as legitimate, indeed valuable, modes of illumination and elucidation. The eighteenth century took it for granted that an illustration should not only explain a passage—literally illuminate it—but should focus, because of its special quality, upon the poem's subject matter and unity. The illustration, therefore, was expected to be more than decorative; it was a mode of explanation and enlightenment intended "to create a coherent imaginative entity of the poem."[7]

Cohen's conclusions point to the interpretive function of Blake's illustrations, but they also enable us to establish a canon of Blake's criticism, verbal and nonverbal. That canon includes, first of all, Blake's formal commentaries—*Descriptive Catalogue* and *Public Address*—and, second, the many critical asides that appear in letters and in the marginalia to Dante, Bacon, Reynolds, Wordsworth, and others. Still further, there are the reported conversations of Robinson, Palmer, and Dibdin. Moreover, Blake's *Milton,* Plates 5-6 of *The Marriage of Heaven and Hell,* and Plate 3 of *Jerusalem* are of particular interest for their reference to Milton.[8] And if we accept Blake's dictum that imitation is criticism and couple it with S. Foster Damon's perception that behind every major poem by Blake is a major work of Milton's the canon swells considerably.[9] Add to this verbal criticism the illustrations to Young's *Night Thoughts*, Blair's *The Grave*, Vergil's *Eclogues*, Chaucer's *Canterbury Tales*, and Dante's *Commedia*; those to the Book of Job, Shakespeare's plays, Bunyan's *Pilgrim's Progress*, and Spenser's *Faerie Queene*; those to Gray, Defoe, and Gay; and the illustrations to Milton.[10] We are then confronted with a canon of criticism surpassed quantitatively by very few critics of the Romantic era and qualitatively by fewer yet.

Clearly, a full study of Blake's achievement as a critic requires a book, perhaps several. Even the subject of Blake's Milton illustrations demands more space than is ordinarily occupied by an essay. Therefore, this discussion of the illustrations to *Paradise Regained* should be considered only as a preliminary study. The illustrations done before those to *Paradise Regained* will be alluded to in the pages that follow, but only insofar as they shed light on Blake's method of illustrating. The illustrations to *Paradise Regained* are especially suited to this study inasmuch as they are the last set of illustrations to Milton that Blake completed and, thus, may be supposed to contain Blake's final crystallization of the Miltonic vision. Moreover, inasmuch as Blake did multiple sets of illustrations to *Comus, Paradise Lost*, and the *Nativity Ode* —each new set differing significantly from the one it superseded in detail and sometimes in subject matter—the problems of interpretation are minimized by choosing the illustrations to *Paradise Regained*.

The only assumptions about these illustrations that we bring with us are that they are inextricably involved with Milton's poetry, whatever their relationship to Blake's, and that they have an interpretive function, forming a series of perceptions that comment importantly and originally on the poems they illuminate. These assumptions are encouraged by Blake himself, who expected a great picture to contain great ideas: "Shall Painting be confined to the sordid drudgery of fac-simile representations of merely mortal and perishing substances . . . ? No, it shall not be so! Painting . . . exists and exults in immortal thoughts."[11] At the very moment when illustration was becoming mere decoration, when the intimate relationship between text and design was broken, Blake was asserting the integrity of that relationship. Instead of ushering in the new era of decorative design, Blake culminates the great tradition of interpretive illustration that flowered during the Renaissance. Neither mere ornament nor mere facsimile reproduction, Blake's designs impress a whole complex of images upon the mind so as to reveal the higher conceptions and deeper meanings of the texts they accompany.

The illustrations to Milton are "the end of a golden string"[12] by which we may wind our way through the intricate mazes of Milton's poetry, and they introduce the paradox that involves all the illustrations Blake did for the works of other authors. These illustrations are too laden with symbolism to allow the designs to be dismissed simply as literal renderings; yet that symbolism is so completely entangled with the poems it illumines that Blake finally comes closer to the text of his author than a "literal" illustrator could. When Blake illustrated the Book of Job, he stated at the lower center of his first design the principle that underlies all his illustrations. Quoting St. Paul, Blake writes, "The Letter Killeth / The Spirit giveth Life" (2 Cor. 3:6). This is not to suggest that Blake ignores textual detail; for such detail, often meticulously rendered, appears in his designs, but usually as the barest suggestion, the merest shorthand. It is to say that Blake is never content with the charming detail for its own sake, but only insofar as it enables him to focus upon those parts of the poem where its spiritual significance is most completely manifested. Blake's illustrations "are presentments of the spiritual essence."[13] In his designs to Milton's poetry in general and in the illustrations to *Paradise Regained* in particular, Blake lifts us to his own level of perception, abstracts the "spiritual essence" of the poem, and lays bare its metaphorical and mythic structures in designs that probe the central issues of Milton's art and resolve those issues in interpretations to which Milton's critics still are strangers.

I

By 1816 Blake had failed magnificently in his effort to compose a diffuse epic under the title first of *Vala* and then of *The Four Zoas*, but he had also succeeded brilliantly in writing a brief epic called *Milton* and was nearly finished with another entitled *Jerusalem*. Still before him were a set of twenty-one illustrations to the Book of Job,[14] a third but unfinished set of illustrations to *Paradise Lost*, a series of twenty-eight illustrations to Bunyan's *Pilgrim's Progress*, and the designs to Dante's *Commedia*. Like Milton, Blake moved from the lyric to the epic mode as his poetical powers developed; and thus *Paradise Regained* was illustrated, as it was written, in the maturity of genius with the intent of presenting a final epitome of Milton's vision. It was probably in 1816 that

Blake illustrated *L'Allegro* and *Il Penseroso* and *Paradise Regained*, presumably in that order.[15] In Milton's twin lyrics Blake found a total pattern of human experience defined in terms of contrary states and progression. In *Paradise Regained* he found more. Milton's brief epic laid down for him not only the main lines of his conception of epic poetry but the very basis of "the Romantic myth"[16] of which he, under the guidance of Milton, was a primary shaper.

Nine years later the series of twelve designs to *Paradise Regained*, each measuring 17 x 13 cms., was purchased by John Linnell, in whose collection it remained for nearly a century.[17] On March 15, 1918, the series, now in the Fitzwilliam Museum, was sold to Mr. T. H. Riches. The first recorded comment on the *Paradise Regained* illustrations comes in a letter, addressed to Mrs. Gilchrist and dated December 13 [1862], from William Michael Rossetti. Rossetti writes, "I will consider about the Paradise Regained. The designs were shown to me by John Linnell as being more than usually beautiful, and I do not directly *dissent* from the terms used in the slip you send me; only my feeling is that Blake has here been less inspired than usual, and the result comparatively tame."[18] The "slip" to which Rossetti refers is apparently the comment on the series published in Gilchrist's *Life of Blake* the following year. That comment suggests that the illustrations to *Paradise Regained* are "a sequel to those from the *Paradise Lost*" and are "of great beauty, refined in execution, especially tender and pure in colour, and pervading feeling";[19] and elsewhere in his *Life* Gilchrist describes the illustrations as possessing "a remarkable affinity to the character of the poem, which is more distinguished by stately and elaborated method than by inspiration."[20]

In our own time the illustrations to *Paradise Regained* have been twice reproduced and three times discussed. Darrell Figgis, the first commentator on this set of illustrations, reaches three conclusions about them: (1) Blake expresses himself more fully in his illustrations to *Paradise Regained* than in those to *Paradise Lost*; (2) in execution the illustrations to *Paradise Regained* seem to stand between the first and second sets to *Paradise Lost*; and (3) the theme of the illustrations is Christ's initiation. Marcia Pointon, the most recent student of the illustrations, is also poignantly conscious of the stylistic differences between them and Blake's earlier illustrations, a difference which she defines in terms of their "symbolic . . . iconic quality." And finally Geoffrey Keynes says that the task of the editor-commentator is not great when it comes to the Milton illustrations, since Blake was content "to illustrate almost literally."[21] With Keynes' remark our discussion may begin, but to the concerns of Figgis and Pointon it must eventually return.

Keynes' contention runs counter to what students of Blake's illustrations have been telling us. Others stress the discontinuity between design and poem, thereby emphasizing Blake's departures from the text so as to direct attention to his own mythology,[22] whereas Keynes underscores "the literal character of the [Milton] illustrations," which, he thinks, require "little 'interpretation.'"[23] Both positions simplify beyond accuracy. What we discover is that the early sets of illustrations possess an immediately apparent literal character; the later ones, however, move in the direction of symbolism—but a symbolism that grasps the spiritual content and aesthetic unity of the poem Blake illustrates. The point is demonstrated easily by turning to the designs for *Comus*, then those for the *Nativity Ode*, or by turning to the first set of illustrations to *Paradise Lost* and considering it in relation to the second set.

Blake made two sets of illustrations for *Comus*, one in 1801, the other in 1809. Each set contains eight designs that are the same in subject but different in detail. These illustrations are characterized by their literal quality, and, significantly, where Blake has deviated from Milton's text in the first set he returns to it in the second. The initial illustration is a case in point. In the first set, Blake depicts Comus and his revellers, headed like sundry sorts of wild beasts, with the Lady seated in the foreground and the Attendant Spirit descending from the sky. The illustration draws upon the first two hundred forty-three lines for its details and, in fact, conflates three separate episodes from that part of the poem within a single design—the descent of the Attendant Spirit, the rout of the monsters, and the Lady's entrance into the woods. This illustration departs from the text in two significant details. The Attendant Spirit, who descends and enters the woods, concludes his prologue with the words, "I must be viewless now" (l. 92); and the Lady appears to be observing a scene that she does not observe in Milton's poem. If the Attendant Spirit is not "viewless" in the illustration to the first set he is made so in the same design for the second set; and the Lady, who in the first set has her head bent toward the scene, has it turned away in the second set, making clear that her experience of it is imaginary rather than actual. Similarly, in the illustration to the first set, the reveller on the far left of the drawing is carrying the cup, Blake apparently forgetting Milton's directive, "*Comus enters with a Charming Rod in one hand, his Glass in the other.*"[24] This departure from the text is, likewise, corrected when Blake illustrates the poem a second time.

To turn from the *Comus* illustrations to those for the *Nativity Ode* is to turn from a literal to a symbolic mode of interpretation. As with *Comus*, Blake made two separate sets of illustrations for the poem, both probably in 1809, and both those sets deviate from Milton's text. Again the subjects are the same, but in detail the illustrations differ decidedly. Here, as before, the first illustration may serve as an example. In both sets the first design presents in tableau the Nativity scene with Peace descending and Nature, having shed her gaudy trim, reclining below. The central episode in both is the birth of Christ. In the first design the stable scene is bisected, with oxen eating from the manger on the viewer's left and Mary cradling Jesus in her arms, Joseph standing beside her, on the right. In the same illustration to the second set, the manger has disappeared altogether, the oxen are only dimly visible, Mary is slouched over with astonishment in Joseph's arms; and the child, springing from the lap of Mary into a blaze of light, dominates the center. Both designs are interesting interpretively, but both also depart conspicuously from the poem Milton has written.

Nowhere before the last stanza of his poem does Milton describe the Nativity scene, but Blake makes it central to the first three of his six depictions for the poem. Yet this scene, as we move from the first to the third design, seems to have diminishing importance. The absolute focus of the first illustration, the Nativity scene is obscured in the second by the marginal clutter and in the third recedes into the background as our attention is riveted to the heavenly choirs above and to the shepherds in adoration below. By giving central importance to the Nativity scene, Blake reveals the celebrative rather than descriptive character of Milton's poem. By depicting the infant springing miraculously from his mother's arms, Blake suggests even further that the poem is a celebration not of the Nativity per se but of the mystery of the Incarnation. And by relating the Nativity scene to both the descent of Peace and the purification of Nature, and particularly by pushing the Nativity scene farther and farther into the distance with each successive illustration, Blake implies that the poem's subject is not primarily the Incarnation but its effects upon human history. That theme all his illustrations share.

This movement from literal to symbolic interpretation is complicated but nonetheless apparent when we turn to the two sets of illustrations to *Paradise Lost*. These sets differ in detail and, unlike the previous series of designs, they differ in subject matter as well. The Huntington set is composed of twelve subjects; the Boston set, as it now exists, of only nine. Whereas the former group of designs commences with "Satan Calling His Legions" and "Satan Coming to the Gates of Hell," the latter begins with the depiction "Christ Offers to Redeem Man." And whereas the second group omits the subjects of "Satan's and Raphael's Entries into Paradise" and "Judgment of Adam and Eve," it contains a new design, "Adam and Eve Sleeping." The matter is more complicated than it seems, however.

Martin Butlin has recently asserted the merest suggestion by Gilchrist as hard fact.[25] Gilchrist had observed of a second depiction of "Satan Coming to the Gates of Hell" that it "may presumably have belonged at first to the set of Nine Designs from 'Paradise Lost.' "[26] Butlin, without providing any supporting evidence, declares that both sets originally contained twelve illustrations: the larger of the two Huntington depictions of Satan, Sin, and Death belongs to the second set, he contends; so do the designs of "Satan Calling His Legions," now in the Victoria and Albert Museum, and of the "Judgment of Adam and Eve," now in the director's office at the Houghton Library. It is almost certain that the "Judgment of Adam and Eve" belongs to the second set; it is dated 1808 and is of the same size and quality as the other designs in that set. The other two designs are more questionable. Both are larger than any design in the Boston set. Both are exceedingly conventional in subject matter. Moreover, "Satan Calling His Legions" was, in Blake's words, "painted at intervals" as an "experiment Picture."[27] It is highly probable, given Blake's early but dissipating interest in the first two books of *Paradise Lost*, that these two illustrations were done as independent designs never intended to accompany the second set of illustrations. Very possibly, then, the second set of illustrations is a broken set but one which originally contained ten, not twelve, designs.

The motives that inspired Blake's illustrations to *Paradise Lost* contrast strikingly with those that produced the designs to Dante's *Commedia*. From Blake's point of view, Dante's entire vision was built upon the fundamental error of punishing sins rather than forgiving them. Blake's illustrations to Dante, therefore, are largely concerned with *correcting* the poet's vision. Blake's principal objection to Milton, even as early as *The Marriage of Heaven and Hell*, was somewhat different. *Paradise Lost*, Blake understood, was written in part to criticize the very theology it postulated; Milton's difficulty lay not so much in what he said but in how he said it. Blake believed that epic poetry had both a narrative and a visionary dimension, and he thought that in *Paradise Lost* the narrative got in the way of Milton's vision. With this observation in mind, Blake set out to illustrate Milton's epic and in those illustrations to illuminate the visionary experience that Milton's poem contains—an experience that Milton's own narrative and eighteenth-century commentaries obscured. One may reasonably conjecture that being dissatisfied with his first set of illustrations Blake felt compelled to try again. With the aim of retrieving the visionary poem Milton had written, Blake quite possibly recalled that *Paradise Lost* appeared first as a ten-book epic and, for that reason, settled upon doing ten illustrations for the second set. As Blake turns from one set to the other, interest is deflected from the first two books of Milton's epic to Christ who is at its center. Blake, in short, casts off his early Satanism as he apprehends the Christocentric character of Milton's diffuse epic. Christ is Milton's hero, the ethical nucleus of Milton's poem, and most fittingly becomes the spiritual focus of Blake's second set of designs to *Paradise Lost*.

Both sets of designs reveal Blake's close adherence to Milton's text. That concern is paramount from the initial designs for the first set to the last design for the second set. With customary accuracy, Samuel Taylor Coleridge has observed that "sundry painters have attempted pictures of the meeting between Satan and Death at the gates of Hell; and how was Death represented? Not as Milton has described him," says Coleridge, "but by the most defined thing that can be imagined— a skeleton, the dryest and hardest image that it is possible to discover; which, instead of keeping the mind in a state of activity, reduces it to the merest passivity."[28] The exception, of course, is Blake. His depiction of Satan, Sin, and Death reveals how scrupulously he, in comparison with his predecessors, followed Milton's text. Unique among eighteenth- and early nineteenth-century illustrators of Milton, Blake preserved Milton's conception of Death as a shadow. Blake would not have known Coleridge's feelings, but he doubtless shared with his contemporaries an admiration for the sublimity of Milton's allegory—a quality that some eighteenth-century commentators denied it. Indeed, Blake may owe something to Hogarth and Gillray, but his most important debt in this illustration is probably to Cowper, for whose edition of Milton he began illustrating Milton's poetry.[29] In his notes for a commentary on *Paradise Lost*, later published by William Hayley, Cowper observes that Milton's Death is "a decided shadow . . . a kind of intermediate form between matter and spirit, partaking of both, and consisting of neither. The idea of its substance," continues Cowper, "is lost in its tenuity, and yet, contemplated awhile as a shadow, it becomes a substance. The dimness of this vague and fleeting outline is infinitely more terrible than exact description, because it leaves the imagination at full liberty to see for itself, and to suppose the worst."[30] Under the influence of Cowper, Blake translated the amusingly grotesque representations of Hogarth and Gillray back into the sublime of Milton.

The succeeding designs, presumably belonging to a later date, are more symbolic and seemingly less precise renderings of Milton's text, as the final illustration to both sets may suggest. In the last lines of Milton's poem, there are no horsemen, no stems of thorns, no thunderbolts; there is no coiled serpent. Yet all these images figure in Blake's concluding illustration to the poem. Blake's depiction of the Expulsion, of course, is more than another design; it constitutes an epilogue to Milton's poem and is, therefore, an epitome of its action. The serpent recalls the fall (its cause), the thunderbolt the action that immediately ensues (the judgment); and the fall and judgment together point to the ultimate consequence of transgression (man's expulsion from Eden). Moreover, the four horsemen and the stems of thorns are faithful in spirit if not in letter to the poem Milton has written. The thorns at once symbolize the world of experience—its misery, fever, and fret—that Milton so vividly portrayed in the biblical visions of Book XI and that man now enters;[31] and they anticipate the coming of Christ who, through his passion and death, will restore man to a paradise happier far than the one from which he has been exiled. Correspondingly, Milton makes no reference to the Four Horsemen of the Apocalypse[32] as he draws his poem to its period, but he does allude to the Book of Revelation. Of Adam and Eve Milton says, "Some natural tears they dropp'd, but wip'd them soon" (XII.645), thus looking forward to the time when "God shall wipe away all tears from their eyes; and there shall be no more death, neither sorrow, nor crying" (Rev. 21:4). What Milton does verbally Blake does visually: both dramatically juxtapose the worlds of experience and higher innocence, the worlds of tragic defeat and spiritual triumph.

Even so, certain details in the final illustration to the first set seem to contradict both the letter and the spirit of the poem's ending. Speaking of "Blake's resistance to Milton and 'reformation' of him," Kester Svendsen says that Blake's Expulsion scene is as "faithful in fact (the clasped hands) as it is creatively free." Whereas Milton's emphasis is on fallen humanity moving into an alien and hostile world, Blake's is on the "hope" in expulsion. Blake misses, says Svendsen, the "paradox of banishment."[33] Reaching conclusions about Blake's illustrations on the basis of Svendsen's article and thus the *first* set of designs to *Paradise Lost*, Merritt Hughes believes that Blake distinguishes himself from Milton's other illustrators by "interpreting the Expulsion in terms of

1. The Baptism Of Jesus

2. The First Temptation

3. Andrew And Simon Peter

4. Mary Watched By Two Angels

5. *Satan In Council*

6. The Banquet Temptation

7. *The Second Temptation*

8. The Tempter Inspiring Jesus's Ugly Dreams

9. Morning Chasing Away The Spectres Of The Night

10. The Third Temptation

11. Jesus Ministered To By Angels

12. Jesus Returning To Mary

redemption and possible joy." Blake's illustration, "solemnly symbolic of redemptive joy," presents "hope and love in the faces of Adam and Eve."[34] Two details in this illustration support the conclusions of Svendsen and Hughes. Adam and Eve seem to be moving swiftly (Milton says they leave Paradise "with wand'ring steps and slow" [XII.648]); and they seem, with heads turned upward, replete with joy.

With these facts and interpretations in mind, it is instructive to consider the final illustration to the second group of designs. The subject is the same, but the details are altered. The heads of Adam and Eve are bent downward; motion is arrested as a thorn punctures the left foot of Adam. If the first depiction of the Expulsion seems overwrought with joy, the second is more in keeping with the sense of sorrow that pervades the closing lines of Milton's poem. Thus even as Blake pushes relentlessly toward symbolic interpretation by making Christ the focus of the second set, his interest is clearly in the poem another has written and not in a poem he wishes to rewrite.

In the set of twelve illustrations to *Paradise Regained*, the last complete set of illustrations to a poem by Milton, there are only minor departures from Milton's text, but those few alterations are of real interest. Keynes has drawn our attention to three of the four contradictions of Milton's poem. He properly observes that in Figure 3, the depiction of Andrew and Simon Peter, "the attendant angels are not mentioned in Milton's text"; nor are they mentioned—and this point Keynes does not make—in the illustration of Mary meditating that immediately follows. Still further, Keynes tells us in his note to Figure 6 that "the crown held in Satan's left hand has been added by Blake's imagination" and in his note to Figure 12 that Blake "has added on either side the figures of Andrew and Simon Peter who are not mentioned in the text."[35]

Keynes poses a question regarding the relationship of Blake's illustrations to Milton's text that should not go unanswered. The illustrations to *Paradise Regained* fall into four groups. There are, first, the purely literal renderings. But there are also conflations as well as anticipatory designs. There are, finally, the symbolic interpretations. Most of the designs are literal renderings of symbolic events. But Figure 4, for instance, conflates two episodes through the merest shorthand into a single design. Mary is meditating upon the meaning of the baptism she has just beheld; but, as she does so, her mind wanders back to the Nativity. Jesus, who made one descent in order to become man, is in process of making another descent, this one a descent into himself in order to become God. Through the faintest suggestion, Blake allows two events, typologically related, to conflate within a single design and thereby calls attention to Milton's suggestion that all of Christ's descents are implied in this one. Figure 6, if not a true conflation of events, is at least an anticipatory design. The banquet serves as a prelude to, may even be regarded as the first stage of, the second temptation. By introducing the image of the crown, Blake allows this design to anticipate the long sequence that immediately follows.[36] The last design in the series, on the other hand, requires symbolic interpretation. Blake, as we shall see later, was concerned finally with the Christ myth as it is presented and interpreted by Milton's poem. That myth involves withdrawal, temptation, and return. Through the inclusion of Andrew and Simon Peter in the design Blake allows the beginning and the end of that myth to converge, with the suggestion that the real force of Milton's poem derives not from its rhetorical but from its symbolic structure and that the end of Milton's poem constitutes a new beginning.

From the foregoing discussion we may conclude that Blake's illustrations assiduously follow Milton's text, but they are also more than literal renderings of it. Blake evolves a symbolic method of illustrating that paradoxically forces him beyond the text so as to capture its spiritual content with greater force of imagination and with sharper precision of pictorial language. Blake's illustrations, then, are both intellectual and utilitarian: they are something to be understood in their own right and, once understood, to be used as a gloss on the poem they adorn; they are pictorial criticisms that greatly increase the intelligibility of Milton's poetry. The main thrust of the discussion thus far has been toward this realization, but the discussion yields yet another conclusion.

One perceptive student of book illustration observes that "the essence of good pictorial narrative is not so much the concentration of a single event in a comprehensive picture . . . as to divide an episode into a series of consecutive phases in which the protagonist is repeated again and again. The aim is to have the changes of action represented in such a dense sequence that the beholder can read the pictorial story almost without resorting to the text for supplementary information."[37] The critic is talking about early illustrators of Homer and Vergil, but the essence of what he has to say pertains to Blake's Milton illustrations as well. At the same time that Blake's designs, individually and collectively, provide a gloss on the text just as a medieval or Renaissance commentary provides a gloss on the words of a poem or a scriptural text, those designs also comprise a "totality." The fact that Blake, in most cases, abandoned the practice of binding his illustrations with the text of the poem they illuminated, or even of indicating passages or line references on the illustrations themselves, has caused some confusion. Many have concluded that the illustrations, wrenched from the text of poems they ostensibly adorn, illuminate Blake's own poetry rather than that of the poet he is illustrating. However, this fracturing of the customary relationship between text and illumination may serve another purpose: it encourages the beholder to see the illustrations, for the moment at least, as a totality, as a related sequence of perceptions that comment on a single momentous event in several consecutive stages. If turning from Blake's illustrations for *Comus* to those for *Paradise Regained* is, in one sense, moving from a literal into a symbolic mode of illustration, it is, in another sense, moving away from the eighteenth-century habit of illustration, in which various events are condensed within a single picture, toward a mode of illustration in which a great event is fragmented and represented in a series of related designs. But this observation leads us into yet another matter that should be broached before embarking upon an interpretation of the illustrations to *Paradise Regained*—the contention that Blake works within traditions of Milton interpretation and illustration.

II

Jean Hagstrum believes that in Blake's illustrations to Milton's poems, "Milton is interpreted as the pictorialist school of the Wartons would have wished";[38] that is, Blake interprets Milton as the eighteenth century wanted to interpret Milton, not as Milton would have wanted to be interpreted. *Paradise Regained*, of course, did not attract the same amount of attention or inspire the same volume of commentary as did *Paradise Lost*; but despite assertions to the contrary, it did not fall into total neglect either. Not only was *Paradise Regained* frequently reprinted in the eighteenth century, and often illustrated, but as early as 1690 the poem was translated into Latin; in 1740 it inspired a poem entitled *On the Resurrection* and five years later one called *Jesus*.[39] Moreover, *Paradise Regained* was the subject of three separate commentaries before 1750 and later in the century was printed separately on various occasions, both in England and America.[40] And in 1752 Thomas Newton offered a new edition of the poem, which was liberally annotated by various hands. *Paradise Regained*, the initial note to this volume suggests, "has not met with the approbation it deserves," largely because of its narrowness of plan, though in its kind the poem is no less excellent than *Paradise Lost*.[41]

Newton himself raises a new issue in the criticism of *Paradise Regained*—the nature of its genre—and allows the commentators he quotes to raise some others. In this respect, the notes by Thyer and Warburton require more attention than they ordinarily receive. Thyer writes,

> It may seem a little odd at first, that Milton should impute the recovery of Paradise to this short scene of our Saviour's life upon earth, and not rather extend it to his agony, crucifixion &c; but the reason no doubt was, that *Paradise regain'd* by our Saviour's resisting the temptations of Satan might be a better contrast to *Paradise lost* by our first parents too easily yielding to the same seducing Spirit. Besides he might very probably, and indeed very reasonably, be apprehensive, that a subject so extensive as well as sublime might be too great a burden for his declining constitution, and a task too long for the short term of years he could then hope for. Even in his Paradise Lost he expresses his fears, lest he had begun too late, and lest *an age too late, or cold climate, or years should have damp'd his intended wing*; and surely he had much greater cause to dread the same now, and be very cautious of launching out too far.

Warburton comments in a similar vein:

> It is hard to say whether Milton's wrong notions in divinity led him to this defective plan; or his fondness for the plan influenced those notions. That is whether he indeed supposed the redemption of mankind (as he here represents it) was procured by Christ's triumph over the Devil in the wilderness; or whether he thought that the scene of the desert opposed to that of Paradise, and the action of a temptation withstood to a temptation fall'n under, made *Paradise Regain'd* a more regular sequel to *Paradise Lost*. Or if neither this nor that, whether it was his being tired out with the labour of composing Paradise Lost made him averse to another work of length . . . is very uncertain. All that we can be sure of is, that the plan is a very unhappy one, and defective even in that narrow view of a sequel, for it affords the poet no opportunity of driving the Devil back again to Hell from his new conquests in the air. In the mean time nothing was easier than to have invented a good one, which should end with the resurrection, and comprise these four books, somewhat contracted, in an episode, for which only the subject of them is fit.[42]

Newton's edition of *Paradise Regained* opens a new chapter in the history of the criticism of Milton's poem. It raises the whole question of the poem's genre, the matter of its relation to *Paradise Lost*, and the propriety of Milton's complementing the fall with the temptation in the wilderness. These questions lie behind much Romantic criticism of the poem and are deeply involved in the illustrative criticism of William Blake.

Unquestionably Blake and the writers of the Romantic era displayed the greatest sensitivity to and appreciation for *Paradise Regained*.[43] If Newton's edition raised the issues that occupied readers of *Paradise Regained* during the last half of the eighteenth century, William Hayley, together with Charles Dunster, formulated the ones that were to engage students of the poem during the Romantic period. Whereas the eighteenth century stressed the continuity between *Paradise Lost* and *Paradise Regained*, Hayley attempted to dissociate the two poems in order to assert the integrity of the latter. In the first poem, Hayley tells us, Milton "seems to emulate the sublimity of Moses and the prophets"; but in *Paradise Regained* he attempts "to copy the sweetness and simplicity of the milder Evangelists." Not wanting to encroach upon Cowper's critical edition of Milton, Hayley confines himself to biographical details except when he leaps into the province of criticism to formulate an elaborate defense of *Paradise Regained* against its detractors. There is "no poem of epick form," concludes Hayley, "where the sublimest moral instruction is so forcibly and abundantly united to poetic delight: the splendour of the poet does not blaze indeed so intensely as in his larger production"; but despite that, *Paradise Regained* embodies "the truest heroism, and the triumph of Christianity."[44] Hayley is not necessarily dealing with issues different from those that Newton's edition posed, but he does present a new and distinctively Romantic attitude toward them. Hayley, like Newton, recognizes that *Paradise Regained* is different in kind from *Paradise Lost*; but he realizes, too, that its form is not necessarily a constraining influence upon the poet. Hayley asserts the integrity of Milton's brief epic, which is to say that he regards the poem as neither companion nor sequel to *Paradise Lost*; and he sees *Paradise Regained* as the culmination of Milton's genius, the final embodiment of his radically new version of Christianity.

In 1795 a separate edition of *Paradise Regained* appeared with notes by various hands, its editor Charles Dunster explaining in his preface that although *Paradise Regained* has been only "negligently and

scantily illustrated" a new appreciation of the poem "begins to prevail." If Newton had tried *to assert* an understanding of *Paradise Regained*, Dunster was intent upon furnishing new perspectives on the
poem, thereby encouraging the kind of critical inquiry from which a
new understanding might eventually emerge. And if Hayley had sought
to dissociate Milton's two epics, Dunster argued instead that "the Paradise Regained is so necessary a sequel to the Paradise Lost, that we
cannot but imagine that Milton, when he wrote the one, was not without
an intention . . . of producing something of the kind for the purpose of
completing his subject. Accordingly, the two poems mutually coincide
with, and admirably illustrate, each other. . . ."[45] But like Hayley, Dunster apprehends the poem's perfection and unity; like Hayley he insists
that failure to appreciate the poem stems from a failure to comprehend
the poem's genre.

If Hayley and Dunster managed to present new attitudes to *Paradise Regained*, they did not succeed in dispelling the old ones. In both
his 1801 and 1809 editions of Milton, Henry John Todd, though he
praises *Paradise Regained*, finds it lacking when compared to *Paradise
Lost*: "The plan," he says, "is faulty: For to attribute the Redemption
of Mankind solely to Christ's triumph over the temptations in the wilderness, is a notion not only contracted but untrue."[46] And Charles Sym-
mons, after asserting that *Paradise Regained* "possessed no charms for
the multitude," suggests that "the voice of the public, which on the question of poetic excellence cannot for a long time be erroneous, has ir-
revocably decided" the fate of *Paradise Regained*.[47] The poem, he
concludes, suffers from extreme narrowness of plan, little action, too
much disputation and didactic dialogue, paucity of character and poetic
imagery. Moreover, the content of the poem does not fulfill the expectations created by the title: *Paradise Regained* should be about the
death and resurrection of Christ, not about his temptations.

This is the shape of the critical tradition with which Blake was
probably familiar. Hayley, whom Charles Dunster considered to be the
"best critic" of *Paradise Regained*, owned various editions of Newton;
he owned an inscribed copy of Dunster's 1795 edition, which included
many of the notes used by Newton; his library also contained various
copies of his own *Life of Milton*. If Blake did not read these works, he
may, indeed, have become acquainted with their contents through discussions with Hayley, who did read them.[48] In any event, it is Hayley
who seems to provide the critical perspective that is manifested in
Blake's illustrations to *Paradise Regained*.

Regarded as a form of nonverbal criticism by Blake and his contemporaries, illustration was also an essential part of the critical tradition accumulated by *Paradise Regained* during the eighteenth century. With this tradition, too, Blake seems to have had at least nodding familiarity. Just as Jean Hagstrum sees Blake working within the tradition of eighteenth-century criticism of *Paradise Regained*, so Morse Peckham contends that Blake works within the same tradition of illustration (the "minute particulars" of that tradition are provided in Appendix A). The nature of that tradition, especially for Blake's "illustrative, nonvisionary, and nonprophetic works," says Peckham, "provided a place for 'imitation,' copying, using other men's ideas." Thus Peckham concludes that "when we have resurrected and studied the work of forgotten illustrators and painters of his time . . . we shall be in a position to understand far better both the nature and the quality of Blake's genius."[49] We may now turn to Blake's illustrations to *Paradise Regained* to see to what extent they were affected by these traditions of criticism and illustration.

III

The most recent and, to my mind, the most important general statement about the tradition of Milton illustration is provided by J. B. Trapp, who, though he does not single out Blake by name, argues that from the sixteenth century onward "little that is new and significant is added to the Fall [or the Redemption] in any medium, including book-illustrations." For Trapp, Milton's illustrators—and he does not except Blake—are best viewed in the light of traditional biblical illustration, where any single illustration is laden with typology. In any individual depiction of the Fall, Trapp contends, there will be "a more or less explicit proleptic reference to Redemption and/or Judgement"; or conversely, in any depiction of the Redemption, there will be reference, direct or oblique, to the Fall. Indeed, "the whole drama of Salvation is condensed into a single picture: Salvation, or its means, writ large, but its antecedent crime merely stated, as it were, in the margin."[50] Trapp's conclusions take us a long way toward understanding Milton's eighteenth-century illustrators but not far at all if our intention is to explicate the illustrations by Blake. The aim of Blake's predecessors was to tie Milton's poem firmly to traditional theology. This meant relating *Paradise Regained* not only to the Fall but to the drama of Crucifixion and Resurrection.

A cursory look through the illustrations to *Paradise Regained* that preceded Blake's brings into bold relief the extent of Blake's departures from the tradition that Trapp describes. For instance, two of Pigné's five designs deflect attention from the temptation per se in order to recall events typologically related to it—the finding of Jesus in the temple and Christ's bruising the head of the serpent by his death on the cross.[51] Two of Chéron's illustrations do the same, namely, his depictions of the Nativity and the crown of thorns. Another noteworthy use of typology occurs in a depiction by an unknown artist in 1779. Upheld by an angel, Christ is shown in mid-air. On the ground below are Adam and Eve clapping their hands. Death, depicted as a skeleton, is for the viewer in the far left corner, hurling his dart; and coiled at the feet of Adam and Eve is a serpent. Three apples lie on the ground. This tradition of typological interpretation Blake, for the most part, eschews in his illustrations to *Paradise Regained*. While Blake's predecessors were concerned with conveying through their illustrations the grand lines of scriptural history, whether or not it pertained to the poem they were illustrating, Blake seems to have been intent upon discerning doctrinal subtlety, upon showing through his illustrations the extent to which Milton subdued a Christian theme to unorthodox purposes.

Seven of Blake's subjects for Milton's brief epic are traditional, and five of the subjects he illustrates for the first time—"Andrew and Simon Peter," "Satan in Council," "The Second Temptation,"[52] "Morning Chasing Away the Spectres of the Night," and "Jesus Returning to Mary." Of the traditional subjects, only "Mary Meditating" is first depicted in the nineteenth century. However, in the six illustrations with subjects of long-standing tradition, Blake makes reference neither to the loss of Paradise by Adam nor to the regaining of it on the cross. By omitting any allusion to the Fall, Blake stresses the integrity of Milton's poem and fastens attention to the myth of reintegration; by omitting reference to the Passion, Crucifixion, and Resurrection, he remains more faithful than his predecessors to the emphases of Milton's poem.

With the exception of Hayley, Blake is the only critic of *Paradise Regained*, before the twentieth century, to expose the sequel fallacy. The view that Milton's poem is a companion poem to the diffuse epic, an extension and an epitome of it, was firmly established by the beginning of the Romantic period. But for Hayley and Blake, that proposition was also the chief stumbling block to an appreciation of the poem. In his illustrations to *Paradise Regained*, Blake elects to note differences rather than similarities between the two epics—differences that are both stylistic and thematic. *Paradise Lost* is portrayed as a song of woe, *Paradise Regained* as a song of joy; the first poem is presented in a highly ornamented style, the second in a plain, almost austere, style. In dissociating the two poems Blake also spurns the bounds of the critical tradition that had grown up around them and without knowing it identifies himself with a small band of dissenters whose chief spokesman is Don Cameron Allen. "It is difficult not to read *Paradise Regained* as an immediate poetical continuation of *Paradise Lost*," says Allen, "but if we indulge in such a reading, if we constantly return to *Paradise Lost* for annotations, we confuse our judgment of the short epic and distort, if we do not destroy, the central issues of the second poem."[53]

Blake's illustrations to *Paradise Regained* are not in any sense a continuation of those to *Paradise Lost*. If these illustrations seem "comparatively tame" in relation to those for the preceding poem, it is because Blake sought to make the same kinds of differentiations visually that Milton made verbally. This meant finding a style less luxurious than the one used to illustrate *Paradise Lost*—a style that in its plainness and severity duplicates the one Milton used in writing his brief epic. It meant capturing the sense of joy that pervades *Paradise Regained* and opposing it to the bitter-sweet ending of *Paradise Lost*. It also meant distinguishing between the characters in the two poems: Satan has lost his former glory in the brief epic; and Christ is present in the poem, at least until the moment on the pinnacle, in his human aspect. In this regard, it is interesting to turn to Blake's portrayal of the First Temptation (fig. 2) and especially to his representation of Satan. The subject is extremely popular among biblical illustrators, and Blake's general conception for the design does not differ radically from theirs, except in minute particulars and especially in the depiction of Satan. Most Renaissance portrayals of the First Temptation accentuate Satan's physical hideousness. Milton's eighteenth-century illustrators, remaining "true" to Milton's poem but still reluctant to eschew the older tradition, present Satan in his rural weeds but not without some of his attributes—horns, claws, or a tail trailing from under his robes. In Blake's depiction, however, Satan's attributes silently disappear; and the tempter, even if he lacks his former glory, is represented as an attractive, if aged, man. Interestingly, this was not the case in Blake's initial attempt at illustrating the First Temptation in *Paradise Regained*. That design, bound with the twenty-eight illustrations to Bunyan's *Pilgrim's Progress*, is an exceedingly grotesque rendering of Milton's Satan (see Appendix B).

Like many other students of *Paradise Regained*, Blake was inclined
to see Milton's poem as the fulfillment of his plan to write a brief epic
and as the poem in which Milton managed to extend and ennoble the
province of epic poetry. Before Barbara Lewalski's magnificent study,[54]
Blake himself attempted, through his illustrations to *Paradise Regained*
and also through his imitations of that poem in *Milton* and *Jerusalem*,
to make that label meaningful. Mrs. Lewalski reminds us that the
brief epic of the Middle Ages and the Renaissance generally dealt with
New Testament subjects while using narrative, structural, and stylistic
devices of the classical epic. Primary attention, then, is focused upon the
life of Christ while a complicated typology recalls the whole of biblical
history. For Mrs. Lewalski, and for many of Milton's illustrators before
Blake, typology was the chief hallmark of the brief epic. The "epic"
dimensions of the brief epic, in other words, were implied rather than
clearly articulated; biblical history was gathered together in the typology rather than explicitly recounted as in the diffuse epic. Thus readers
and illustrators alike saw all of biblical history collapsing in the moment on the desert. Blake, however, was neither a typical illustrator nor
a typical interpreter of Milton's poem. Traditional typology is virtually
ignored in his illustrations to *Paradise Regained*.

Though acutely aware of the fact that the brief epic involves drastic reduction and severe compression, Blake realized, too, that the brief
epic is not a miniature epic in the strictest sense. It is not for Blake—
nor was it for Milton—a scale model of the diffuse epic; but, rather, reduction and compression are accompanied by distortion and exaggera-
tion. Prologues and foreshadowings are abbreviated; epic paraphernalia
are held to a bare minimum. Yet the epic action is magnified. Blake recalled, no doubt, that Milton had concentrated the drama of *Paradise
Lost* within the ninth book, whereas in *Paradise Regained* he allowed
it to extend over the entire four books of the poem. It is the dramatic
element that Blake, following Milton, seems to regard as the salient
characteristic of the brief epic poem.[55] One of the new subjects Blake
adds, "Satan in Council," recognizes the one epic convention that Milton
utilizes prominently in *Paradise Regained*, but without the same detail
and variety that characterize the corresponding scene in *Paradise Lost*;
another, "Morning Chasing Away the Spectres of the Night," points to
the introspective and psychological character of Milton's poem. In recognition of the fact that Milton's drama of the mind gathers intensity as
it drives toward the epiphany on the pinnacle, Blake concentrates his
designs within the fourth book of *Paradise Regained*, thereby defining

the poem's thematic and dramatic center. But Blake also underscores the epiphanic character of *Paradise Regained* through the symbolic "stationing" of Christ in the designs that deal specifically with the temptations. In Figure 2, Christ, wandering into the wilderness, is seen from the back; only the right half of his face is visible. In Figure 7, Christ is seen from the side; this time the left half of his face is visible. Then in Figure 10, which depicts the epiphanic moment, Christ is seen as the full man poised triumphantly on the pinnacle as Satan—stripped of his garments, exposed for what he is—falls.

Blake's illustrations to *Paradise Regained* deviate conspicuously from the traditions of criticism and illustration that surround the poem. Blake makes no effort to impose the Passion, Crucifixion, or Resurrection upon a poem that underplays those events. Through this omission of traditional typological reference, Blake brings us closer to the poem Milton has written than any previous illustrator. Like his predecessors, Blake recognized Milton's departure from the usual view of the Incarnation, which locates the central contest of Christ and Satan between the Crucifixion and the Resurrection and which asserts that Paradise was recovered when Christ died upon the cross. But Blake seems also to have grasped the theological significance of that departure more completely than his contemporaries or, for that matter, his successors.

For years, James Holly Hanford told his students that Milton was never mature enough to handle the Passion and thus chose a subject within his limited abilities. Elizabeth Pope argues, on the other hand, that Milton simply rejects one tradition in favor of another, pointing out that in some Cluniac art, recently unearthed, the Fall and the Temptation in the Wilderness are paired.[56] Neither explanation is to the point. Hanford disparages the poet by dwarfing the quality of his mind, and Pope unwittingly deprecates the poem. For admittedly, a poem that makes sense only in terms of an atrophied tradition is severely limited both in its appeal and in its achievement. Two further points complicate the matter: first, Milton always guarded against shifts in scriptural emphasis; and second, in all previous instances, departure from Scripture involved embellishment rather than contradiction of it. Therefore, it would seem that the revision of biblical emphasis in *Paradise Regained* is calculated and meaningful.

Milton avoids the subject of the Passion for aesthetic *and theological* reasons. The aesthetic reasons were grasped by Blake's contemporaries, the theological reasons understood by Blake alone. Milton avoids the Passion because it is too fully elaborated in Scripture; thus, to choose the subject is to choose the most intractable material imaginable. Besides, the emphasis on the Passion is wrong. It illustrates Christ's triumph at the divine rather than the human level. The obvious disadvantages inherent in the story of the Passion and Crucifixion are avoided by dealing with the temptations. The risk of contradicting Scripture is checked inasmuch as the accounts by Matthew, Mark, and Luke are brief, and each contradicts the others. Significantly, however, Milton departs from his sources on four occasions—in three instances by elaborating upon Scripture, in the last by bold contradiction of it. The banquet scene, the storm scene, and Satan's falling from the pinnacle are Milton's own contributions to the tradition, contributions that Blake would have recognized and that he chooses to emphasize in four of his twelve illustrations (see figs. 6, 8, 9, and 10). A fourth departure from tradition, also depicted by Blake (see figs. 3 and 12), requires closer attention.

In the Prologue to Book II of *Paradise Regained*, Milton introduces the figures of Andrew and Simon Peter who "Began to doubt, and doubted many days" (l. 11). Milton has authority for presenting Andrew and Simon Peter in the context of the baptism (John 1:40), but it is curious that he should do so. Throughout *Paradise Regained*, Milton has been following the accounts of Matthew, Mark, and Luke; here he turns to John, whose account he contradicts. In the Gospels by Matthew, Mark, and Luke, Andrew and Simon Peter are represented as the first disciples Christ gathers *after* his ministry begins (see Matt. 4:18, Mark 1:29, Luke 5). In John, Andrew and Simon Peter are portrayed as recognizing Christ's messiahship at the baptism. John identifies the Lamb as the leader and suggests that spiritual vision is granted to those who follow him. By contradicting Scripture on this one point, by presenting Andrew and Simon Peter in the posture of doubt, Milton calls further attention to the human context in which Jesus appears until the triple epiphany on the pinnacle when Satan, Christ, and the reader simultaneously apprehend Christ's divinity. Blake not only illustrates this seemingly innocuous episode in the second book (one of two episodes, the other being Mary meditating, that the eighteenth century considered to be "little digressions") but allows Andrew and Simon Peter to figure in his final illustration as well. Jesus returns to Mary *and to Andrew and Simon Peter*. Blake's intention here is twofold: wishing to underscore yet another of Milton's departures from Scripture, he first illustrates the scene for Book II, then recalls it in the final illustration, thereby suggesting that Christ gathers his disciples only after his ministry begins; but Blake wishes also to stress that it is only through repetition of Christ's experience, only through a corresponding journey to the very center of being, that spiritual vision is achieved. *Paradise Regained* involves the gradual awakening of Jesus to his mediatorial offices and culminates in a general acknowledgment of his divinity. Until that acknowledgment, the Lamb cannot lead; and until we, like Andrew and Simon Peter, repeat that experience we cannot apprehend.

These elaborations of Scripture and this contradiction of it pave the way for Milton's audacious departure from the tradition of complementing the Fall and the Crucifixion—a departure from tradition that is announced boldly in the final lines of the second verse paragraph in *Paradise Regained*. Describing his poem not as an "advent'rous Song" but as a "prompt'd Song," Milton says that he will tell of things "unrecorded . . . through many an Age, / Worthy t'have not remain'd so long unsung" (I.16–17). The Crucifixion is referred to twice in the poem, both references coming in the first half. Jesus tells Satan that "a Crown, / . . . is but a wreath of thorns" (II.458–459); and he recounts earlier that the scribes in the temple told him, "this chiefly, that my way must lie / Through many a hard assay even to the death, / Ere I the promis'd kingdom can attain" (I.263–265). Even so, Milton can hardly be referring to the atonement on the cross as Christ's "unrecorded" deed, for it is clearly not in keeping with the main thrust of the poem. The proem asserts that Paradise is "Recover'd . . . / By one man's firm obedience fully tried / Through all temptation . . . ," that Eden is "rais'd in the waste Wilderness" (I.3–5, 7). With similar assertions the poem ends. "By vanquishing Temptation," Milton says, Christ "hast regain'd lost Paradise"—"A fairer Paradise is founded *now* (IV.607–608, 613; italics mine).

C. A. Patrides has pointed out, quoting from J. S. Whale, that

> "no theological theory is binding upon Christians, no explanation of the Cross is a Christian dogma. We may reject all the theologies of the Atonement . . . on the ground that they are inadequate to the mystery of the Crucifixion of Him who was God as well as man, but the mystery itself is at the heart of the Christian faith." It is a mystery whose capital aim is to uphold the "at-one-ment" of God and man—"the creation of the conditions whereby God and man come together"—through the Christ Jesus.[57]

Blake is alone among critics and illustrators of his time in inviting us to consider what Milton's attitude toward the atonement may have been. With the exception of the explanation offered by Bernard of Clairvaux,

all previous rationales for the atonement stressed the wrath of God, his
dreadful anger, his awful aspect.[58] Blake seems to have understood that
the prevailing Protestant sentiment by the mid-seventeenth century
was that all theories of the atonement were inadequate to the mystery
and that many came to regard the whole notion of the atonement
as immoral. What Patrides admits somewhat reluctantly Blake would
probably assert emphatically:

> We cannot be absolutely certain whether some such notion had
> not occurred to Milton as well; we can only suspect that it might
> have, principally because nearly every time God appears in *Para-
> dise Lost* the poetry responds adversely, becoming flat, dull,
> monotonous. Certainly an impressive number of Milton's contem-
> poraries were quite troubled by the "fire and bloud" so often inti-
> mated by their God, while even before the middle of the sixteenth
> century the very word "satisfaction" was . . . "hated to al christen
> eares." By 1661 finally, only six years before the publication of
> *Paradise Lost*, George Rust protested that "Modern Theology,"
> suffering from "an excess of complement to the Justice of God,"
> had become "as rude and troublesome as the Ass in the Fable, who
> did not fawn upon, but invade his masters."[59]

Blake grasped that Milton's "prompted Song" was an attempt to re-
organize Christian precepts, dispelling the specious orthodoxy of recovering Eden on the cross and hardening into a new orthodoxy the idea
that Paradise was regained on the desert.

Blake's knowledge of Milton was sufficiently deep to suggest that
Milton's departures from tradition were as significant as his uses of it.
By deviating from the tradition of presenting the Fall and the Crucifixion together, Milton suggested that *Paradise Regained* was a criticism
of the very theology he had postulated in *Paradise Lost*. Blake himself
strove to return to a purified version of Christianity based upon the values of love and forgiveness, and he detected in *Paradise Regained* the
same impulse. Milton omitted reference to the Passion and Crucifixion
not because he lacked the ability to handle the subjects but because he
found those subjects uncongenial to him and alien to the spirit of Christianity that his poem enshrined. Not enjoying the doctrine of the atonement, Milton deflected interest from it, thereby eradicating the "torture" and "horror" of Christianity. In *Paradise Regained* Milton is not
concerned with a God who deserts his champion and allows him to be
taunted; he is concerned rather with Christ as Redeemer, not of man-

kind only but of the Christian religion. Like Hayley, Blake found in Milton's poem a "purer religion" accompanied by "greater force of imagination" than had been presented in *Paradise Lost*;[60] he saw poetic imagination triumphing over popular orthodoxy. Through his illustrations to *Paradise Regained* Blake was able to bring into sharp focus Milton's radical Christian vision and to proclaim with Shelley that Milton was a bold and inquiring spirit who "shook to dust" the most oppressive forms of the Christian religion.[61]

If Blake insists upon symbolic reading of his illustrations, he also compels us to read Milton's poem in the same fashion. Taken literally, the poem's action is absurd; understood symbolically, that action has momentous significance. As Blake interpreted the temptations in the wilderness, they revealed Christ's "energy of mind" and the "majesty" of his human nature. This Blake makes clear in his marginalia to Lavater's *Aphorisms on Man*. In his initial illustration, Blake depicts the baptism of Jesus, in the second the temptation to turn stone into bread. The third, fourth, and fifth illustrations call attention to the poem's genre, to the human context in which Jesus appears, and to the poem's meditative character; but the sixth illustration, with its depiction of the banquet temptation, returns us to the poem's central event—the temptation. In the seventh illustration, Blake conflates the entire sequence of the kingdom temptations. The eighth and ninth illustrations accentuate the psychological character of the poem's action. The tenth illustration, Christ on the Pinnacle, returns us to the temptation sequence; and the final two illustrations deal with the aftermath of temptation—Christ being ministered to by the angels and his return to his mother's house. A rising crescendo until the pinnacle scene, the poem drives unremittingly toward that moment of self-discovery. Not only does the preponderance of illustrations to the fourth book fix our attention to that moment, but the fact that all the designs, except Figure 10, possess a static quality causes that illustration to distinguish itself from the rest. Through this concentration of illustrations within the fourth book, Blake places himself in the company of those who believed that "all the poems ever written must yield, even *Paradise Lost* must yield, to the *Paradise Regained* in the grandeur of its close."[62]

Blake's illustrations to *Paradise Regained*, then, serve various functions. They establish the human context in which Christ moves; they illuminate the poem's genre by pointing to its meditative, psychological character; they give an architectonic clarity and vigor to Milton's verbal expression. But they also bring into focus the three major events of the

poem—baptism, temptation, and return. This is the great pattern Blake
discerned in Milton's poem and the one to which his illustrations give
formal substance. It is the poem's myth that fascinates Blake, and his
interpretation of that myth must finally elicit our attention.

IV

Blake's illustrations to *Paradise Regained* exist, in large part, to express the poet's dissatisfaction with the critical tradition that grew up
around the poem, just as Northrop Frye's observations, and Howard
Schultz's, exist to express dissatisfaction with the same tradition, not
significantly altered, that extends into the twentieth century.[63] Like
Frye and Schultz, Blake seems to think that the chief trouble with the
criticism of *Paradise Regained* is that those who read the poem do not
bring to it sufficient mythic perceptions. With the mythic aspect of Milton's poem Blake's illustrations are ultimately concerned.

Blake understood that in *Paradise Regained* Milton subscribed to
the Hero-Christology of the Bible which yields the tradition of Jesus
as the hero of heroes.[64] Milton's descriptive phrases in Book I of *Paradise Regained*—"deeds Above Heroic," "th' exalted man," "man of
men," "the perfect Man," and "victorious deeds . . . heroic acts"—and
his fierce insistence upon Christ's heroic acts of virtue, heroic capacity
for love, heroic magnitude of mind, are calculated to recall that tradition and to bring forward the idea that Jesus, enacting his human career, epitomizes the pattern of the "Most perfect *Hero*" (*The Passion*,
l. 13). It is this pattern of perfection and beauty that Blake sees Milton
celebrating and exalting in his brief epic.

Blake understood, too, what has eluded many recent critics,
namely, that the life of Jesus submits to various interpretations. On the
one hand, we may regard Jesus as a man who by virtue of his auster-
ities and meditations attained wisdom. This view implies that we should
follow the myth literally, that paradoxically contemplation and abstraction are the way to life and that action and involvement are the way
to death. On the other hand, we may regard Jesus as a God descended
who took upon himself the enactment of a human career. Such a view
suggests that Jesus is a symbol, a revelation of the indwelling life, and invites us to meditate upon our own immanent divinity. This view implies that all men are human forms divine and that retreating into the
self culminates not in estrangement but in communion.

Joseph Campbell provides us with at least two observations on
the Christ myth that are anticipated, if not clearly articulated, by Blake.

Campbell tells us, first, that there are essentially two degrees of heroes: those who return to the world as emissaries and those who return with the knowledge that "I and the father are one." The heroes of this "second, highest illumination" are the world-redeemers, the incarnations, whose "myths open out to cosmic proportions."[65] And Campbell suggests even further that there are three significant ways through which the hero may enact his destiny: he may renounce the world, he may become an emperor in the world, he may redeem the world. Most heroes appear in one of these roles, but Milton's Christ as "Most perfect *Hero*" appears in all three. He rejects the kingdoms of Satan in order to rule over the Kingdom of God; he returns to the world of civilization in order to become its spiritual leader and redeemer. If *Paradise Lost* recounted the story of loss and fragmentation, *Paradise Regained* countered with one of recovery and reintegration. The finding of a paradise within, Blake understood, preceded the recovery of one without.

This theme, no less prominent in the illustrations to *Paradise Regained* than in Blake's imitations of that poem, is conveyed most forcibly in Figures 2, 3, 8, and 9, all of which emphasize the introspective nature of Milton's poem. The one interpretively important subject that was contributed to the tradition of illustrations to *Paradise Regained* during the early nineteenth century was the depiction of Christ with a "swarming multitude of thoughts" wandering into the desert. For Blake's contemporaries, and for Blake himself, the central act in *Paradise Regained* was Christ's "tracing the Desert wild . . . with holiest meditations fed" and then "into himself" descending (II.109–111)—an act that is immediately preceded and thus punctuated by the introspection of Andrew and Simon Peter and the extended meditation of Mary. In Blake's *Milton*, his most exacting imitation of *Paradise Regained*, Milton assumes the role of Jesus, goes "guarded within," and "wanders lost in dreary night" (15:16, 20). One third of the illustrations to Milton's brief epic drive the same theme. Andrew and Simon Peter wandering and doubting, Mary meditating, and Christ dreaming, then awakening "with untroubl'd mind"—all these subjects combine to suggest that the human mind itself is the arena for epical activity. Through these designs, Blake suggests that *Paradise Regained* is a poem of definition and discovery: Christ *defines* himself by *discovering* his roles as prophet, king, and priest and by recovering the knowledge of which he has been "emptied."

Like *Milton*, *Paradise Regained* is the story of "gathering self-awareness."[66] The dramatic center of Blake's epic involves a sudden change in attitude, which enables the hero to come to full self-knowledge. Milton casts off Selfhood, goes to Eternal Death, and recovers the values of love and forgiveness. These are the same values that Christ acquires in the desert. In resisting the temptation to turn stones into bread, Christ adheres to the authority of the Law; in rejecting the temptation on the pinnacle, he embraces the power of Love. The ethical nucleus of Milton's poem, as Blake reads it, involves the casting aside of the primitive ethic of the Old Testament in favor of the more humane ethic of the New Testament. By 1798 Blake had come to believe that the whole purpose of Christ's Incarnation was to "abolish the Jewish Imposture." "Was not Christ marter'd," Blake asks, "because he taught that God loved all Men & was their father & forbad all contention for Worldly prosperity . . . ? Christ died as an Unbeliever [a rejector of the Law and the wickedness attendant to it] & if Bishops had their will so would Paine. . . . Let the Bishops prove that he has not spoken against the Holy Ghost, who in Paine strives with Christendom as in Christ he strove with the Jews."[67] This "striving" against the Law in order to redeem Life Blake saw represented by the moment in the desert—the moment recorded and celebrated in Milton's poem. The whole process of *Paradise Regained* is one wherein Christ, turning within himself, consolidates in the figure of Satan the errors of primitive Christianity and then annihilates them. Blake uses his interpretive designs to assert that Milton's poem must be read symbolically; its myth must be deciphered before the poem can be understood.

Within Milton's poem, there are three major events—Christ's baptism, his temptations, and his return. Significantly, the first event to appear in each of the synoptic Gospels, the first event referred to in Milton's poem, and the first event illustrated by Blake, is the baptism of Jesus. That event figures prominently in the two prologues to *Paradise Regained*, where it is presented as an announcement of a threshold experience, which characteristically involves the hero's withdrawal from civilization for the purpose of illumination. Jesus is baptized and leaves behind the wisdom of the law to embrace the wisdom of love. He makes his private departure into the wilderness where, by withstanding Satan's temptations, he achieves full self-knowledge and learns of his mediatorial offices. Christ's experience on the desert—the long temptation he undergoes—becomes for Blake, as it was later to become for Jung, a "sacred symbol": "the prototype of the only meaningful life, that is, of a life that strives for individual realisation."[68] That experience, entailing the birth of personality, has restorative effects both upon the individual and upon society: the individual acquires wholeness of being; society acquires an illuminated man to lead it.

Not only are there three significant events in *Paradise Regained* that Blake draws into focus, but there are also three scenes of activity —the desert, the mountain-pinnacle, and the world of civilization. Related to these regions of tension and repose are the patterns of descent and ascent that dominate the poem. In retreating to the desert, Jesus separates himself from the world and symbolically journeys into the depths of his mind, where he experiences consciously the elemental struggles of existence. This descent is followed by an ascent, by the appearance of Christ on the pinnacle. Blake suggests that this descent into the self enables Christ to return to the plane of contemporary life, to re-entrench himself in civilization as one of its leaders and teachers. This return and the life this return implies are exactly proportionate to the depth of the hero's descent.

With gathering energy Milton's poem drives toward the climax on the pinnacle when Christ tells Satan, "Tempt not the Lord thy God," and Satan "smitten with amazement" falls (*PR* IV.561–562). Blake focuses on that moment of triumph and complete self-realization, first by clustering five of his twelve illustrations within the fourth book of Milton's epic and then by making the illustration of Christ on the pinnacle (fig. 10) the central design for that book. Christ's words on the pinnacle are, of course, the most ambiguous words in the entire poem. They have been taken to mean only that one must not make unnecessary demands upon God. But Blake, it seems, took them to mean much more. The poem began with an epiphany that Satan did not understand; it ends with an epiphany he does understand. Thus, stricken with the realization that he has been tempting divinity, Satan falls. At the same time, the pinnacle scene involves an epiphany for the reader; he now knows what has been suppressed throughout the entire poem. And most importantly, Christ's words indicate his own coming to awareness; he now comprehends that which he did not know before.

Blake is one of the very few illustrators, one of the very few interpreters, of *Paradise Regained* to recognize that Milton's poem does not end with the epiphanies signaled by the pinnacle scene. Those epiphanies are followed by the most heroic act of all.[69] Having learned of his divinity, Christ instead of passing away into ecstasy returns to humanity. This is Christ's deed above heroic, what Blake would call his "unexampled deed." By withstanding the temptation on the pinnacle

Christ displays his enormous love for God; by returning home he displays his enormous love for man. He can "Now enter, and begin to save mankind" (IV.635).

Paradise Regained contains what was for Blake the highest, the fullest, the most intense, the most valuable mental experience imaginable. That internalized drama was, he thought, the center of the poem's interest and the basis of its unity. He adumbrates those modern critics who locate "the really revolutionary moment in the history of the epic"[70] in Milton's poetry; but he would also resist the notion, all too common, that the "revolutionary moment" occurs with the publication of *Paradise Lost*. From Blake's point of view, Milton's brief epic was the first example of the truly modern *heroic* poem. If Milton's devastating treatment of the epic tradition in *Paradise Lost* had the effect of silencing the epic talent of future generations, the psychodrama of *Paradise Regained* had the opposite effect. Milton had taken the Book of Job as the model for his brief epic; his Romantic successors, the first of whom was Blake, took *Paradise Regained* for theirs, and for two reasons. The poem was free from the impedimenta of the classical epic tradition, and as Blake read the poem it retracted the terrifying theology of *Paradise Lost*, revealing Milton to be a broader and wiser man than usually acknowledged, a more humane and moral man than ordinarily thought.

From the few previous commentaries on Blake's Milton illustrations, some crucial questions have emerged: How closely related are Blake's illustrations and Milton's text? Do those illustrations move away from Milton's poetry in the direction of Blake's own private mythology, or are they instead literal renderings? To what exent is Blake working within traditions of illustration and criticism? What is the meaning of Milton's poetry as Blake understood it? And closely related to that question: Do Blake's illustrations offer valid interpretations, or are they rather an index to the reigning critical attitudes about Milton at the end of the eighteenth century, the errors of which modern criticism has already exposed? With these questions this essay has been largely concerned.

The conclusions of this study, pointing toward a methodology for studying Blake's illustrations, enable us to approach his Milton illustrations anew. Besides dispelling the old notion that when multiple sets of illustrations exist the early one relentlessly follows Milton's text and the later ones move steadily away from it, this essay has shown that although the later sets become more symbolic they do so as they push even closer to the text of Milton's poetry. It is, therefore, the last set of illustrations to *Comus*, the *Nativity Ode*, and *Paradise Lost* that provides the most complete statement on the poem and offers the most reliable guide to interpretation. Moreover, while Blake is obviously cognizant of various traditions of illustration, and of traditions of interpretation as well, he works *with*, not *within* them. Blake preserves the notion of interpretive illustration that he inherited from the Renaissance biblical illustrators and saw practiced by eighteenth-century illustrators of Milton's poetry, but he also refuses to impose a typological interpretation upon a poem that resists it, or that may be confused by it. Aware of the corrective function of much interpretive design, Blake invoked that tradition, in his Milton illustrations at least, to correct mistaken readings of Milton's poetry developed by eighteenth-century commentaries. He thereby returns to the visionary experience of Milton's poetry that, though sometimes clouded by the disfiguring mist of a cumbersome narrative, was most often lost by the critic whose doors of perception remained closed.

Blake's illustrations to *Paradise Regained* are more than literal renderings of random episodes and inconsequential details. These illustrations, greatly enlarging the possibilities for criticism on the poem, are symbolic interpretations which follow Milton's poetry through its most complicated metaphors and its subtlest musings. So doing, these illustrations add a major dimension to criticism of Milton's brief epic. Northrop Frye has written that through the illustration of other poets' works Blake "found a formula for uniting the work of the creator with that of the teacher, of combining mythopoeic art with instruction in how to read it." Through a sequence of visions, Blake recreated the archetype "into a tradition, then into a Scripture."[71] No comment uttered on Blake the illustrator comes closer to explaining his achievement in illustrating *Paradise Regained*. In a series of twelve designs, Blake has presented with magnificent clarity the grand lines of the myth that informs Milton's poem and has explored, then defined, Milton's relation to both theological and poetical traditions. Far from restating orthodox theology or reiterating scriptural history, Milton embodied in a revolutionary form his radical version of Christianity. Blake's illustrations exist, in part to probe the doctrinal subtlety of Milton's poem, in part to illuminate the genre in which that vision is contained. Through the agency of these illustrations, the Miltonic vision burns into lucidity.

In *Areopagitica*, Milton wrote that "revolutions of ages do not oft recover the loss of a rejected truth."[72] Our own age has produced a revolution in Blake studies that has taken us far beyond the place where the nineteenth century left Blake, the poet-painter. But in the process it has managed to shun one perception about Blake that emerges from our antecedent century—the realization that Blake was a critic of major stature and keen perception, whose illustrations constitute an imaginative and intelligent interpretation of the texts they adorn. It is this "truth"—formulated in the nineteenth century but rejected in our own —that this essay has sought to recover.[73]

NOTES

This essay was researched during my tenure as a Summer Fellow at the Henry E. Huntington Library and written during a leave-semester provided by the University of Wisconsin Graduate School. To both institutions I am deeply indebted. I should also like to express thanks to my student Jefri Ruchti, who presented me with a provocative paper on Blake's illustrations to Milton and thereby enabled me to sharpen some of my own conclusions.

1. Guy Eglington, *Reaching for Art* (Boston and London, 1931), p. 113.
2. The most significant recent appraisal of Blake as a literary critic is by Karl Kiralis, who suggests that "Blake's genius as a literary critic has yet to be explored fully enough and so remains insufficiently appreciated" ("William Blake as an Intellectual and Spiritual Guide to Chaucer's *Canterbury Pilgrims*," *Blake Studies*, I [1969], 139).
3. See *The Works of William Blake, Poetic, Symbolic and Critical* (3 vols.; London, 1893), II, 308–311; and *A History of Criticism and Literary Taste in Europe* (3 vols.; Edinburgh and London, 1904), III, 266–269. After the Yeats-Ellis edition and the Saintsbury history, there is a steady decline in Blake's reputation as a critic. He is ignored entirely by William K. Wimsatt, Jr., and Cleanth Brooks in *Literary Criticism: A Short History* (New York, 1965); he is mentioned only once, and then not importantly, by Walter Jackson Bate in *Criticism: The Major Texts* (New York, 1952), p. 270; and he is used only for illustrative purposes by Meyer H. Abrams in *The Mirror and the Lamp: Romantic Theory and the Critical Tradition* (New York, 1953). Finally René Wellek, who offers some provocative suggestions, treats Blake as an eccentric (see *A History of Modern Criticism: 1750–1950, The Later Eighteenth Century* [London, 1955], pp. 4, 110). The one dissenter, among students of literary criticism, is R. A. Foakes (*Romantic Criticism 1800–1850* [London, 1968], pp. 17–18).
    The nineteenth century was more sensitive to Blake's critical talent and more penetrating in its evaluation of that talent; see esp. Alexander Gilchrist, *Life of William Blake with Selections from His Poems and Other Writings*, 2nd ed. (2 vols.; London, 1880), I, 276, 344; and William Michael Rossetti, "Prefatory Memoir," *The Poetical Works of William Blake, Lyrical and Miscellaneous* (London, 1874), p. lxx. This is not to deny that a few enlightened Blakeans have commented suggestively in our own time; see esp. Northrop Frye, *Fearful Symmetry: A Study of William Blake* (Princeton, 1947), pp. 414–418; S. Foster Damon, *Blake's Grave: A Prophetic Book* (Providence, 1963), pp. [1–10]; also "Introduction," *Blake's "Job"* (Providence, 1966), pp. 3–7.
4. I adopt language from Clyde Taylor's review of John Beer's *Blake's Humanism* in *Criticism*, XI (1969), 101.

5. *The Art of Discrimination: Thomson's "The Seasons" and the Language of Criticism* (Berkeley and Los Angeles, 1964), esp. pp. 2–5, 441–448.

6. "Annotations to Sir Joshua Reynolds's Discourses," *The Complete Writings of William Blake, with Variant Readings*, ed. Geoffrey Keynes (New York and London, 1966), p. 453.

7. Cohen, *The Art of Discrimination*, p. 253.

8. Blake's Milton criticism is conveniently collected in my edition, *The Romantics on Milton: Formal Essays and Critical Asides* (Cleveland and London, 1970), pp. 33–101. The first note to the Blake section lists various studies of Milton and Blake that are especially useful for providing a context for this essay. For a list of books in which Blake's illustrations to Milton are reproduced, see the headnote to Appendix B of *this* volume.

9. "Blake and Milton," in *The Divine Vision: Studies in the Poetry and Art of William Blake*, ed. Vivian de Sola Pinto (London, 1957), pp. 91–96.

10. See Appendix B.

11. "A Descriptive Catalogue," *Complete Writings*, p. 576.

12. *Jerusalem*, plate 77, in *Complete Writings*, p. 716.

13. Philippe Soupault, *William Blake*, trans. J. Lewis May (New York, 1928), p. 48. Nor should one forget Blake's remark that many of his visions were translated into "pictures . . . all containing mythological and recondite meaning, where more is meant than meets the eye" (*Complete Writings*, p. 566). Suppositions like this one that underlie Blake's paintings may be expected to underlie his illustrations as well.

14. It is interesting that Blake turned from the illustrations for *Paradise Regained* to those for the Book of Job, particularly when we recall, as Blake may have done, Milton's comment in *Reason of Church-Government* that the Book of Job is a "model" for the brief epic (see *John Milton: Complete Poems and Major Prose*, ed. Merritt Y. Hughes [New York, 1957], p. 688). All quotations of Milton's work are from this edition, and hereafter citations of poetry will be given parenthetically within the text of this essay.

15. If there is not total agreement on the date for the illustrations to *Paradise Regained*, there is at least a consensus. In *The Art of William Blake* (Morningside Heights, N.Y., 1959), Anthony Blunt postulates a later date, ca. 1820–1821 (p. 83); in *The Paintings of William Blake* (London, 1925), Darrell Figgis suggests a much earlier date, ca. 1808 (p. 69); so does George Wingfield Digby in *Symbol and Image in William Blake* (Oxford, 1957), p. 65. But Geoffrey Keynes in *John Milton: Poems in English with Illustrations by William Blake, Miscellaneous Poems* (London, 1926), p. 278, Thomas Wright in *The Life of William Blake* (2 vols.; Olney, 1929), II, 26, and Mona Wilson in *The Life of William Blake* (New York, 1932), p. 220, agree that the illustrations were made ca. 1816.

16. The phrase is Northrop Frye's; see *A Study of English Romanticism* (New York, 1968), pp. 3–49. I do not discount the possibility that Spenser importantly influenced the development of Blake's mythology; see my essay, "The Epic Designs of Hayley and Blake," *Studies in Philology* (forthcoming).

17. According to Gilchrist, Linnell tried unsuccessfully to sell the illustrations to Sir Francis Chantrey (see *Life* [1880], I, 378, 400). See also G. E. Bentley, Jr., *Blake Records* (Oxford, 1969), pp. 338–339, 604, 607.

18. *Letters of William Michael Rossetti Concerning Whitman, Blake, and Shelley to Anne Gilchrist and Her Son Herbert Gilchrist*, ed. Clarence Gohdes and Paull Franklin Baum (Durham, N.C., 1934), p. 11.

19. *Life of William Blake*, "Pictor Ignotus" (2 vols.; London and Cambridge, 1863), I, 335. The passage quoted is underscored by Rossetti in his copy of Gilchrist's *Life*, which is now in the Houghton Library, Harvard University (see Catalogue No. °EC75/B5815/W863g [B]).

20.   Ibid., II, 215.

21.   Figgis discusses Blake's illustrations to *Paradise Regained* in *The Paintings of William Blake* (pp. 69–71). Pointon comments incidentally on the series of illustrations in *Milton & English Art* (Manchester, 1970), pp. 164–165. Keynes' remark is quoted from "Notes on the Illustrations," *On the Morning of Christ's Nativity: Milton's Hymn with Illustrations by William Blake* (Cambridge, 1923), p. 32; but he reiterates those sentiments in "Notes on Blake's Illustrations to Milton's Poems," *Poems in English*, pp. 271–279. For incisive remarks on Milton's illustrators, many of which involve Blake's Milton illustrations, see the following: C. H. Collins Baker, "William Blake, Painter," *Huntington Library Bulletin*, no. 10 (Cambridge, Mass., 1936), pp. 135–148, and "The Sources of Blake's Pictorial Expression," *Huntington Library Quarterly*, IV (1940), 359–367; Ruthven Todd, *Tracks in the Snow: Studies in English Science and Art* (London, 1946), passim; C. H. Collins Baker, "Some Illustrators of Milton's *Paradise Lost* (1688–1850)," *The Library*, 5th ser., III (1948), 1–21, 101–119; Thomas Balston, "Some Illustrators of Milton's *Paradise Lost*," *The Library*, 5th ser., IV (1949), 146–147; Adrian Van Sinderen, *Blake: The Mystic Genius* (Syracuse, 1949), pp. 45–47; C. B. Tinker, "Blake: Dreams of Milton," *Art News*, XLIX (1950), 22–25, 64; Morse Peckham, "Blake, Milton, and Edward Burney," *The Princeton University Library Chronicle*, XI (1950), 107–126; Frederick B. Adams, Jr., "Blake Water-Colors for Poems by Milton," in *First Annual Report to the Fellows of the Pierpont Morgan Library* (New York, 1950), pp. 56–60; Helen Gardner, "Milton's First Illustrator," *Essays and Studies*, N. S., IX (1956), 27–38; Anthony Blunt, *The Art of William Blake*; Kester Svendsen, "John Martin and the Expulsion Scene of *Paradise Lost*," *Studies in English Literature 1500–1900*, I (1961), 63–73; Marcia Allentuck, "Fuseli as Illustrator of Milton," *Studies in English Literature 1500–1900*, II (1962), 151–153; Merritt Y. Hughes, "Some Illustrators of Milton: The Expulsion from Paradise," *Milton Studies in Honor of Harris Francis Fletcher*, ed. G. Blakemore Evans et al. (Urbana, 1961), pp. 62–71; Jean Hagstrum, *William Blake, Poet and Painter: An Introduction to the Illuminated Verse* (Chicago and London, 1964), pp. 123–126 and passim; J. B. Trapp, "The Iconography of the Fall of Man," *Approaches to Paradise Lost: The York Tercentenary Lectures*, ed. C. A. Patrides (Toronto, 1968), pp. 223–265; Edward J. Rose, "Blake's Illustrations for *Paradise Lost*, *L'Allegro*, and *Il Penseroso*: A Thematic Reading," *Hartford Studies in Literature*, II (1970), 40–67; John E. Grant, "From Fable to Human Vision: A Note on the First Illustration [*L'Allegro*]," *Blake's Visionary Forms Dramatic*, ed. David V. Erdman and John E. Grant (Princeton, 1970), pp. xi–xiv. But see also the following for pertinent discussions of Blake's illustrations to other poets: Paget Toynbee, "The Earliest English Illustrators of Dante," *Quarterly Review*, CCXI (1909), 395–417; Philippe Soupault, *William Blake*; Guy Eglington, *Reaching for Art*, pp. 106–120; Albert S. Roe, *Blake's Illustrations to the Divine Comedy* (Princeton, 1953); John Beer, *Blake's Visionary Universe* (Manchester and New York, 1969) pp. 312–335; and Thomas H. Helmstadter, "Blake's *Night Thoughts*: Interpretations of Edward Young," *Texas Studies in Language and Literature*, XII (1970), 27–54; also Ben F. Nelms, "Text and Design in *Illustrations of the Book of Job*," *Blake's Visionary Forms Dramatic*, pp. 336–358.

22.   In *Blake's Vision of The Book of Job* (London and New York, 1924), Joseph Wicksteed writes that Blake's illustrations assume a "strange independence" from the texts they accompany (p. 13); Blake, says Wicksteed, "seldom illustrates literally" (p. 45). A year later, Darrell Figgis suggests in *The Paintings of William Blake* that "in general . . . the changes [between different sets of illustrations] are such as to make Blake less dependent on Milton, more fully expressive of himself, and of that which he wished to utter" (p. 69). In "Blake, Milton, and Edward Burney," Morse Peckham comments more pertinently: "Whenever he [Blake] designs illustrations

for a work which he did not write himself, he departs from the text of the author in the direction of symbolism. The habit of most illustrators, of course, is to depart from the author in the direction of their own imaginative construction of the scene" (p. 118). Some time later, in *Blake's Illustrations to the Divine Comedy*, Albert S. Roe declares that at times Blake is "no longer primarily illustrating the poem; rather he seeks for incidents which recall his own mythology, and then makes drawings which present his own ideas much in the manner of the designs of his prophetic books" (p. 37). For similar statements, see Anthony Blunt, *The Art of William Blake*, pp. 63, 64n.; Anne T. Kostelanetz, "Blake's 1795 Color Prints: An Interpretation," p. 124, and Morton D. Paley, "Blake's *Night Thoughts*: An Exploration of the Fallen World," p. 137—both essays are in *William Blake: Essays for S. Foster Damon*, ed. Alvin N. Rosenfeld (Providence, 1969). But for a view that accords with Keynes', see S. Foster Damon, who writes, "No other illustrator was ever so precise in following the text" of the author he illustrated (*A Blake Dictionary: The Ideas and Symbols of William Blake* [Providence, 1965], p. 275); and for a view that accords with the one in this essay, see Rose, who insists that Blake's illustrations to Milton are "as much of a commentary on Milton as his poem *Milton*" ("Blake's Illustrations for *Paradise Lost*, *L'Allegro*, and *Il Penseroso*: A Thematic Reading," p. 40). Yet Rose's essay, not published until my own essay was completed, seems far more concerned with demonstrating the commonplace that "Blake inserts in his pictorial images much of the subject matter and point of view of his own poems . . . while illustrating the work of other writers" (p. 61).

23. *Poems in English*, p. 272.

24. *Complete Poems and Major Prose*, p. 92.

25. "Blake's Illustrations to *Paradise Lost*," *Blake Newsletter*, III (1969), 57.

26. *Life* (1880), II, 249. But see also C. H. Collins Baker who suggests that the same design "was drawn in the torment of the late 1790's and repeated less strikingly in 1807" ("William Blake, Painter," p. 144).

27. "A Descriptive Catalogue," *Complete Writings*, p. 582.

28. *Seven Lectures on Shakespeare and Milton by the Late S. T. Coleridge*, ed. John Payne Collier (London, 1856), pp. 65–66. The comment was frequently repeated by Coleridge.

29. Blake mentions the edition in a letter to James Blake, dated January 30, 1803 (*Complete Writings*, p. 821). In *The Life of William Blake*, Mona Wilson suggests that this illustration to *Paradise Lost* "follows closely Hogarth's treatment of the same subject" (p. 210); however, Geoffrey Keynes was the first critic to postulate that debt (see "The Nonesuch Milton," *The Nation and Athenaeum*, XXXIX [1926], 697). But in *Blake: Prophet Against Empire*, rev. ed. (Garden City, N.Y., 1969), David Erdman argues that Blake's largest debt is to James Gillray (pp. 221–223). Hogarth's design is reproduced by Samuel Ireland in *Graphic Illustrations of Hogarth from Pictures, and Drawings, in the Possession of Samuel Ireland* (2 vols.; London, 1794–1799), I, opp. 179; Gillray's is reproduced as Plate 50 in *The Works of James Gillray: 582 Plates and a Supplement Containing the 45 So-called "Suppressed Plates"* (London, 1851; reissued in New York and London, 1968).

30. *Milton's Life and Poetical Works with Notes by William Cowper*, ed. William Hayley (4 vols.; Chichester, 1810), II, 453–454.

31. John E. Grant reminds us that before painting his sets of illustrations to *Paradise Lost* Blake did a separate design of "The Lazar House" in which he attempted "to analyze the human consequences of the Fall" ("You Can't Write About Blake's Pictures Like That," *Blake Studies*, I [1969], 196).

32. In *William Blake, Poet and Painter*, Jean Hagstrum writes (I think mistakenly), "Even the four Zoas, who appear broodingly in the sky at the time of

the expulsion, are not the four horsemen of the Apocalypse, but fallen gods yearn-
ing for the day that will restore their primal unity" (p. 126).

33.   "John Martin and the Expulsion Scene of *Paradise Lost*," p. 70.

34.   "Some Illustrators of Milton: The Expulsion from Paradise," pp. 65–66.

35.   *Poems in English*, pp. 278–279.

36.   The image of the "crown" looks forward to the kingdoms sequence that
follows and makes clear that Blake saw Milton compressing the entire temptation
sequence within the second temptation. For an insightful discussion of the temptation motif—its tradition and Milton's deviations from that tradition—see Elizabeth
Marie Pope, *Paradise Regained: The Tradition and the Poem* (Baltimore, 1947),
pp. 51–69.

37.   Kurt Weitzmann, *Ancient Book Illumination*, Martin Classical Lectures, No.
XVI (Cambridge, Mass., 1959), p. 31. Blake's interest, of course, is less in the narrative than in the vision accompanying it; Karl Kroeber's essay is pertinent (see "Gra-
phic-Poetic Structuring in Blake's *Book of Urizen*," *Blake Studies*, III [1970], 7–18).

38.   *William Blake, Poet and Painter*, p. 10.

39.   Weitzmann reminds us that book illustration, in ancient times *and now*,
"begins only after it [the poem] has become sufficiently popular and widespread"
(p. 2). "The first condition for a text to be illustrated," he reiterates, "is its popularity" (p. 31).

See the Latin translation by William Hog, *Paraphrasis Poetica in Tria Johannis
Miltoni, Viri Clarissmi, Poemata, viz. Paradisum Amissum, Paradisum Recupera-
tum, et Samsonem Agonisten* (London, 1690); also [anon.], *On the Resurrection in
Imitation of Milton*, in Francis Peck's *New Memoirs of the Life and Poetical Works
of Mr. John Milton* (London, 1740), separate pagination, and [anon.], *Jesus: A Poem
in Blank Verse* (London, 1745). There are, in addition, numerous eighteenth-
century translations of Milton's brief epic into both French and German.

40.   See [Bernard Routh], *Lettres critiques a Mr Le Comte sur le Paradis Perdu
et Reconquis de Milton* (Paris, 1731); Richard Meadowcourt, *A Critique on Milton's
Paradise Regain'd* (London, 1732); [anon.], *An Essay upon Milton's Imitations of
the Ancients in His Paradise Lost, with Some Observations on the Paradise Regain'd*
([London], 1741). A second edition of Meadowcourt's critique was published in 1748
under the title *Critical Dissertation with Notes on Milton's Paradise Regain'd*. An
anonymous prose translation of *Paradise Regained*, *The Recovery of Man*, was published in 1771 [London?]; but the first separate English edition of the poem, published in London by Toplis and Bunney, did not appear until eight years later.
The first American edition of *Paradise Regained*, published along with *Paradise Lost*,
was issued in Philadelphia in 1777.

41.   (London, 1752), pp. 3, 49. Newton is quoting from John Jortin's *Remarks on
Spenser's Poems* (London, 1734), p. 172; but see also Newton's "Preface," p. [i],
and his note, pp. 186–187.

42.   Ibid., pp. 3–4. With this comment, Warburton brings into focus an objection to *Paradise Regained* implied earlier (1705) by John Dennis, who thought that
Milton in his brief epic "err'd wildly" from religion (*Milton: The Critical Heritage*,
ed. John T. Shawcross [London, 1970], p. 134). Comments like these reveal E. L.
Marilla to be quite mistaken when he says that Denis Saurat was "the first to recognize the problem" in Milton's omitting the subject of the Crucifixion from *Paradise Regained*. On the other hand, Marilla is quite right in saying that "there is a
need for a clear definition of Milton's conception of the Crucifixion" ("Milton and
the Crucifixion," *Études Anglaises*, XXII [1969], 7). I question, however, whether
a very "clear definition" emerges from Marilla's essay, which takes into account *De
Doctrina Christiana* and Books III and XII of *Paradise Lost* but dismisses the "negative evidence" supplied by *Paradise Regained* as irrelevant: the Crucifixion "does

not appear" in *Paradise Regained*, says Marilla, "for the simple reason that the context provides no place for it" (p. 10). Lurking behind this conclusion, and indeed the entire essay, is the assumption that Milton once he formulated an attitude never changed it. A statement by Blake is pertinent: "The man who never alters his opinion is like standing water, & breeds reptiles of the mind" (*Complete Writings*, p. 156).

Also pertinent is Edwin Panofsky's reminder that in Christian painting and poetry, especially that of Protestant artists, "conspicuous omission" is an important element of meaning ("Comment on Art and Reformation," in *Symbols in Transformation: Iconographic Themes at the Time of the Reformation* [Princeton University Art Museum, 1969], p. 11). The remark has special application to Milton when we recall not only the importance of the Crucifixion to Protestant theology of the Renaissance but also its popularity as a subject for Renaissance artists. In this same volume, for instance, Craig Harbison observes that between 1560 and 1660 the Crucifixion, along with the Last Supper, was the most popular subject for artists depicting events from the life of Christ—*popular* because of its centrality to "Protestant doctrine" (p. 24). Still further, Panofsky's comment has relevance to my discussion of Blake the illustrator, especially in Section III of this essay, insofar as it establishes a tradition of "conspicuous omission" in illustration and attests to the fact that such omissions provide a vehicle for asserting dogmas and beliefs peculiar to the individual artist. I hasten to add, however, that in this instance Blake is representing a belief "peculiar" to Milton's poem rather than one "peculiar" to his own understanding of it.

43. Wordsworth is reported to have thought *Paradise Regained* "the most perfect in *execution* of anything written by Milton" (*The Prose Works of William Wordsworth*, ed. Alexander B. Grosart [3 vols.; London, 1876], III, 430); and Shelley's enthusiasm for the poem is communicated in a letter to John Gisborne: Byron's *Cain*, he says, "contains finer poetry than has appeared in England since the publication of Paradise Regained" (*The Letters of Percy Bysshe Shelley*, ed. Frederick L. Jones [2 vols.; Oxford, 1964], II, 388). For other appraisals of *Paradise Regained* by the major Romantic poets and critics, see the index to my edition *The Romantics on Milton*.

44. *The Life of Milton*, in *The Poetical Works of John Milton* (3 vols.; London, 1794–1797), I, cxxv-cxxvi. Hayley's distinction between Milton's two epics probably caught the eye of Blake, as it caught the eye of Coleridge who marks the passage thus ($\sqrt{} \sqrt{} \sqrt{}$) in his 1796 copy of Hayley's *Life*. Coleridge's copy is now in the Henry E. Huntington Library (Catalogue No. 144952).

45. (London, 1795), pp. i, iv (a second edition of Dunster's volume was issued in 1800). But Dunster also refers to *Paradise Regained* as a "companion" poem to *Samson Agonistes* (p. v). For fuller discussion of the critical tradition accumulated by *Paradise Regained* during the eighteenth century and Romantic period, see the introduction to my facsimile edition of Meadowcourt's *Critique* and Dunster's edition of the poem (Gainesville, Fla., 1971).

46. *The Poetical Works of John Milton* (London, 1801), IV, 355; (London, 1809), V, 310.

47. *The Prose Works of John Milton, with a Life of the Author* (London, 1806), VII, 487, 489.

48. From 1800 to 1803, Blake lived on Hayley's estate at Felpham. During that time, Hayley taught Blake Latin and Greek, and the two probably discussed Milton from time to time. For a list of the holdings in Hayley's library, which contained a sizable Milton collection, see *A Catalogue of the Very Valuable and Extensive Library of the Late William Hayley, Esq.* (Sold at auction by Mr. Evans), February, 1821. Hayley's copy of the Dunster edition is in the William Andrews Clark Memorial Library, Los Angeles. And for discussion of Blake's reading of Milton, see Beer, *Blake's Visionary Universe*, pp. 23–25.

It is impossible, with our present knowledge, to ascertain exactly with what editions and critics of Milton Blake was familiar. We can assume that in knowing Hayley Blake knew his opinions of Milton, certainly, and probably his works. The only other lead is provided by Crabb Robinson, who says that "as he [Blake] spoke of frequently Seeing Milton, I ventured to ask . . . which of the three or four portraits in *Hollis's Memoirs* . . . is the most like [.]—He answ^d [']They are all like, At different Ages [']" (Bentley, *Blake Records*, p. 543). Hollis, who refers repeatedly to "the divine Milton," describes the poet as a great "hero" and "an asserter of British liberty." In his memoir of Milton, Hollis distinguishes between the "two Miltons," the poet and the politician who, he asserts, were "two different men." In defending Milton as the hero of political radicalism, the creator of "the *mode* of the Revolution, as well as the *principles* of it" that then pertained, Hollis prints two answers to criticism of *Paradise Lost* from the *London Chronicle*, both of which make clear that by 1764 it was a cliché to refer to the Whigs, or the republicans, as belonging to "the party" of Devils or the "diabolical party" (*Memoirs of Thomas Hollis, Esq.* [London, 1780], esp. pp. 621, 625). The references suggest an unperceived political dimension to Blake's famous claim in *The Marriage of Heaven and Hell* that Milton was "of the Devil's party without knowing it" (plates 5–6 in *Complete Writings*, pp. 149–150). By the end of the century the designation had been extended to the dissenters. In short, Blake's phrase from *The Marriage* may be translated to mean that Milton was both a political radical and a religious dissenter—an idea first suggested to me by Jacqueline Di Salvo, a student of mine at the University of Wisconsin.

49.   "Blake, Milton, and Edward Burney," pp. 114, 126. In *The Art of William Blake*, Anthony Blunt postulates that Blake "borrowed more extensively and more systematically from the work of other artists than did any of his contemporaries" (p. 32); see also *Blake's Pencil Drawings*, ed. Geoffrey Keynes, 2nd ser. (London, 1956), p. ix.

50.   "The Iconography of the Fall of Man," in *Approaches to Paradise Lost*, pp. 253, 224–225. Trapp's conclusions are easily borne out by looking through the sixty-volume, extra-illustrated *Kitto Bible* in the Henry E. Huntington Library (Catalogue No. 49000). The temptations of Christ, as represented by Matthew, Mark, and Luke, are copiously illustrated—especially the first one—by biblical designers. The illustrators of *Paradise Regained* rely so heavily upon this tradition that in many instances their designs are scarcely more than copies of earlier biblical illustrations. But Blake, even when he uses a traditional subject, importantly transforms the concepts that he inherits from tradition; his greatest debt to the traditions of biblical illustration and eighteenth-century Milton illustration lies not in his borrowing of detail but in his adaptation of a technique. Acutely sensitive to traditional typology, which relates the temptations of Adam to those of Christ and which sees in any one of the latter temptations the whole sequence, the biblical illustrator customarily brings only the first temptation of Christ into focus but at the same time may represent the others marginally (see, e.g., *Kitto Bible*, XXXIV, 6362; XXXIX, opp. 7184, 7183 verso, 7207; XLVIII, 8636, 8750). Blake, on the other hand, uses the technique but not to conflate all scriptural history into the moment on the desert, not to see all the events in Christ's life contained in that event, not even to gather into the first temptation all the others; his concern is with using the devices of typology to define Milton's departures from tradition. Thus, where the technique appears in Blake's illustrations, as in Figures 6 and 7, it serves to suggest the continuity of the banquet and kingdoms temptation (in the first instance) and to call attention to Milton's gathering of the three temptations into the extended second temptation (the second instance). See also n. 36 above.

51.   As C. H. Collins Baker observes, Blake is the first illustrator to present the Crucifixion, with Christ bruising the head of the serpent, as a subject for *Paradise Lost* (see "Some Illustrators of Milton's *Paradise Lost*," p. 119); however, Blake is

not the first to use the subject in his Milton illustrations. Blake's predecessors often chose the subject as the first illustration (generally a frontispiece) to *Paradise Regained*, thereby stressing the continuity between the two epics (see Appendix A). Blake, on the other hand, uses the subject only where Milton's text fully justifies its use, that is, in Book XII of *Paradise Lost*. That illustration is obviously affected by those done previously for *Paradise Regained*, but in conception and execution it surpasses those earlier renderings. Previous illustrators show the serpent twined around the foot of the cross and a skull lying to the side of it (Christ is ordinarily carrying the cross rather than suspended from it); Blake shows the nail piercing Christ's foot also piercing the head of the serpent. The only comparable conception that I have seen is in the *Kitto Bible*, XLI, 7673, where the base of a crude cross is shown going through the head of the serpent. The illustration, designed by P. J. de Loutherbourg, may have been known to Blake, since de Loutherbourg, a contemporary of James Barry, exhibited a design for *Paradise Lost* at the Royal Academy in 1782.

52.   See n. 36 above. Many previous illustrators depicted different phases of the long second temptation, but Blake is the only illustrator of the poem, so far as I know, to conflate the entire kingdoms sequence within a single design. For this reason, I have thought it appropriate to treat the design as a new subject.

53.   *The Harmonious Vision: Studies in Milton's Poetry* (Baltimore, 1954), p. 110. This is not to say that Blake and Hayley could not join with Charles Dunster in perceiving points of contact between *Paradise Lost* and *Paradise Regained* when the two poems are seen together: the emblematic serpent which moves through the designs to *Paradise Lost* as a kind of "visual melody" (the phrase is Rose's) reappears, less magnificently to be sure, in the designs to *Paradise Regained* (figs. 8 and 9); the winged Lucifer of the *Paradise Lost* series turns up in Figure 5 of the *Paradise Regained* designs but without his earlier grandeur. Blake, then, is emphasizing dissimilitude rather than similitude between the two poems; and his primary concern seems to be with showing the unity, connection, and perfection that exists in *Paradise Regained* and which the view of the poem as simply a sequel to *Paradise Lost* denies it ordinarily. Blake, of course, apprehends the entanglement of the poems in Milton's canon which together comprise his "vision." His point is simply that *Paradise Regained*, and every other poem, retains its own integrity at the same time that each contributes to a larger vision that the poems together comprise.

54.   *Milton's Brief Epic: The Genre, Meaning and Art of Paradise Regained* (Providence and London, 1966), esp. pp. 3–129.

55.   Northrop Frye perceives the dramatic aspect of brief epic poetry in *Fearful Symmetry*, p. 405.

56.   *Paradise Regained: The Tradition and the Poem*, p. 51. What Miss Pope neglects to point out is that many biblical illustrators before Milton paired Adam's temptations and Christ's (see, e. g., *Kitto Bible*, XLVIII, 8634). Orthodox theology, however, is undisturbed, since the temptation in the wilderness is seen merely as a "type" of the Crucifixion at which time Paradise is recovered. In other words, the suggestion implicit in this pairing—that Paradise was regained in the desert—never was absorbed into orthodoxy. Milton does not exploit this typological association between the temptation and the Crucifixion, though, of course, he exploits others as the proem to the brief epic indicates and as Mrs. Lewalski (see n. 54 above) so competently demonstrates.

57.   *Milton and the Christian Tradition* (Oxford, 1966), p. 132. In this passage Patrides is quoting from J. S. Whale's *Christian Doctrine* (Cambridge, 1941), p. 75.

58.   Ibid., pp. 132–142.

59.   Ibid., pp. 141–142.

60.   I adopt language from Hayley's *Life of Milton* (1796), p. 277.

61.   "Preface to *Prometheus Unbound*," *Shelley's Prometheus Unbound: A Variorum Edition*, ed. Lawrence John Zillman (Seattle, 1959), p. 123.

62.   I quote from Calton's note reprinted by Dunster in his edition of *Paradise Regained*, p. 262.

63.   For Frye's comments, see *Anatomy of Criticism: Four Essays* (Princeton, 1957), p. 96, and *The Return of Eden: Five Essays on Milton's Epics* (Toronto, 1965), pp. 118–143; and for Schultz's see "A Fairer Paradise? Some Recent Studies of *Paradise Regained*," *ELH*, XXXII (1965), 275–302.

64.   For an excellent discussion of this point, see Patrides, *Milton and the Christian Tradition*, pp. 149–152.

65.   *The Hero with a Thousand Faces*, Bollingen, XVII (New York, 1949), p. 349; but see also pp. 315–364.

66.   Carl G. Jung, *The Development of Personality*, trans. R. F. C. Hull, Bollingen, XX (New York, 1954), p. 181.

67.   "Annotations to Watson," *Complete Writings*, p. 387.

68.   The phrase is Harold Bloom's; see *Blake's Apocalypse: A Study in Poetic Argument* (Garden City, N. Y., 1963), p. 362.

69.   For Blake, it seems, Christ's deed above heroic is his decision to return to civilization as its leader and redeemer; contemplation, then, is merely a prologue to action. Interestingly, Blake's *Milton* takes *Paradise Regained* as its model in a more exact, but also in a much different, sense than is usually acknowledged. Both poems involve the interior journey, the descent into the self, which ends with the hero's return to civilization. The focus of the poets is different, however: Milton concentrates upon the journey, whereas Blake stresses the idea of return. In a very real sense, *Milton* begins where *Paradise Regained* leaves off. I would argue, then, that it is the illustrations to *Paradise Regained* that provide the best guide for reading *Milton*, although Susan C. Fox has recently suggested that if *Milton* is "derived from any Miltonic pattern, it is from the two brief poems which reflect and reinforce each other, 'L'Allegro' and 'Il Penseroso' " ("The Structure of a Moment and Parallelism in the Two Books of Blake's *Milton*," *Blake Studies*, II [1969], 21).

70.   Peter Felix Hägin, *The Epic Hero and the Decline of Heroic Poetry: A Study of the Neoclassical English Epic with Special Reference to Milton's 'Paradise Lost'* (Basel, 1964), p. 44.

71.   *Fearful Symmetry*, p. 415.

72.   *Complete Poems and Major Prose*, p. 720.

73.   After I completed this study, Marcia Pointon's *Milton & English Art* (Manchester, 1970) appeared, and I have revised my own essay so as to include references to this volume. Our conclusions about Blake's Milton illustrations occasionally agree, but generally I have provided the kinds of discriminations and demonstrations that Pointon's study avoids. A lengthy section of the volume (pp. 135–166) considers Blake's illustrations to Milton, but that consideration is valuable chiefly as a summary of conclusions reached by earlier critics. For those searching for a fresh perspective on Blake's illustrations, Pointon's volume is disappointing.

The Mental Pinnacle: *Paradise Regained* and the Romantic Four-Book Epic

STUART CURRAN

UNIVERSITY OF WISCONSIN

> Oft in these moments such a holy calm
> Would overspread my soul, that bodily eyes
> Were utterly forgotten, and what I saw
> Appeared like something in myself, a dream,
> A prospect in the mind.
>
> Wordsworth, *The Prelude* (1850), II.348–352.

In a recent and provocative essay on *Paradise Lost*, T. J. B. Spencer concludes by forcing from hiding a clandestine critical assumption that has for years lurked behind Milton commentary—the notion that this great poem is the last of its kind in English. *Paradise Lost*, he asserts,

> is the anti-epic. Wherever we turn we find the traditional epic values inverted. It closed the history of this poetic genre in England. . . . Never was the death of an art form celebrated with such a magnanimous ceremony, splendid in ashes and pompous in the grave. The death of tragedy was a mere decline into a whine and a whisper. But the death of epic was, in Milton's hands, a glorious and perfectly staged suicide.[1]

If in the present state of literary aesthetics, under the concerted siege of Barth, Borges, Nabokov, and Robbe-Grillet, we have become acutely conscious of the value of serious parody, it is, perhaps, especially incumbent upon us to avoid high drama and to pursue the "anti-form" to its sometimes mundane, but ever more subtle roots. Centuries of baf-

133

fled critics have questioned whether *Paradise Regained* is a proper sequel to Milton's grand epic: if the first was an "anti-epic"—a "suicide"
—what, indeed, are we to term the second? *Paradise Regained* not only
follows *Paradise Lost* in inverting the traditional conventions of the
European epic,[2] but steadfastly refuses even to comply with the high
style of its epic predecessors. If Milton's second epic has not until recently attracted either the veneration or the critical attention accorded
the first, it could suggest that all of us are sufficiently attached to conventional epic values to feel deprived of our expectations when the
sublime is exiled to a fruitless wilderness and heroics become harangues.

The truth of Spencer's assertion is also dubious, however, on a
second and more significant count. We have no need to exhume the
mouldering remains of eighteenth-century epics best forgotten in order
to prove the continuation of the genre in English poetry after Milton.
The eighteenth century attended to the consolidation of the rules of the
genre, a study whose finest fruits can be seen in the polish of Pope's
translations and the structural solidity of Fielding's "comic epics in
prose," but the actual writing in the form fell to the likes of Blackmore,
Glover, and Wilkie, poets whose sense was measured out in inverse
proportion to their pretension. For all the debate over the correct application of conventions, the epic, for more than a century after Milton's
death, slumbered in venerable senility. Its second birth was presided
over by the English Romantics, and, if its life was as brief as many of
theirs, it was equally varied and intense. The epic is, in fact, the major
poetic genre of the Romantic period, attempted—and generally more
than once—by every major poet writing between 1795 and 1825.[3] Moreover, the remarkable self-consciousness that the Romantics consistently displayed toward their craft invests their epic adventures with a
controlled recreation of convention unequalled except by Milton—and
clearly indebted to him for its aesthetic base. In terms of both numbers
and insight into the potential of the genre, the Romantic period represents the heyday of the English epic.

Recent studies of Romantic narrative poetry have argued, sometimes too tentatively, against the views of more traditional critics of the
epic tradition. But in adopting an often defensive posture, they do not
do full justice to the central importance of the epic genre for the Romantics. Brian Wilkie, whose *Romantic Poets and Epic Tradition* is
the fullest treatment of the subject, pays such detailed attention to the
transmutation of convention that he often neglects the far more significant matter of the habitual Romantic mode for epic.[4] And Karl Kroeber,

in emphasizing the revolutionary character of *The Prelude* as a "personal epic," which "has given its form to much of the heroic literature of revolution that has succeeded it," greatly underestimates the potential of the alterations in epic form realized by Milton and certainly understood by Wordsworth.[5] Milton's impact on the imaginative efforts of this time is everywhere evident—in Wordsworth's plans for an epic trilogy, in Blake's prophetic books, in Keats' epic style and subject. The Romantics read *Paradise Lost* with an excitement and perception unmatched in English literary history, and one must assume that their endeavor to seize the long poem for philosophical purposes owes much to Milton's success with the form. A. C. Bradley long ago remarked on the general failure of the Romantics in this endeavor, and, if he greatly generalizes what Blake would have termed the "minute particulars" of the case, his criticism is essentially just.[6] The Romantics were less interested in the dramatic potential of the epic than they were in its capacity for projecting philosophical unity in an encyclopedic form. The two exceptions to Bradley's rule are *The Prelude* and *Don Juan*, both of which, in defining the epic hero as the artist laboring to redeem his culture by subsuming its chaotic stresses within the unity of his personality, derive their mode from Milton's seminal intrusions into the structure of *Paradise Lost*. *The Prelude*, it should be noted, however, was not published until the middle of the century; and *Don Juan* lost Byron much of his contemporary audience. More characteristic of the long poem in this period are the *longueurs* of Southey's epics, or of *The Revolt of Islam* and *The Excursion*, and the virtually impenetrable multi-layered structure of *The Four Zoas*. Radically different from each other as these poems are (and all of them are more or less epic in structure and intent), they fail from an inability to reconcile the conflicting demands of epic action and thought. That is not to say that the authors lacked the requisite poetic gifts, but rather that the philosophical epic embodies a basic contradiction in terms. Had Milton not written a masterpiece in *Paradise Lost*, the form might have subsisted as the generic equivalent of the unicorn, true in conception if impossible in fact.

The eminence of *Paradise Lost* as a model for succeeding epics—and this has been affirmed by all students of the Romantic epic—has obscured the equal, if not greater, significance of *Paradise Regained*. That both Miltonists and Romanticists have hitherto neglected its influence is especially curious, since in many respects *Paradise Regained* is purer in form, perfecting the revolution in the epic genre that is implicit in *Paradise Lost*.[7] In the brief epic Milton no longer felt com-

pelled to reform the pagans: he cast off from the Vergilian main, reliev-
ing himself of even a parodic dependency in order to forge a philosophical epic complete in itself. The development was not lost on the
Romantic poets. If they looked to *Paradise Lost* for inspiration, the form
they consistently modified, even in their long poems, was that of the
internalized epic of *Paradise Regained*. And, whereas in the long poem
the demands of narrative and theodicy were frequently in opposition,
when the Romantic poets constrained themselves to a tighter form
where invention was less often put to the test, the results could be mas-
terful. The brief epic, as defined by *Paradise Regained*, is clearly the prototype for the four-book epics of the Romantic period: Keats' *Endymion*, Blake's *Jerusalem*, and Shelley's *Prometheus Unbound*.[8] In each
there is a struggle for mastery of the self. In each the issue is the recreation of Paradise.

  After centuries of refinement we have come to expect definite characteristics of the epic poem: panoramic vision, encyclopedic knowledge, a heroism that defines human possibilities, a sense of the ultimate
nature of the cosmos, and a justification of the cosmic order as propi-
tious to human life. The brief epic, in narrowing its compass and elimi-
nating many of the usual conventions, must necessarily limit its panoramic vision (though surely Blake would have denied such a drastic
consequence), but no other expectation of the diffuse epic is omitted
except its diffuseness. The brief epic is not a scale model but a concentrated form of its grander counterpart; and just as it tends to turn in
upon itself in shape, so, too, there is a comparable internalization of
idea. The struggle between good and evil, which is the basic component
of all epics, becomes centered in a single individual representative of
man, and from his internal conflict emerges the scope of human life,
its triumphs and limitations. From it, too, emerges a cultural redefinition
of the means by which Paradise can be regained upon earth.

  This is the subject of both Keats' epics, though the scheme is more
obvious in his last, unfinished effort. *Hyperion* is an essentially Christian epic, cast, like numerous brief epics of the Renaissance, in the
mold of classical mythology.[9] Though Keats was in no way as insistent
on his freedom from Christian orthodoxy as Shelley, his muse was not
as thoroughly pagan as he, Leigh Hunt, and his contemporary critics
might have thought. The subject of *Hyperion* is that of *Paradise Lost*,
with the Adamic fall transposed into the descent from the Golden Age.
The Titans are sadly uncomprehending counterparts of primordial
Adam and Eve; the new race of gods, counterparts of the fallen race.

"Apollo shriek'd" (III.135) upon being cruelly visited with knowledge: he must "Die into life" (III.130), into the ambiguous mixture of ideal and real which dominates human existence. Keats ended his first attempt at *Hyperion* on this point, because, however much he treasured negative capability, the center of the conflict, as he saw it, was more modern than ancient, residing in the poet-priest he was striving to become. Returning to the myth in *The Fall of Hyperion*, he began with the lengthy induction in which the link between himself and Apollo's birth trauma was firmly established.

In *Endymion*, Keats' only completed poem of a major length, the Apollonian struggle is even more deeply explored, and, what has surprisingly escaped critical observation, the myth is as indelibly Christian beneath its pagan trappings as *Hyperion* is. If *Hyperion* is Keats' *Paradise Lost*, *Endymion* is his *Paradise Regained*. In the unfinished epic, the poet is a Christ-Apollo figure who must assume mortal knowledge and suffering as his redemptive pledge to man.[10] In *Endymion* we see the rigorous efforts of the incarnate Christ figure to redeem himself before entering upon his priestly function. Such a reading invests the preface, in which Keats apologizes for his youthful work, with a greater significance than it has generally been accorded: "The imagination of a boy is healthy, and the mature imagination of a man is healthy; but there is a space of life between, in which the soul is in a ferment, the character undecided, the way of life uncertain, the ambition thick-sighted. . . ."[11] This is the period in which the secular savior enters the wilderness to purge the dross from the true self and to return revitalized, liberated, a mature and active voice for society.

If *Paradise Regained*, as we have come to see its tradition, derives from the Gospel according to Luke, the Gospel of John, the most metaphysical of the accounts of Christ's life, might be taken as the biblical text most illuminating to *Endymion*.[12] Keats' focus—and his hero's—is, in brief, the Word, the divine spirit infusing all life. Endymion's epic journey, the journey of the poet from novice to mature advocate, comprises a search for the means by which the Word can be made incarnate. Its consummation is a marriage between mortal and immortal, man and God. The famous philosophical passage of Book I, renowned equally for its suggestiveness and its obscurity, in this context becomes clarified:

> Wherein lies happiness? In that which becks
> Our ready minds to fellowship divine,

> A fellowship with essence; till we shine,
> Full alchemiz'd, and free of space. (I.777–780)

To submit to the "fellowship divine" is to know the immensity and om-
nipresence of the divine spirit, to join in "a sort of oneness, [wherein]
our state / Is like a floating spirit's" (I.796–797). But, just as God's
word issues in the love of Christ, so in Keats' "Pleasure Thermometer,"
the ultimate state, "the chief intensity" (I.800), is a conjunction of the
human and divine through the agency of love. The epic purpose, thus
obscurely enunciated toward the end of Book I, is realized through the
baroque allegory that follows. No reader, even Keats himself, has found
the conclusion of the poem an entirely satisfactory resolution to the
questions Keats raises: *Endymion's* claims to greatness lie in the moral
perceptions of the allegorical quest.[13]

Paradise Regained spans the two epiphanies in which Christ's divinity is revealed and realized. The ritual of the baptism, a second birth,
stands in structural juxtaposition to the ritual of the assumption of
divine knowledge, the ministry. These are the formal polarities of *Endymion* as well, symbolized by the ritual sacrifice of Book I, the Hymn
to Pan, in which Endymion cannot fully participate, and the celebration of rebirth in Book III, the Hymn to Neptune, which he leads. The
mental wilderness through which the king wanders between these
points results from the sudden knowledge visited upon him by the descent of his goddess in a dream. In the celebration of Pan, as God of
generation, Endymion intrudes the sole discordant note, one "of yellow
leaves, of owlets' cry, / Of logs piled solemnly" (I.182–183). Amid
the effluence of spring, he alone sees the coming of winter. His knowledge is tragic, the mark of man's fallen state. In contrast, the end of
Book III is comedic in the Dantean sense: the events and image patterns reinforce our sense of an allegorical event of immense significance.
As Endymion performs for Glaucus the sacred ritual, his friend exclaims, "The spite of hell is tumbling to its grave" (l. 760). The dead
lovers arise in amazement, and, though the verse is clumsy, the biblical
extrapolation is clear:

> Death felt it to his inwards: 'twas too much:
> Death fell a-weeping in his charnel-house. (III.787–788)

Freed through "This mighty consummation" (III.828), the resurrected
lovers gather with Endymion before the throne of Neptune, who is

seated with Venus (as the Holy Spirit) on his left and Love (as Christ) on his right. The Hymn to Neptune seals this perversely "aesthetic" apocalypse. The course of the first three books of *Endymion*, then, is a secular equivalent of the Christian pilgrimage from the Fall to the Resurrection.

The vale of Latmos over which Endymion rules is a natural paradise, fertile, enclosed, and innocent. Keats' divergence from the normative conception of Eden, such as we find in the Happy Valley of *Rasselas*, is immediately apparent. The seeds of discontent are implicit in the Hymn to Pan, Keats' first major ode, which suggests the paradoxically inseparable character of the natural and supernatural later developed so intensely in the odes of 1819. The Hymn begins on a strangely ominous note: the province of Pan is dark, inscrutable, productive of death as well as life. The three central stanzas retreat from this forbidding conception to praise nature in terms suggestive of the ode "To Autumn": as granting "the fresh budding year / All its completion" (I.259–260), as magical and endlessly creative, as provider for man's bodily and mental health. In the great last stanza, the Hymn characterizes the natural world as compelling the mind to higher, supernatural conceptions. Endymion, alone of the assembled celebrants, knows the truth and the sorrow of this compulsion, for his receptive mind, visited by glimmerings of perfection, is no longer content with the cyclical "green world" (I.16) praised in the opening lines of the poem. The visionary poet and the natural man are at war within him: from such mutually exclusive cravings, only despondency (a premonition of the more fully realized Cave of Quietude in Book IV) results. Endymion has become what he sees, a universe of death.

In the king's subsequent interview with his sister Peona the rival claims gain sharper definition. Endymion, lost in his personal struggle of allegiances, has forsaken his "high and noble life" (I.758) and "high-fronted honour" (I.759), his public obligations as leader of his people. The visionary union with his goddess, the high imaginative ends to which he is now dedicated, have ironically rendered him impotent and incapable of rule. Peona, in counselling his return to the active life, speaks for the natural world; but to retreat from the ends to which Pan, the "symbol of immensity" (I.299), has led him is to forsake the higher obligations derived from nature itself.

Opposing commitments to natural and spiritual man, elevated to an acute pitch, produce the "crisis" of the Romantic brief epic, as they had produced the crisis of *Paradise Regained*. Milton's central importance for the new epic tradition, however, is nowhere more distinctly etched than in what issues from the spiritual crisis. Not action, not Achilles bursting from his tent to lay waste the battlefield, but meditation, an internal search for the means of reconciling conflicting demands. Like Christ withdrawn from human society, Endymion in crisis "Into himself descended" (*PR* II.111). Before Endymion's plunge into the underworld, the imagery of pool and of flower prepares us for the allegorical significance of his descent: to see beyond his own reflection, to find his way through the layers of the personality to the central selfhood. The "Brain-sick shepherd-prince" (II.43), as he is described upon reappearing in the second book, alone can unravel his future possibilities. If he is to discover "the silent mysteries of earth" (II.214), he must begin with the mysteries of his own internal landscape. And the rigor, even peril, of the descent is a necessary condition for attaining knowledge of the self.

This distinctive focus of the Romantic epic, central to *Jerusalem* and *Prometheus Unbound* as well as to *Endymion*, derives its justification from the psychological profundity of Milton's portrait of Christ. *Paradise Regained* is a dialogue of self and soul, waged over the future of humanity and thus deserving of the most heroic proportions—"Above Heroic, though in secret done" (I.15). Assuredly, one cannot ignore the orthodox Christian traditions upon which Milton founds his superstructure, nor suggest that he is wilfully and heretically casting Satan as a dual aspect in Christ's personality. But, by the same token, one cannot ignore the fact that none of these Romantic poets was an orthodox Christian and that each was primarily concerned with the conflicts and paradoxes of the human psyche. Furthermore, if Milton stops short of heresy, he frequently plunges into audacity. As Christ's victory is a triumph over the agent of evil, the progress to the exaltation demands the capitulation of Christ's selfhood as man to his selflessness as God. Satan, we learn immediately, is "the Spiritual Foe" (I.14), a condition of the fallen mentality with which the "inward Oracle" (I.463) of God's grace wages unremitting battle: "his great duel, not of arms, / But to vanquish by wisdom hellish wiles" (I.174–175). Ironically, the last of Satan's rationalizations for the annoyance of Christ is the only one that bears real merit: it suggests Milton's purpose in writing the poem, not to say Christ's in remaining in the wilderness:

> Thenceforth I thought thee worth my nearer view
> And narrower Scrutiny, that I might learn

> In what degree or meaning thou art call'd
> The Son of God, which bears no single sense. . . . (IV.514–517)

In modern parlance, the struggle in the wilderness is a crisis in identity, during which Christ analyzes the unique personality of the man-God and resolves the nagging duality by assuming the Godhead, thereby accomplishing his entry into human ministry absolved from human frailty.

Troubled by the revelation at his baptism, Christ wanders into the wilderness, "Musing and much revolving in his breast, / How best the mighty work he might begin . . ." (I.185–186). In such circumstances, the first temptation arises: the search for purpose suggests its antithesis, the distrust of purpose.[11] From the symbolic wandering of Christ's thought in Book I, we turn immediately in Book II to the doubts of Andrew and Simon, whose questions sharpen our understanding of the mental conflict Christ is experiencing in the wilderness. Mary's worries about her Son also serve to frame his own worries. But the retreat from societal and family obligations to accept God's will is necessary to the purgation of Christ's humanness. Far more arduous is the subsequent retreat from the demands of the Self. It is not Satan who broaches the question of hunger, but Christ himself (II.244), or rather the Satanic aspect of the fallen man. The internal resolution ironically furnishes the impetus for the succeeding temptation, which Christ suggests even as he testifies to his release from the temptations of the flesh:

> Yet he who reigns within himself, and rules
> Passions, Desires, and Fears, is more a King;
> Which every wise and virtuous man attains:
> And who attains not, ill aspires to rule
> Cities of men, or headstrong Multitudes,
> Subject himself to Anarchy within,
> Or lawless passions in him, which he serves. (II.466–472)

And the final line of Book II—"to gain a Scepter, oftest better miss't" (l. 486)—only emphasizes the crucial problem of how Christ is to assume the kingship of man, the focus of the third and fourth books.

Endymion's variations from this pattern result mainly, one supposes, from the lateness of his revelation: he has been led by natural causes to a supernatural apprehension, not singled out from birth. But the underlying paradox of the two heroic minds is the same: both experience spiritual separation, alienation, only to find a higher integration. Yet, if the self cannot coexist fruitfully with present society, it is obvious that the future society will not be capable of coexisting with that self, either. Endymion's solitary descent into a lifeless world— equivalent to the wilderness—shatters the equilibrium of his mental life, obliterating external support:

> And thoughts of self came on, how crude and sore
> The journey homeward to habitual self!
> A mad-pursuing of the fog-born elf,
> Whose flitting lantern, through rude nettle-briar,
> Cheats us into a swamp, into a fire,
> Into the bosom of a hated thing. (II.275–280)

This is "The goal of consciousness" (II.283); and the greater part of the second book illustrates the unhappy results of "habitual self." An inverted parallel to Endymion's relationship with his goddess forms the most memorable episode in Endymion's underground exploration: the descent of Venus to awaken Adonis. Unlike Endymion, Adonis did not strive for immortality, fearful of the consequences when he ascertained through an indelibly Keatsian perception that an immortality of joy presupposes the immortality of sorrow. Venus, unlike Cynthia, did not fear granting apotheosis to Adonis, but her infatuation produced ominous results for Endymion's future happiness. He is told "how the sea-born goddess pin'd / For a mortal youth, and how she strove to bind / Him all in all unto her doting self" (II.458–460). The immortal confluence of joy and sorrow implicit in the lines of the myth ironically derives from a failure by both Venus and Adonis to comprehend the true nature of love. Their imperfect relationship is central to the cyclical recurrence of the natural world they symbolize, their gesture toward perfection rendered tragic by mutually selfish ends. From her suffering, Venus like Dido has learned compassion: in her kindness to Endymion, the selfless nature of love is quietly underscored. So, at the end of Book II, he will repeat her act by praying ironically (Keats' desire for a stunning denouement makes *Endymion* perhaps the most oppressively ironic poem in English literature) to Diana, his dream-goddess, to relieve Alpheus and Arethusa, further symbols of selfish love, from the tortured eternality of impassioned desire and chaste fear. The darkest symbol of the book, the mythological figure who appears as a structural fulcrum between the two pairs of lovers, is also the most briefly sketched. It is possible that the sudden vision of Cybele, the ancient earth-mother, is here to illustrate "the silent mysteries of earth," the springs of life in the wasteland of subterranean rock.[15] But that is to ignore the sometimes twisted personality of the goddess in mythological legend. Cybele, too, distrusted love, transforming Hippomanes and Atalanta into lions and yoking them to her chariot for having, with their love, profaned one of her sacred temples. She is, to anticipate Blake's terminology, Vala, the principle of the Selfhood embodied in the natural world.

If Book II can be seen as Endymion's education in the ubiquitous snares of personal love, whereby he learns the sources of its true integrity, Book III represents his introduction into the realm of public love, humanitarianism. It is in this book that the emphases of the Gospel of John seem especially relevant. Keats' sudden and virulent attack on social and political leaders is organic to the enlarging themes of his allegorical epic, for "the light shineth in darkness; and the darkness comprehended it not" (John 1:5). The severe and all but Manichean conflict of darkness and light in John is not alleviated by any of the sensuous embellishments the young Keats lavishes on his epic, but the poet's underlying conception is similarly stern. In Book II wherever Endymion travels, he finds monuments to the failure of vision: a similar failure is exposed in the narration of Glaucus. In secular terms it is a failure to comprehend and, comprehending, incorporate into one's life the universal truths of the Spirit. The imagination, which Endymion worships as his goddess and Keats as the moon, both (as Endymion is to learn) being the same, is the Logos, the creative word invested with the universal Spirit, the beneficent grace that quickens men's souls: "thy benediction passeth not / One obscure hiding-place, one little spot / Where pleasure may be sent . . ." (III.61–63). Endymion, in love with a goddess, laments that she has surpassed the moon in his affections (III.175 ff.) —which is to say, that immortal love excels the immortal imagination. His task is to discover that his goddess is actually Cynthia, that love and imagination are ultimately one. Glaucus' mission is that of a precursor, one who has learned truth but awaits a greater man to realize it. His opening address (III.234–255) is rich with echoes of John: "Thou art the man," he exclaims both at the beginning and the end, suggesting the Baptist's revelation of the Messiah, as well as the crowning of Christ with thorns and Pilate's presentation of Christ to the Jews: *Ecce homo!* (see John 1:29–36; 19:5). The regenerative function of the Logos —"Except a man be born again, he cannot see the kingdom of God" (John 3:3)—suggests the significance of Glaucus' impassioned exclamation: "O Jove! I shall be young again, be young" (III.238). Glaucus' biography, furthermore, reveals how very much a precursor he is, for his

life is correlative and corrective to Endymion's. An Endymion of the
sea, Glaucus also had immortal longings, but they were debased; his
pursuit of Scylla was as criminal as Alpheus' of Arethusa, and as productive of ill. The servant of self-gratification finds himself in the power of
Circe, "arbitrary queen of sense" (III.459), and the price for his escape
is banishment to the barren rock, another wilderness, he has inhabited
for ages. The book, which comes to his hands through his selfless concern for the shipwrecked mariners, is the Word of God, the resurrection
and the life (John 11:25–26), in secular form:

> If he utterly
> Scans all the depths of magic, and expounds
> The meanings of all motions, shapes and sounds;
> If he explores all forms and substances
> Straight homeward to their symbol-essences;
> He shall not die. (II.696–701)

Glaucus' mission is a deeply poetic one, to become one with the Spirit
through comprehension of the Word, the universal symbolism of earth.
Endymion, Glaucus' second self, is committed to the same quest; and
his ritual resurrection of the lovers, like the miracle of the raising of Laz-
arus (John 11:1–44), testifies to the selfless brotherhood of men beneath
the Spirit: "A new commandment I give unto you, that ye love one another; as I have loved you, that ye also love one another" (John 13:34).
At the conclusion of the sacred rite Endymion learns that he has won
"immortal bliss" (III.1024) for himself and his goddess.

　　　Endymion's education in "symbol-essences" has freed him from the
trammels of selfish love and has prompted his commitment to human
brotherhood, but his goal of interior regeneration has not yet been attained. He has still to learn the means by which human longing for the
infinite can be realized. The resolution is as simple as it is profound.
Endymion, compassionate to sorrow, finds himself in love with the Indian maid, who as a bacchante is representative of human passion. The
dilemma of opposing commitments central to Book I now returns with
renewed force. The contradictory impulses within Endymion's mind
strive toward a sensitive adjustment. On the one hand, he must learn
that ideal love is not an abstraction, but is grasped through the real:
Book IV begins with consecutive prayers by the poet, the Indian maid,
and Endymion, each suggesting the necessity for the Spirit to be incarnate within the flesh.[16] But on the other hand, it is just as crucial that
Endymion "from this mortal state . . . / Be spiritualized (IV.991–993).
Without that he is trapped in the labyrinthine paradoxes of the Cave of

Quietude, to which, in an exact parallel to the climax of *Paradise Regained*, he plunges when he resists the call to divine marriage with Diana. The only recourse for one who thus surrenders to the Satanic element of the personality is the suicide Endymion subsequently contemplates. In rejecting this defeat and perceiving the identity of the Indian maid and Diana, Endymion surmounts the contradictions of his mortal state. At last he is prepared to undertake the temporal mission of the poet. Once again, the sophisticated paradoxes of the Gospel of John clarify the basic harmony of Keats' vision. If, as Christ repeatedly insists in John, the Father can only be realized through the Son, the super-real through the real, the reality of Christ is nevertheless refined from mortal dross to become a pure, if earthly, Spirit. Without unnaturally violating the integrity of *Endymion*, one might claim that, as the first three books parallel Christ's discovery of his divinity, the fourth book is an attempt to render in dramatic terms the final line of *Paradise Regained*. Christ's return to his mother's house is as spiritual liberator, whose ministry Keats grants to the poet, the visionary, who comprehends and communicates the identity of love and the Logos: "In the world ye shall have tribulation: but be of good cheer; I have overcome the world" (John 16:33).

The unity of *Endymion* as epic theodicy is manifest, even though a number of causes serve to disrupt it: the complications of the romantic allegory; a myth and a mind that do not lend themselves easily to the subordination of the senses; a temperament less gifted than Shelley's for the extraction of subtle philosophical distinctions from a narrative form; and the natural obstacle to de-Christianizing a theodicy as essentially Christian as Milton's. There is a further problem stemming from Keats' evident lack of belief, when he came to write it, in the happy ending he had planned. But if Keats asks much of a reader, he is subdued in his demands in comparison with Blake, who creates an original, abstruse mythology and simultaneously redefines and enlarges Christian mythology through his own system. The longest and most rigorously complicated of four-book epics, *Jerusalem* nonetheless is a narrative of mental adventures that subsumes all history and of a spiritual revelation that conflates all time into "a pulsation of the artery" (*Milton* 28:62). The struggle of the epic hero is to achieve this infinity of time and space within the finite moment, an event synonymous with apocalypse.

Jerusalem is the culmination of Blake's lifelong struggle with epic form. Written over a period of some fifteen years, it subsumes the themes and characters of its predecessors, from *America* to *Milton*, refining what even in the early miniature epics was abstruse and subtle into a grand coherence that defies the logic of the natural world and replaces it with "Visionary forms dramatic" (*Jerusalem* 98:28). The vast panorama of history and space given imaginative form within the epic structure corresponds to the microcosmic imaginative form itself, the human mind. *Jerusalem* does not simply record, it *is* the attempt of the visionary mind, as "a repetition . . . of the eternal act of creation in the infinite I AM,"[17] to create a universe and bring it to everlasting life. As *Jerusalem* is thus the ultimate reduction of the internalized epic form, so it is also its final extension, able in its teleological fulfillment of the imaginative *eschaton* to surmount the cyclical, if similarly encyclopedic, unity of its closest rival in the epic tradition, *Finnegan's Wake*.

The epic tradition itself is largely mirrored in the development of Blake's literary art. His initial attempt to convert historical forces into epic necessity was *The French Revolution*, of which only one of the seven projected books was written (or has survived). Turning to *America*, Blake enlarged his scope in order to treat more than simply the mechanisms of history; but still the form was inadequate to his needs. A theodicy, after all, must encompass more than an explanation of why revolutions occur and why revolutionary struggles are more debilitating to the oppressor than to those claiming their freedom. With *Europe*, the richest of the historical epics, Blake began to work out the cultural flaws that were, seemingly, forcing the Christian era into apocalyptic eruptions. But in *Europe*, too, Blake makes explicit the subterranean ironies of *America*: a social revolution by its nature does not free those involved in the struggle; it merely gives the dynamic forces a new turn, whereby the cycle begins again. What Blake sought now was an epic structure by which he could root social and cultural forces within the psyche, the only arena in which revolution could be transformed into apocalypse. The nascent mythology of the historical epics was transferred to the ontological questionings of the Urizen-Los sequence. It took the five years that span *The French Revolution* and *The Book of Los* for Blake to develop a mythology capable of representing both psychological states and historical forces simultaneously. With customary fervor he next attempted to draw all his themes together in a diffuse epic, *The Four Zoas*, which would arch created time and conceive both fall and apocalypse within the tensions and resolutions of the human personality. That mighty undertaking is, as Northrop Frye has noted, "the greatest abortive masterpiece in English literature,"[18] a monument of intellectual scope and artistic vision, continually falling apart and being hammered into new form by the dialectical force of Blake's mind.

The last two epics, *Milton* and *Jerusalem*, are Blake's crowning achievements, fully conceived and deftly finished. Harold Bloom has suggested *Paradise Regained* as the source of *Milton*,[19] and certainly there are numerous and intentional resemblances. The struggle of Milton to descend from eternity, to become incarnate on earth in William Blake, and annihilate the Satanic aspect of himself, his Spectre, is a free version of the materials of *Paradise Regained*; and the similarity of conclusions is marked. Like Satan, Milton's Spectre falls shrieking into the sea, as all of creation prepares "To go forth to the Great Harvest & Vintage of the Nations" (*Milton* 43:1).[20] In important respects, however, *Milton* is less obliged to *Paradise Regained* than *Jerusalem* is. It is Blake's most personal major poem, a domestic epic recording Blake's incarnation and redirection of Milton's genius to truly humane ends. Lacking the sublime austerity of *Paradise Regained*, as well as its graduated enlargement of focus, it treats the apocalypse as an essentially internal phenomenon. *Milton* is an epic concerned with the creation of poetry. *Jerusalem*, in which the internal and external are fused from beginning to end, is concerned with the creation of eternity.

Jerusalem may have fewer actual echoes of *Paradise Regained*, but it does have truer symbolic ones. Blake expands the symbolic encounter of Christ and Satan in the wilderness to cosmic dimensions without altering the basic dramatic antipathy. His epic of the regaining of Paradise is a contest for the soul of man waged literally from the beginning to the end of things. Christ's victory on the pinnacle is, in Blake's terms, the casting out and dissolution of the Antichrist, which is the Spectre, the principle of Self in all living things. The holy wedding with Jerusalem is the everlasting embrace of all life with pure, spiritual freedom, for "JERUSALEM is Named Liberty / Among the Sons of Albion" (26:1).[21]

Just as Blake expands the struggle in the wilderness until it encompasses the history of life on earth, so he correspondingly deepens the nature of the conflict. In so brief a compass it is impossible to do justice to Blake's mythology of the psyche, but some account of its fourfold nature and of the proliferation of mental archetypes is essential. The dichotomy between hero and Spectre, between soul and self, has a corresponding split in the potential, the capability rather than mere actuality, of the psyche. Each personality (male) has such an Emanation (female), and the Emanation is also inherently capable of division into a fixed state, so that a Shadow, the counterpart of the Spectre, arises. To turn into abstraction (Blake's greatest loathing) what he realizes in mythology, Albion is man's soul; Albion's Spectre is his "Rational Power

. . . the Great Selfhood / Satan" (29:5, 17–18); Jerusalem is the supreme freedom to realize perfection; Vala, the Shadowy Female Will, is the earth-mother, Nature. In a perfectly balanced psyche neither Spectre nor Shadow would appear; and fact and capability would be united in perfect harmony. The fall produces mental bifurcation and alienation, a fourfold, internecine striving for dominance that can be catastrophic. The complication of this Jungian mental landscape is that the four temperaments of the mind, the four Zoas, are each capable of such a four-way split as well. These four—Luvah, Urizen, Los (Urthona), and Tharmas—represent, respectively, sexual energy, abstract form, imaginative form, and unifying energy, the last (Tharmas) being dormant until the resurrection.

The dynamic forces of *Jerusalem* are thus of greater complexity than those of *Paradise Regained,* as Blake attempts to portray simultaneously, as it were, both Christ's and man's assumption of divinity. Since, to Blake, Christ is the divine vision in man, man's salvation directly depends upon clarifying that vision—surely Milton's point in terming such a process the regaining of Paradise. In turn, Blake continually emphasizes Milton's metaphor of the wilderness. The epigraph of the poem, which appears on the first plate of the poetic text, Μονος ὁ Ιεσους, bears in Greek as in English a dual sense: "Jesus alone"—unique, but forsaken and in solitude as well. The metaphor is enriched as Blake follows Milton's example in *Paradise Lost* and identifies as epic poet with the struggle he depicts.

> Trembling I sit day and night, my friends are astonish'd at me.
> Yet they forgive my wanderings, I rest not from my great task!
> To open the Eternal Worlds, to open the immortal Eyes
> Of Man inwards into the Worlds of Thought: into Eternity
> Ever expanding in the Bosom of God. the Human Imagination
> O Saviour pour upon me thy Spirit of meekness & love:
> Annihilate the Selfhood in me, be thou all my life!
>
> (5:16–22)

The epic poet is the man between, striving for the epiphanic moment by which he is remade in the bosom of God, the Imagination, but forced to labor toward that revelation in the land of Albion, which is a spiritual wilderness.

> But all within is open'd into the deeps of Entuthon Benython
> A dark and unknown night, indefinite, unmeasurable, without end.

Abstract Philosophy warring in enmity against Imagination
(Which is the Divine Body of the Lord Jesus. blessed for ever).
                                                        (5:56–59)

It is only after he has fixed his own crucial position—that of Christ in
Book IV of *Paradise Regained*, preferring visionary prophecy to the
heathen abstractors invoked by Satan—that Blake calls forth the great
imaginative protagonist of his poem, Los, who will strive against his
Selfhood and fallen man for the redemption of Albion. If that conflict
occupies all history, it is also centered in William Blake. The four chapters of *Jerusalem* are the gospels of his mental life and of the life of
humanity. That Los is incarnate within Blake is manifest in Plate 15,
his second invocation which follows Blake's survey of the spiritual realm
and his introduction of the monstrous Polypus of the twelve sons of
Albion who oppose it:

> I see the Past, Present & Future, existing all at once
> Before me; O Divine Spirit sustain me on thy wings!
> That I may awake Albion from his long & cold repose.
>   (15:8–10)

The first episode of *Jerusalem* is Los' effort to subordinate his Spectre to his will. Driven by materialist logic, the Spectre turns on Los for
his fruitless attempts to save the sinful Albion, who refuses salvation
on Los' terms. The Spectre, Los' "Pride & Self-righteousness" (8:30), demands his freedom from painful servitude to so ungrateful a task, suggesting that Albion's continued defiance merits his destruction. To this
end the Spectre argues, like the Satan of *Paradise Regained*, in "temptations of doubt & despair" (10:33) against the divine purpose Los has
undertaken:

> To lure Los: by tears, by arguments of science & by terrors:
> Terrors in every Nerve, by spasms & extended pains:
> While Los answer'd unterrified to the opake blackening Fiend[.]
>   (7:6–8)

Blake derives both the Spectre's superb rationality and his subtle method
of intellectual harassment from *Paradise Regained*; but his psychological prototype is the Satan of *Paradise Lost*. In the Spectre's long lament
for his condition, Blake rhetorically and symbolically echoes Satan's
soliloquy in the fourth book:

I said: now is my grief at worst: incapable of being
Surpassed: but every moment it accumulates more & more
It continues accumulating to eternity! the joys of God advance
For he is Righteous: he is not a Being of Pity & Compassion
He cannot feel Distress: he feeds on Sacrifice & Offering:
Delighting in cries & tears, & clothed in holiness & solitude
But my griefs advance also, for ever & ever without end
O that I could cease to be! Despair! I am Despair
                                      . . . Life lives on my
Consuming: & the Almighty hath made me his Contrary
To be all evil, all reversed & for ever dead.
                                     (10:44–51; 55–57)

With the conflict unresolved, plagued by raging self-doubt, Los returns to his forge and the creation of his great imaginative city of God,
Golgonooza—the spiritual, fourfold London that must be hammered out
upon Los' anvils in eternal mental labor. Despite his isolation and discomfort, Los is reconciled to the necessity under which he strives. Blake's
emphasis thus turns to the even more dire condition of Albion, unable
either to endure the fallen state or to alter it. The second movement of
Chapter 1 records the efforts of the sons of Albion to cast out Jerusalem,
who is conceived as responsible for man's fallen condition. Spiritual
freedom, Albion defines as "Inward complacency of Soul" (23:15), and
he banishes, as he hopes, all temptation to sin through acceptance of a
rigid moral code. If he cannot make the wilderness bloom, man can at
least mark out its boundaries, its topography, its terrors. The chapter
ends with an epiphany for Albion: in accepting the wilderness of Ulro,
the single vision of law, he has denied the imaginative redemption of the
Lamb of God:

O Human Imagination O Divine Body I have Crucified
I have turned my back upon thee into the Wastes of Moral Law.
                                     (24:23–24)

Christ's refusal to succumb to temptation arose not from a moral code
but from imaginative insight. In Blake's terms, Christ entered the desert
to the end that he might redeem man from the original wanderer in the
wilderness, Moses.

As Chapter 1 began with the struggle between Los and his Spectre.
Chapter 2 pursues the conflict on a less hopeful level, reduced to the
schizophrenic state of Albion's soul. He has assumed God's providence
to end the assumption of God's providence (sin) in his sons: as moral

arbiter, his seat is overhung by the branches of the Tree of Moral Virtue, which themselves send down roots to form a vast and impenetrable prison of natural law. A dialectical materialism ensues, progressively circumscribing man's capabilities until his mind is adapted to the natural law he has invoked: a cycle dependent on revenge, a civil war in nations and in minds. To forestall the logical outcome of this strife, suicide, the Savior must intercede and repose Albion in deathlike sleep upon the Rock of Ages:

> Hark! & Record the terrible wonder! that the Punisher
> Mingles with his Victims Spectre, enslaved and tormented
> To him whom he has murderd, bound in vengeance & enmity
> Shudder not, but Write, & the hand of God will assist you!
> Therefore I write Albions last words. Hope is banish'd from me.
> (47:14–18)

Los' function in the second and third chapters has no exact parallel in *Paradise Regained*, but if one were to treat the central temptation as wholly symbolic of Christ's future office in replacing human power struggles with the divine kingdom, the central half of *Jerusalem* would have its counterpart in Christ's gathering awareness of where his public duties lie. Albion must thread his way through the maze of his own error: no external agency but Truth and that Providence which forestalls universal devastation can be an effective aid to this end. So in the great 42nd plate of *Jerusalem*, Los, spurning Albion's demand for "righteousness & justice" (42:12), confronts Albion with his own hypocritical evil and counters, as Christ does, the charge that he has been ineffectual in redeeming man from its consequences. The argument has its decided parallel in *Paradise Regained*, for a redemptive Christ must nevertheless refuse intrusion into Satan's wars on earth.

>   . . . am I to be only
> Merciful to thee and cruel to all that thou hatest [?]
> Thou wast the Image of God surrounded by the Four Zoa's
> Three thou hast slain! I am the Fourth: thou canst not destroy me.
> Thou art in Error; trouble me not with thy righteousness.
> I have innocence to defend and ignorance to instruct:
> I have no time for seeming; and little arts of compliment,
> In morality and virtue: in self-glorying and pride.
>   . . . do thou be righteous,
> And I will return it; otherwise I defy thy worst revenge:
> Consider me as thine enemy: on me turn all thy fury

But destroy not these little ones, nor mock the Lords anointed:
Destroy not by Moral Virtue, the little ones whom he hath chosen!
The little ones whom he hath chosen in preference to thee.
He hath cast thee off for ever; the little ones he hath anointed!
Thy Selfhood is for ever accursed from the Divine presence[.]
                                                    (42:21–28; 38–45)

   With the soul now dormant, the third chapter focuses on Los' efforts to force the sons and daughters of Albion to free themselves from
the spiritless realm they have embraced. That realm is under the tyranny
of the Satan of *Paradise Regained*:

Where is that Friend of Sinners! that Rebel against my Laws!
Who teaches Belief to the Nations, & an unknown Eternal Life
Come hither into the Desert & turn these stones to bread. (54:19–21)

To create an exit from the spectrous world of Ulro, the rockbound nadir
of vision, Los fashions the perpetual cycle of generation, presided over
by the Druidic deities of Tirzah and Rahab, Nature and Religion, dependent on female chastity and slaughter.[22] The central event is the construction of the petrific Stonehenge:

The Building is Natural Religion & its Altars Natural Morality
A building of eternal death: whose proportions are eternal despair[.]
                                                        (66:8–9)

Again, Los' imperative is comprehension, sufficient clarity to be able
to discover the means for converting despair into apocalypse. With the
daughters of Albion uniting in Rahab and the sons in the warrior Hand;
with Luvah, the Zoa of fertility, crucified on Albion's tree; with the
continents measured and national limits formed, "the Great Polypus of
Generation covered the Earth" (67:34) in a vast parody of the imaginative structure of Golgonooza. As Chapter 3 moves to its climax, the
antithetical forces of the modern world are drawn into array: on the one
hand the rationalists, deists, and feudal aristocracy of the earth, all
"Created by Rahab & Tirzah in Ulro" (73:39); on the other hand, the
patriarchs and prophets, the idealist philosophers and poets, created by
Los "to preserve them from Eternal Death" (73:40). The ultimate conflict is simple, the central conflict of all of Blake's work: between nature and the imagination. Blake once more intrudes to pray, like Los,
for comprehension, and in sudden awareness sees that the natural

London, this perversion of Golgonooza built by the twenty-seven her-maphroditic churches of state religion, is Babylon, presided over by the unholy spirit—Rahab:

> thus Rahab is reveald
> Mystery Babylon the Great: the Abomination of Desolation
> Religion hid in War: a Dragon red, & hidden Harlot
> But Jesus breaking thro' the Central Zones of Death & Hell
> Opens Eternity in Time & Space; triumphant in Mercy[.]
> (75:18–22)

Chapter 4 thus opens on the equivalent of Christ's encompassing vision of the Romans and Parthians, the night of Rahab's dominion, a universal naturalism that bears within it the seeds of its own destruction and redemption. Jerusalem, lamenting the decline of man, is answered by Vala, the earth-mother, who laments in terms startlingly like those of Shelley's Prometheus, chained to his rock:

> I walk in affliction: I am a worm, and no living soul!
> A worm going to eternal torment! raisd up in a night
> To an eternal night of pain, lost! lost! lost! for ever! (80:3–5)

Vala's self-justification, to expiate her own divorce from spiritual reality, brings on universal slaughter. The daughters of Albion, the passive vortex to which the sons must return, now attack the independence of the male principle, in fear seeking to gain dominion over it. Thus the natural principle leads to its own negation, a deism that denies individual will and locks man into a wholly deterministic, wholly meaningless cycle. For Los the end is in sight, but that understanding precipitates a sudden, catastrophic threat to his integrity. Overconfident in his enthusiasm, Los sings a sublime hymn to Jerusalem, which produces the jealous fragmentation of his own Emanation, Enitharmon, who fears the effect of the transcendent love Los envisions. Like one of the daughters of Albion, Enitharmon turns on Los' masculinity, demanding power over him, claiming—as Satan implicitly does—the integrity of becoming against being. Confronted with this sudden revolt, Los immediately understands its cause:

> A sullen smile broke from the Spectre in mockery &
>   scorn
> Knowing himself the author of their divisions &
>   shrinkings. . . . (88:34–35)

Los is himself now the epitome of the universal struggle between Satanic pride and liberated capability, "the victim of their love / And hate" (88:46–47), in his impotence the possible agent of man's destruction. Jerusalem has accepted the poison of jealousy proffered by Vala, and the Covering Cherub, who bars Eden from man's grasp, has arisen bearing the tabernacle of Tirzah and Rahab: Holy War to the last man impends.

So involved an account of the gathering climax of *Jerusalem* is necessary in order to intimate how fully Blake has recreated the final combined temptation and realization of *Paradise Regained*. Satan's act of violence against Christ necessitates not just firmness of purpose and strength of will, but a spiritual act of survival for Christ and, through him, for mankind. There is only one means to this: the casting off of his humanity and the assumption of divinity. To Blake the Enlightenment was a dark, Satanic act of violence against the character of man, a deistic reduction into the Ulro of absolute materialism. The alternatives it presupposed were world conflagration—the Napoleonic wars—or self-redemption. In the "Sublime Allegory" of *Jerusalem*, the climax comes through Los' recognition of his divided nature and his resolution to annihilate the division.[23] He turns upon his spectre (plate 91), suddenly aware that it was this Spectre, demanding adherence to its own law, that had produced the vast and inhuman framework of Natural Religion. When the Spectre, refusing to accept its culpability, defies Los' command that it dissolve deism through the love of God, Los, like Christ on the pinnacle, denies the Satanic integrity:

> . . . Los beheld undaunted furious
> His heavd Hammer; he swung it round & at one blow,
> In unpitying ruin driving down the pyramids of pride
> Smiting the Spectre on his Anvil & the integuments of his Eye
> And Ear unbinding in dire pain, with many blows,
> Of strict severity self-subduing, & with many tears labouring.
> (91:41–46)

The Spectre is compelled into annihilating identity with Los, and Enitharmon laments the eradication of potential in the attainment of the *eschaton*: "The Poets Song draws to its period & Enitharmon is no more" (92:8). The converging unity of Blake's conception reflects the selfless harmonizing of Los' personality: the apocalypse has come; and Albion is regenerate, saved by Christ's offering of himself for man's soul: "And the Divine Appearance was the likeness & similitude of Los" (96:7).

The poem has here attained its ultimate epiphany, as Los, "The labourer of ages in the Valleys of Despair" (83:53), denies his Selfhood to become divine redeemer. The regained paradise into which all living things enter in a spiritual state will endure "for ever / In Forgiveness of Sins which is Self Annihilation. it is the Covenant of Jehovah" (98:22–23).

Jerusalem, for all its complexity, is predicated on a principle of utmost simplicity: if in the natural world we are defined by our constantly altering individuality, in the spiritual world all beings are one. When the richness of narrative and symbolic patterns is reduced to the singular spiritual reality that underlies them, we are left with the plot of *Paradise Regained*. In other words, *Jerusalem* enlarges the vision of *Paradise Regained* to encompass all of humanity and all of human history. The fallen man leaves Eden to encounter a wilderness in which, through the mental struggle with his Selfhood, he rises slowly toward the pinnacle where he must undergo his final and most critical spiritual test, his willingness to annihilate his individual humanity and undertake the divine giving of self which is eternal forgiveness. Christ and Satan—imaginative vision and rationalizing Selfhood—are antipodes in the spiritual life of all men. But, whereas the Selfhood is a negation of the personality and must be destroyed, the Emanation, the Heavenly City of infinite promise, is a contrary with which the soul unites in holy nuptials after its purgation of the Selfhood. The penultimate engraving of *Jerusalem*, Plate 99, depicts this ecstatic union of man and God.

Jerusalem was finished no later than 1820, the year Shelley printed his masterpiece *Prometheus Unbound*. Although no possibility exists of influence between either work, the poems bear a remarkable coincidence in archetypal patterns. In both, there is a single protagonist whose various manifestations occur as fully articulated characters. In both, too, the Selfhood is cast out; and a divine union of masculine and feminine characteristics signals the regeneration of the universe. In his use of mythology, Shelley represents something of a bridge between Keats and Blake. For though, like Keats, he rejects Christian archetypes in favor of classical ones, he explicitly establishes the Christian context of *Prometheus Unbound* through frequent allusions to the later mythology. Such a procedure was natural to this writer, whose devotion to Greek thought and literature was as strong as his detestation of institutional Christianity. To suggest analogies in the life of Christ to his Greek original allowed Shelley to pay his profound respect to the Christian mythology without compromising the integrity of his sometimes stridently defended agnosticism.

Although *Prometheus Unbound* is the most original reworking of
the materials of *Paradise Regained* among the three poems under discussion, it is in some respects also the most consciously indebted of them.
Indeed, the originality of Shelley's conception of his myth is most
clearly portrayed in the instance where his debt is also the most pronounced. The brief opening scene of Act III, in which Demogorgon
overthrows Jupiter, is actually the climax of the dramatic conflict; but,
like the climax of *Paradise Regained*, it has frequently disturbed those
readers anticipating inflated histrionics.[24] Shelley carefully follows Milton in making the last battle no contest at all. Jupiter's final act, like
Satan's, is one of arrogant folly; his overstepping of eternal bounds confirms a self-delusion bordering on stupidity. Jupiter's sudden fall "on
the wide waves of ruin" (III.i.71), after challenging Demogorgon, is an
exact parallel to Satan's fall from the pinnacle, "whence he stood to see
his Victor fall" (IV.571). But Demogorgon is an agent of the logical
necessity deriving from another's act; and the event which occasions the
fall occurs at the very beginning of the drama, in Prometheus' expression of pity for Jupiter's deranged and power-hungry mind (I.53).
That the pinnacle episode in this work thus spans two acts suggests a
divergence from Milton's conception of his myth, a conscious attempt
on Shelley's part to create an eschatology inclusive of Christian principles, but based in a secular humanism that envisions the apocalypse as
within the capabilities of a godless race of men.

Prometheus Unbound does not concentrate upon the struggle between self and soul preceding a conscious assumption of divinity, the
subject of *Paradise Regained* and its Romantic successors. Its focus is
more positively ethical, directly centered on the impact of an ethical decision on the world we inhabit. Prometheus, against all the values he
has sustained through thirty centuries of torture, must make a choice
which stems from the deepest sources of human nature.[25] Aware that
he is betraying the conflict he has waged so long—his mental act rebuked
by the Earth and superciliously defended by Ione as a momentary lapse
—Prometheus must nonetheless grant forgiveness to all creation, including Jupiter: "I wish no living thing to suffer pain" (I.305). This fundamental ethical assertion is man's claim to divinity, even though it is
neither conceived nor understood as such until late in the drama. The
period between the decision and its paradoxical consequence, the fall
of Jupiter, marks Prometheus' attempts to realize within himself its
logical implications and resolve the conflict between his humanity and
the will it has seemingly betrayed.

The three sets of visitors to the scene of Prometheus' torture in the first act intrude upon the mental landscape of his mind the alternatives following upon his decision. The sycophantic Mercury, who is in the deepest sense of the term a time-server, presents Prometheus with the opportunity to reconcile himself with Jupiter: in Blake's universe this would be tantamount to Los' becoming servant to the net of natural morality spread by Tirzah and Rahab. To reject so patent a temptation to evil is easily within the determination of one who has withstood Jupiter's tyranny for centuries. But the Furies who descend to tempt Prometheus next as manifestations of his darkest fears are not so comfortably dismissed. Even as Prometheus surmounts the doubts that arise from his ethical decision—asserting, "Yet am I king over myself, and rule / The torturing and conflicting throngs within" (I.492–493)—his fears intensify into external threats. The rapidly accumulating visions of human depravity, state repression, and the failure of liberating influences rise to the epitomizing symbol, the crucifixion of Christ in a martyrdom without meaning or effect. Thus tempted to renew his defiance of Jupiter, Prometheus withstands the terrifying visions of his own mind: "I pity those they torture not" (I.633). Deprived of substance, the Furies of his mind vanish, and are replaced by contrasting visions of hope. The revelation toward which the entire act has driven Prometheus comes in the pause between these contrary projections of mental turmoil. Repeating the despairing refrain of his torture—"Alas! pain, pain ever, for ever!" (I.635), Prometheus at last assigns its cause.

> I close my tearless eyes, but see more clear
> Thy works within my woe-illuméd mind,
> Thou subtle tyrant! (I.636–638)

The curse with which Prometheus denounced the tyrannical Jupiter when he abused the knowledge the Titan brought to earth, revoked in pity at the beginning of the drama, was paradoxically responsible for maintaining Jupiter on his throne. Jupiter *is* Prometheus' defiant selfhood, a tyrannical force because of the negative nature of defiance.[26] But if Prometheus' withdrawal into forgiveness must dethrone the tyrannical principle, this can only occur when Prometheus has regained his active nature. Torn between the fears and aspirations of his own mind, Prometheus at the end of Act I has risen from hell to limbo, a state in which mental power is of itself insufficient to resolve the inner conflict. Prometheus' allegorical role, as a figure for the mind of man, is thus a truly functional one. The mind has been illuminated, but the revelation accompanies its ethical certitude with a sharpened understanding of the inadequacies of the mere intellect. If it is faith that enables Christ to transform himself from man to God, an equivalent force is necessary in Shelley's universe. For a sceptic, faith is too easily capable of perversion to be the active and therefore redemptive virtue: the necessary correlative to intellect in Shelley's terms is the simultaneously passionate and idealized love of Asia.

Act II is less obviously epiphanic in movement than Act I of *Prometheus Unbound*, but it is no less truly devoted to an awakening in Asia corresponding to that in Prometheus. The passions, too, must come to know themselves, to understand that when the mind is dormant, its capability to love is similarly restricted (so Asia has remained in her Indian vale during Prometheus' long imprisonment); but that upon the liberation of the mind, love becomes the active principle compelling all before it. In a complicated series of dreams within dreams Asia descends to Demogorgon's cave, the epipsyche which is Shelley's version of the Christian unity of center and circumference, there to ask the fundamental metaphysical questions of *Prometheus Unbound*. Demogorgon's oblique responses have been troubling to many readers, who have been misled, perhaps by too much pedagogy, to expect that the one questioned should provide acceptable answers. It is not, however, Demogorgon who answers: it is Asia—"I feel, I know it" (II.iv.31)—who has attained the knowledge at the center of her being, the seat of Love which is Demogorgon. In this state she projects the restitution of Paradise. Asking, "When shall the destined hour arrive?" (II.iv.128), she sees it arrive. Demogorgon, who is the antithetical extension within Asia of the Jupiter within Prometheus, is thus the emissary who dismisses Jupiter from his throne. The fourfold, almost mathematical, relationship between the faculties of humanity is remarkably Blakean in concept, though diverging in actual terms from Blake's. The four stages through which Shelley's drama moves mark a progress from the finite to the infinite, similar to Blake's four stages of vision.[27] The central figure of Act I is Jupiter (although he, himself, never actually appears); that of Act II, Asia; of Act III, Prometheus; of Act IV, Demogorgon.

Prometheus Unbound, rather than revising the prototypal structures Milton built in *Paradise Regained*, subsumes those structures by concentrating on the internal and eternal psychological verities of the revelation on the pinnacle and then by extending its vision into the necessary relationship between such a revelation and a humanist apocalypse. There are dual epiphanies in the drama, that of Prometheus near the beginning of Act I (who is, with brilliantly imaginative literalness, crucified upon the pinnacle of a mountain), and that of Asia, his counter-part, within the corresponding depths of the earth near the end of Act II. Jupiter's fall from his pinnacle at the beginning of Act III is similarly balanced by Demogorgon's organization of eternity at the end of Act IV. As in *Paradise Regained*, the movement is one of continually ex-panding consciousness, proceeding from the physical torments of Act I to the social and political democratizing of the end.

The clear relevance of *Paradise Regained* to the subtly interwoven structures of *Prometheus Unbound* may be, at this point, more obvious than the pretentious assumption that Shelley's poem is an epic. Drama and epic have been polarized forms in the minds of critics ever since Aristotle chose them as the antitheses around which to construct his *Poetics*. And of the Romantic poets Shelley's understanding of and commitment to formal genres was the most highly refined. It is, how-ever, interesting to note that the work most closely resembling *Prome-theus Unbound* among the poems of his contemporaries, Byron's *Cain*, received Shelley's encomium as "finer poetry than has appeared in En-gland since the publication of Paradise Regained.—Cain is apocalyptic. . . ."[28] Shelley's point of comparison is just, if overly modest, for though more fundamentally dramatic than *Prometheus Unbound* and written in three acts, *Cain* in its lengthy metaphysical dialogues between Cain and Lucifer is more directly modelled after the dramatic mode of *Para-dise Regained* than any of the epics of the Romantic poets. Perhaps what Shelley was attempting in *Prometheus Unbound* is most apparent when one realizes that after the Romantic period only one major literary venture has copied the form Shelley created in *Prometheus Unbound*— Thomas Hardy's hybrid epic-drama, *The Dynasts*.[29]

The formal generic designation Shelley gave to *Prometheus Un-bound* was "lyrical drama." That term has stood without serious ques-tion for a century and a half despite its oxymoronic nature. Shelley's "lyrical drama" is a careful contradiction in terms, an *exemplum* of how the Romantic imagination, as Coleridge conceived it, could unite intel-lectually irreconcilable elements. Drama is time-bound, conceiving the world as a scene of action understandable within the framework of a linear progression. Lyric, on the other hand, strives to destroy time, to render it irrelevant through epiphanic moments, what Wordsworth called "spots of time," in which time is literally stopped and the instant is expanded into a metaphorical eternity. The fourth act of *Prometheus*

Unbound opens upon a chorus of dead hours who "bear Time to his tomb in eternity" (IV.14), and the drama is exquisitely poised between its conflicting allegiances to time and eternity, to the psychological development of comprehension in Acts I and II as well as to the climax that occurs at the beginning of the play and is simultaneously Demogorgon's call to eternity at the end.

The difference between stage drama and "lyrical drama" is exactly parallel to the distinction between the diffuse epic and the brief epic Milton created in *Paradise Regained.* The diffuse epic derives its archetypal models from men of action, whose heroism and honor depend upon their single-minded commitment to a linear projection of time even while aware of its transitory nature. If that is pathetic, it is not sublime. In *Paradise Regained,* on the other hand, the dialogues between Christ and Satan are subsumed by the epiphanic moment on the pinnacle, which is literally for Milton *the* moment divorced from time, irreversible, apocalyptic. Christ himself is further and further separated from a time-bound world as he progresses from a victory over the basic necessity of food to a triumph over the most fundamental of all human necessities, the ego. The romantic brief epic, in following Milton's example, concentrated on the metaphysical as well as aesthetic possibilities of a form thus defined.[30] It was, to them as to Milton, an internalized genre, instinct with prophetic truth, adopting as hero a type of Christ and equating his ritual of self-purification with the regaining of Paradise on earth. Evil, as self-motivated, could be self-destroyed. The form is thus profoundly personal in character, radical in its social implications, and apocalyptic in its literary as well as philosophical intentions. In contracting the grand stage of encyclopedic thought and action to the epitome of sublime awareness, it destroyed the diffuse epic, as inadequate to human vision, to build eternity in its place.

NOTES

1. *"Paradise Lost*: The Anti-Epic," in *Approaches to Paradise Lost,* ed. C. A. Patrides (Toronto, 1968), p. 98.

2. Note, for instance, the epic catalogue of Rome's possessions—IV.44–79—an ironic survey of the known world discovering only encyclopedic bondage. This, except for Satan's council scene, is the only major use of epic convention in *Paradise Regained.*

3. Obvious objection can be raised to Coleridge as an epic poet; but see Karl Kroeber, " 'The Rime of the Ancient Mariner' as Stylized Epic," *Transactions of the Wisconsin Academy of Sciences, Arts, and Letters,* XLVI (1957), 179–187.

4. (Madison and Milwaukee, 1965). Wilkie's opening chapter is the pertinent statement on the debt of the entire Romantic movement to previous epic traditions; for a discussion of epic traditions as they impinge on Blake's work, see Wilkie's "Epic Irony in *Milton*," in *Blake's Visionary Forms Dramatic*, ed. David V. Erdman and John E. Grant (Princeton, 1970), pp. 359–372.

5. *Romantic Narrative Art* (Madison, 1960), p. 103. The ensuing discussion of the influence of *Paradise Regained* on the Romantic epic is illuminated by Kroeber's description of the archetypal narrative pattern that, he claims, descends from *The Prelude*: "Its hero rejects, or is rejected by, his civilization; hence his journey is above all a spiritual journey through 'The Heart of Darkness' to a personal salvation that may—but need not—be Christian salvation" (p. 103). This is the pattern of each of the epics to be discussed, all of them of course, including *Paradise Regained*, antedating publication of *The Prelude*.

6. "The Long Poem in the Age of Wordsworth," *Oxford Lectures in Poetry*, 2nd ed. (Bloomington, 1961), pp. 177–205.

7. This was Coleridge's view, expressed in 1807: "Readers would not have been disappointed in [*Paradise Regained*], if they had proceeded to it with the proper preconception of *the kind* of interest intended to be excited in that admirable work. In its kind, it is the most *perfect* poem extant" ("Annotations to Hayley's *Life of Milton*," in *The Romantics on Milton: Formal Essays and Critical Asides*, ed. Joseph Anthony Wittreich, Jr. [Cleveland and London, 1970], p. 175). Some years later, in 1836, Wordsworth made much the same point, praising *Paradise Regained* to Henry Crabb Robinson as "surpassing even the *Paradise Lost* in perfection of execution, though the theme is far below it and demanding less power" (Wittreich, p. 138).

8. Citations from the four works will occur parenthetically within the text. The editions referred to are: *John Milton: Complete Poems and Major Prose*, ed. Merritt Y. Hughes (New York, 1957); *John Keats: Selected Poems and Letters*, ed. Douglas Bush (Cambridge, 1959); *The Poetry and Prose of William Blake*, ed. David V. Erdman (Garden City, N. Y., 1970); *The Complete Poetical Works of Percy Bysshe Shelley*, ed. Thomas Hutchinson (London, 1905).

9. See Barbara Kiefer Lewalski, *Milton's Brief Epic: The Genre, Meaning, and Art of Paradise Regained* (Providence and London, 1966), p. 55.

10. It should be noted that *Hyperion's* structure seems to presuppose a four-book form in its finished state: see Ernest de Selincourt's note to his edition of the *Poems of John Keats* (London, 1926), pp. 488–489.

11. "Preface" to *Endymion*, Bush, p. 38.

12. Mrs. Lewalski begins her study with the relevant passages from the Gospel according to St. Luke; however, Elizabeth Marie Pope—in *Paradise Regained: The Tradition and the Poem* (Baltimore, 1947), p. 5—suggests, after comparing the Gospel accounts, that Milton's chief source was Matthew.

13. The generic hurdle of "romance" should be confronted, if only that it may be safely left behind. *Endymion*, subtitled "A Poetic Romance," looks back to Spenser for its allegorical mode; yet, just as Spenser's allegory forces *The Faerie Queene* into epic dimensions, so the internalized allegory of *Endymion* establishes the poetic reality not in a rarefied world of legend, but in the actual and most immediate domain of the psyche. Exactly the same shift occurs in *Childe Harold's Pilgrimage*, also "A Romaunt," which could, with some stretching, be claimed as a four-book epic whose concerns are similar to those discussed herein. But since it attained its four divisions more by chance than original design, it would seem wise to leave it to its unique place in English literary history.

14. Interestingly, Christ's recapitulation of his history in order to reveal the unified coherence by which he will shape the future of man (I.196–293) furnishes the archetypal pattern of Wordsworth's *Prelude*.

15.   Or, as Bernard Blackstone puts it in *The Consecrated Urn* (London, 1959): Cybele "is the ultimate vision in the chthonic world, the supreme dispenser of the mysteries. She represents the nadir of Endymion's descent. And because she is the ultimate, she is also the inexplicable" (p. 143). Blackstone's last comment may suggest why most writers on the poem quietly ignore this scene.

16.   Keats' prayer comes in his impassioned invocation to the Muse for enlightenment and thus protection from despondency. The similarity of Milton's invocations in Books III and VII of *Paradise Lost* is obvious.

17.   Samuel Taylor Coleridge, *Biographia Literaria*, ed. J. Shawcross (London, 1907), I, 202.

18.   *Fearful Symmetry* (Princeton, 1947), p. 269. Frye's analysis of the epic in this study is one of the most illuminating and valuable that exists; see pp. 313–325.

19.   *Blake's Apocalypse* (Garden City, N.Y., 1963), p. 304.

20.   A further testament to Blake's indebtedness to *Paradise Regained* is the curious reworking of the final line of Milton's poem scrawled on the back of a drawing for Plate 42: "Father & Mother I return from flames of fire tried & pure & white" (Erdman, p. 730).

21.   One wonders whether Tasso's title, *Gerusalemme Liberata*, was not instrumental to Blake's identification of Jerusalem with Liberty. Whatever the source, the underlying conception of Liberty is an extension of Milton's thoughts in *Paradise Lost*, Book XII, and *Paradise Regained*, Books III and IV.

22.   Against this rapidly increasing horror, Blake places the digression of Plates 61 and 62. There, the Lamb descends to comfort Jerusalem and sends her forth into the wilderness under his protection.

23.   "Sublime Allegory" is a term Blake uses to define his epic mode in a letter to Thomas Butts of July 6, 1803—*The Complete Writings of William Blake*, ed. Geoffrey Keynes (London, 1966), p. 825. It is also a particularly apt term for the tradition of the brief epic emanating from *Paradise Regained*.

24.   This is especially the case in *Prometheus Unbound*, inasmuch as this is Jupiter's only actual appearance in the drama.

25.   It must be understood that Prometheus, as man's immortal intercessor with the tyrant Jupiter, represents an archetypal human figure.

26.   The identification of Jupiter as Prometheus' *doppelgänger* in Act I, I have traced at greater length in "Manfred in the Caucasus," a paper read to the English 9 meeting of the Modern Language Association (Denver, 1969). The present reading of *Prometheus Unbound* is a greatly compressed version of that to be included in my forthcoming study of Shelley's 1819 poems.

27.   In Blakean terms, Shelley's order would reverse the central stages: Ulro, Beulah, Generation, Eden.

28.   Letter to John Gisborne, January 22, 1822 (Wittreich, *The Romantics on Milton*, p. 541). *Cain*, written a year after *Prometheus Unbound* and heavily indebted to it for expanding the too restrictive landscape of *Manfred*, has yet to be investigated in relationship to Shelley's drama.

29.   It should be noted that the first introduction of formal dramatic dialogue into the English epic occurs in Southey's *Thalaba* (1801). If neglected today, the Southey epics had a remarkable influence on his contemporaries.

30.   The generic proximity of *Samson Agonistes*, less a closet drama than a psychodrama, to *Paradise Regained* has its counterpart in the close relationship of *The Cenci* to *Prometheus Unbound*; indeed, of Romantic drama to the Romantic epic.

The Date of *Samson Agonistes* Again

WILLIAM RILEY PARKER
1906–1969

I first thought of calling this paper "Dalila, or the Problem of Dating Samson."[1] This I abandoned as not only undignified but positively misleading, for Dalila had little trouble dating Samson, and I have had a great deal. I mention my temporary aberration only as a prelude to noting that this is the second time I have written a paper with my present sober title. My first attempt to date *Samson Agonistes* was in a talk at Johns Hopkins University in 1937. I did not know, then, the right answer to the question I was raising—and I do not know it now. But I knew enough, then, to recognize a real problem, the existence of which had not even been suspected before; and I know enough now, after thirty-two years of thinking about it, and talking about it in graduate seminars, and looking constantly for additional clues, to feel confident that somebody, someday, is going to come up with that single piece of missing evidence that will make everything else fit together and finally reveal its secret. It has been my personal extremely humbling experience, not once but often, to read for the 534th time a line of Milton, or a statement made about him by an early biographer, and suddenly realize what it really says. I last had this experience in connection with the date of *Samson*, eleven years ago, and had to apologize in print for being so stupid in an earlier article. I am prepared to suffer this humiliation again if it will eventually result in discovering the truth. My purpose here, in other words, is to explain the problem, and then to put into my reader's possession all the relevant bits of evidence as I now see them.

Samson Agonistes, Milton's successful attempt to imitate Greek tragedy, was published in 1671—three hundred years ago. It was published as the second piece in a volume that began with *Paradise Regain-*

ed. The signatures are continuous, but *Samson* has its own title page and pagination. When was it written?

If you open almost any book on Milton, or read almost any article published before 1950, you will find an answer given so confidently that the question may seem absurd. *Samson Agonistes*, you will be told firmly, is the last of Milton's poems, and was written in the years 1667–1669, after the publication of *Paradise Lost* and after the composition of *Paradise Regained*. If any space is devoted to the tragedy, the book or article will go on to generalize about how it exhibits Milton's art and thought at the end of his career. But there is a queer thing about all this which it took me about five years to discover. If you go on reading books about Milton, and articles too, you will never come to one that troubles to give a coherent argument for the date that everyone repeats so confidently.

This was a jarring discovery, but a profitable one too, for it taught me to expect and look for this curious phenomenon of our scholarship, and I have found it elsewhere. Montaigne was right: "Nothing is so firmly believed as what we least know." Too many scholars are all too ready to believe the words of the Bellman in *The Hunting of the Snark*: "What I tell you three times is true." Let a conjecture be repeated often enough and it comes to seem a fact.

Of course, *this* conjecture might be true. Since no one else had bothered, I next felt it necessary to find what evidence existed for dating the composition of *Samson Agonistes* in 1667–1669—or in any other period. I began with an important fact: neither in his preface to *Samson Agonistes* nor elsewhere in print did Milton himself say anything explicitly about the date of composition of his dramatic poem. There is, however, a tantalizing sentence in the preface in which Milton speaks of the stage and says, parenthetically: "to which this work never was intended." Why didn't he say: "to which this work *is not* intended"? It could not have been intended for the stage in the period 1642–1660.

I looked next for external evidence. The book in which *Samson Agonistes* was printed in 1671 was licensed July 2, 1670, and registered September 10, 1670. That seemed to account for the years of 1667–1669 instead of 1667–1670. But it proved nothing about the date of composition. Back in the early eighteenth century, someone must have figured: *Samson Agonistes* was printed last, ergo it was written last—a dubious logic that no one would dream of applying to some of Milton's prose, which we know to have been written early and published late. What did Milton's earliest biographers have to say about the matter? I went through the eight earliest with a fine-toothed comb. It later turned out that the comb wasn't fine enough, but I made an immediate discovery, which led me to write that paper at Johns Hopkins so many years ago.

Milton's nephew, Edward Phillips, was a member of his uncle's household during the years 1640–1646 and was later one of the amanuenses for *Paradise Lost*; in his biography of Milton he declares that he paid his uncle "frequent visits to the last." He helps us to date many things. Of *Paradise Lost* he says, "I had the perusal of it from the very beginning." Of *Paradise Regained* he is confident that it was "begun and finished and printed after the other [*Paradise Lost*] was published [1667], and that in a wonderful short space considering the sublimeness of it." What of *Samson Agonistes*? This is what Phillips has to say: "It cannot certainly be concluded when he wrote his excellent tragedy entitled *Samson Agonistes*." Now this statement seemed to me to carry a rebuke to the easy assumptions of later biographers and modern editors. Phillips says, frankly, that he does not know when the tragedy was written. Moreover, he does not guess. Moreover, his confession, taken with the connected remarks about *Paradise Regained* and the "wonderful short space" of its composition, makes it quite clear that he, for one, does not believe *Samson* to have been written after *Paradise Lost*.

Thus released from presupposition, I started wondering when the tragedy might have been written, and Edward Phillips was an obvious wild goose to chase. If he didn't know, clearly *Samson* was written at some time when he was not around. I worked on his biography, and on Milton's too, for it was highly unlikely that *Samson Agonistes* was composed in a period when Milton was very busy with other matters. This investigation was not really fruitful, even though I pressed it to the point of supervising an excellent Ph.D. dissertation on Phillips that turned up other interesting things. The best I could do, by way of establishing a working hypothesis, was to rule out, with Phillips, the traditional years 1667–1669, and also rule out the earlier years, 1640–1646, when Phillips lived with his uncle—and then pinpoint the years 1647–1648 and 1653, as times when Milton might have worked on the tragedy without Phillips' knowledge.

Temporarily frustrated—for all too little is known about Milton's nephew—I cast about for other kinds of evidence. Perhaps the poem itself contained clues. It was at this point that I completely convinced myself that, whatever the correct date, the traditional date is wrong. For *Samson Agonistes* contains rhyme. There is not much—only about 150 lines—but it is there, quite conspicuous at the close, and there are three completely rhyming stanzas in the choral odes. Now, it was in 1668, right in the middle of the period that everyone thought *Samson Agonistes* to have been written, that Milton publicly denounced rhyming verse. All the occasion called for was an explanation and defense of the blank verse of *Paradise Lost,* but Milton went out of his way to damn rhyming in general. He could have limited himself to heroic poetry, but, no, he mentioned drama too. In view of this I concluded, and still conclude, that *Samson Agonistes* could not have been composed in the years immediately preceding or immediately following this public rejection of rhyme.

This was my little argument back in 1937. It was all so tentative, and I was so optimistic about carrying it further, that I did not commit my views to print until a dozen years had passed. Meanwhile, I talked hopefully with other Milton scholars about my suspicions. Some, like Holly Hanford, were horrified; if I was right, an appalling number of books would have to be rewritten. Others, like Allan Gilbert and Harris Fletcher, were sympathetic. Overlooking my conclusions about Edward Phillips, they thought the tragedy might even have been begun early in the 1640's, when Phillips was a student in Milton's household. Fletcher stated this briefly in his edition of the *Poetical Works* in 1941, and Gilbert casually mentioned it in 1947. Both of them also put graduate students to work on the problem. This was more than I had bargained for, and taught me something useful about friendly conversations at MLA meetings. In 1949, therefore, with considerable reluctance, I published an article, "The Date of *Samson Agonistes,*" rehearsing what I have already related and adding some other arguments which we shall come to in a minute. I thought I was careful to make no exaggerated claims in that article, but rather to state my conclusions tentatively and with diffidence. Since then, however, I have sometimes been unable to recognize myself in published summaries of my position. A case in point is the text I am currently using in my Milton classes, edited by my old friend Merritt Hughes. He is obviously upset by the fact that three of his good friends and colleagues, Professors Gilbert, Woodhouse, and Parker—otherwise sane, sensible people—want to date the composition of *Samson Agonistes* earlier than its traditional niche in the chronology, and, what's more, cannot agree among themselves where it should be placed.

Gilbert's position, that *Samson Agonistes* was begun (if not completely written) in the early 1640's, has never been fully, coherently argued, and I do not believe that it can be. It rests largely on some verbal parallels between the preface to *Samson Agonistes* and a tract published in 1642, and on the fact that Samson is among a hundred possible topics for dramas which Milton jotted down in this same period. A compelling argument against it is Edward Phillips' avowed ignorance of the date of composition (and his very evident awareness of compositions actually begun in the disputed period), and also the fact, proved up to the hilt in several unpublished dissertations, that any drama begun by Milton in the early 1640's would have resembled Italian neoclassical drama rather than Greek tragedy. On the other hand, it is surely significant that our only evidence of Milton's interest in dramatic composition is from the period 1641–1645. *Paradise Lost* was begun then, as a drama, but not a Greek drama. The theaters were closed in 1642, but earlier that year Milton had announced publicly his interest in writing a tragedy, and on the title page of his 1645 *Poems* the muse Melpomene appears. At what point did Milton decide to imitate the Greeks, and why? If we could determine this, we would know something important. Of only one thing I am sure: it was not after *Paradise Regained*, with its attack on Hellenic culture, including Attic drama. I would particularly like to know when Milton decided that Aeschylus, as well as Sophocles and Euripides, was a worthy model. This was probably after 1644. In both 1642 and 1644, he had written of Greek tragedy in terms of Sophocles and Euripides alone. Milton's Euripides, purchased in 1634, is now in the Bodleian Library. If his copy of Aeschylus ever comes to light, we may have the missing link in our chain of evidence. Pending that discovery, I am ready to bet that he bought it after, and near, 1645.

Woodhouse's position is that *Samson Agonistes* was written immediately after the Restoration. He argues this cogently and coherently, but from my point of view, also ironically and unconvincingly. Before trying to justify these uncomplimentary words, let me backtrack a little. How was it possible that so many excellent scholars, for so many years, could so confidently assert that *Samson Agonistes* was written in the late 1660's? Behind this uncritical assumption was another, dating from 1746, that had become almost an article of faith. No one, it seems, has ever before doubted for a moment that *Samson* contains a number of hidden (but easily discoverable) allusions to post-Restoration events. Now, I don't know which came first, the chicken or the egg. If you begin by finding these allusions, as John Upton did in 1746 (while finding political allusions also in Shakespeare), then *Samson Agonistes* is of course post-Restoration. Or, if you begin by assuming *Samson* to be post-Restoration, there follows an open season on allusion-finding. What troubles me, not only about *Samson* but also about many other literary works, is the lack of rules for playing this particular game. If I find a topical allusion in something I'm reading, and you cannot see it, how do you prove me wrong? You can't, I'm afraid, unless you can prove that the literary work was composed *before* the event that I am reading into it. Otherwise, my private intuition defies all refutation. I see it; therefore, it is there.

A few illustrations will help. By my count, there are thirteen lines or passages in *Samson Agonistes* in which commentators have seen personal, autobiographical allusions which argue late composition,[2] and nine other lines or passages in which they have seen political allusions to post-Restoration events.[3] Naturally, I have studied all these with great care, for interpretation of them is crucial to dating the poem. The Chorus, in a memorable ode, complains that God, having exalted certain individuals, "Oft leav'st them to the hostile sword / Of heathen and profane, their carcasses / To dogs and fowls a prey" (ll. 692–694). Here we have, according to almost every editor since 1751, a historical allusion to the disinterment and disgrace of the remains of Cromwell, Bradshaw, and Ireton in January 1661. No one has ever objected that the passage says nothing about disinterment, or that the bodies were actually hanged, or that Cromwell, Bradshaw, and Ireton were never victims of the "hostile sword of heathen and profane." But ignore this cavilling. Is it not more to the point that tearing and devouring by dogs and fowls are often God's threatened punishment of the erring Hebrews in the Old Testament? And should we utterly forget what happened to so many crusaders and pilgrims? Indeed, since Milton is Milton, and the passage in question occurs in a Greek tragedy, should we utterly forget the opening lines of the *Iliad*, where the Achaean heroes are described as spoil for dogs and fowls? I think not. But look at almost any recent edition of *Samson* and you will learn how lonely I am in my view. Cromwell, Bradshaw, and Ireton have been seen in that passage, and there seems to be no way of exorcising them.

It is the same way with the alleged personal allusions in the poem. If we are to believe the commentators, Milton is writing about himself when he has the Chorus accuse God: "perhaps in poverty / With sickness and disease thou bow'st them down, / Painful diseases and deformed." The usual footnote on this passage is, to my way of thinking, pathetic: it reminds us that Milton suffered from the gout in his old age. It does not quote Aubrey, the earliest biographer, who writes: "He was very healthy, and free from all diseases, and only towards his later end he was visited with the gout, spring and fall. He would be cheerful even in his gout-fits, and sing." I am not seriously arguing that this would make an appropriate note on the passage; seriously, I would prefer a reminder of Job, who is surely on Milton's mind here and in a number of other passages alleged to be autobiographical.

To get back to the question of date, all twenty-two of the passages supposed to contain personal or political allusions to post-Restoration events refer, if we may believe the editors, to nothing later than 1662. This being so, a handful of scholars have felt that the poem must have been written immediately after the Restoration, rather than in 1668–1669, the traditional date. William Hayley argued this in 1796, and Charles Dunster agreed in 1809. They were pretty much ignored; their dating would not only upset the traditional order, it would put the writing of *Samson Agonistes* squarely in the midst of the composition of *Paradise Lost*. A. J. Church revived the argument in 1872, and he too was ignored. Apparently unaware of these earlier arguments, Arthur Woodhouse came to the same conclusion in 1949; he had been worried about putting *Samson* and *Paradise Regained* so close together, when they clearly differed greatly in doctrine, temper, and tone. But he too, I prophesy, will be ignored. A great difficulty implicit in his argument is that he must pronounce *Samson* eloquently expressive of immediate experience in some respects, but retrospective in others, e.g., Samson's reactions to blindness and unhappy marriage.

Where, then, does all this leave us? It sends us, thank heaven, back to the poem, for closer, more attentive reading than ever before. It also sends us, hunting for clues we may have missed, back to Milton's other writings, and to the words of the early biographers.

Take the so-called Anonymous Biographer, whom I now believe to be Milton's friend and former student Cyriac Skinner. In 1949 I pronounced his comment on *Samson Agonistes* "unhelpful"—words I later had to eat. He cites a group of five works begun by Milton at some unspecified time but all "finished after the Restoration." Three of these, Milton's *History of Britain*, *Accedence Commenc't Grammar*, and *Artis Logicae*, although published from 1669 to 1672, were, we know, begun in the 1640's or earlier. In this same group is *Samson*. The biographer may be mistaken, but it is clear that he believes *Samson* was begun before 1660. This qualifies as documentary evidence. How I missed it I shall try to explain before I close.

Take next Milton's prose. Does it reveal any developing interest in the Samson story? I have already noted that, around 1640 and 1641, Samson turns up among a hundred other topics for possible dramatic treatment. In early 1642, in a 235-word passage, Samson and Dalila are the subjects of a crude little political allegory on King Charles and the bishops. A few years later, in *Areopagitica*, England is described as "a noble and puissant nation rousing herself like a strong man after sleep, and shaking her invincible locks." In 1649, Samson is still a useful analogy, his hair symbolizing the strength of law. All this is highly conventional and unrevealing; no psychological development—so important in the drama—is anywhere implied. In the *Defensio Prima* of 1651, however, a new interest is apparent: Samson is now the lonely champion who fought his country's enemies while his countrymen blamed him. This is a theme of the tragedy. Moreover, in this same passage we find Milton raising, but not answering, a question crucial to the tragedy: Was Samson's warring against the Philistines instigated by God or by his own valor only?

Now let us look at the other poetry. In *Samson Agonistes* Dalila is Samson's wife; in *Paradise Lost* she is mentioned as a harlot (IX.1060–1061)—and her name is spelled differently. What are we to make of this? In *Paradise Regained* Milton not only goes far out of his way (and out of the Christian tradition too) to have the devil praise Greek drama; he also, quite gratuitously, denies a basic assumption of *Samson Agonistes*, which as a tragedy depends upon the truth of something that Milton's divorce tracts of 1643–1645 insist upon repeatedly: that the wisest men can fall victim to feminine charms. *Samson* insists upon this too, and twice expresses the idea by shipwreck imagery (ll. 198–200, 1044–1045). In *Paradise Regained*, however, we are told that "many" men have "easily scorned" the lure of beauty, which stands "in the admiration only of weak minds," and that the Son's constancy must be steered instead against "Rocks whereon greatest men have oftest wrecked." Now, obviously, Milton had to avoid the impropriety of tempting the Son with sex; but there was no need to mention the possibility, nor, having mentioned it, did he need to reject it in language which so strikingly denies to Samson truly heroic stature. That volume of 1671 containing both *Samson Agonistes* and *Paradise Regained* is truly ambivalent, and I, for one, am convinced that *Paradise Regained* was written later than *Samson Agonistes*.

But we have not exhausted all the evidence. We may talk, for example, about the mood and dominant ideas of *Samson*, and try to relate these to Milton's experience. Both Woodhouse and I have attempted this, but we have not succeeded in convincing each other, and perhaps we have cancelled each other out. This kind of evidence tends, of course, to be subjective, and while it cannot be disproved, it rarely persuades those starting with presuppositions that are irreconcilable.

Spelling may turn out to be a clue. The 1671 edition of *Samson Agonistes* contains many spellings that are distinctively Miltonic but many more that are not. Since no manuscript survives, we can only infer that the manuscript sent the printer was in the hand of several amanuenses, and recognize the possibility (it can be nothing more) that part of the manuscript was in Milton's own handwriting—dating, therefore, no later than 1651. A former student of mine who has done an exhaustive study of Milton's spelling has at least convinced himself that *Samson Agonistes* was composed early.

There are a number of individual words or phrases in the poem that may constitute clues. I shall not muster these for you—they will all be discussed in my forthcoming variorum edition of *Samson Agonistes* —but take one as an example. In *Paradise Lost* Milton carefully explains that "Ashtaroth" is a plural form and "Astoreth" a singular (I.422, 438). But in *Samson Agonistes*, as in the *Nativity Ode*, "Astaroth" is a singular. What are we to make of this?

You have probably been wondering when, if ever, I will get around to mentioning prosody. I have saved this for the last, not as a sweet, but, in British fashion, as a savory. Let me serve it with a reminder that the prosody of *Samson* has not, to this day, yielded up its secret to us; that there are more bridges to cross; that the rhythms of Milton's choruses in his tragedy have baffled and delighted critics from the beginning. When we finally solve the mystery of the prosody, the date of composition may reveal itself—and may seem so obvious that we shall marvel that we ever missed it.

In his preface to *Samson*, Milton has the following, self-conscious comment on one aspect of the prosody: "The measure of verse used in the chorus is of all sorts, called by the Greeks *monostrophic*, or rather *apolelymenon*, without regard had to strophe, antistrophe, or epode . . . or, being divided into stanzas or pauses, they may be called *allaeostropha*." Let me translate this. He is saying, in effect, that in the choruses of *Samson Agonistes* he has abandoned all regular stanzaic or strophic divisions. He has felt free to vary the line length and the meter in irregular stanzas to suit the sense or the effect wanted. *Monostrophic* means "single stanza" as contrasted with stanzas that correspond to and parallel each other. *Apolelymenon* means "free from the restraint of correlation."

Now, what prompted Milton to write a Greek tragedy with choral odes lacking strophe and antistrophe? Perhaps there is a clue in Edward Phillips' *Theatrum Poetarum* (1675); he speaks there of "the *Monostro-*

phic, or *Apolelymenon*, used in the choruses of Aeschylus his tragedies."
But let me quote another passage from Milton himself: "A poem of this
kind," he writes, "should perhaps more properly be called *monostrophic*. The meters are in part regular and in part *apolelymenon*." What I
have just cited is a note of explanation appended, not to *Samson*, but to
a Latin ode which Milton composed on January 23, 1647. Which do we
have here, coincidence or clue?

Having followed me thus far, some of you may be thinking that
there are more objective and scientific methods of resolving this problem of date. Why not subject Milton's poetry to the same kind of
detailed analysis of prosody that has proved so useful in the metrical
dating of Shakespeare's plays? Why not produce statistics on the fre-
quencies of strong pauses (terminal and medial), run-on lines, feminine
endings, pyrrhic endings, etc., in the blank verse of, say, *Comus, Paradise Lost, Paradise Regained, Samson Agonistes*? Well, this, too, has
been done. In 1953 Ants Oras, nettled by my suggestion that *Samson*
might have been written early, published sixty-eight pages of statistical
analysis. His conclusion is that I am quite mistaken, and that the traditional chronology of Milton's major poems is firmly established.

Now, I have had a little experience with statistics. I rather enjoy
playing with them. Let's take a look at Oras' statistics. He examines
strong pauses in the major poems. Here are his figures on terminal
pauses: *PL* 49.7, *PR* 65.3, *SA* 69.5. Here they are on medial pauses: *PL*
50.3, *PR* 34.7, *SA* 30.5. These are his figures on run-on lines: *PL* 58.8,
PR 45.2, *SA* 42.1. And so on, with his other statistics. You can see how he
convinced himself: starting with the preconceived notion that the order
of composition was *PL-PR-SA*, he was able to show that this or that
prosodic characteristic either increased or decreased. Being a careful,
thorough scholar, he had also analyzed the prosodic features of the
blank verse of *Comus*, which is indisputably the earliest of the major
poems. Now, let me rearrange his statistics, not to suit any preconceived
notion, but simply to start with *Comus* and show either progression or
regression, increase or decrease.

Here are the terminal pauses again: *Comus* 69.5, *SA* 69.5 (the
same), *PR* 65.3, *PL* 49.7. Here are the medial pauses: *Comus* 30.5, *SA*
also 30.5, *PR* 34.7, *PL* 50.3. Here are the run-on lines: *Comus* 39.9, *SA*
42.1, *PR* 45.2, *PL* 58.8. Here are strong pauses used in run-on contexts:
Comus 52.9, *SA* 62.0, *PR* 75.0, *PL* 78.8.

Why did not so good a scholar as Oras see this? I submit that it was
because it was inconceivable to him that *Paradise Regained* could have

preceded *Paradise Lost*. But now let's go back to that word "Astaroth." In *Paradise Lost* Milton explains that it is a plural form, and that one should use "Astoreth" as a singular. But "Astaroth" is singular in the *Nativity Ode* and *Samson Agonistes*—and, we may now note, also in *Paradise Regained*. Let's go back also to the Anonymous Biographer of Milton, whose words I had misinterpreted back in 1949. I promised to try to explain my stupidity—so let me confess that I was guilty of the very same mistake as Professor Oras. For in naming five works that were begun before and finished after the Restoration, the Anonymous Biographer included, not only *Samson Agonistes*, but also *Paradise Regained*.[4]

Is it, then, really possible that this alleged "sequel" to *Paradise Lost* was written first? That, I'm afraid, must be another topic, for another paper, at another time.

NOTES

1. Originally this paper was a talk delivered on February 7, 1961. The only alterations made were the removal of audience-directed remarks and the updating of chronological references. Those alterations were made by John T. Shawcross, who kindly undertook the task of editing this essay. The significance of the topic to Milton studies and the summary of ideas with its attendant suggestions for further research have prompted me to include the paper in this collection.

2. Appended to Professor Parker's manuscript is the following list of alleged personal allusions in *Samson Agonistes* [JTS]:

ll. 1–11	Samson, released from prison and sitting outdoors, is Milton himself.
ll. 30–33	Milton's stress on Samson's special education as a Nazarite is an allusion to his own education.
ll. 67–109	Samson's soliloquy on blindness is autobiographical, particularly in its references to helplessness and mistreatment by others. (Editors ignore the facts that Milton's loss of sight was gradual and was not a violent punishment.)
ll. 191–193	Samson's complaint that "most" of his former friends have deserted him.
ll. 697–702	Poverty and disease.
l. 709	Samson (Milton) prays for death.
l. 1366	Samson submits quietly to his captors.
l. 1457	The reactions of the Philistines to old Manoa's efforts to ransom Samson are an allusion to the Royalists at the Restoration when Milton's friends tried to save him.
ll. 1687–1707	Samson's revenge is Milton's grim prophecy of his own poetical revenge.
l. 1758	Katharsis.
	Samson=Milton
	Dalila=Mary Powell
	Harapha=Salmasius

3. Also appended is the following list of alleged political allusions [JTS]:

l. 40   Samson eyeless in Gaza is an allusion to the once victorious republican party, after the Restoration. (But the Puritans had actually succeeded in overturning monarchy for more than a decade, as Samson had not.)

l. 240   Samson reproaching his countrymen for not supporting him is Milton doing the same. (But Samson nowhere refers to a restoration of tyranny; Israel is not returning to servitude.)

ll. 268–276   Corruptness brings servitude. (Milton's belief, early and late, based on classical beliefs. Krouse: political overtones integral to Samson tradition. Cf. Judges.) "Deliverer" rejected=Milton (Masson), Cromwell (editors), Lambert (other editors). Why not Moses? Chorus supplies other illustrations.

ll. 368–372   "Foul indignities" suffered by living Samson equal the disgracing of Cromwell's remains. (Samson immediately rebukes his father and pronounces his punishment just.)

ll. 667–709   Ode on God's injustice—an allusion to the fate of the Good Old Cause. Details worked out: dissensions among leaders, imprisonment of Lambert and Martin ("captived"), trial and execution of Sir Henry Vane ("unjust tribunals").

ll. 1268–1299   Ode of thanksgiving—a panegyric to the memory of Cromwell, as solitary Deliverer.

l. 1653   Ladies, captains, priests at Philistine festival—an allusion to Restoration court.

l. 1659   The "vulgar" who escaped are the English people as contrasted with the court.

4. Compare the preceding with John T. Shawcross, "The Chronology of Milton's Major Poems," *PMLA*, LXXVI (1961), 345–358. For Parker's other discussions of the date of *Samson Agonistes*, see "The Date of *Samson Agonistes*," *Philological Quarterly*, XXVIII (1949), 145–166; "The Date of 'Samson Agonistes': A Postscript," *Notes & Queries*, N. S., V (1958), 201–202; and "On the Date of *Samson Agonistes*," in *Milton: A Biography* (2 vols.; Oxford, 1968), II, 903–917. The essay published in *this* volume has the virtue of gathering together observations scattered through the biography and of presenting information that otherwise would be unavailable until the *Samson* variorum is published, sometime after 1974 according to the current schedule. The following articles also comment on the dating of Milton's tragedy: Allen H. Gilbert, "Is *Samson Agonistes* Unfinished?" *Philological Quarterly*, XXVIII (1949), 98–106; A. S. P. Woodhouse, "*Samson Agonistes* and Milton's Experience," *Transactions of the Royal Society of Canada*, 3rd ser., XLIII (1949), 157–175; Ernest Sirluck, "Some Recent Changes in the Chronology of Milton's Poems," *Journal of English and Germanic Philology*, LX (1961), 749–785. The traditional view, that *Samson* was published last and therefore written last, is argued by Ants Oras, first in "Milton's Blank Verse and the Chronology of His Major Poems," *SAMLA Studies in Milton*, ed. J. Max Patrick (Gainesville, 1953), pp. 128–197, then in *Blank Verse and Chronology in Milton*, University of Florida Monographs, Humanities No. 20 (Gainesville, 1966).

"Passions Well Imitated": Rhetoric and Poetics in the Preface to *Samson Agonistes*

JOHN M. STEADMAN
HENRY E. HUNTINGTON LIBRARY

Obliquely introduced in his preface to *Samson Agonistes* in order to support another point—the moral utility of tragedy—Milton's brief allusion to catharsis has proved, on a smaller scale, almost as controversial as Aristotle's own remarks on the subject. Unwittingly Milton plunged his twentieth-century readers into the midst of a sixteenth-century conflict. In modern scholarship on his preface we may recognize yet another skirmish in that Cinquecento battle of the books—the war of commentaries fought over the text of the *Poetics*, uneven but fiercely disputed terrain.

Frequently translated, frequently reprinted, and still more frequently annotated, Aristotle's treatise had engaged not only the foremost Italian critics but also scholars in northern Europe. To the elucidation of his text they had brought the exegetical and philological methods acquired from humanistic or scholastic disciplines, literary concepts inherited from intensive rhetorical training and the study of Horace and Terence, and a predisposition (unacknowledged and perhaps unconscious) to interpret the "new" and relatively unfamiliar Aristotelian principles in terms of "older," more familiar patterns already established in late-medieval and early-Renaissance theory. The result, as Bernard Weinberg has cogently argued, was "one of the strangest misunderstandings of a basic text in the history of ideas, and the formation of that very curious complex of notions which we call the neoclassical doctrine."[1]

In retrospect, this controversy may seem mere windy disputation, more productive of words than of matter; but, on the whole, it was by

175

no means barren. Critical disputes over Aristotle's text remolded literary criticism and decisively influenced the theory of painting, sculpture, and music. Serving to define problems (even if it did not provide definitive answers to them), formulating issues (even if it did not satisfactorily resolve them), this controversy left its imprint not only on epic and drama, but also on the visual arts.

It is against this background that Milton's scattered remarks on poetics and all of his major poetry must be placed. The *Poetics* Milton quotes is, in a sense, a Cinquecento document; to understand what it meant to him, one must approach it through Italian commentors—Tasso, Mazzoni, and their contemporaries—rather than through late-Victorian and twentieth-century explicators. In seeking the Aristotle Milton knew, one must in large part divest oneself of interpretations derived from recent Aristotelian scholarship and turn instead to the less accurate but perhaps more relevant observations of Renaissance scholars. One must endeavor to visualize the *Poetics* as it appeared to Castelvetro, Minturno, and Piccolomini rather than to Butcher and Bywater.

The conflicts of these Cinquecento and Seicento critics are still relevant for the Miltonist. Contemporary studies of Milton's interpretation of the *Poetics* are essentially a recapitulation of the earlier Renaissance debate. They have, moreover, inherited the ambiguities of this controversy along with its issues. If students of the preface are still undecided as to what its author meant to say or how he interpreted Aristotle, it is partly because students of the *Poetics* have not yet reached agreement as to what Aristotle himself had intended.

Recent scholarship on Milton's preface has been preoccupied with the problem of ascertaining his sources. Verbal or doctrinal parallels have been noted in the works of Minturno, Guarini, Heinsius, and (more recently) the Italian musician and theorist Monteverdi.[2] Nevertheless, with the exception of recent studies by Sellin and Mueller, few efforts have been made to compare and evaluate these alleged sources. To assess their comparative merit as evidence lies beyond the scope of this study. Most of the "key" concepts in Milton's remarks on catharsis were Renaissance commonplaces. The analogues hitherto noted in Minturno and other sixteenth-century theorists are less unconventional than they appeared to be a generation ago. The scholar should be reluctant to accept these (or other parallels he may discover) as evidence of Milton's positive indebtedness to a particular author.

The rhetorical structure of the preface also needs to be explored. Far from being an ingenious, if cryptic, tissue of critical novelties or a systematic exposition of poetic theory, this "Epistle" is essentially a rhetorical document, an apology defending the poet's choice of genre and his preference for classical models over contemporary conventions. The preface is (in Milton's own words) a "self defence, or explanation," and its statements concerning catharsis (or any other subject) must be read and interpreted in this light.[3]

I

Milton's remarks on catharsis occur within the immediate context of a defense of tragedy on the grounds of its dignity and utility, and within the larger context of an apologia for his own practice. Structurally, the preface falls into two divisions—a defense of tragedy itself and a defense of his own dramatic models. The two sections are linked, however, by the qualifying clause in the opening sentence: "Tragedy, *as it was antiently compos'd*, hath been ever held the gravest, moralest, and most profitable of all other Poems. . . ." In this way Milton made even his praise of tragedy contingent;[4] its excellence was relative to the *stile antico*, to tragedy as the *ancients* composed it. This qualification, in turn, provided the foundation for his subsequent self-defense: "In the modelling therefore of this Poem, with good reason, the Antients and *Italians* are rather follow'd, as of much more authority and fame. . . . of the style and uniformitie, and that commonly call'd the Plot, . . . they only will best judge who are not unacquainted with *Æschulus*, *Sophocles*, and *Euripides*, the three Tragic Poets unequall'd yet by any, and the best rule to all who endeavour to write Tragedy."

His condemnation of the moderns provides a further link between the two parts of his essay; it effects the necessary transition between Milton's eulogy of tragedy as anciently composed and his defense of his own practice in following the ancients and the Italians: "This is mention'd to vindicate Tragedy from the small esteem, or rather infamy, which in the account of many it undergoes at this day with other common Interludes; hap'ning through the Poets error of intermixing Comic stuff with Tragic sadness and gravity; or introducing trivial and vulgar persons. . . ."

Like most apologies, moreover, Milton's preface includes both a *confirmatio* and a *refutatio*. The first comprises his citation of authorities and classical examples affirming the gravity and profitableness of tragedy. The second he has telescoped into a single sentence denouncing contemporary drama. Like most refutations, this rebuttal depends on a distinction in terms. The current indictments of tragedy spring (the poet argues) from its corruption by the moderns; in seeking popular appeal rather than tragic gravity, they have violated the cardinal principle of decorum. Such charges apply therefore only to the contemporary stage, not to ancient tragedies—nor (significantly) to modern tragedies modelled on those of the ancients. This argument was conventional; Milton had already employed it against contemporary poetasters in *The Reason of Church-Government*, Sidney had directed it against Elizabethan dramatists, and Lomazzo had turned it against contemporary painters.

Milton's *confirmatio* occupies the greater part of the first section. In this part of his defense he makes extensive use of the same type of arguments that other Renaissance apologists had employed in defending the arts and sciences. Like Bacon in *The Advancement of Learning* and Sidney in *An Apologie for Poetrie*; like Leonardo and Alberti and Lomazzo in their defenses of painting; or like Alessandro Piccolomini in the "Proemio" to his *Annotations* on Aristotle's *Poetics*, Milton appeals to the conventional topics of *honestas* and *utilitas*.[5] He attempts to "vindicate" tragedy by emphasizing its dignity and profitableness—to counter the "small esteem" in which it is currently held by demonstrating the high esteem bestowed on it by "gravest Writers" and "Men in highest dignity."

In confirmation of his initial statement or thesis he relies heavily on examples (a form of induction) and on the testimony of the ancients (a form of inartificial proof), adducing a list of authorities that would normally seem disproportionate in so short an essay. These range from Scripture (a Pauline epistle and the Book of Revelation) to pagan worthies (Dionysius, Cicero, Augustus, Caesar, Seneca, Plutarch) and "a Father of the Church" (Gregory Nazianzen). It is within this context that the allusion to Aristotle occurs; it is a part—indeed the most important part—of the *confirmatio*. Introduced specifically to support the general statement that precedes it, it is designed primarily to demonstrate the gravity, morality, and utility of tragedy rather than to set forth a theory of tragic effect.

Aristotle's name heads the list, and Milton devotes considerably more space to his opinion than to those of other authorities. For several reasons this reference was especially vital for Milton's rhetorical strategy. Not only was Aristotle the principal authority on tragedy. He was also virtually the only classical philosopher who ranked with Plato and could refute the latter's indictment of tragedy; he could therefore serve as a useful ally against possible opponents—adversaries of the drama who might support their condemnation by appealing to *The Republic.*

In considering Milton's remarks on tragic effect, one should bear in mind the following points. In the first place, they are subordinated to the principal intent of his apologia—to defend his own practice. The doctrine of "purgation" is instrumental to his rhetorical strategy only insofar as it enables him to argue the gravity and profitableness of tragedy "as it was *antiently* compos'd." (He does not even mention the Greek term *katharsis*; instead he employs the Latin equivalent *lustratio* —in the epigraph to his work—and the English verb form "purge" in the text itself.)

In the second place, his remarks on this subject are partial; they attempt neither a comprehensive definition of tragedy nor a balanced statement of tragic effect. Elsewhere he alludes, in fact, to the role of dramatic action in arousing the passions, and to the interconnection between passion and thought (*dianoia*): "whatsoever hath passion or admiration in all the changes of that which is call'd fortune from without, or the wily subttleties and refluxes of mans thoughts from within. . . ."[6] This allusion to fortune's "changes" clearly refers to the tragic incidents portrayed in the fable—a point especially vital in Aristotle's theory of tragedy, but omitted in the preface to *Samson Agonistes*. Milton obviously held a broader view of tragic effect than the preface alone would appear to indicate. As he recognized, the proper "delight" of tragedy arose not only from imitation of the passions but also from imitation of an action. Indeed the epigraph on the title page begins with Aristotle's definition of tragedy as "μίμησις πράξεως σπουδαίας," "imitatio actionis seriae."

The remarks in the preface provide a severely limited selection rather than a representative summary of Milton's views on tragic effect; and the basis of this selection appears to have been primarily rhetorical. To regard his preface as a miniature treatise on poetics rather than a brief defense of his own practice is to mistake its genre. To interpret his observations as an epitome of his tragic doctrine is to mistake the part for the whole.

The third point to keep in mind is that the novelty of Milton's statements on tragic effect has been greatly exaggerated. The principal features of his discussion of purgation—the imitation of the passions, their reduction to "just measure" instead of complete eradication, the analogy between poetry and medicine—have numerous parallels in the critical treatises of the period.

Finally, the particular aspects of tragic purgation that Milton se-
lects for emphasis may have been chosen partly for their relevance to
the principal argument commonly directed against tragedy—that it ex-
cites the passions, and is therefore morally dangerous.

II

Having briefly examined the context of Milton's statement, let us
return to the text itself. Tragedy is "said by *Aristotle* to be of power by
raising pity and fear, or terror, to purge the mind of those and such
like passions, that is to temper and reduce them to just measure with a
kind of delight, stirr'd up by reading or seeing those passions well imitated." In support of Aristotle's "assertion" Milton then turns to medicine for an analogous kind of purgation: "for so in Physic things of
melancholie hue and quality are us'd against melancholy, sowr against
sowr, salt to remove salt humours."

To modern observers this passage obviously contains much more
(and much less!) than was actually "said by *Aristotle*." It confronts us,
accordingly, with several interrelated problems. First, how well did
Milton understand Aristotle? How far does this passage reflect views
explicitly stated in the *Poetics*? And how far is it merely a Renaissance
gloss, derived from earlier commentators or from Milton's own study of
the treatise? Second, what are the sources of the "non-Aristotelian"
elements in this passage? Third, how much of this passage did Milton
intend to represent as Aristotelian statement—as actually "said by *Aristotle*"—and how much is his own commentary or exposition on Aristotle's text? Though these questions cannot yet receive definitive answers, they are not unanswerable. Thanks to the research of previous
scholars, we may perhaps approach a tentative solution.

The first part of Milton's statement offers little difficulty. That tragedy is "of power by raising pity and fear . . . to purge the mind of those
and such like passions" seems, on the whole, a fairly accurate paraphrase
of the Aristotelian definition translated on the title page of Milton's
drama: "Per misericordiam & metum perficiens talium affectuum lustrationem." Except for its reference to "the mind" Milton's statement is
a faithful rendering of what was explicitly "said by *Aristotle*"—perhaps,
indeed, more faithful than most modern translations.

Nevertheless, whatever Aristotle actually "said" in this passage, he
clearly left much more *un*said. His brief definition of tragedy did not
specify how or why it accomplished its catharsis; and his commentators
were quick to remedy his omission. They debated whether all or only a

few of the passions were to be purged; whether or not the emotions purged were identical with those that effected the purgation; whether the passions were to be eradicated entirely or merely moderated and reduced to just measure. They glossed this passage in the *Poetics* with others from the same work, with the discussion of "purgative melodies" in the *Politics*, and with medical theory. Though some of the interpretations they imposed on the text may seem exaggerated when judged by twentieth-century interpretations of Aristotle, these critics nevertheless arrived at such views by well-tried exegetical methods. Their deficiencies can be partly attributed to the aims and techniques of Renaissance scholarship itself.

The essential difficulty for the twentieth-century reader lies not in Milton's paraphrase of Aristotle, but in his own gloss on his Aristotelian paraphrase. This is his own exegesis (albeit an incomplete exegesis) of a notoriously ambiguous passage in the *Poetics*; as such it does not pretend to be what was actually "said by *Aristotle*" but what the commentator thought Aristotle meant by what he *did* say; it is Milton's attempt to resolve an ambiguity that he and many others had encountered in the text, to explain how and why tragedy achieves its *lustratio* or purgation.

His statement that tragedy is able "to temper and reduce them [i.e., the passions] to just measure with a kind of delight, stirr'd up by reading or seeing those passions well imitated" is essentially his own gloss on the Aristotelian text he has just paraphrased. It could, accordingly (as he well knew), seem plausible only insofar as it did not contradict the text itself. Before analyzing his gloss, therefore, let us turn first to the text and to his translation and paraphrase.

According to late-nineteenth- and twentieth-century interpretations of the *Poetics*, the tragic emotions are essentially the product of events. Arising out of the development of the fable, they result from the dramatist's skill in plotting and his mastery of dramatic structure. The fable itself—the "soul" of the poem—is an imitation of an action; and from the evolution and unravelling of this action, in accordance with verisimilitude and probability, the poem derives its emotional force. Character and thought—*ethos* and *dianoia*—are secondary to plot; to the latter belong the three elements principally responsible for tragic effect—reversal, discovery, and suffering (peripeteia, anagnorisis, pathos).

Such an interpretation would appear to be justified by the strong emphasis that Aristotle places on the fable (*mythos*) throughout his treatise; but it is not explicitly stated in the phrase that Milton translates on the title page, paraphrases near the beginning of his preface, and proceeds in due order to explicate. Though elsewhere in the *Poetics* Aristotle stresses the types of action most suitable for arousing pity and fear, his statement on catharsis makes no mention of "deeds" or "actions" as the means of exciting these emotions. More than one translator, however, regarded this meaning as implicit in Aristotle's statement and accordingly introduced it into his own translation. Bywater, for instance, renders this passage as "with incidents arousing pity and fear, wherewith to accomplish its catharsis of such emotions." The word "incidents" does not, however, occur in Aristotle's text (δι᾽ ἐλέου καὶ φόβου περαίνουσα τὴν τῶν τοιούτων παθημάτων κάθαρσιν).[7] Earlier, as Bywater acknowledged, Goulston had advanced a similar interpretation, inserting the qualifying phrase "factis expressum" after the words "per Misericordiam, Metumque";[8] but he had placed his own addition in italics, to indicate that the reference to "deeds" did *not* occur in the text. His version of the *Poetics* was not only a literal translation; it was also (in a sense) a paraphrase.

Bywater's translation would, of course, tend to rule out Milton's interpretation; but in actuality Milton's translation ("Per misericordiam & metum perficiens talium affectuum lustrationem") is closer to Aristotle's actual words than Bywater's rendering. The text, as he renders it, retains its original ambiguity and is therefore capable of multiple interpretations—including the meaning he ascribes to it in his own paraphrase and explanation.

Though Renaissance commentators sometimes showed considerable freedom in paraphrasing and explaining Aristotle's text and in elaborating their own definitions of tragedy after his precedent, they usually strove for strict verbal accuracy in translating his text and they generally preserved the distinction between a literal translation and a paraphrase. Goulston, as we have observed, italicized his own additions. Though other commentators—Maggi, Robortello, Castelvetro— might advance very different theories of tragedy and hold highly divergent views as to how Aristotle's text ought to be interpreted, they normally differentiated their own paraphrases or explanations from the text itself. Maggi, for instance, reproduced Pazzi's translation of this passage, "per misericordiam verò atque terrorem perturbationes huiusmodi purgans,"[9] and then added his own (and Lombardi's) "explanation" and finally his own "annotations" or commentary. Robortello likewise accepted Pazzi's translation as the basis for his own commentary.[10] Castelvetro rendered the same passage as "induca per misericordia, &

per ispavento purgatione di così fatte passioni"[11] and then proceeded to advance, in his commentary, a theory of tragedy that is in several respects radically different from that of his predecessors. In Milton's approach to Aristotle we encounter a similar regard for verbal accuracy in translating the words of the text, and a similar freedom in explaining them. He provides us first with a literal translation, then with a paraphrase, and finally with a brief explanation or commentary.

His paraphrase of what was "said by *Aristotle*" is less accurate than his translation, but it is still considerably less free than the paraphrases written by many of his predecessors and near-contemporaries. The first addition he makes to Aristotle's text in paraphrasing it is his allusion to "the mind." This was scarcely a major addition, and perhaps he felt it advisable in view of the notorious ambiguity of the word *pathēma* and its Latin and English equivalents "passion" and "perturbation." His qualification, moreover, had already become a commonplace in Aristotelian commentary. Goulston had employed the same word (again in italics to indicate that it represented his own addition), "eiusmodi *vehementes animorum* Perturbationes";[12] and Maggi and Lombardi had introduced it into their own "explanation" of the text: "MISERICORDIAM VERó ATQUE TERROREM PERTURBATIONES HUIUSMODI PURGANS: hoc est animum liberans à perturbationibus, misericordiae & terrori similibus."[13]

The second addition Milton makes is more substantial. The word "those" ("those and such like passions") does not occur in the text he is paraphrasing. On the contrary Aristotle employed only the ambiguous term τοιούτων (which Milton renders as "talium" and "such like"), and thereby gave rise to one of the major debates in Cinquecento criticism.[14] Which of the emotions does tragedy attempt to purge? Granted that it arouses pity and fear, does it also *purge* them—or does it (on the contrary) arouse them only to purge other, more harmful emotions? Does catharsis apply only to pity and fear? does it exclude pity and fear? or does it comprehend a variety of emotions including pity and fear?

On this issue critics were divided. Maggi, for instance, explicitly denied that the end of tragedy could be the purgation of pity and fear, for these emotions could, in his opinion, have highly beneficial results. His view was that tragedy employs pity and fear to purge the mind from other, more harmful passions—wrath, avarice, and lust (*luxuria*): "His itaque rationibus haudquaquam dubito, Aristotelem nolle Tragoediae finem esse animam humanam à terrore misericordiave expurgare;

sed his uti ad alias perturbationes ab animo removendas: ex quarum
remotione animus virtutibus exornatur. nam ira, verbi gratia, depulsa,
succedit mansuetudo. expulsa avaritia, inducitur liberalitas. atque ita
de caeteris."[15]

Piccolomini, on the other hand, denies that pity and fear are ex-
cluded from purgation. Surveying the eleven passions of the mind discussed in Aristotle's *Rhetoric* (five belonging to the irascible faculty
and six to the concupiscible appetite), he declared that tragedy arouses
pity and fear by portraying grievous events that have befallen great
persons and thereby purges and liberates the mind from excess of emotions (*affetti*). Pity and fear are included in this purgation, inasmuch
as tragedy tempers fear and moderates pity.[16] Castelvetro, in turn, explicitly asserts that tragedy utilizes pity and fear to purge "these passions" and drive them from the heart. By "its example and its frequent
representation" of things worthy of pity, fear, and cowardice (*viltà*), it
confers magnanimity on an ignoble audience, lends courage to fearful
men, and makes compassionate men severe. Tragedy diminishes fear
and pity by accustoming the spectator to fearful and pitiable objects—
just as in a pestilence pity and fear are stirred by the first few deaths,
but cease after hundreds and thousands have perished.[17] If "terrible
and pitiable actions are uncommon they move men the more to terror
and to compassion, but if they are less frequent they move them the
less, and because of their frequency are able to purge the terror and
compassion of mortal lives."[18] Guarini similarly insists that tragedy
purges pity and fear ("terror purges terror") but draws a sharp distinction between good and evil aspects of these emotions. The "terror of
internal death . . . excited in the spirit of the spectator by the image of
what is represented, interprets the injurious evil tendency as a calamity"; but reason, "abhorring the bad tendency . . . drives it out, leaving
behind only the beneficial fear of infamy and of internal death, which is
the foundation of virtue."[19]

Against this background Milton's additions to Aristotle's assertion
seem modest indeed. He does, to be sure, introduce into his paraphrase
two concepts that are not explicitly stated in the passage he is paraphrasing; in the eyes of some of his predecessors, moreover, one of these
would scarcely have seemed even implicit. By inserting the word
"those" into his paraphrase he took a positive stand against commentators who, like Maggi, had dogmatically denied that tragedy purges pity
and fear. Unlike many Cinquecento critics, Milton does not elaborate
this point into a systematic theory or qualify it by new and novel dis-

tinctions. He does not endeavor to define and catalogue "such like passions" or to distinguish between the beneficial and injurious modes of pity and terror. In comparison with theorists like Castelvetro and Guarini, the views expressed in the paraphrase and in the brief *explicatio* that follows it are conservative.

Except for two insertions—one of them a commonplace, the other a debatable but widely accepted interpretation—Milton's paraphrase is an accurate restatement of the passage he had already translated literally on the title page. Thus far he has not been unfaithful to what was actually "said by *Aristotle.*"

III

As the passage that follows this initial statement has sometimes proved a stumbling block for recent criticism, let us consider first its general nature and function and then examine some of its basic ideas. Strictly speaking, it is not a *paraphrase*, but a commentary. It amplifies and elucidates the statement in the Greek text and in Milton's own paraphrase. It is an explication of Aristotle's dictum rather than a restatement.

The five principal ideas advanced in this explication, moreover— (1) moderation rather than extirpation of the passions, (2) imitation as the source of tragic delight, (3) delight as an attendant of purgation, (4) the imitation of the passions, and, finally, (5) the medical analogy —are by no means novel additions to Renaissance critical thought. They had already become familiar and even widespread doctrines in neo-Aristotelian theory. All of them had found plausible, though still debatable, support in the works of Aristotle—his *Ethics*, *Politics*, and *Rhetoric* as well as his *Poetics*. In varying degrees, these concepts had become part of the Renaissance Aristotelian tradition; few Cinquecento critics would have regarded any of the five as either novel or "un-Aristotelian." Some of them, indeed, had become near-commonplaces.

In declaring that tragedy may "temper and reduce" the passions "to just measure," Milton commits himself, once again, to a positive stand on a long-standing controversy. The question of the degree of purgation—whether tragedy effected a total or merely partial reduction of the passions—was another of the highly debatable issues arising out of the ambiguities of Aristotle's text. In asserting the latter view, Milton advances essentially the same interpretation that he had expressed earlier in *The Reason of Church-Government*: poetry can "allay the perturba-

tions of the mind, and set the affections in right tune."[20] This conception
was by no means rare in Renaissance criticism; nor could it be regarded
as un-Aristotelian. Though it is never explicitly stated in the *Poetics*, it
is nevertheless consistent with views expressed in the *Nicomachean
Ethics* as to the nature of the passions and their relation to virtue and
vice. Moreover, it was consistent with Milton's own views on this subject. For Milton as for Aristotle, virtue consisted in a mean or "just measure" between extremes. For both, the passions or affections constituted
the common subject matter of vice and virtue. Though other philosophical schools—notably the Stoics and certain neo-Pythagorean or neo-
Platonic philosophers—regarded a complete eradication of the passions
as essential for perfect virtue, the ataraxy of the Stoic sage and the pas-
sionless perfection of the neo-Platonic *anima purgata* were, on the
whole, alien to Renaissance Aristotelianism and indeed to Christian
humanism.

One of the strongest arguments for this interpretation, then, would
seem to be its fidelity to Aristotelian ethics.[21] The alternative view, which
regarded tragic purgation as the complete eradication of the passions,
would fit a Stoic or neo-Pythagorean ethical system but would hardly
accord with the moral principles of the Peripatetics. Several of Milton's
predecessors, moreover, had emphasized this point, affirming that catharsis denoted an Aristotelian moderation of the passions, not the total
eradication demanded by the Stoics.

For Piccolomini the principal end of tragedy (as of all other species
of poetry) is utility or instruction, delight serving merely as a secondary
aim and as a means to the principal end. The greatest utility, he continues, is to possess a true tranquillity of mind. As such tranquillity cannot be stained or disturbed except by the flow of passions through the
mind, tragedy is most useful insofar as it moderates the emotions and
thereby fosters peace of mind. Distinguishing sharply between Stoic and
Peripatetic conceptions of the passions and their relation to tranquillity,
Piccolomini observes that the latter school does not regard total eradication of the emotions as a prerequisite of tranquillity. For the Peripatetics it is enough to purge, moderate, and reduce them to a certain
"good temperament." The rule and measure of this purgation or "tempering" belongs to reason; when the passions conform to reason, they are
said to be "moderated" and purged.[22]

Guarini similarly observes that "the word *purge* has two meanings.
One means *to blot out completely*"; the second sense, however, "does
not mean to blot out . . . but to rid . . . of all vileness and make [a thing]

perfect in its nature. In this second sense is to be taken the *purge* of tragedy, as also the physicians take it. . . . A tragic poem . . . does not purge the affections in Stoic fashion, by removing them totally from our hearts, but by moderating and reducing them to that proper consistency which can contribute to a virtuous habit." Pity and fear "need to be purged, that is, reduced to a proper mixture, and this is done by tragedy."[23]

In elucidating obscure or ambiguous passages in the *Poetics*, Renaissance commentators not uncommonly sought clarification from other writings by the same author. To explain Aristotle's theory of purgation, Cinquecento critics ransacked the *Ethics*, the *Rhetoric*, and the *Politics* for the philosopher's views (relevant or irrelevant) on the passions. Maggi, for instance, explained the word *pathē* (which occurs near the beginning of the *Poetics*) in terms of Aristotle's ethical theory: "Sunt autem affectus omnes, virtutum materiae quaedam, circa quarum moderationem rationalis animae pars versatur: quae dum eosdem fraenans, ad mediocritatem ducit, virtutum habitus omnes in animo procreat."[24]

In a more modest—and perhaps more sensible—way, this is precisely what Milton has done in his preface. He has glossed an obscure passage in the *Poetics* with concepts derived from the *Ethics* and (as we shall see later) from the *Politics*. He explains Aristotle's poetic doctrine—the purgation of the passions—by citing the ethical doctrine advanced by the same author—the moderation of the passions. By reducing the emotions to just measure, tragedy performs an ethical function comparable to that of reason itself; like reason, it governs the passions and thereby serves as an agent of moral virtue. This argument, needless to say, is vital to Milton's rhetorical strategy, for it supports, and demonstrates, his initial thesis. To prove that tragedy is indeed the "moralest" of all other poems he turns appropriately to the central thesis of the standard treatise on moral philosophy, the *Nicomachean Ethics*.

Milton's observation on the origin and function of tragic delight is by no means new, but the tradition behind it is complex and requires some elucidation. Like many of his contemporaries and predecessors, he has clearly subordinated delight to utility; pleasure serves the graver, moral ends of tragedy. This view, of course, antedates the Renaissance Aristotelian tradition; it is essentially an inheritance from classical rhetoric with its threefold end—to teach, delight, and move—and from Horatian poetics with its dual emphasis on utility and delight.[25] From Horace's injunction to mix the *utile* and *dulce* and from his statement that poets ought to aim either at instruction or at pleasure "aut prodesse

volunt aut delectare poetae") medieval and Renaissance poetics had
evolved the ideal of poetry as a mode of delightful teaching, a form of
instruction all the more effective because it employed pleasure in order
to teach and to persuade. Delight served the end of utility. The poet
combined the *utile* of moral doctrine with the *dulce* of verse, rhetorical
ornament, or invented fable. In rhetorical terms, the poem served as
inductive proof; it was a moral or political *exemplum*.

The rediscovery of Aristotle's *Poetics* might force a reappraisal of
well-established poetic theories, but on the whole it did not displace
them. Instead, neo-Aristotelian theory tended to absorb them or (by
introducing new and partially understood concepts) to stimulate them
to new developments; in this way it gave them a new vitality, a second
youth. The traditional subordination of delight to utility remained, but
with a wider application. The traditional sources of poetic *delight* were
broadened by adding Aristotelian interpretations of imitation. The
conventional ideas of poetic *utility* were enriched by the Aristotelian
doctrine of catharsis.[26] Thus in Tasso's "Allegory" to the *Gerusalemme
Liberata* one finds a fusion of Aristotelian and medieval poetics; poetry
pleases (he declares) through its imitation but instructs by means of its
allegory.[27] In the opening stanzas of his epic, however, he returns to the
older conception of poetry as delightful teaching; "truth convey'd in
verse of gentle kind" is like a sweetened medicine administered to sick
children:

> Anoint with sweets the vessel's foremost parts,
> To make them taste the potions sharp we give;
> They drink deceived; and so deceiv'd they live.[28]

In Renaissance discussions of the nature and ends of the poetic art
it is not uncommon, therefore, to find a mixture of Aristotelian and
medieval concepts. In Varchi, Mazzoni,[29] Minturno, Tasso, Sidney, and
numerous other critics one encounters definitions of poetry that have
been partially modelled on Aristotle's definition of tragedy but which
nevertheless incorporate the traditional twofold or threefold "ends" of
poetry inherited from the Horatian and Ciceronian traditions. These
specifically define the ends of poetry as delight, instruction, and (in
those cases where the critic has been most strongly influenced by rhetorical theory) persuasion. In most of these cases, moreover, delight is
clearly subordinated to utility—to instructing and moving the poet's audience.

This subordination of delight to utility could find at least a limited textual support in Aristotle's own works. Besides subordinating poetics to ethics, and ethics to politics, he had argued that music may have a nobler "use" than pleasure. "In addition to this common pleasure," he had declared in his *Politics*, "felt and shared in by all (for the pleasure given by music is natural, and therefore adapted to all ages and characters), may it not have also some influence over the character and the soul? It must have such an influence if characters are affected by it." Even "in mere melodies there is an imitation of character, for the musical modes differ essentially from one another, and those who hear them are differently affected by each." Music has therefore "a power of forming the character, and should therefore be introduced into the education of the young."[30]

Even that time-honored cliché—the conception of poetry as a sugared medicine, making instruction palatable through delight—could derive support from the *Politics*: "The study [of music] is suited to the stage of youth, for young persons will not, if they can help, endure anything which is not sweetened by music, and music has a natural sweetness."[31]

The conception of delight as a secondary end of poetry—both subordinate and instrumental to utility—was, then, thoroughly conventional in Renaissance criticism; and it was within this framework that Milton (like many of his predecessors) interpreted the Aristotelian concepts of mimesis and catharsis. Imitation was delightful; purgation was morally useful. In treating the delight aroused by imitation as an assisting cause in achieving catharsis, Milton was adapting the ideas he encountered in the *Poetics* to a frame of reference already thoroughly conventional in Renaissance thought. He was, in effect, subordinating delight to utility.

In regarding pleasure as subservient to usefulness, he was in fundamental agreement with the majority of Renaissance critics. Few of them shared Castelvetro's opinion that delight alone was the principal end of tragedy. Some of them specifically linked neo-Aristotelian concepts of imitation with older theories concerning the poetic or rhetorical *exemplum*. Many of them regarded poetics as the handmaid of moral and civil philosophy—or indeed of theology—and accordingly stressed the ethical, political, and religious functions of tragedy.

Milton's allusion to the "delight" stirred up by tragic imitation would have raised few eyebrows among his contemporaries; Aristotle himself had declared that it is "natural for all to delight in works of imitation."[32] Moreover, Milton's further suggestion—that such delight might actually assist purgation—was not uncommon, even though many of his predecessors held sharply divergent views on this subject. In the *Politics* (they observed) Aristotle had discussed the influence of the so-called "purgative melodies" on "feelings such as pity and fear"—the very emotions excited by tragedy—in terms that clearly associated purgation with delight:

> Some persons fall into a religious frenzy, whom we see as a result of the sacred melodies—when they have used the melodies that excite the soul to mystic frenzy—restored as though they had found healing and purgation. Those who are influenced by pity and fear, and every emotional nature, must have a like experience, and others in so far as each is susceptible to such emotions, and all are in a manner purged, and their souls lightened and delighted.[33]

The context as well as the contents of this passage made it a convenient gloss on the text of the *Poetics*. Preceded by an extensive discussion of music as imitation of character and passion[34] and followed by the recommendation that "purgative melodies" should be performed at the theater inasmuch as they "give an innocent pleasure to mankind,"[35] it seemed equally relevant to the drama. Moreover, it appeared to provide a foundation for several of the principal commonplaces of "pre-Aristotelian" poetic theory—the combination of utility with delight and the analogy between poetry and medicine. Maggi[36] quoted it to elucidate Aristotle's definition of tragedy, specifically noting its parallel between musical and medical catharsis and its emphasis on utility and pleasure. In his version one encounters, indeed, some of the very *topoi* that Milton himself subsequently employed—concepts that had not been explicitly stated in Aristotle's definition of tragedy but that were nevertheless read into it by critics familiar with the *Politics*. First, Milton alludes to the power of tragedy "to purge the *mind*." This word (as we have seen) does not occur in the relevant passage in the *Poetics*, but it does appear in the analogous passage in the *Politics* ("animum . . . expiant"). Secondly, Milton asserts that tragedy purges pity and fear ("those . . . passions"). In the *Poetics* this idea may be implied, but is not explicitly stated; for many Renaissance critics, Aristotle's term τῶν τοιούτων was ambiguous, and the precise identity of the emotions to be purged was subject to doubt. The *Politics*, on the other hand, refers *explicitly* to the purgation of pity and fear as well as to other emotions: "quod idem pati necesse est eos, & qui commiseratione, & qui metu, & generatim sunt affecti. . . ." Thirdly, though the medical parallel, so common in Renaissance poetic theory, does not occur in the account of catharsis provided by the *Poetics*, it *does* appear in the political treatise: "idoneumque reddunt . . . carminibusque ita constitui, ut si medicinam, purgationemque reperissent. . . ." Finally, Milton alludes to purgation "with a kind of delight." The definition of tragedy given in the *Poetics* makes no mention of pleasure as accompanying catharsis (though such a view may be implicit in other sections of the treatise). The *Politics*, on the other hand, offers a close verbal parallel: "omnesque aliqua ex parte purgari, & allevari cum voluptate."[37]

Milton's remarks on tragic purgation seem, on the whole, to represent a conflation of Aristotle's definition of tragedy with opinions on catharsis advanced in the *Politics*. These he amplified and explained, in turn, with doctrines likewise derived from Aristotelian sources—the moderation of the passions, from the *Ethics*; imitation of the passions, from the *Poetics* and the *Politics* alike; mimesis as the source of pleasure, from the *Poetics*. The medical analogy, explicit but still undeveloped in the *Politics*, he elaborated as other critics had done before him.

Milton's expression "with a kind of delight" is not entirely free from ambiguity. Does it mean that purgation is accomplished "by aid of" pleasure, or merely "accompanied with" pleasure—or both?[38] A similar ambiguity is inherent in the *Politics*. Aristotle's phrase μεθ' ἡδονῆς ("with delight") could mean both "by aid of" and "in conjunction with"; the Latin equivalent *cum voluptate* was likewise ambiguous.[39] Whichever meaning Milton intended (and it is quite possible that he may not have recognized the ambiguity or else did not want to split hairs over this point), his interpretation could hardly be regarded as original.

On the relationship between tragic purgation and tragic pleasure Renaissance critics held sharply divergent views; some regarded purgation as "accompanied with" pleasure, others as accomplished "by means of" delight. On the one hand, for instance, Giacomini (in a passage clearly influenced by the *Politics*) maintained that "this lightening or purgation of the soul is accompanied by a feeling of pleasure."[40] On the other hand, Denores declared that pleasure serves as the instrument or agent of catharsis; poetry endeavors to purge the listeners "col mezzo del diletto da' più importanti affetti dell' animo. . . ."[41] Whichever meaning Milton meant to signify by his phrase ("with . . . delight"), his interpretation would appear to be thoroughly traditional.

In asserting that tragic pleasure springs from imitation, Milton was partly following Aristotle's doctrine that "the tragic pleasure is that of pity and fear, and the poet has to produce it by a work of imitation.

. . ."[42] There is nevertheless one significant difference between them: whereas Aristotle stresses the actions or "incidents" imitated in the story, Milton emphasizes the "passions . . . imitated." In the context of Renaissance poetic theory, however, this divergence would have appeared less glaring; in the eyes of many Cinquecento critics (as we shall see later) Milton's remarks on the imitation of the passions would have seemed impeccably Aristotelian.

Milton's reference to Aristotle's mimesis at this point could, moreover, serve a rhetorical purpose as well as a doctrinal end. By alluding to the role of imitation in arousing delight, he was indirectly reinforcing his defense of his own practice in following the ancients. The passions may be dangerous if ill imitated (in *The Reason of Church-Government* he censures the moderns for imitating badly and accordingly communicating "vitious principles in sweet pils"),[43] but if "well imitated" they may be truly medicinal. Tragedy can be morally useful only if it arouses the proper delight; it can purge the passions only if it imitates them well.

Milton's reference to the delight "stirr'd up" by imitation provides a fuller and more comprehensive explanation of tragic effect. But it also serves as a rhetorical argument to support his apologia for tragedy "as it was antiently compos'd."

IV

From the delight aroused by imitation (a thoroughly conventional doctrine in neo-Aristotelian poetics) let us turn to the fourth major idea in Milton's *explicatio*, the imitation of the passions. For many twentieth-century critics, this doctrine would *not* seem Aristotelian; and John Arthos, observing that Aristotle had defined tragedy as an "imitation of an action," not of passion, has advanced the interesting but not altogether convincing suggestion that Milton may have derived this "modification of Aristotle" from Italian musical theory. Monteverdi, for instance, "spoke insistently of his work as imitation, and as imitation of the passions."[44]

In actuality, like most of the ideas in Milton's preface, this was a Renaissance commonplace. Though it did not pass unchallenged,[45] it entered neo-Aristotelian criticism virtually at the beginning—in Maggi's lectures on the *Poetics*[46]—and it was reaffirmed by numerous other commentators—Tomitano, Robortello, Lionardi, Tasso, Segni, Piccolomini, Gambara, Varchi, and Zabarello.[47] Other authors, such as Dolce, Lomazzo, Leonardo da Vinci, and the Quattrocento artist Alberti, had adapted the concept of poetry as emotional representation to the arts of design. The painter and sculptor (they argued) must attempt, like the poet, to depict the passions of the mind, albeit by different means. Some of the readers of Milton's preface, moreover, would have encountered this doctrine already—if not in Cinquecento criticism, then surely in Dryden's essay *Of Dramatic Poesy*,[48] published three years before *Samson Agonistes*.

One hardly needs, therefore, to look to Italian musical theory for the sources of Milton's allusion to "passions well imitated." The doctrine that poetry imitates the passions was already well established in Italian critical theory and had already been introduced, by a major poet and critic, into English criticism. Similarly, it was in all probability to Cinquecento poetics that the musical theorists, like the theorists of the arts of design, were indebted for the doctrine that art is an imitation of the passions.

The theory that poetry represents the passions antedates the Renaissance Aristotle. In various forms, this doctrine appears in classical and medieval rhetoric, in late classical commentaries on Horace and Terence, and in medieval poetic theory. These antecedents, however, lie outside the scope of this study. Our immediate concern is with the *Poetics*. What justification for this doctrine did Milton's predecessors find in Aristotle's treatise and related works? What verbal authority, if any, did they find for their assertions that poetry imitates the passions?

The principal support for this view was to be found in Aristotle's discussion of choreographic imitation, near the very beginning of his treatise. "Rhythm alone," he declares, "without harmony, is the means in the dancer's imitations; for even he, by the rhythms of his attitudes, may present men's characters, as well as what they do and suffer."[49] In this passage the author mentions three distinct objects of imitation—characters, "passions," and actions: μιμοῦνται καὶ ἤθη καὶ πάθη καὶ πράξεις.

The word *pathē* ("passions") is ambiguous, and Aristotle does not always employ it in the same sense. Like its Latin equivalents *passio* and *perturbatio*, it could denote sufferings—the torments inflicted on a man—or alternatively the emotions. In his note on this passage, as in his translation, Bywater interprets it in the former sense.[50] Many Renaissance commentators, on the other hand, preferred the latter meaning. In their *explanatio* on the *Poetics*, Maggi and Lombardi interpret this term as an allusion to the passions: "Per perturbationes autem Aristoteles, iram, furorem, odium, & reliqua eiusmodi intelligit." More significant, however, is the fact that in his "Annotations" Maggi specifically attributes the same objects of imitation—characters, passions, and actions—to the poet: "Illud etiam adnotandum, poetas omnes, cùm mores, perturbationes, atque actiones imitentur, inde tamen potissimùm nomen sumpsisse, quòd actiones humanas imitentur, ut inferius ex Aristotele constabit."[51] Robortello,[52] Vettori,[53] Piccolomini,[54] and Goulston[55] all interpreted this term as denoting the emotions. The dancer imitated actions, passions, and character.

This, then, is the textual authority for the triad—*mores, perturbationes, actionesque*—so common in Renaissance definitions of poetry and the objects of poetic imitation. Occurring first in Pazzi's translation of the *Poetics*, it was subsequently taken up by Maggi, Robortello, and others, and thus entered the mainstream of the Italian critical tradition. For many critics, Aristotle's definition of tragedy ("imitatio actionis") seemed incomplete in comparison with his earlier remarks on choreographic imitation. If the dancer imitated character and passion, could not the poet imitate them as well? In their commentaries, accordingly, they frequently broadened Aristotle's definition of tragedy to include the imitation of passion and character in addition to action.

In support of this interpretation, moreover, critics could point to the discussion of music in the *Politics*, where again Aristotle appeared to speak of the imitation of emotion and character: "Rhythm and melody supply imitations of anger and gentleness, and also of courage and temperance, and of all the qualities contrary to these, and of the other qualities of character, which hardly fall short of the actual affections, as we know from our own experience, for in listening to such strains our souls undergo a change." When "men hear imitations, even apart from the rhythms and tunes themselves, their feelings move in sympathy." Or again, "even in mere melodies there is an imitation of character. . . ."[56]

Scarcely less important, as a foundation for the view that poetry imitates the passions, were Aristotle's remarks on passion in relation to diction. In constructing his plot and adding appropriate diction, the poet ought (Aristotle declares) to place the actual scene before his eyes, to act out his story with "the very gestures of his personages," and to experience personally the emotions he plans to represent: "Given the same natural qualifications, he who feels the emotions ($\pi\acute{a}\theta\epsilon\sigma\acute{\iota}v$) to be described will be the most convincing; distress and anger, for instance, are portrayed most truthfully by one who is feeling them at the moment. Hence it is that poetry demands a man with a special gift for it, or else one with a touch of madness in him; the former can easily assume the required mood, and the latter may be actually beside himself with emotion."[57]

Though Maggi suggested that this passage might refer to the actors and the gestures that accompanied their delivery of the words, he saw in it an application of the principle of decorum: "Dixit modum, quo decorum invenire commodè possimus: cui etiam figuris, ac gestibus opitulari debemus."[58] Robortello emphasizes the principle of decorum (*tò prépon*) in diction. In order to express the emotions ("animi motiones, ac perturbationes") of individual persons and clothe them in appropriate words, the poet ought to visualize their habits of body, eliciting from these habits the mores and speech appropriate to such individuals. As the diction must seem natural (proceeding as it does from men in calamity and agitated by passion) the poet ought himself to feel emotion in order to imitate it correctly: "alioqui non rectè imitari potest, nam iratus melius irati exprimit sermonem, ac vultum. Dolens dolentis, & amans amantis."[59]

Piccolomini similarly declares that the poet must arouse in himself the same passions (*affetti*), moral states (*costumi*), and qualities that he wishes to portray in his dramatic personages. To depict an irate man he must himself feel anger; to portray a fearful man, he must himself feel fear. Distinguishing three modes of passionate discourse, Piccolomini finds only one that is truly imitative and is capable therefore not only of arousing but also of *expressing* emotion. The first kind of pathetic discourse, by describing atrocities and torments, arouses such horror that it disturbs the delight of imitation. The second kind is Aristotle's pathetic proof; the speaker attempts to arouse emotion not for his audience's instruction or delight but in his own interest. The third mode, however, represents the passion of the speaker and therefore appears to be the natural expression of emotion: "Quando il parlare tiene convenientia, & conformità con l'affetto, che si truova in colui, che parla, o vuol mostrare, ch' in lui si truovi conciosiacosache solendo la natura guidar l'huomo à mandar fuora le parole conformi agli affetti, che in lui si truovano, & massimamente se son molto potenti. . . ." Such discourse is imitation, especially if the speaker does not actually feel the emotion he attempts to portray.

Like the expression of character (*costumi*), the expression of emotions (*affetti*) is necessary for the poet, but especially, Piccolomini argues, for the writer of comedy or tragedy. The dramatist must impart verisimilitude to his imitation by adapting his language to the emotions he desires to express and imitate ("esprimere, & far' imitando apparire").

Just as the actor imitates by adapting voice and gesture to the words he must deliver, so the poet imitates by making his words conform to the passions of the mind ("affetti dell' animo") and thereby arouses "maraviglioso diletto" in his audience. This third type of passionate discourse seems rather to express than to excite the emotions: "non motiva, ò escitativa d'effetti, . . . ma più tosto significativa, & espressiva d'affetti, la domandiamo."[60]

Goulston, finally, specifically links this passage with the three objects of imitation mentioned in Aristotle's discussion of choreography: ēthē, pathē, and praxeis. His glosses refer respectively to the imitation of actions ("Sive Res-ipsas oratione imitere") and to the imitation of character and emotion ("Sive Personarum Mores & Adfectus").[61]

V

In recent scholarship the medical image that concludes Milton's explicatio has overshadowed other, and perhaps more fundamental, aspects of his doctrine. In particular, critics have been preoccupied with the problem of sources—citing parallels in Minturno and Guarini—and with the alleged resemblance to modern "pathological" interpretations of catharsis. In his valuable essay on this subject Paul Sellin has called attention to some of the weaknesses of this approach. There are (as he points out) significant differences between Milton's view and those of Minturno and Guarini. Milton's own statements elsewhere in the preface and in his brief translation of Aristotle's definition seem, moreover, to indicate that he held a predominantly "moral" rather than "pathological" conception of catharsis. Finally, in emphasizing this "homeopathic analogy," the "modernistic view of Milton's catharsis" has failed to give adequate attention to "the rest of his remarks on catharsis. . . . Indeed, it would seem that the analogy, rather than the preceding text, is sometimes taken as though it were Milton's explanation of what tragic catharsis is."[62]

As an argument from analogy, the medical image constitutes logical proof. Milton is demonstrating the validity of a relatively obscure poetic doctrine by means of a more familiar medical doctrine. From a purely rhetorical viewpoint, moreover, this analogy bears a double relationship to the preceding passage. It not only demonstrates that like may cure like; it also amplifies the image of "temper[ing]" the passions in an easy transition from the ethical to the physiological meaning of this term. Milton's image emphasizes precisely the interpretation of catharsis that he wanted to stress—not the eradication of the passions, but their reduction to just measure. Illustrating moral and psychological "tempering" through analogy with the physiological "temperaments" or "complexions" associated with the traditional four humors, he supports his initial statement that tragedy (as anciently composed) is the "moralest and most profitable" form of poetry.

In overstressing the significance of this analogy, scholarship has not only distorted Milton's theory of catharsis (as Sellin justly observes); it has also obscured the rhetorical function of this image. The comparison between poet and physician is far older than Renaissance neo-Aristotelian criticism; almost from the beginning, moreover, it had been closely associated with two principles most frequently invoked in discussions of the ends of poetry—utility and delight. In the *Laws* Plato refers to plays and songs as "charms for the spirit." Since the "spirits of the young cannot bear seriousness, we use the terms *plays* and *songs* and employ our charms as games, just as in treating those who are sick and weak, physicians attempt by using pleasant foods and drinks to give them proper nourishment. . . . In the same way the good lawgiver will persuade . . . the poet to work as he should, and present in his beauteous and well-wrought rhythms and harmonies the gestures and accents of men who are wise, strong, and altogether good."[63]

Though Proclus inferred from this passage that "poetry should be rather a medicine than a pastime," Mazzoni interpreted it as advocating "moral instruction flavored with poetic sweetness." While agreeing with Proclus "that Plato has sometimes called poetics a medicine as that which seeks to render souls healthy, and consequently has the useful as its end," Mazzoni also credits Plato with the opinion that "by means of delight it introduces also the useful."[64] In further support of this view he cites Lucretius' *De Rerum Natura*:

> . . . on a dark subject I pen such lucid verses o'erlaying all with the Muses' charm . . . even as physicians when they propose to give nauseous wormwood to children, first smear the rim round the bowl with the sweet yellow juice of honey . . . so I . . . set forth to you our doctrine in sweet-toned Pierian verse and o'erlay it as it were with the pleasant honey of the Muses, if haply by such means I might engage your mind on my verses, till such time as you apprehend all the nature of things and thoroughly feel what use it has.[65]

Lucretius' doctrine, clearly subordinating delight to utility, became Renaissance orthodoxy, along with Horace's precept to mix the *utile* and the *dulce*. Tasso, as we have observed, echoes Lucretius in the opening lines of his epic, and Sidney employs a similar image in his *Apologie for Poetrie*:

> . . . our Poet . . . beginneth not with obscure definitions . . . but
> hee commeth to you with words sent [*sic*] in delightful propor-
> tion. . . . And, pretending no more, doeth intende the winning of
> the mind from wickedness to vertue: even as the childe is often
> brought to take most wholsome things by hiding them in such
> other as have a pleasant tast: which, if one should beginne to
> tell them the nature of *Aloes* or *Rubarb* they should receive,
> woulde sooner take their Phisick at their eares then at their
> mouth.[66]

Beni similarly compares the poet to the physician. In a passage that reveals the influence of both Lucretius and Horace, he declares that poetry mixes the precepts of life with pleasure, "tempering with sweet-ness the bitterness of a medicine."[67] Puttenham alludes to the poet's ability "to play also the Phisitian, and not onely by applying a medicine to the ordinary sicknes of mankind, but by making the very greef it selfe (in part) cure of the disease."[68]

Gosson, on the other hand, converts the medical analogy into a weapon against the poets: "Where honie and gall are mixt, it will be hard to sever the one from the other. The deceitfull phisition geveth sweete syrroppes to make his poyson goe downe the smoother. . . ."[69] Milton similarly turns the same image against his contemporaries, "libidinous and ignorant Poetasters" who violate decorum and "doe for the most part lap up vitious principles in sweet pils to be swallow'd down, and make the tast of vertuous documents harsh and sowr."[70]

In its traditional forms, this parallel between poetry and medicine usually referred to the wholesome but harsh doctrine disguised by verse or fable and made palatable by delight. It did not as a rule involve ca-tharsis. Once the impact of the *Poetics* had begun to be felt, however, it was only natural that the medical analogy should be extended to in-clude tragic delight and tragic purgation. Not only had Aristotle appar-ently introduced the medical parallel into his discussion of catharsis in the *Rhetoric*, but catharsis was itself already a familiar medical term. Scientific and poetic interpretations stood side by side in Renaissance dictionaries; and (as Sherman Hawkins has clearly demonstrated)[71] these medical senses of catharsis were widely known in seventeenth-cen-tury England.

From a rhetorical viewpoint the analogy with homeopathic medicine is essentially a variation of an older, more familiar *topos*—the metaphor of poetry as sugared medicine and of the poet as physician. For neo-Aristotelian critics, the homeopathic variant was useful primarily as an instance of the principle that like purges like; whether they interpreted Aristotle's phrase τοιούτων as meaning "the same" or "similar" or "such like," the analogy could still apply. For some (though not all) of these critics, however, the image still retained its original associations with the *topoi* of delight and utility. In comparing the tragic poet to the physician, Minturno alluded to "the force of the passions charmingly expressed in verses";[72] similarly, in comparing tragic and medical catharsis, Giacomini emphasized the pleasure that accompanies purgation.[73] Both of these writers may reflect the influence of Aristotle's *Politics.*[74]

Milton's medical image is, then, conventional, not only in explanations of Aristotle's tragic theory but also in more generalized discussions of the utility of poetry. It derives additional force from the very ambiguity of the word *catharsis*; of all the multiple senses of this term the medical was probably the most widely known. Finally, this image brought into clearer focus most of the ideas Milton wished specifically to stress—the distinction (as well as the analogy) between the perturbations of the mind and the sufferings of the body; the conception of excess passion as itself a disease or *morbum animi*;[75] the principle that like purges like; and the moderation of painful emotions by mixing them with pleasure, thereby rendering the images of these very passions delightful through imitation.

VI

If Milton's remarks on catharsis have been overstressed, it is partly because they have been taken out of context. Their context (as we have attempted to demonstrate) is essentially rhetorical; and in ignoring their rhetorical function one runs the risk of distorting them. Even Milton's allusion to Aristotle is (as Sellin points out) "conditional"; it is intended to support his preceding statement that tragedy as *anciently* composed "hath been ever held the gravest, moralest, and most profitable of all other Poems. . . ."[76] Milton introduces his allusion to Aristotle's doctrine obliquely, in order to prove and support a generalization already made. The rhetorical relevance of this subject is secondary rather than primary; and it is significant perhaps that (except for its English and Latin equivalents) the term *catharsis* does not occur in this volume at all. The preface is not a systematic treatise on tragic theory, but an apologia or defense of the genre as *anciently* composed—and of Milton's practice in following the ancients.

Ex pede Herculem. Perhaps a competent sculptor can reconstruct an entire statue from a single marble foot, but it is dangerous business for the literary scholar. Milton's remarks on tragedy are too fragmentary, and perhaps too oblique, to enable us to deduce a complete and coherent dramatic theory from them. Whether he ever arrived, tacitly, at such a theory is doubtful; and, if we may believe his own words, the "best rule to all who endeavour to write Tragedy" was to be found rather in the tragic poets themselves—"*Æschulus, Sophocles,* and *Euripides* . . . unequall'd yet by any"—than in any systematic treatise on poetics. (In this respect Milton was, it would seem, faithful to one of the cardinal principles of Renaissance humanism—the stress on example over and above precept, and the emphasis on close study and imitation of classical authors.)

The preface does indeed throw some light on his concept of tragedy, but it is light of one wavelength; it does not include the entire spectrum. This work obviously omits certain highly important aspects of poetic imitation and purgation that receive expression in his other writings. Most of Milton's remarks on poetics, in fact, are strongly conditioned by their rhetorical context. *An Apology for Smectymnuus, The Reason of Church-Government,* and the *Second Defense* are polemical treatises; in these works Milton generally introduces his ideas on poetry as a form of ethical proof. In the tractate *Of Education,* poetics receives tantalizingly brief attention. The preface to *Samson Agonistes* is, as he himself declares, an apologia or defense. Even in his verse and prose epistles his remarks on his literary tastes or his literary plans appear to be partly conditioned by his awareness of the personality and interests of the men he is addressing.

His statement on "passions well imitated" obviously does not exhaust his opinions on the objects of tragic imitation. His remarks are selective, and the selection has been made primarily for rhetorical purposes. In defending tragedy on the ground of its utility (as the "moralest" and "most profitable" of all poetic genres), he had the best possible reason for stressing the passions (rather than action or character or thought) as the object of poetic imitation. Expressed in this form, his argument anticipated, and refuted in advance, one of the most common ethical objections raised against tragedy—that it imitates the passions and corrupts character. In *The Republic* Plato had condemned tragedy on this and other grounds, and his verdict had been boisterously echoed by later opponents of the stage. To these charges Aristotle's *Poetics* was widely regarded as the most authoritative—and, in the opinion of many Renaissance critics, the definite—answer.[77]

Milton does not, of course, summarize the views he is refuting, nor does he mention Plato by name. He was far too competent a rhetorician to cite the very authority whom the enemies of the theater generally regarded as one of their strongest supports. It was common rhetorical practice, however, to anticipate an opponent's arguments and thus forestall him by refuting them in advance. Several of Milton's arguments in defense of tragedy could serve, accordingly, as replies to the objections a hostile reader might raise under the shadow of Plato's authority. In particular, his remark on "passions well imitated" could forestall an appeal to Plato's strictures against dramatic imitation of the passions. His medical image, moreover, enabled him to answer Plato with Plato, pitting the poet-physician simile of the *Laws* against the statements in *The Republic*. His allusion to the poet's ability to "temper" and moderate the passions might likewise rebut Plato with one of his own arguments. For in *The Republic* the philosopher had asserted that "a good man, who has the misfortune to lose his son" will indeed feel sorrow; but "though he can not help sorrowing, he will moderate his sorrow."[78] Similarly, Milton's long catalogue of rulers who had composed tragedies might constitute a reply to Plato's contention that tragedy would corrupt the future guardians of the state.[79]

In investigating Milton's sources, one should also consider the factor of rhetorical conditioning. Like most rhetoricians, Milton knew the persuasive force of a commonplace, and the evidential value of an authority. As yet we have no clear-cut evidence that he took his theory intact from any single author; though in certain respects it resembles those of Minturno, Guarini, Giacomini, Bartolommei, Piccolomini, and Heinsius, on other points it diverges from their views. To isolate the principal ideas in his preface and to trace each of them to its source is unrewarding. Parallels are too numerous, and at best one can merely amplify one's list of analogues. These may add to one's knowledge of the variegated and complex traditions that underlie Milton's assertions, but they do not as yet enable one to pinpoint his actual sources with any degree of precision.

The principal source of Milton's statements would seem, indeed, to be Aristotle himself—though Aristotle as seen and interpreted through Renaissance eyes. Milton's discussion is (it would appear) a skillfully composed mosaic of ideas and phrases derived from Aristotle's own writings, from the *Ethics* and *Politics* as well as the *Poetics*. Even his medical analogy, though conventional in Renaissance poetic theory, is in a sense "authorized" by the medical comparison Aristotle had employed near the end of his *Politics*.

On the whole, Milton was nominally faithful to the authority he cited in introducing his short account of purgation. Like many other critics of his period, he utilized Aristotle to explain Aristotle. Much of the opening section of the preface reveals Aristotelian influence either in diction or in doctrine. Most of its principal ideas were, in varying degrees, conventional in Renaissance neo-Aristotelian criticism. All of them had been accepted, by one critic or another, as implicit or explicit in the *Poetics*.

Recent criticism of Milton's preface has, perhaps, placed an exaggerated, if paradoxical, emphasis on both its originality and its orthodoxy. One doubts that Milton would have been flattered by either term. None of the major ideas in the preface was really original; all were derivative, and most were conventional. Novelty and paradox might command an audience's attention, but they were not always the most effective instruments of persuasion. Though they undoubtedly had their place in mock-defense and mock-encomium, the apologist normally appealed to accepted opinions, to acknowledged authorities, and to commonplaces. In the context of Renaissance critical theory, on the other hand, "orthodoxy" is not an altogether valid concept. Cinquecento criticism was, in a sense, constantly in *quest* of poetic orthodoxy (or "right opinion") without ever quite managing to find it. For many Cinquecento critics the norm or standard was the text of the *Poetics* itself, but this was sometimes too ambiguous to serve as a "rule" without extensive commentary. The text had to be explicated and interpreted, and the explicators rarely agreed. One can hardly speak, therefore, of an orthodox interpretation of the *Poetics*—only of a variety of zealous, painstaking, and sometimes opinionated efforts to ascertain what the orthodox tenets really were, what the classic and most widely accepted canons of poetic doctrine actually meant.

NOTES

1. "From Aristotle to Pseudo-Aristotle," in *Aristotle's "Poetics" and English Literature: A Collection of Critical Essays*, ed. Elder Olson (Chicago and London, 1965), p. 200.

2. Cf. J. E. Spingarn, *A History of Literary Criticism in the Renaissance* (New York, 1925), pp. 79–81; Allan H. Gilbert, *Literary Criticism, Plato to Dryden* (Detroit, 1962), pp. 517, 593; Paul R. Sellin, "Sources of Milton's Catharsis: A Reconsideration," in *Milton Studies in Honor of Harris Francis Fletcher* (Urbana, 1961), pp. 104–122. (Except where otherwise noted, all further references to Sellin cite this study.) See also Sellin, "Milton and Heinsius: Theoretical Homogeneity," in *Medieval Epic to the "Epic Theater" of Brecht*, ed. Rosario P. Armato and John M. Spalek (Los Angeles, 1968), pp. 125–134; also *Daniel Heinsius and Stuart England* (Leiden, 1968), pp. 164–177; John Arthos, *Milton and the Italian Cities* (New York, 1968), pp. 129–205; Martin Mueller, "Sixteenth-Century Italian Criticism and Milton's Theory of Catharsis," *Studies in English Literature*, VI (1966), 139–150; also "Pathos and Katharsis in *Samson Agonistes*," *ELH*, XXXI (1964), 156–174.

3. For rhetorical considerations underlying Milton's remarks on poetry and poetics in *The Reason of Church-Government*, cf. William Riley Parker, *Milton: A Biography* (Oxford, 1968), I, 210. In Parker's opinion, Milton's brief autobiographical sketch, though "startling in its revealing irrelevance," is nonetheless "a subtle argument, designed to convince the nonconformist or Presbyterian reader that poetry has religious sanction. . . ."

4. As Sellin correctly observes, Milton treats "Aristotle's assertion . . . as a conditional statement. He says that Aristotle conceived of tragedy as effecting catharsis *because* tragedy (as constructed by the ancients) had always been considered the most serious, moral, and useful of poetic forms" (pp. 108–109).

5. Cf. Cicero, *De Inventione*, trans. H. M. Hubbell (London and Cambridge, Mass., 1949), pp. 324–327, on *honestas* and *utilitas* in deliberative oratory. The *Rhetorica ad Herennium*, on the other hand, treats *honestas* as a subdivision of *utilitas*; *Ad. C. Herennium de Ratione Dicendi*, trans. Harry Caplan (Cambridge, Mass., and London, 1954), pp. 160–161.

6. *The Reason of Church-Government*, in *Complete Prose Works of John Milton*, ed. Don M. Wolfe (New Haven, 1952), I, 817 (hereafter cited as *Yale Prose*).

7. Aristotle, *On the Art of Poetry*, ed. and trans. Ingram Bywater (Oxford, 1909), pp. 16–17.

8. Theodorus Goulston, *Aristotelis de Poetica Liber, Latinè Conversus, et Analytica* [sic] *Methodo Illustratus* (London, 1623), pp. 11–12; cf. Bywater, p. 151; Sellin, p. 118. Bywater interprets Aristotle's phrase as meaning "practically . . . 'by piteous and alarming scenes.'"

9. *Vincentii Madii Brixiani et Bartholomaei Lombardi Veronensis in Aristotelis Librum de Poetica Communes Explanationes: Madii Vero in Eundem Librum Propriae Annotationes* (Venice, 1550), p. 96. According to Girolamo Tiraboschi, *Storia della Letteratura Italiana* (Milan, 1824), XIII, 2156, Lombardi had been "surprised by immature death" and Maggi had continued the work alone, adding notes and comments "scritti sul far di que' tempi, cioè spiegando Aristotile co' passi di altri antichi scrittori, e fondando i precetti più sull' autorità che sulla ragione e sulla natura."

10. *Francisci Robortelli Utinensis in Librum Aristotelis de Arte Poetica Explicationes* (Florence, 1548): "Per misericordiam verò atque terrorem perturbationes huiusmodi purgans" (p. 52).

11. Lodovico Castelvetro, *Poetica d'Aristotele vulgarizzata, et sposta* (Basel 1576), p. 113.

12. Goulston, pp. 11–12; Sellin, p. 118.

13. Madius, p. 97; cf. ibid., p. 50, "Quod graeci πάθος, affectum nos, aut animi perturbationem dicemus."

14. Cf. Spingarn, pp. 74–81; Bernard Weinberg, *A History of Literary Criticism in the Italian Renaissance* (New York, 1961), passim. (Except where otherwise stated, all further references to Weinberg cite this work.) See also Sellin, pp. 111–115.

15. Madius, p. 98.
16. *Annotationi di M. Alessandro Piccolomini nel libro della poetica d'Aristotele* (Venice, 1575), pp. 102–103.
17. Castelvetro, p. 117; Gilbert, pp. 315–316.
18. Gilbert, p. 316.
19. Gilbert, p. 517; cf. Weinberg, I, 627, on Giacomini's lectures about catharsis. These summarized three different theories of tragic purgation (that tragedy purges only pity and fear; that it purges the *opposites* of those passions; that it "moderates" *all* the passions through its spectacle of "the instability of human affairs") and offered a fourth explanation, that the passions are "purged by exteriorization." Mueller (p. 148) calls attention to the "very striking" resemblance between Milton's views and Giacomini's ideas on "general politics," the "theory of moderation," and the combination of "purgation with tragic delight."
20. *Yale Prose*, I, 816–817. For poetry's ability to "temper" the affections and set them in "right tune," see Aristotle's remarks on the power of music: "There seems to be in us a sort of affinity to musical modes and rhythms, which makes some philosophers say that the soul is a tuning, others, that it possesses tuning." Aristotle, *Politica*, trans. Benjamin Jowett, in *The Basic Works of Aristotle*, ed. Richard McKeon (New York, 1941), p. 1312.
21. Cf. Aristotle, *Ethica Nicomachea*, trans. W. D. Ross, in McKeon: "Virtue must have the quality of aiming at the intermediate. I mean moral virtue; for it is this that is concerned with passions and actions" (p. 958). Cf. also pp. 954, 956.
22. Piccolomini, pp. 101–102. Cf. Spingarn on Sperone Speroni's conviction that "Aristotle cannot refer to the complete eradication of pity and fear—a conception which is Stoic rather than Peripatetic, for Aristotle does not require to free ourselves from emotions, but to regulate them, since in themselves they are not bad" (p. 81); and Weinberg, I, 343, on Borghesi's belief that poetry is "moderatrice di trasandanti affetti." Quoting Heinsius' statement that "defectum quoque eorum atque excessum expiant ac purgant. mediocritatem verò . . . relinquunt," Sellin adds that "Milton could find in Heinsius an elaborate version of Aristotle's mean systematically applied to the *Poetics*" (p. 120).
23. Gilbert, pp. 516–517. Though Gilbert calls attention to the parallel between Guarini's phrase "ridotti a vertuoso temperamento" and Milton's "to temper and reduce them to just measure" (p. 517n.), Sellin observes that "having thus reviewed this idea, Guarini *rejects* it and turns back to the first alternative (extirpative catharsis)" (pp. 115–116).
24. Madius, p. 51.
25. For the syncretistic methodology of Renaissance criticism and the influence of Horace on interpretations of Aristotle, see Weinberg in Olson, pp. 199–200; Weinberg, *History*; and Marvin T. Herrick, *The Fusion of Horatian and Aristotelian Criticism, 1531–1555* (Urbana, 1946).
26. Cf. also the combination of delight and utility in Antonio Posio's view of catharsis (Weinberg, I, 17).
27. Torquato Tasso, "Allegoria della *Gerusalemme Liberata*," in *Le Prose diverse di Torquato Tasso*, ed. Cesare Guasti (Florence, 1875), I, 301: "L'eroica poesia, quasi animale in cui due nature si congiungono, d'imitazione e d'allegoria è composta. Con quella alletta a sè gli animi e gli orecchi degli uomini, e maravigliosamente gli diletta; con questa nella virtù o nella scienza, o nell'una e nell'altra, gli ammaestra."
28. Torquato Tasso, *Jerusalem Delivered*, trans. Edward Fairfax, ed. John Charles Nelson (New York, n.d.), p. 2; Book I, stanza 3.
29. Cf. Gilbert, pp. 377–385.
30. Aristotle, *Politica*, pp. 1311–1312.

31. Ibid., p. 1312.
32. Bywater, p. 9.
33. Aristotle, *Politica*, p. 1315.
34. Ibid., pp. 1311–1312.
35. Ibid., p. 1315.
36. Madius, p. 98: "Videmus eos, cùm animum ad sacrorum cultum expiant, idoneumque reddunt, sacris modulationibus, carminibusque ita constitui, ut si medicinam, purgationemque reperissent: quod idem pati necesse est eos, & qui commiseratione, & qui metu, & generatim qui aliqua perturbatione sunt affecti, atque alios, quatenus aliquid huiusmodi singulis iniicitur. omnesque aliqua ex parte purgari, & allevari cum voluptate. Haec Aristoteles."
37. The phrase *cum voluptate* is, of course, a literal translation of Aristotle's expression meth' hēdonēs ($\mu\epsilon\theta$' $\dot{\eta}\delta o\nu\hat{\eta}s$). Cf. Segni's version of the same passage: "E per l'armonie sacre veggiamo noi disporsi gli uomini in tale modo, quando e'cantano i versi, che purgano l'anima, come se e'confidassino in tal medicina e in tal purificazione.—Un medesimo effetto per necessità interviene in chi ha misericordia, e in chi teme, e finalmente in chiunque ha uno affetto. . . . *Chè tutti per tal mezzo si purgano, e alleggeriscons l'animo con piacere*; e similmente le musiche purgative porgono letizia agli uomini senza nocumento." Bernardo Segni, *Trattato de' Governi d'Aristotile*, Nuova edizione, ed. Casare Bini (Milan, 1864), p. 208 (italics mine).
38. Though several earlier critics regarded delight as an effect or by-product of catharsis, Milton explicitly asserts that imitation is the cause of tragic pleasure. Castelvetro (unlike Milton) held that by "delight" Aristotle meant purgation—the expulsion from the human mind of pity and fear by means of these very emotions. Castelvetro, p. 299.
39. Cf. Liddell and Scott on the preposition μετά (*with*); when accompanied with the genitive, it signifies (1) *"In the midst of, among, between"*; or (2) *"in common, along with, by aid of* (implying a closer union than σύν)", or *"in conjunction with."* Cf. Gildersleeve and Lodge (nos. 392, 399) on *cum* as ablative of attendance and as ablative of manner.
40. Weinberg, I, 627; cf. Mueller, p. 148.
41. Weinberg, I, 625.
42. Bywater, p. 39.
43. *Yale Prose*, I, 818.
44. Arthos, pp. 155–186.
45. See Weinberg, I, 534–535, 555, on the views of Sassetti and Del Bene.
46. In discussing Sardi's manuscript notes on lectures given by Maggi on Aristotle's *Poetics* at the University of Ferrara, Weinberg observes that the 1546 lectures were "very close in context to the ones that Maggi began giving in 1541; hence by all odds the earliest extant commentary on Aristotle's *Poetics*" (I, 375 ff.). The definition of poetry as an imitation not only of actions, but of *passions* and *mores* as well appears in Sardi's notes (quoted by Weinberg, I, 380): "imitatio actionum, passionum, et morum."
47. Cf. Weinberg, I, 22, 206–207, 302, 385, 389, 429, 544, 567, 592; Tasso, ed. Guasti, I, 301; *Dialogo di Messer Alessandro Lionardi, della inventione poetica* (Venice, 1554), p. 81; Giovanni Paolo Lomazzo, *A Tracte Containing the Artes of Curious Paintinge Carvinge & Buildinge*, trans. R.H. (Oxford, 1598), p. 13; Lodovico Dolce, *L'Aretino. Dialogo della Pittura*, ed. D. Ciampoli (Lanciano, 1913), p. 13; Leon Battista Alberti, *On Painting*, trans. John R. Spencer, rev. ed. (New Haven and London, 1966), pp. 77–79; *The Works of Leonardo da Vinci*, ed. Jean Paul Richter, 2nd ed. (London and New York, 1939), I, 38–39, 50, 55, 342. For further discussion of the passions in art, see Anthony Blunt, *Artistic Theory in Italy, 1450–1600* (London and New York, 1968), pp. 12, 34–35, 52–78; Rensselaer W. Lee,

Ut Pictura Poesis: The Humanistic Theory of Painting (New York, 1967), pp. 22–29, 41, 64–75. Though many of the late Renaissance treatises on painting (or on poetry) claim to base the doctrine of the imitation of the passions on Aristotle's *Poetics*, the relatively early date of Alberti's treatise (which antedated the influence of the *Poetics*) indicates that this doctrine had long been established in the theory of painting. It had, moreover, become conventional in late medieval or early Renaissance poetic theory, largely through the influence of Horace.

48. Cf. John Dryden, *Of Dramatic Poesy and Other Critical Essays*, ed. George Watson (London and New York, 1962), I, 25, for the definition of a play as "a just and lively image of human nature representing its passions and humours, and the changes of fortune to which it is subject, for the delight and instruction of mankind." Again (p. 56), "imitation of humours and passions" is the soul of poetry. The Greek tragic poets attempted to express "the πάθος of mankind" (p. 73); and both tragedy and epic depict "human nature, in its actions, passions, and traverses of fortune" (p. 87). Morris Freedman has already raised the question of a possible relationship between Dryden's essay *Of Dramatic Poesy* and Milton's preface to *Samson Agonistes*; "Milton and Dryden on Rhyme," *Huntington Library Quarterly*, XXIV (1961), 337–344.

49. Bywater, pp. 2–5.

50. Bywater, p. 105. Though he observes that the term *pathē* is "generally assumed . . . to denote in this passage 'feelings' or 'emotions,'" Bywater prefers to interpret it in the sense of "what they [the personages represented] have done to them," citing analogous instances of the word elsewhere in the *Poetics*: "The words πάθη καὶ πράξεις cover the whole ground of the story in the dance; so that Aristotle . . . might have said here, without difference of meaning ἤθη καὶ μύθους." Cf. p. 204 on "the variety of senses attaching to" the term *pathos*.

51. Madius, pp. 50–51.

52. Robortello (pp. 11–12) bases his commentary on Pazzi's translation ("mores, perturbationes, actionesque imitantur"), explaining that "ratio aut paret, aut imperat, si imperat, parent cupiditates. Si paret, imperant cupiditates. Ex priore habitu, existunt ἤθη. Ex altero existunt πάθη." He also observes that the same triad (*ēthē, pathē, praxeis*) recurs in the *Paedagogus* of Clement of Alexandria, and he further cites Cicero's *Tusculan Questions* on the meaning of *perturbationes*.

53. Cf. Vettori: "imitantur & mores, & affectus, & actiones" (p. 10).

54. Cf. Piccolomini: "cerchino d'imitare i costumi, gli affetti; & le attioni degli huomini" (p. 13). In commenting on this passage Piccolomini dismisses Vettori's doubts and defines imitation as representation of the actions, mores, and passions of men: "intendendo io per l'imitation, che fanno, quella, che rappresenti, & esprimi i costumi, gli affetti, & le attioni de gli huomini, come aviene, quando saltando s'imita l'ira, la pazzia, la fortezza, la crudeltà; & insiememente i fatti di chiunque sia. . . ."

55. Goulston, p. 2: "imitantur & Mores, & Affectus, & Actiones."

56. Aristotle, *Politica*, pp. 1311–1312.

57. Bywater, p. 49.

58. Madius, p. 187, observes that several manuscripts contained the phrase, καὶ ὅλως ἐν ὑποκρίσει. Cf. Piccolomini's account of Madius' view (p. 245).

59. Robortello, pp. 197–198.

60. Piccolomini, pp. 245–248.

61. Goulston, p. 40.

62. Sellin, p. 108. Warning against mistaking Milton's medical analogy for "Milton's formulation of Aristotle's assertion" concerning purgation, Sellin regards the first sentence in the preface as "a rather careful specification of what Milton thought τὴν τῶν τοιούτων παθημάτων κάθαρσιν means. The analogy, however,

serves an entirely different purpose: it only bolsters the likelihood that the assertion is true. . . ."

63. Gilbert, p. 57.

64. Gilbert, pp. 379–380.

65. Lucretius, *On the Nature of Things*, trans. H. A. J. Munro, in *The Stoic and Epicurean Philosophers*, ed. Whitney J. Oates (New York, 1940), p. 137.

66. *English Literary Criticism: The Renaissance*, ed. O. B. Hardison, Jr. (New York, 1963), p. 117.

67. Weinberg, I, 343.

68. Hardison, pp. 172–173.

69. Ibid., p. 87.

70. *The Reason of Church-Government, Yale Prose*, I, 818.

71. Hawkins addressed the Milton Society of America at its annual meeting in New York on December 27, 1968. His topic was "Catharsis in *Samson Agonistes*." For the published version of this paper, see "Samson's Catharsis," *Milton Studies*, II (1970), 211–230.

72. Gilbert, p. 290.

73. Weinberg, I, 627; Giacomini compares tragic purgation to the effect of "medicinal purgatives which drive out certain humors from the body, provided that the purgatives have some natural appropriateness to the humors." Cf. Mueller, p. 148, on analogies between Milton and Giacomini.

74. Like Aristotle, Minturno employs the medical image not only in close association with the notion of delight, but also in connection with the purgative effect of sacred melodies. Giacomini, like Aristotle, alludes to the "lightening" effect associated with purgation and says that it is "accompanied by a feeling of pleasure."

75. Cf. Vettori: "perturbationem & quasi morbum animi" (p. 112). Mueller has called attention to Vettori's "use of the medical—if not the homeopathic—analogy" in his use of terms like "remedy" and "cure" (p. 145). Arthos notes that the seventeenth-century poet and critic Girolamo Bartolommei likewise "speaks of catharsis in homeopathic and therapeutic terms" and suggests the possibility that Milton may have been influenced by Bartolommei's views (p. 192).

76. Sellin, pp. 108–109.

77. Cf. Weinberg, I, 281, on Parthenio's opinion that the type of imitation Plato had criticized was "that of the passions"; cf. Gilbert, pp. 314–315, on Castelvetro's view of Aristotle's attempt to refute Plato's criticism of poetry as passionate and hence injurious.

78. *The Works of Plato*, trans. B. Jowett (New York, n.d.), II, 391–392; *The Republic*, Book X.

79. Among Plato's arguments against dramatic poetry was the charge that the poet prefers the "passionate and fitful temper, which is easily imitated," instead of attempting to please the "rational principle in the soul." Even the "best of us . . . when we listen to a passage of Homer, or one of the tragedians, in which he represents some pitiful hero who is drawling out his sorrows in a long oration, or weeping, and smiting his breast—the best of us . . . delight in giving way to sympathy, and are in raptures at the excellence of the poet who stirs our feelings most" (Jowett, II, 278, 382, 394).

Time, Light, and the Phoenix:
The Design of *Samson Agonistes*

ALBERT R. CIRILLO

NORTHWESTERN UNIVERSITY

I

In spite of its format *Samson Agonistes* is really a dramatic poem rather than a drama;[1] and it is about human, moral endurance, or fortitude, and the manner in which this leads to the triumph over despair which is regeneration. In this poem such endurance is a virtue within a specifically Christian dispensation. I am aware that this is not a unique view of the work, but it is one that needs to be reaffirmed by way of locating my particular concerns in context. For, although the poem is set in a historical situation and time which antedates Christianity, it was written by a professed Christian poet whose Christian consciousness, no matter how heterodox, colored virtually everything he wrote. Historical setting becomes one aspect of Milton's concern with time in this poem (as in many of his others), and with controlling his materials so as to impress his "fit" audience with the fact that the *essential* action depicted in the fiction is eternal in nature.

Milton relies on what Nicolas Berdyaev calls the "transfiguring action of memory" which is characteristic of eschatological Christianity, a memory which does not restore, or attempt to restore, the past but transforms it into something which is eternal.[2] The external forms of history become vehicles for illustrating the startling immediacy of the moral actions which those forms project. If one may label history as man's pathway toward eternity,[3] Milton's use of historical setting is a rich illustration of such a concept, for the setting merely empha-

sizes the fact that the patterns of the Christian dispensation transcend
the particular historical moments in which they transpire, to become illustrations in time for eternity. It is what I shall call our "responsive
memory" as well as Milton's "creative memory" which enables the poem
to achieve this effect.

There often seems to be current in critical circles an insidious lit-
eral-mindedness that makes it necessary—at the risk of belaboring what
should be obvious to readers of *literature* where the meaning of "imaginative" ought to have some force—to state formally that I am not suggesting that *Samson Agonistes* is a religious tract, or propaganda in
the patently didactic sense. What I am saying is that Milton is an author
conscious of the resonances certain materials would have in the minds
of his particular audience; by using a historical/biblical (the two would
have been synonymous for Milton) situation from the Old Testament,
particularly one so widely known and commented upon, in such a way
that he infuses it with his Christian consciousness, Milton works into it
certain informing contexts and patterns which provide the life-force of
the poem according to his own insights and ends. These were ends
which were always concerned with the perspective which human action, historical action, had in eternity. "Creative memory," then, is the
art of bringing recognizable nuances and contexts to a work so as ac-
tively to transfigure and transform the past, which is the setting for the
work's action, in order to make that past as present as today in suggesting the meaning and application of the work; "responsive memory"
is the reader's recognition of and response to the patterns of "creative
memory" in the work.

To argue Milton's insights and ends at length in this age of enlightened Milton studies would, one hopes, be redundant; but it would
not be overstating the case, by way of summary, to repeat D. C. Allen's
epitomization of Milton's poetic career as an attempt to recapture the
harmonious vision lost at the Fall.[4] The restoration of this vision Milton
sees not only in the era of grace instituted by Christ, but in what that
grace makes possible for man, if only through the voice of a chosen
poet-prophet. This poet-prophet can apply his own particular, inspired,
vision to past history and see it in terms of the era of grace; make its
drama relevant and contemporary because of its implicit relation to
what is, for him and for every Christian, an eternal, ever-present drama.
It is in this sense that *Samson Agonistes* is a typological poem;[5] not
that Samson is a Christ figure in any rigid sense, but that his action and
triumph are of a particular kind which, controlled by what I have

called the "creative memory" of the prophetic author, can be seen as an image of the endurance, the strength of soul and character, which Christ exemplified for all time, present and past.

The endurance or fortitude which I mentioned at the very beginning of this essay, then, is a quality of character rather than simply physical strength. It is an *inner* virtue, the strength of mind and soul to resist softness and *luxuria*, on the one hand, even when they *seem* inviting and proper (as they always do), even when they have the approval or urging of the populace; it is, too, the strength to resist, ultimately, despair about one's physical and moral lot. This is the fortitude exemplified by Guyon, for example, in *The Faerie Queene*, when he passes through the Bower of Bliss without succumbing to its delights; when he imprisons Acrasia, unmoved by her loveliness and apparent feminine fragility and the sweet ease which her charms induce. What is at issue here, obviously, is the essence of Christian heroism as it was understood in the Christian humanistic tradition. Just as the allegorizers of Homer and Vergil could exercise their creative imagination to see Achilles' strength and Aeneas' purposefulness as indicative of the qualities of soul necessary for the Christian in the New Law, so Christian heroism came to apply particularly to strength of spirit rather than to strength of body. In this sense, it becomes more "heroic" to refuse to fight than to fight; to turn the other cheek than to strike back.[6] Although, in general, my view of the poem would agree with that which sees it primarily as a drama of the mind,[7] I would particularize that setting as the soul, or the whole spiritual dimension of man. The drama is about an inner struggle which is not a particular struggle, but all moral struggles; its dimension is spiritual and it therefore transcends time and space, although these are the immediate aspects of the "fiction."

When Georges Poulet explains the phrase "Un punto solo" in the last canto of Dante's *Paradiso* in terms of an instant of duration, the instant when one remembers having seen God, he sees this as occurring at precisely that moment when Dante is ready to apprehend the point of eternity. Human duration and the divine Point become one, even as the poem itself comes to the end of its movement: "The final object of the poem is no longer an object around which one can turn and toward which one tends; it is an object one possesses, a point with which one coincides. And if one coincides with it, that is because it is no longer now an exterior and remote object. The divine Point is the very center of the soul, it is God interiorly possessed in a human moment."[8] This possession of God in a human moment is what Samson moves toward in his struggle and interior motions: to see what is God's plan for him and in what terms it is to be expressed, to free himself from the feeling that he has betrayed God and thus has been abandoned by him, is the particular course of this motion and of the movement to possess God. This pattern makes Samson's drama ours, which is only to say, in terms of this poem, what Poulet has said in general about the movement by which, according to the mystical tradition, the soul is said to approach God: by means of a centered motion that takes place in the interior of the soul.[9] Not only is this motion within Samson, but the entire poem becomes a projection, a generalization, of this motion toward the apprehension of God in a single moment, at the noon climax of the Feast of Dagon.

Milton's art (or his vision) effectively makes time and place no time and no place, or all time and that "placelessness" which is the soul or the moral dimension. Time becomes blurred because Samson's struggle is our struggle, just as it is Adam's struggle, and Christ's struggle. Such action looks back to the past (even as it is "past" in terms of the reader's place in human time) and forward to an indeterminate and potentially endless future. The physical action, the physical details which make up the data of the work, are projections of spiritual states; Samson's physical blindness represents his spiritual blindness as an aspect of his motion through the darkness to the light. His physical strength wanes and waxes as his spiritual strength does. In this sense, the poem not only depends on typology for its essential "form"; it *is* typology.[10]

II

I have already mentioned the general typological relations between Samson and Christ and have alluded to the fact that the type of moral struggle which is Samson's becomes timeless, in one particular, because it is, as our "responsive memory" (on which Milton relies) reminds us, one version of the struggle which all men undergo, even the God who became man. It may be merely circumstantial that *Samson Agonistes* was first published together with *Paradise Regained*, but it was a fortuitous circumstance nevertheless, for the two poems are remarkably similar in the nature of their essential actions and, indeed, in the setting of those actions.

The action of these two poems is really internal, or introspective, to the exclusion of any *particularly* defined external landscape: *Paradise Regained*, in spite of the vague wilderness where the temptations occur, being concerned with the inner struggle which shows both Christ's manhood and divinity. *Samson Agonistes*, set in the light, and in the dark shadows before the prison in Gaza, also projects its locale into the inner being of Samson in such a way that the light-dark contrast becomes a universalization of the implications of this internal "action." What is essentially remarkable about the joint publication of these two poems is the fact that one deals with the moral struggle as it was defined for the Christian dispensation, while the other deals with it in a context that precedes yet prefigures that dispensation. Both are the same, united in a continuum of eternally meaningful, spiritual action. Samson's ultimate spiritual triumph is possible by virtue of the coming of Christ and his triumph.

The drama of *Paradise Regained* presents the pattern by which the paradise within is recovered; it is a pattern set for us at a moment in time by a man whose actions transcend time. Further, it is a pattern which is established in terms of moral action or development within meditation—in the larger sense, of a mind moving toward an apprehension of the divine.[11] Insofar as this is a model capable of infinite repetition throughout time (and, in fact, should be repeated throughout time, the narrative would suggest), its mode is timeless. As a model of psychic and moral struggle the situation is an existential one, what Berdyaev refers to as "an irruption of the eternal into the temporal, and also a fulfilment" in the "time of the world of subjectivity."[12] The plane of time on which the action is located is the plane of eternity as it exists within the human spirit; and the temptations of Christ contain all temptations, past, present, and future. Indications of this occur early in the first book of *Paradise Regained* where Milton repeats, proportionately compressed in the space of a hundred-odd lines, the council in Hell and the council in Heaven that we saw on a grander scale in Books II and III of *Paradise Lost*. Both Satan's brief council "in mid air" (I.39 ff.) and the Father's "in full frequence bright / Of Angels" (I.128–129)[13] represent expressions of intent in eternity: the temptation occurs once, but it is for all time. This is the real force of the Father's concluding statement:

> But first I mean
> To exercise him in the Wilderness;
> There he shall first lay down the rudiments
> Of his great warfare, ere I send him forth
> To conquer Sin and Death the two grand foes,
> By Humiliation and strong Sufferance:

His weakness shall o'ercome Satanic strength
And all the world, and mass of sinful flesh;
That all the Angels and Ethereal Powers,
They now, and men hereafter, may discern
From what consummate virtue I have chose
This perfect Man, by merit call'd my Son,
To earn Salvation for the Sons of men. (I.155–167)

The milieu of Christ's temptation is one of solitude, a wilderness
in which time seems to be suspended. In this landscape, in which he
"walk'd alone," distinctions are not precise and clear, only shadow and
light stand out:

And his deep thoughts, the better to converse
With solitude, till far from track of men,
Thought following thought, and step by step led on,
He enter'd now the bordering Desert wild,
And with dark shades and rocks environ'd round,
His holy Meditations thus pursu'd. (I.190–195)

This landscape of temptation is also the interior landscape of moral
choice, the moral choice which leads to regeneration; and the very meaning of "regeneration in Christ" is what is at issue here, not simply that
Christ's merits earned mankind the possibility of redemption, but, more
specifically, that it is this action, repeated throughout time in the landscape of the individual soul, which secures *individual* redemption. One
moves, existentially, from the wilderness and darkness of the desert up
into the light and civility of a revitalized spirit. What we see in the
drama of *Samson Agonistes* is much the same thing—the "Humiliation
and strong Sufferance" by which Samson, through his weakness, overcomes the Satanic strength of Dagon which has seized his spirit in the
form of despair—even if the setting is pre-Christian. The typology which
would be a part of Milton's inherited "language," as well as that of his
audience, would demand that the triumph of Samson be seen in the light
of the triumph of Christ: "creative memory" and "responsive memory"
would be perfectly complementary. The drama is an internally oriented
one about a man's regeneration, which is every man's possibility of regeneration because of the example and action of "one greater Man."

This is not to force the comparison between Samson and Christ but
to emphasize the way in which the figure of Samson, as used by a poet
whose thinking is influenced by a Christian typological tradition which
saw Christ as the center of the universe—all time before his coming as

looking toward it, all time after his coming as looking back to it[14]—can represent Christ-like action. Samson's death, the "resurrection" of his spirit in the image of the Phoenix, as I shall suggest, has its *meaning* in the death and resurrection of Christ—which was a triumph. In the Christological companion-piece *Paradise Regained*, there is the same coming-to-awareness of a sense of mission, the same consciousness of being a divine instrument, that Samson articulates early in his despondency, when Christ recalls his mother's words during his youth:

> High are thy thoughts
> O Son, but nourish them and let them soar
> To what height sacred virtue and true worth
> Can raise them, though above example high;
> By matchless Deeds express thy matchless Sire.
> For know, thou art no Son of mortal man;
> Though men esteem thee low of Parentage,
> Thy Father is th'Eternal King, who rules
> All Heaven and Earth, Angels and Sons of men.
> A messenger from God foretold thy birth
> Conceiv'd in me a Virgin; he foretold
> Thou shouldst be great and sit on *David's* Throne,
> And of thy Kingdom there should be no end. (I.229–241)

Christ is always conscious that the way to his triumph will be the way of tribulation:

> my way must lie
> Through many a hard assay even to the death,
> Ere I the promis'd Kingdom can attain,
> Or work Redemption for mankind, whose sins'
> Full weight must be transferr'd upon my head. (I.263–267)

In comparison with Christ, Samson represents a similarity with a difference, as befits a more fully human instrument and precursor. At the beginning of the action, Samson is not conscious of the means by which he is to be used, of the manner in which he is to be God's instrument; he cannot reconcile the suffering and humiliation in which he finds himself with his knowledge of his special particularity among the chosen people. This is what makes him despair:

> O wherefore was my birth from Heaven foretold
> Twice by an Angel, who at last in sight
> Of both my Parents all in flames ascended

From off the Altar, where an Off'ring burn'd,
As in a fiery column charioting
His Godlike presence, and from some great act
Or benefit reveal'd to *Abraham's* race?
Why was my breeding order'd and prescrib'd
As of a person separate to God,
Design'd for great exploits; if I must die
Betray'd, Captiv'd, and both my Eyes put out,
Made of my Enemies the scorn and gaze;
To grind in Brazen Fetters under task
With this Heav'n-gifted strength? (ll. 23–36)

The drama of *Samson Agonistes* is the drama of man's triumph over this despair; and, as the Chorus recognizes, this is the realization of God's plan:

All is best, though we oft doubt,
What th' unsearchable dispose
Of highest wisdom brings about, .
And ever best found in the close. (ll. 1745–1748)

It is, too, an aspect of the same eternal plan which will be fulfilled in Christ—indeed, *has been fulfilled* in terms of the audience which confronts the poem.[15] Samson has to learn what Christ knows even at the beginning of his ordeal, that "All things are best fulfill'd in their due time, / And time there is for all things" (III.182–183); but the difference which makes Christ aware of this at the beginning and makes Samson have to learn it through experience and suffering is the difference between the Old Law and its fulfillment, between a completely human type who is to be a divine instrument and the "true Image of God"[16] who is to make good that instrumentality. In this sense, the interior action of the one who came first in time is relevant only because it partakes of the interior action that is to come, only because it derives its value from the physical and moral action of one who, in terms of human time, is to come later.[17]

From the perspective of eternity, however, this action is always present, for the redemption was promised from all eternity, as Milton had described in *Paradise Lost* (III.236 ff.); in the scheme of *eternal* providence—which was one of the principal concerns of Milton's poetic ideology—Samson's triumph is present in eternity because the Son's offer of redemption is made in eternity: it is to be a historical act with eternal validity.[18] If we see eternity as endlessly extended time, "the linking of an unlimited series of limited world periods, whose succession only God is able to survey,"[19] the reader can identify, in this succession, the linkage between Samson, Christ, and himself: all are men, and all are involved, within God's survey, in those movements of the soul which cannot be said to be confined to time. The past becomes present in that the movement of Samson's soul, potentially at least, is the movement of our soul; and it becomes more so in the reader's recognition of this potential identity in the act of reading, an act of human consciousness which affectively involves the reader in the work. This is an inclusive, but no less real and valid, use of typology: that an "event" in the past becomes a shadow or type of an "event" in the present or future.[20]

III

History moves forward in its own historical time, but it cannot either remain in it, or come to an end in it. It moves on either into cosmic time, in which case it makes an affirmation of naturalism and is in tune with the final objectification of human existence, when man takes his place as merely a subordinate part of the whole world of nature. Or it issues into existential time, and this means moving out from the realm of objectification into the spiritual pattern of things.

Existential time, which is known to everyone by experience . . . is evidence of the fact that time is in man, and not man in time, and that time depends upon changes in man. At a greater depth we know that temporal life is consummated in eternity. The development of the spirit in history is supratemporal. Hegel is of opinion that in historicity the spirit overcomes history and realizes eternity, but he does not understand the tragedy of history. In existential time, which is akin to eternity, there is no distinction between the future and the past, between the end and the beginning. In it the eternal accomplishment of the mystery of spirit takes place. In consequence of events which occur in existential time there is development and enrichment of history, and a return to the purity of its sources. From time to time limpid springs are brought into view which well up from existential depths and then an illusion is created by which the revelation of the eternal is transferred to the far distant past. Time is not the

> image of eternity (as in Plato, Plotinus), time is
> eternity which has collapsed in ruin. Cosmic time
> and historical time do not resemble eternity. But,
> nevertheless, Christianity attaches a meaning to time
> and to history within time.
>
>   Nicolas Berdyaev, *The Beginning and the End*,
> pp. 206–207.

Up to this point I have been concerned with the general configuration of *Samson Agonistes* as a dramatic poem which focuses on the eternal (and internal) movement of the soul by which it triumphs over despair. The controlling design of the poem—the typological pattern which relates Samson's triumph to the triumph of Christ, in time for eternity—fixes the "action" as transpiring in the interior infinity of the soul, the common ground which the reader shares with the type and with its fulfillment; it is this common ground, this relationship, which puts such action beyond any particular time and locale to make it part of all time (or the time that is in man, according to Berdyaev), and, by implication, *one* time which is eternity, or the endless continuum of historical periods which only God can survey. For the rest of this essay I shall attempt to trace the pattern by which this design is executed in terms of three principal and related images: time, light, and the Phoenix.

In an embryonic footnote to another essay, some years ago, I prepared the way for my considerations here.[21] At that time my interest in *Samson Agonistes* was ancillary to an examination of the temporal structure of *Paradise Lost*; and I should like, now, to flesh out the skeletal design I furnished there with some additional considerations on the larger aspect of *Samson Agonistes*, related to the long passage from Berdyaev with which I have prefaced this section.

Let us begin with the most obvious data. The action of *Samson Agonistes* begins at daybreak (l.11) and ends with the Messenger's account of Samson's death at high noon (l.1612). The day itself is the Feast of Dagon and the atmosphere of religious ritual becomes important both within the action of the poem and in the poem's affective structure. It takes no real stretch of the imagination to see the temporal span—from daybreak to noon—even within the convention of the "circumscription of time" announced in the preface, as an epitome, or compression, of a moral lifetime set in the context of ritualistic enactment which takes us from darkness to light. Since the real concern in the poem is the struggle within, and the movement of the spirit from darkness to light, it is appropriate that Samson himself voice this pattern in a kind of liturgical pronouncement of a formulaic ritual:

A little onward lend thy guiding hand
To these dark steps, a little further on;
For yonder bank hath choice of Sun or shade,
There I am wont to sit, when any chance
Relieves me from my task of servile toil,
Daily in the common Prison else enjoin'd me,
Where I a Prisoner chain'd, scarce freely draw
The air imprison'd also, close and damp,
Unwholesome draught: but here I feel amends,
The breath of Heav'n fresh-blowing, pure and sweet,
With day-spring born; here leave me to respire.
This day a solemn Feast the people hold
To *Dagon* thir Sea Idol . . . (ll. 1–13)

As Samson slowly makes his way, we follow the movement of a soul
from darkness to light. (This design has been well established at the
outset, not only by the suggestion that the day is beginning, but also by
the very setting: *before* the Prison in Gaza; the opening lines make it
clear that Samson has just *emerged* from the actual prison to a place
outside, just as he will emerge from the prison of his mind.) Incipient
in these lines is the course of the entire moral drama, and its fulfillment.
In the light, he feels "amends" from the "breath of Heav'n fresh-blowing," and this *respiration* (re-breathing, or new breath) comes with the
light of day.[22]

The contrast between outward light and inner darkness, which
is simultaneously physical and moral, and the indication that movement into the light, no matter how blind his eyes, gives Samson some
feeling of "amends" from the breath of heaven, makes Samson not
unlike the narrator of the great prologue to Book III (ll. 1–55) of *Paradise
Lost*, who just as intensely feels his own blindness but, with proportionate intensity, feels the inward shining of the "Celestial Light."[23]
The significant difference—and it is both a difference and a significant
one—is that Samson has not yet achieved the knowledge and wisdom
which the narrator of *Paradise Lost* has from the very beginning; hence,
Samson's famous lament underlines the fact that he has not yet reconciled the physical blindness, the inability to see external reality, with
his own place in the providential scheme. This realization will *be* the
inner light:

O dark, dark, dark, amid the blaze of noon,
Irrecoverably dark, total Eclipse
Without all hope of day!

O first created Beam, and thou great Word,
"Let there be light, and light was over all";
Why am I thus bereav'd thy prime decree?
The Sun to me is dark
And silent as the Moon,
When she deserts the night,
Hid in her vacant interlunar cave.
Since light so necessary is to life,
And almost life itself, if it be true
That light is in the Soul,
She all in every part; why was the sight
To such a tender ball as th' eye confin'd?
So obvious and so easy to be quench't,
And not as feeling through all parts diffus'd,
That she might look at will through every pore?
Then had I not been thus exil'd from light;
As in the land of darkness yet in light,
To live a life half dead, a living death
And buried . . . (ll. 80–101)

Implicit here is Samson's sense of his own error in being dazzled by a false light ("land of darkness yet in light") most aptly represented by the day of celebration to a false god. As yet, however, this sense is confined to the purely physical aspects of his situation, to the purely physical nature of his blindness. But inherent here, too, is the knowledge that will come later, that in yielding to the temptation which led to his capture, he yielded to the false light that flooded him with inner (spiritual) darkness. This speech works together with his actual emergence from his dark prison ("a life half dead, a living death / And buried . . .") into the gradually intensifying light of the morning.[24] Samson must move into the light, as in *Paradise Lost* the blind narrator *already* has. The *motion* (Samson himself uses this term: "what I motion'd was of God" [l. 222]) is that to which the reader bears witness. It is a movement out of the darkness of night, through the glimmer of daybreak, to the highest light of noon: a narrative investiture of an inward journey by which the soul approaches God. From another perspective, this is a movement in and through time, to its fulfillment in eternity, or the eternal moment in which God is possessed in the soul.[25]

In the development from the darkness and glimmers of dawn to the high intensity of noon-light—simultaneously a literal movement that is the temporal setting of the action—we witness the increasing crescendo of inner light that signals Samson's spiritual rebirth. He suf-

fers, for truth's sake, to achieve fulfillment in his real action at noon
when he destroys the Temple of Dagon. To return to the example of
Adam who, after his vision of the "Race of time" at the end of *Paradise
Lost*, sees the true perspective of divine Providence whereby all time,
change, and suffering will "stand fixt"—we may see Samson's suffering
and its direction in the pattern Adam sees:

> . . . suffering for Truth's sake
> Is fortitude to highest victory,
> And to the faithful Death the Gate of Life;
> Taught this by his example whom I now
> Acknowledge my Redeemer ever blest. (*PL* XII.569–573)

Adam's is a vision of the perspective of events in eternity whereby death
becomes life; darkness becomes light. Samson, as he moves toward his
action at noon—the moment of greatest light—is, so to speak, approach-
ing the "Gate of Life" in terms of that light, that moment (high noon)
which was, in a famous Renaissance analogy, the image of eternity.[26]
Time, which is literal in the poem, is typological in terms of Samson's
interior struggle; it is the action of timeless moral struggle from death
to life, and the basic metaphor for expressing this timeless struggle is
light-darkness.

Samson thus speaks of himself at the beginning of the poem, within
images of death and darkness, as a "Sepulcher, a moving Grave" (l. 102);
and the Chorus glosses this sentiment as an expression of despair by
which he has plunged his soul into darkness. It is difficult to read this
passage without seeing in it the parallel between his literal imprisonment and his spiritual one:

> Thou art become (O worst imprisonment!)
> The Dungeon of thyself; thy Soul
> (Which Men enjoying sight oft without cause complain)
> Imprison'd now indeed,
> In real darkness of the body dwells,
> Shut up from outward light
> To incorporate with gloomy night;
> For inward light, alas,
> Puts forth no visual beam
> O mirror of our fickle state . . . (ll. 155–164)

These lines describe the imagistic pattern by which we shall eventually
see Samson move out of the midnight darkness of his despair into the

noon-light of grace. The emphasis on darkness at the opening of the
poem—the actual darkness of the night which is just blending into
the light of sunrise—serves to make the intense nature of noon and its
light at the end of the poem more realizable, particularly because of the
image of the Phoenix which plays an important and integral part there.[27]

Everything in the poem is effectively pointed toward the great climax which brings together, in a single complex image, the theme of
time and its relation to light-darkness. Throughout, there has been an
emphasis on Samson's despair, which is provoked, primarily, by his
feeling that he was destined from birth for greater things than the lot to
which he now is confined. In addition, this despair is not unrelated to
Samson's sense that his mission has something to do with some kind of
strife or contest (what Crashaw calls "A commerce of contrary powres")
between God and Dagon, whose "thrall" he now seems to be. The fact
that it is the Feast of Dagon—the false god whose light is really spiritual
darkness—consequently takes on genuine importance in the overall
symbolic texture. The interview with his father, Manoa, concentrates
on this tension when Manoa reminds Samson of the ultimate humiliation which awaits him:

> A worse thing yet remains.
> This day the *Philistines* a popular Feast
> Here celebrate in *Gaza*; and proclaim
> Great Pomp, and Sacrifice, and Praises loud
> To *Dagon*, as their God who hath deliver'd
> Thee, *Samson*, bound and blind into thir hands,
> Them out of thine, who slew'st them many a slain.
> So *Dagon* shall be magnified, and God,
> Besides whom is no God, compar'd with Idols,
> Disglorified, blasphem'd, and had in scorn
> By th' Idolatrous rout amidst thir wine;
> Which to have come to pass by means of thee,
> *Samson*, of all thy sufferings think the heaviest . . . (ll. 433–445)

Recognizing his fault and his anguish in this situation, Samson sees it
now as a contest between God and Dagon in which Dagon "must stoop"
(ll. 461–468). The irony here, realizable at the end, is that God's victory
over Dagon comes about through Samson, through the very celebration
of the feast in which Samson will eventually participate, in a ritual action whereby he becomes the image of God—as everyone who triumphs
over evil does—in defeating Dagon. Humiliation becomes triumph,

just as darkness becomes light; or, as in this case, just as light *flows* out
of darkness.

Later, in one of his most important and impressive speeches, Samson indicates that his despair involves a kind of death, a spiritual
night which darkens his "inmost mind" (l. 611):

> My griefs not only pain me
> As a ling'ring disease,
> But finding no redress, ferment and rage,
> Nor less than wounds immedicable
> Rankle, and fester, and gangrene,
> To black mortification.
> Thoughts my Tormentors arm'd with deadly stings
> Mangle my apprehensive tenderest parts,
> Exasperate, exulcerate, and raise
> Dire inflammation which no cooling herb
> Or med'cinal liquor can assuage,
> Nor breath of Vernal Air from snowy *Alp*.
> Sleep hath forsook and giv'n me o'er
> To death's benumbing Opium as my only cure.
> Thence faintings, swoonings of despair,
> And sense of Heav'n's desertion. (ll. 617–632)

This attitude, maintained throughout, lends a dark tonality to the whole
poem which the imagery underlines in visual terms. We are over-
whelmed by an impression of a complete plunge into the depths, especially at the moment when the Chorus aligns Samson's descent with the
sin of pride—and thus with the sin of Adam—in terms of the noon imagery which reminds us of Adam's fall at noon:[28]

> God of our Fathers, what is man!
> That thou towards him with hand so various,
> Or might I say contrarious,
> Temper'st thy providence through his short course,
> Not evenly, as thou rul'st
> Th'Angelic orders and inferior creatures mute,
> Irrational and brute.
> Nor do I name of men the common rout,
> That wand'ring loose about
> Grow up and perish, as the summer fly,
> Heads without name no more remember'd,
> But such as thou hast solemnly elected,
> With gifts and graces eminently adorn'd

> To some great work, thy glory,
> And people's safety, which in part they effect:
> Yet toward these, thus dignifi'd, thou oft,
> Amidst thir height of noon,
> Changest thy count'nance and thy hand . . . (ll. 667–684)

The Chorus' conviction that Samson has been cast down at the height of his glory, at the point when he himself was most proud of his singularity or "election," is both true and false: true in the sense that Samson's fall has been the fault of his own pride and blindness, but false in that the working out of Providence will bring a rising from this fall, even *through* this fall. The "noon" which, to the Chorus, is an image of the height of Samson's former glory will become, instead, an image of the height of his ultimate glory, his resurrection from the death of despair at a symbolic moment in time that is the image of all time.

That Samson himself shares the responsibility for his own movement into light is apparent from his statement to Dalila that he was false to himself before she was false to him (l. 824), a self-conscious recognition of his blame for his plight and a classic step toward his "resurrection" or renovation.[29] After he has been through the series of confrontations which make up the "middle" of the poem by developing our recognition of the depths of his despair and of his eventual acceptance of his responsibility for it, together with the glimmers of hope that issue from that acceptance of responsibility, one is not surprised that Samson again feels the stirrings of grace within him ("I begin to feel / Some rousing motions in me which dispose / To something extraordinary my thoughts" [ll. 1381–1383]) and a renewed sense of himself as especially chosen. Significantly, this is expressed in terms which emphasize that his sense of self will be vindicated on *"this* day"—a particularization of the day on which all takes place (the Feast of Dagon), and an implicit allusion to the image of light inherent in the idea of "day":

> If there be aught of presage in the mind,
> This day will be remarkable in my life
> By some great act, or of my days the last. (ll. 1387–1389)

The long speech of the Messenger (l. 1596 ff.) which describes the great act by which Samson makes the day remarkable epitomizes the action of the entire poem; for, in it, the Messenger announces that his own entrance into the gates of the city coincided with the sunrise, or with the same glimmerings of light with which the poem opened. In addition, he emphasizes the ceremonious nature of the day as "The morning Trumpets Festival proclaim'd / Through each high street" (ll. 1598–1599). In the background of Samson's anguish—even from the very beginning, when he sought choice of "Sun or shade"—has been the motif in which the increasing intensity of light parallels the increasing intensity of the ceremonies of the day until the great spectacle at noon: Samson's spiritual awakening is counterpointed by the progress of the day which is the very setting of the poem. Milton seems to be providing an exceptionally apt symbolic action that moves and progresses as Samson moves and progresses, until, at the climactic moment, Samson transforms the light of Dagon, which is equivalent to the darkness of his own blindness, into the light of his own triumph as the executor of the true God's providence.

But the Messenger's speech emphasizes other points important in underlining this convergence of elements in a single moment of time that epitomizes the entire action of the poem and suggests that here is where its meaning is concentrated. The principal ceremony of this great feast takes place in what is described as a "spacious Theater" (l. 1605) as the "Feast and noon grew high and Sacrifice / Had fill'd thir hearts with mirth, high cheer, and wine" (ll. 1612–1613).[30] Just as he had done with the scene of the Fall in *Paradise Lost*, Milton weaves the symbolic temporal occasion of this action—even the crescendo of intensity from sunrise to noon—into the entire framework here so that everything comes together in one meaningful climax. The description of the reveling Philistines filled with wine, awaiting the appearance of their blind captive, in a context which carefully locates the situation at noon, sets the scene in the tradition I explored some years ago, a tradition which saw noon not only as the image of eternity, but thereby as the moment when the divine is most apt to manifest itself to man; conversely, it was also the moment when man was believed to be most susceptible to *luxuria* (sensual indulgence) and a general relaxation of his moral guard.[31]

At this moment, too, the Messenger's description suggests, Samson achieves his closest communion with God, as the actual intense light of noon becomes the inner light which displaces the darkness of his despair:

> And eyes fast fixt he stood, as one who pray'd,
> Or some great matter in his mind revolv'd. (ll. 1637–1638)

What this ritual stance presages is the return of that light "in the Soul" (l. 92) which Samson had earlier despaired of receiving. It comes at this moment, in this temple-theater of a false god whose light is darkness; and it is externalized in the climactic ritual of Samson's whole series of ritualistic actions in the poem, the "rousing motions" of physical power which lead to the destruction of the temple and, thereby, of the false god and his works which had possessed him in the form of despair until his own inner "rousing motions" brought him from darkness to light. The Semichorus describes the sacrifice of the Philistines in terms that recall the earlier description (ll. 1612–1613) of the mob flush in its orgiastic rites at the hour of noon:

> While thir hearts were jocund and sublime,
> Drunk with Idolatry, drunk with Wine,
> And fat regorg'd of Bulls and Goats,
> Chanting thir Idol . . . (ll. 1669–1672)

The great religious epitome of the Feast of Dagon, realized in terms of sensual rites which reach their climax at noon with the appearance of the humiliated Samson, is subsumed into another rite, the celebration of the one true God, as Samson rises out of his humiliation, feels once more the light of God within him—appropriately, at the hour of noon— and asserts His power. This is the triumph of eternity in that human moment which is an image of eternity. At this moment, the Semichorus indicates, *internal blindness* afflicts the Philistines (l. 1686) as *internal illumination* fills Samson (ll. 1687–1689).

Wilkenfeld suggests that this marks Samson's "transformation as a mythical event";[32] and it seems as if Milton does this in a clear, though symbolic, way. That this is the Feast of Dagon, a religious festival, has been insisted upon since the beginning of the poem (l. 12). In his study of sacred time and myths Mircea Eliade sees religious rite, and particularly religious festival, as the means by which man passes from ordinary temporal duration to sacred time; a festival is time which has become ritualized, commemorated as an ever-present event (see Donne's "Good Friday, 1613. Riding Westward" for a concise development of this idea) which therefore represents a perpetual recovery of the event commemorated. As Eliade says, it is *"primordial mythical time made present"* ritually, or reactualized by the festival.[33]

Samson's entire course of action throughout the poem has been ritualistic, from the opening ceremony of moving from shade to sun,

through his three major confrontations with Manoa, Dalila, and Harapha, to the final appearance in the temple-theater. All of this "ritual"
has occurred on the feast day, but the final act, at which point Samson's
communion with God has been reestablished, takes place at high noon
in the center of the temple-theater: it becomes a central celebratory act.
Samson "participates" in the festival in a way that is ironic in respect to
its nature as a celebration of a pagan god. His participation becomes
the focal ceremony which celebrates, not the god whose festival this is
supposed to be, but the God whose instrument he is; it is an act which
asserts the validity and the presence of the true God—at that moment
most like eternity—by the destruction of the dwelling of the false god.
Simultaneously, it is an emblem of Samson's renewed communion, in
eternity, with God, and a sign of the *eternal* punishment visited upon
those who worship the illusory light of false gods. The destruction of
the temple becomes, then, a kind of liturgical, religious act in itself,
made ritually present in and by the poem. As Madsen's study of typology suggests, and as I have iterated earlier, the typology here does not
lie in any explicit reference to Christ vis-à-vis Samson, but in the fact
that we as readers come to this poem with the consciousness that Christ
has lived, suffered, and died, just as Milton wrote the poem with this
consciousness. Samson's act is a type, a prefiguration of Christ's. Just as
our acts of moral courage are said to be accomplished by virtue of
Christ's, to which we look back, so Samson's action, like that of most
Old Testament figures, looks forward to Christ's. All are essentially the
same action, "eternalized" in the spiritual dimension of the human soul,
"ritualized" and commemorated in the festival act at high noon, when
divine and human will become one.[34]

The most important image which fits into this pattern is that of the
Phoenix, which the Semichorus designates in addressing itself to the contrast between the internal blindness of the Philistines and Samson's
internal illumination at noon:

> But he though blind of sight,
> Despis'd and thought extinguish't quite,
> With inward eyes illuminated
> His fiery virtue rous'd
> From under ashes into sudden flame,
> And as an ev'ning Dragon came,
> Assailant on the perched roosts,
> And nests in order rang'd
> Of tame villatic Fowl; but as an Eagle

His cloudless thunder bolted on thir heads.
So virtue giv'n for lost,
Deprest, and overthrown, as seem'd,
Like that self-begott'n bird
In the *Arabian* woods embost,
That no second knows nor third,
And lay erewhile a Holocaust,
From out her ashy womb now teem'd,
Revives, reflourishes, then vigorous most
When most unactive deem'd,
And though her body die, her fame survives,
A secular bird ages of lives. (ll. 1687–1707)

This simile summarizes the entire movement of the poem from darkness
to light; for the Phoenix was associated with the sun and with the
flame of its own spontaneous conflagration by which the new Phoenix
rose out of the ashes of the old. Thus, darkness becomes light in this
cycle in the very image of death becoming life: *Vita mihi mors est,* as
Camerarius' emblem book says about the Phoenix.[35] For Samson, the
death of the body signals the life of the soul, the process by which the
light of noon becomes the light of eternal illumination. The traditional
lore of the Phoenix which associated it with light, with resurrection,
and, indeed, with eternity and noon, all become part of the interplay
of forces here.[36] To this, one ought to add that, according to at least one
popular redaction of the myth, the Phoenix was last seen at the Crucifixion.[37]

The culmination of what has become a ritualistic drama, then, becomes, by control of imagistic and symbolic patterns, an action perpetually commemorative of moral triumph by virtue of the action of the
"One greater Man" (himself a Phoenix) toward whom Samson looks,
and back to whom we look. As Samson moves into history with his act,
the establishment of a relation between him and the image of the Phoenix at high noon fixes him in a moment of time that transcends time;
commemorates his action as that of spiritual rebirth by which the image of God is restored to the soul. To return to my earlier point in the
context of Berdyaev's comments on history and time, we have witnessed,
in a poem that is itself a commemoration, the movement of a historical figure toward eternity; that moment of arrival into eternity has been
fixed for us by the image of the Phoenix and by the commemorative act
of the poem itself which becomes an objectification of what Berdyaev
calls the "transfiguring action of memory," transforming the past into
something which is eternal.[38] The poem exists, then, not only as a kind

of mythologizing (remembering that, as biblical narrative, the historical, literal level must also be accepted as true) of a spiritual action
within the soul, but as a memorialization of a historical action that has
eternal validity by virtue of its relation to another historical action in
which it participates across the gulf of human time.

In the overall design of the poem there remains another significant
aspect to which the image of the Phoenix calls attention: the restoration
of the divine image that comes with regeneration. Milton had spoken
of this in his *De Doctrina Christiana* when he said that "regeneration
is that change operated by the Word and the Spirit, whereby the old
man being destroyed, the inward man is regenerated by God after his
own image . . ." (XVIII.1014–1015) [39] Specifically, this is the image of
Christ, as Milton says when he speaks of the glorification of the regenerate "after the image of Christ" (XXIV.1020). In Chapter XVIII he
quotes 2 Corinthians 5:17, "if any man be in Christ, he is a new creature"
(p. 1015), and divides regeneration into the mortification of the flesh and
the quickening of the Spirit, the latter also used often to signify resurrection. Samson's final act and death take on added significance in this
light. In moving from darkness to light through his humiliation and
mortification, he rises to the inner "rousing motions" which constitute
the quickening of the Spirit. The "old man" is destroyed, both in his
rejection of his father's image for him and in the literal destruction of
his own body. The Phoenix image is a specific emblem of the "new
creature" (related to Christ) which Samson has become through his
action; in mythical terms, this image is also an indication of Milton's
statement, in the *De Doctrina Christiana*, that "the humiliation of Christ
was succeeded by his exaltation"; that "having triumphed over death,
and laid aside the form of a servant, he was exalted by God the Father
to a state of immortality and of the highest glory" (XVI.1010). So, the
death of the Phoenix is succeeded by its life, its fall by its rise, and Samson's humiliation and despair by his triumph and his resurrection into
the light as this new creature, the Phoenix.[40] This has been accomplished at that high-noon point at which all of the elements of the symbolic
design, all of the threads of the narrative, converge—at the ritual festival
toward which the poem has been moving since its opening at sunrise.

IV

By way of conclusion, I should now like to make some comments in
the perspective of the long quotation from Berdyaev with which I
opened the preceding section.

As Milton retells it, the story of Samson is based on what is, for him, objective history. Insofar as the poem has its initiative in that sacred history—no matter how much Milton's creative imagination elaborated on the brief Old Testament account—it is a *true* narrative: that is, Milton's fiction is that this is history. In addition, the story exists as an objective series of symbols (words) on the page. Now, both as objective history and a series of symbols on a page, the poem has been so designed as to move out from what Berdyaev calls the "realm of objectification" into the "spiritual pattern of things." As history, because of Milton's careful and studious control of his narrative threads and because of his evocative language and symbols, the poem transcends its fixation in a particular time to become a narrative embodiment of a spiritual pattern. This is simply to describe with some particularity the way in which Milton has imitated biblical typology. But, further, in its *affective* relationship to the audience, the poem, by means of the same design, involves us in a commemorative rite by which we realize again the force of Donne's statement, "Restore thine Image, so much, by thy grace, / That thou may'st know mee, and I'll turne my face." We have become part of the ritual which Samson undertakes, for we are in him and he is in us. This is the way the spirit overcomes history and realizes eternity in Milton's historicity. If we see it in terms of Berdyaev's existential time which is in man, and which is akin to eternity, "there is no distinction between the future and the past, between the end and the beginning," just as the Phoenix, to which Samson is likened at the end, really has neither future nor past: its past is its future and its future is its past.

In *Samson Agonistes*, perhaps even more pointedly than in *Paradise Lost*, Milton has transferred the "revelation of the eternal" to the "far distant past," a past not quite so distant as the Garden of Eden and the eternal realms of heaven before the angelic fall, but a past, by the same token, not quite so remote in terms of its humanly identifiable participants. The eternity which is time "collapsed in ruin" is significantly realized in the very temple-theater which Samson destroys, along with the Philistine civilization which it represents. The destruction at high noon is the enactment in history, in the historical moment, as a religio-theatrical event, of the eternal action by which man triumphs in time for eternity.[41] This is the meaning which Milton, as Christian poet, attaches to time and its history. In its meaning and in its affective relation to its audience, the story of Samson's death is the story of a death that is a life, a triumph for the reader *now*. In this sense, it is timeless and eternal, for it asserts that man's spirit does rise, like the Phoenix, out of the darkness, out of the death of despair, out of the ashes of the body, and the flesh, and time, into the noon-light of eternal life. To the human spirit—which is eternal, but paradoxically confined to time in the here and now—the poem reaffirms, with freshness and immediacy, the old Christian consolation that "Nothing is here for tears, nothing to wail . . . nothing but well and fair."

NOTES

1. This position has recently been taken by Roger B. Wilkenfeld, "Act and Emblem: The Conclusion of *Samson Agonistes*," *ELH*, XXXII (1965), 161.
2. *The Beginning and the End*, trans. R. M. French (London, 1952), p. 212.
3. Ibid., p. 207. See also Franklin R. Baruch, "Time, Body, and Spirit at the Close of *Samson Agonistes*," *ELH*, XXXVI (1969), 319.
4. "Introduction," *The Harmonious Vision* (Baltimore, 1954), p. xx.
5. On typology see William G. Madsen, *From Shadowy Types to Truth: Studies in Milton's Symbolism* (New Haven, 1968), p. 186.
6. See John M. Steadman, *Milton and the Renaissance Hero* (Oxford, 1967), p. 160.
7. See esp. Arnold Stein, *Heroic Knowledge* (Minneapolis, 1957).
8. Georges Poulet, "Introduction," *The Metamorphoses of the Circle*, trans. Carley Dawson and Elliott Coleman in collaboration with the author (Baltimore, 1966), p. xviii.
9. Ibid., p. xix.
10. Malcolm Mackenzie Ross' statement is applicable here: "History is again made valid. Once again the fact in time seems to participate in values which have no dependence on time" (*Poetry and Dogma* [New Brunswick, 1954], p. 222; see also p. 223).
11. See Isabel G. MacCaffrey's "The Meditative Paradigm," *ELH*, XXXII (1965), 396–397, a review article on Louis Martz's *The Paradise Within* (New Haven, 1964).
12. Quoted by George Seaver, *Nicolas Berdyaev: An Introduction to His Thought* (London, 1950), p. 110.
13. Citations from Milton's poetry are to *John Milton: Complete Poems and Major Prose*, ed. Merritt Y. Hughes (New York, 1957). References are included in parentheses in the text.
14. See Charles S. Singleton, *An Essay on the Vita Nuova* (Cambridge, Mass., 1958), p. 24.
15. On the triumph over despair see Allen, *Harmonious Vision*, p. 94.
16. The phrase is borrowed from Madsen, *From Shadowy Types to Truth*, p. 181.
17. On this point see Arthur E. Barker, "Structural and Doctrinal Pattern in Milton's Later Poems," in *Essays in English Literature from the Renaissance to the Victorian Age, Presented to A.S.P. Woodhouse*, ed. Millar Maclure and F. W. Watt (Toronto, 1964), p. 179. We may also see the story of Samson as a *historical* account in what Roy Daniells calls (in reference to *Paradise Lost*) "a great demonstration and justification of divine purpose, for the sake of which history exists" (*Milton, Mannerism and Baroque* [Toronto, 1963], p. 99).

18. See my " 'Hail Holy Light' and Divine Time in *Paradise Lost*," *Journal of English and Germanic Philology*, LXVIII (1969), 52; and also Baruch's relevant remarks about applying the meaning of the story for "times to come" by gathering time "almost solely into the generalized present" ("Time, Body, and Spirit," p. 319).

19. Oscar Cullmann, *Christ and Time, The Primitive Christian Conception of Time and History*, rev. ed., trans. Floyd V. Filson (Philadelphia, 1964), p. 46.

20. A similar point is made about *Paradise Lost* by John N. Morris, "Milton and the Imagination of Time," *South Atlantic Quarterly*, LVII (1968), 650, 658, as well as by Stanley E. Fish in *Surprised by Sin: The Reader in Paradise Lost* (New York, 1967). See also Jon S. Lawry, *The Shadow of Heaven, Matter and Stance in Milton's Poetry* (Ithaca, 1968), pp. 19–20.

21. "Noon-Midnight and the Temporal Structure of *Paradise Lost*," *ELH*, XXIX (1962), 395, n. 45; reprinted in *Critical Essays on Milton from ELH* (Baltimore and London, 1969), pp. 210–233.

22. Lee Sheridan Cox also comments with different perspective on the pattern suggested by Samson's opening lines, in "Natural Science and Figurative Design in *Samson Agonistes*," *ELH*, XXXV (1968), 74; reprinted in *Critical Essays on Milton from ELH*, pp. 253–276.

23. See my " 'Hail Holy Light' and Divine Time" (n. 18 above), pp. 50–51, for commentary on this.

24. A similar case occurs in Spenser's *Faerie Queene*, I.viii.38–41, when Red Cross Knight emerges from Orgoglio's (Pride's) dungeon, having been saved from the darkness of his sin by Una and Arthur. His imprisonment in that dungeon is described in terms of darkness and death; and his emergence into light is described in terms of life.

25. See Poulet, *Metamorphoses*, pp. xviii–xix; and Dionysius the Areopagite, *On the Divine Names*, trans. C. E. Rolt, Translations of Christian Literature, Series I Greek Texts, new ed. (New York, 1940), p. 171n. The distinctions made in this note are significant, particularly in the discrimination and relation made between eternity and time: "Eternity is timeless as infinite number is superior to all numerical process. According to Plato, Time is 'incomplete life' and Eternity is 'complete life.' Thus Eternity fulfils Time and yet contradicts it, as infinite number fulfils and contradicts the properties of finite numbers. If Time be thought of as an infinite series of finite numbers Eternity is the sum of that series and not its process. But the name may be applied loosely to the process. . . . According to St. Thomas, Eternity measures Rest, and Time measures Motion: Eternity is a *totum simul* and Time is *successivum*."

26. On noon as image of eternity, see my "Noon-Midnight," p. 379 ff.

27. This image has been much discussed, most recently by Lawry, *The Shadow of Heaven*, pp. 349–350; Wilkenfeld, "Act and Emblem," pp. 165–167; and Cox, "Natural Science and Figurative Design," pp. 58–59.

28. See my "Noon-Midnight," pp. 385 ff., and Lawry, *The Shadow of Heaven*, pp. 349–352.

29. See Barker, "Structural and Doctrinal Pattern," p. 172.

30. See Wilkenfeld's interesting comment on this passage in "Act and Emblem," p. 165.

31. "Noon-Midnight," pp. 379–383.

32. "Act and Emblem," p. 165.

33. Mircea Eliade, *The Sacred and the Profane, The Nature of Religion*, trans. Willard R. Trask (New York, 1961), pp. 68–88. This phrase is from p. 68. See also Baruch's remarks about gathering time "into the generalized present" ("Time, Body, and Spirit," p. 337).

34. See French Fogle, "The Action of *Samson Agonistes*," in *Essays in American and English Literature, Presented to Bruce Robert McElderry Jr.* (Athens, Ohio, 1967), p. 195.

35. This emblem is reproduced in Hughes, p. 548. Claudian's famous poem on the Phoenix points out the paradox that its life begins in death. See Jean Hubaux and Maxime Leroy, *Le Mythe du phénix dans les littératures grecque et latine* (Paris, 1939), p. xxii.

36. See my "Noon-Midnight," pp. 387–389; Wilkenfeld, "Act and Emblem," p. 167; and Hubaux and Leroy, pp. 3, 7–9, for more on the relation between the Phoenix myth and time.

37. John Swan, *Speculum Mundi* (Cambridge, 1644), p. 385.

38. *The Beginning and the End*, pp. 207, 212.

39. My citations from the *De Doctrina Christiana*, as translated by Bishop Sumner, are from the text of *The Student's Milton*, ed. Frank Allen Patterson (New York, 1930), which is based on the Columbia edition. I include chapter and page numbers in parentheses in my text, and I have normalized italics.

40. On the restoration of God's image in Milton's theology, see Ira Clark, "Milton and the Image of God," *Journal of English and Germanic Philology*, LXVIII (1969), 422–431; and Barker, "Structural and Doctrinal Pattern," p. 172. One also ought to remember that Christ, who was traditionally compared to the Phoenix, triumphed through his crucifixion at noon.

41. Wilkenfeld speaks of Milton's actualization, through the image of the Phoenix, of an "eternal recovery of God" ("Act and Emblem," p. 160). And Baruch sums up one aspect of the issue: "Milton's metaphoric patterns in the closing section of *Samson Agonistes* support the conviction that the play has been centrally concerned, not with Samson, but rather with the way in which the Old Testament hero's story could be made to figure forth the nature of spiritual strength and insight, and of the kind of activity needed to achieve these objectives" ("Time, Body, and Spirit," p. 319).

Samson Agonistes as Tragedy

IRENE SAMUEL

HUNTER COLLEGE

Virtually all recent discussion of *Samson Agonistes* has assumed that it ends with divine providence vindicated as a regenerate Samson fulfills his appointed mission of delivering the Israelites from their Philistine oppressors. Interpreters largely set themselves to trace the stages by which Samson achieves his regeneration. The dictum of Dr. Johnson, that the tragedy has a beginning and an end but no middle, has elicited a variety of elaborate answers, most of which agree that the sequence of his visitors enables the protagonist to assert a series of virtues, which, annulling his earlier vices, fit him to play his ultimate heroically sacrificial role. Thus Samson, by whatever route of demonstrable ironies, ends as a martyr, a witness to Jehovah's truth, a prototypical saint, one of those who need only await Judgment Day to take their due place among the blessed. Out of a concern to answer Johnson's major charge against the drama, interpreters unwittingly support yet another of his thrusts: "This is the tragedy which ignorance has admired, and bigotry applauded."

Milton's critical and religious thought, his view of tragedy, his habit as a poet, the detail he wrote into the play, the nature of tragedy generally or of tragedies like *Samson* in particular—none of these supports such a reading of the play; it finds its grounds only in the still common notion of Milton as primarily a theologian of the narrowest Puritanism and only secondarily a poet with the full range of a poet's interests in the mimesis of human actions. Although his poetry shows a sensibility hardly narrower than Shakespeare's and a moral vision rather finer, his prose a steady grasp of why men think, speak, and act as they do, and his life in its range of friendships, interests, and achievements anything but the Hudibras mentality, the conviction somehow persists, though increasingly unadmitted and perhaps unaware, that Milton never wrote except to assert divine providence and herald ultimate doomsday with its sure division of the elect from the damned when, of course, his party would be of the elect.

If *Samson Agonistes* demonstrates its protagonist's election in his final vengeance on God's enemies, it can do so only if its author thought such vengeance admirable. The fact is other: though Milton was no pacifist, throughout his pages *peace* is the good word; *revenge* and *vengeance* are regularly linked with the tyrannical and diabolical rather than the divine. Violence, even in legitimate warfare, he abhorred: his sonnets applauding the victorious Fairfax and the victorious Cromwell, far from taking the defeat of the enemy as occasion for rejoicing, assert the unquestionable superiority of the tasks of peace. In *Paradise Lost* God sends the Son to terminate violence in Heaven, declaring that "War wearied hath performed what war can do" and dismissing what war can do as "wild work" without solution (VI.694–695).[1] Again Michael, instructing Adam on the Son's victory over Satan, admonishes, "Dream not of their fight / As of a duel or the local wounds / Of head or heel" (XII.386–388). Most explicitly in *Paradise Regained* the Savior rejects the very offer of military victory as "Much ostentation vain of fleshly arm / And fragile arms" (III.387–388), argues the impossibility of effectively freeing by such means those who would remain "Unhumbled, unrepentant, unreformed" (III.429), and when urged to rescue the entire Roman world from the tyranny of Tiberius asks the pointed question,

> What wise and valiant man would seek to free
> These thus degenerate, by themselves enslaved,
> Or could of inward slaves make outward free? (IV.143–145)

During England's Civil War, "when the assault was intended to the city," Milton for his part could address the possible assailant in courteous and peaceable—if humorous—terms as "Captain, or colonel, or knight at arms"; at the height of the conflict he chose to translate psalms that celebrate or implore God's mercy, not his vengeance; and, the tyrant Charles Stuart having been caught and put to death, he began the preface to *Eikonoklastes* thus: "To descant on the misfortunes of a person fallen from so high a dignity, who hath also paid his debt both to nature and his faults, is neither of itself a thing commendable nor the intention of this discourse" (Columbia ed., V, 63). Little in Milton's verse or even the prose suggests that he enjoyed violence or took the defeat, death, or discomfiture of enemies as providential occasions for triumphant gloating.

In *Paradise Lost* it is significantly Satan who, with his constant vice of attributing his own motives to others, describes victorious God as indulging in "th' excess of joy" over the discomfiture of the vanquished. Satan is also the one who consistently chooses the resort to force, and the one who gloats—even in advance—on the painful defeat of his chosen enemies (IV.533–535; VI.470 ff., 558–567, 609–619; IX.130–134; X.485–493). In marked contrast with that diabolical joy in others' pain, Raphael calls the story he will tell of the defeat of his enemies a "sad task" and speaks with "remorse" of "The ruin of so many glorious once / And perfect while they stood" (V.564–568). He comments with like sorrow on mankind's possible invention of weapons "to plague the sons of men / . . . on war and mutual slaughter bent" (VI.501–506). So too Michael denounces the age to come that will admire nothing but military prowess, confusing it "with valor and heroic virtue" and styling "great Conquerors" those more rightly called "Destroyers . . . and Plagues of men" (XI.689–697). The poet himself contemptuously dismisses the modes of violence that have been deemed the only matter fit for heroic poetry (IX.27–33), and bluntly dubs war, when it first appears in human history, "sword-law" (XI.672).

However necessary Milton found the military struggle of his time against episcopal and royalist tyranny in order that the English nation might gain a government of law and a separation of church and state, he nowhere glorified slaughter. Doubtless that is why the more sensitive interpreters of *Samson Agonistes*, even while tracing the regeneration of its protagonist through and in the catastrophe, carefully avert their eyes from the Messenger's prolonged account of that mass slaying and close their ears to the Chorus' prolonged rejoicing over it. A. S. P. Woodhouse,[2] who gives much the most sensitive of such readings, simply dismisses the fate of the Philistines as irrelevant and even Dalila's motives in visiting Samson as not mattering and therefore left obscure. In his concern to prove the tragedy Christian in its outlook as it takes Samson from sin through repentance to grace, Woodhouse scarcely troubles to mention the Philistines: presumably they, like Dalila, are there "for the sake of Samson and the action," not in their own right. Even so perceptive a reader, once he is intent on showing how properly *Samson Agonistes* demonstrates theological doctrine, can thus ignore large segments of the human action, as well as the human agents, that Milton wrote into his tragedy.

Woodhouse at least does not burden his reading with long citations of every truism Milton ever wrote about God, grace, faith, and regeneration. But most of those who exhaust *Christian Doctrine* to tally its points with the play's supposed vindication of Samson avoid with remarkable skill the distinctively Miltonic sentences that might tell against their arguments:

> Inasmuch . . . as God is best served by internal worship, whereas man stands more in need of outward attention, the external service of God is sometimes to be postponed to our duties towards men. (II.8)[3]

> The opposite of [compassion] is . . . rejoicing in the misfortunes of others. (II.11)

> Opposed to a regard for the life of our neighbor is first the shedding of his blood. Under this head is also included, first every thing by which the life of our neighbor is endangered; as blows, wounds, mutilations, &c. Secondly, hasty anger. Thirdly, revenge. (II.12)

> As the kingdom of Christ is not of this world, so neither is it sustained by force and compulsion. (II.17)

The most that Milton is willing to say of avenging God and his church is that it is "not forbidden" (II.12), as the most he is willing to say for war is that it is "lawful" (II.17). And even with lawful war he adds that it is to be "prosecuted with moderation"—though no mercy need be shown to the merciless. But the whole tenor of *Christian Doctrine* as it bears on the kind of episode with which Samson ends his career shows Milton averse by both temperament and conviction to the mentality that preaches holy wars. Like his views on peace and violence, his very cast of mind precludes his deliberately offering Samson's final act as proof of God's renewed favor:

> surely to every good and peaceable man it must in nature needs be a hateful thing to be the displeaser and molester of thousands; much better would it like him to be the messenger of gladness and contentment, which is his chief intended business to all mankind. . . . (*The Reason of Church-Government*, Columbia ed., III, 231)

And even beyond his ethical bent and his explicitly argued convictions, Milton's view of tragedy of itself might rescue his play from misconstruction. The title page of *Samson Agonistes* begins with a quotation from Aristotle's *Poetics* 6, first in Greek, then in Latin translation: Tragedy is an imitation of a serious action, etc., through pity and terror effecting a purgation of such emotions. The last paragraph of the prefatory note declares that they will best judge *Samson Agonistes* "who are not unacquainted with Aeschylus, Sophocles, and Euripides, the three tragic poets unequalled yet by any." Milton patently takes tragedy as best explained by Aristotle and best illustrated by the Greeks.

In earlier years he had entertained a somewhat different view: "Sometime let gorgeous tragedy / In sceptered pall come sweeping by, / Presenting Thebes or Pelops' line / Or the tale of Troy divine, / Or what (though rare) of later age / Ennobled hath the buskined stage." The author of *Il Penseroso* apparently accepted the Horatian-Renaissance commonplaces that distinguish tragedy from comedy by its dealing solely with princes.

Perhaps because of his antiroyalist sympathies, perhaps because of a growing taste for Euripidean tragedy, by the time he wrote *Samson* he had come to think the "scepter" unnecessary and "gorgeousness" irrelevant. The "pall," however, remains: tragedy by its very nature involves such things. Thus when he explicitly turns his notes to tragic in Book IX of *Paradise Lost* he defines the tone and theme of that poem, and of tragedy generally, as involving

> a world of woe,
> Sin and her shadow Death, and Misery,
> Death's harbinger. (ll. 11–13)

Even those who think *Paradise Lost* provides a happy ending after a fortunate fall cannot mistake the plain equation in those lines of the tragic with a sequence of sin, misery, death—a "world of woe."

Milton called *Samson Agonistes* a tragedy, not a martyr play; its subject cannot be Samson restored to divine favor. The title signifies Samson in his *agon*,[4] his contest, and thus prepares us for a grim struggle proper to tragedy, as the prefatory note prepares us for tragedy of the kind preferred by Aristotle and produced by the Greeks. No doubt Aristotelian theory and Greek practice were variously interpreted in the Renaissance—as now—but the chief variants concerned such matters as the meaning of catharsis, the number of hours permissible in the action, the precise requirements of verisimilitude and decorum, the superiority of tragedy or epic poetry. These are not at issue in our reading of *Samson*. The nature of tragedy as Aristotle understood it is.

True, Aristotle does not require an unhappy ending in tragedy, although he distinctly prefers it. And Greek example gives precedent not only for happy resolutions of tragic actions, but for the specific happy resolution that shows a man who has sinned ultimately reconciled to and mysteriously accepted by the gods in the hour of his death: *Oedipus at Colonus* traces just such a course. Nor has Greek tragedy been without interpreters who take its chief meaning to be that man willy-nilly brings to pass what the gods have decreed. Presumably, then, Aristotelian theory and Greek practice could support the common reading of Milton's *Samson*. Against such argument stand some important facts. Renaissance commentators on the *Poetics*, Castelvetro, for example, if they argued the happy ending preferable for some reason, knew that they were opposing Aristotle's view. More important, Milton cites no theorist on tragedy but Aristotle in his prefatory note to *Samson*. And Aristotle's argument for the single unhappy issue for tragic agents—as against the double issue, good for the good, bad for the wicked—is involved in the definition of tragedy Milton quotes.

As Aristotle works out the relation of tragic form and function in the *Poetics*, the catharsis that tragedy is to effect determines its most effective form. That is why scenes of discovery, reversal, and suffering are the most effective parts of plot: they imitate the fearful and pitiful. That is why these parts must grow out of the plot itself and the plot out of the *ethos* and *dianoia* of the agents: plots that rest on the will of the gods, since they involve the irrational and improbable, are less fearful and pitiful. And that is why the best tragic plot imitates "the case of . . . a man not superlatively good and just, nor yet one whose misfortune comes about through vice and depravity; but a man who is brought low through some error of judgment or shortcoming, one from the number of the highly renowned and prosperous."[5] The *hamartia* in the otherwise good and just agent is so crucial to the probability of tragic events that to accept Aristotle's view of tragedy entails accepting his view of tragic *ethos*, of the undesirability of the *deus ex machina*, and of the distinct inferiority of the double resolution—"a happy and an unhappy ending for the better and the worse agents respectively"—as less appropriate to tragedy than to comedy.

Obviously Milton need not have been a strict Aristotelian in his view of tragedy. He nowhere commits himself to accepting the *Poetics* wholesale. Still, if Aristotle's analysis of how tragedy works is sound, if *Samson Agonistes* is effective, and if Milton gained from his study of the *Poetics* an understanding of what makes tragedy effective, his citation of Aristotle's words on the title page may bear on how *Samson Agonistes* should be read.

Moreover, what Aristotle sees as desirable in plot for reasons of artistic probability, Milton would see as desirable on moral grounds as well. The Aristotelian preference for the flawed tragic agent whose own shortcomings bring him to his doom accords far better with Milton's arguments against predestination as depriving man of moral responsibility for his own deeds than does a mode of tragedy that exploits the workings of providential grace. For Milton argued in *Christian Doctrine* that grace either extended to all men or extended proportionally to free individual choice:

> God explicitly and frequently declares . . . that he desires not the death of any one, but the salvation of all; that he hates nothing that he has made; and that he has omitted nothing which might suffice for universal salvation. . . . no one believes because God has foreseen his belief, but God foresees his belief because he was about to believe. . . . If then God reject none but the disobedient and unbelieving, he undoubtedly gives grace to all, if not in equal measure, at least sufficient for attaining knowledge of the truth and final salvation. . . . he must also will that an adequate proportion of saving grace shall be withholden from no man; for if otherwise, it does not appear how his truth towards mankind can be justified. . . . God excludes no one from the pale of repentance and eternal salvation, till he has despised and rejected the propositions of sufficient grace. . . . (I.4)

All through the section of *Christian Doctrine* in Book I, Chapters XVII–XXVI, where we might expect to find evidence that the regenerate, as they are "justified," "adopted," and "glorified," are dealt with by God in some special way, Milton emphasizes the "general" rather than the "special" calling of men and places its effect in "the service of God and the performing of good works," in "peace and real tranquility of mind." Everything must turn on whether Samson's final deed is to be read as "service of God" and as showing Samson's "tranquility of mind." Against such reading stands Milton's unwillingness to exclude heathen as well as Hebrew from God's sufficient grace: "To those who are not yet regenerate, the law of nature has the same obligatory force, and is intended to serve the same purposes, as the law of Moses to the Israelites" (chap. XXVI).

It would be hard in terms of Milton's explicit comments on grace and election to make a case for the catastrophe of *Samson Agonistes* as stemming from any special illumination afforded Samson by Providence. Milton's is so distinctly the ethic of will and reason freely choosing that a *deus ex machina* resolution of plot would be repugnant to him on theological and moral no less than on artistic grounds. *Comus*, with its fairy lore derived from romance, can use supernatural agencies to bring the Lady and her two brothers triumphantly home "in victorius dance" —but the masque by its very genre involves what Aristotle calls the irrational.[6] *Samson* as tragedy cannot, without forfeiting probability, rely on divine intervention to resolve its complication. A divine intervention that made Samson's death sacrificial would disastrously diminish the homeopathic purgation of pity and terror that Milton took as the meaning of Aristotle's catharsis: "so in physics things of melancholic hue and quality are used against melancholy, sour against sour, salt to remove salt humors."

But the terms tragedy and tragic agent have come in our time to mean something so far from the Aristotelian idea that we must here try to dispel a new illusion that encourages the common misreading of *Samson* as a martyr play. Aristotle—and Renaissance theorists as well —had not been advised by Nietzsche that every tragic hero represents the god whose death provides a Dionysian release into primordial oneness; and no mythologizing critics had led them to see in the tragic agent a scapegoat dispatched to glut the barbaric heritage of man's racial unconscious. Aristotle does not speak of tragic heroes, but of agents; and these he asserts must be men like ourselves, better than average though flawed, but not therefore designed to satisfy in their undoing either our death wish or our unadmitted envies. In Aristotle's assumption we fear for the right tragic agent because of his evident defects; we pity him because of his sufferings; and we thereby win release from pity and fear. Aristotle in short thinks that as we witness tragedy we feel what we think we feel. Nietzsche and the newer schools of anthropological critics may come closer to discovering ultimate sources of tragedy in primitive tribal rites and our unadmitted proclivities; Aristotle comes far closer to explaining our conscious feelings in the process of attending to tragedy. To trace the oak to the acorn hardly defines the oak—much less suggests how to use the wood in building. And to trace artistic forms to their hidden origins as little defines the forms or tells how they work in the building of poems.

Nothing else in Milton's scattered comments on tragedy sheds so much light on *Samson* as the phrase he quotes from Aristotle in the brief preface. His list of possible subjects for tragedy in the Cambridge MS does not greatly help, for a number of reasons. First, we do not know when the list was drawn up, and Milton's views on tragedy may have developed in the course of his life as much as his views on epic. Second, we do not know how he intended to treat the subjects he lists, and in poetry treatment makes a total difference, as we may know by comparing the arguments for *Paradise Lost* with the poem they summarize. Third, we do not even know that he thought all the subjects listed proper for tragedy: next to Number xx, Theristria, he adds "a pastoral out of Ruth," and the subjects from the life of Christ, lvi through lxii, suggest a dramatic mode unlike tragedy. Nor can we be sure that Milton in working out subjects from Scripture intended to emphasize specifically religious or theological themes any more than in working out subjects from British and north British story. We can say only that he was drawn to a greater number of subjects from biblical than from British story, that tragedies on some of his biblical subjects would surely have ended happily, and that some—not always the same—might have demonstrated the workings of divine providence. A great many would have ended unhappily for their chief agents, and a great many suggest no particular involvement of God's ways. The one we could wish he had sketched more fully for its possible bearing on *Samson Agonistes* is his proposed Samson Hybristes.

In any event, given the paucity of Milton's statements on the subject, we need to attend far more to the explicit words on tragedy in the prefatory note to *Samson*. We need also in reading Milton to attend far more both to what he writes and to our own apparent responses, far less to what the narrow dissenter he has been assumed to be must have written and less still to the responses such narrowness presumably demands. Our apparent responses, like the apparent text of *Samson*, suggest that Milton confused tragedy with neither miracle plays nor saints' lives.

Recently William Madsen has demonstrated how far Samson falls short of the ethical ideal presented in the central figure of *Paradise Regained*.[7] But Madsen argues too that Christian typology requires such disparity between type and antitype to make plain the need for the type. His argument hardly accounts for the extent of Samson's failings. Indeed, in Books XI and XII of *Paradise Lost* those who typologically prefigure Christ are presented with emphasis not on their shortcomings but on their resemblance to the ultimate Savior. The Samson of Milton's tragedy would not fit the pattern of Old Testament history

there used to instruct Adam because he has been conceived not as pre-
figuring Christ but as a tragic agent, a flawed man, markedly superior
to those he deals with on stage and off, but of mingled strengths and
weaknesses which have brought him to such a pass that no perfectly
happy issue is possible for him.

No one, I think, questions that the Samson of the play's opening is
flawed, or that his flaws have brought him to the point at which the action begins, or that despite such flaws he is from first to last steadfast
in his conviction of God's absolute rightness and justice. And no one
questions Samson's patent superiority to the other agents in his understanding of God, himself, his countrymen, and all the issues on which
his life and death turn. We need not argue the obvious. But Samson's
absolute understanding of anything we may question. The Samson of
the opening scene changes considerably in the course of the action,
but scarcely to the point where, shedding the flaws that have brought
him to this pass and illumined by "the visitation of God's Spirit,"[8] he
achieves at once victory over himself and his enemies, reconciliation to
God and vindication of divine prediction, a sanctified martyrdom and a
proleptic demonstration of the ultimate triumph of good over evil. Where
precisely do such momentous changes occur?

The Samson we see all through the play could never be content
with any possible kind of life remaining to him. That is the first and
last truth about the protagonist of Milton's tragedy. It is not merely
that he could not—rightly, of course—agree to Dalila's proposal and become her petted lapdog, or even that he could not—less rightly—accept
Manoa's earlier offer to ransom him, but that no peaceable life, however
attained and however full of opportunity to instruct or judge or in any
other nonviolent way deliver Israel, could recompense the Samson of
this tragedy for the indignity of having to continue in life knowing himself to have been physically defeated by the Philistines. Not even a
miraculously restored vision could reconcile Samson to that defeat—
any more than his miraculously restored strength does. Vision, like
strength, can have only one purpose for him: the physical destruction of
the enemy. In that he resembles, among all the portraits Milton drew in
his various poems, Moloch, who "rather than be less" than the power
that struck him down "Cared not to be at all" (*PL* II.48–49). Obviously
the power that struck Moloch down was God's, the power that struck
Samson Philistia's; and still Samson resembles Moloch in preferring
annihilation to any continued existence-in-defeat—surely because Milton
understood the kind of *ethos* that by innermost habit relies on, resorts

to, and glories in brute force. In any other poet such understanding of men would immediately be assumed; only with Milton readers persistently blind themselves to the evidence of his human understanding, ascribing his every word to theological doctrine.

Milton in his own blindness could take comfort in having lost his sight "in liberty's defense"—even had he had "no better guide." Anyone can argue that assertion is not fact, that Milton may have lamented his loss of sight as bitterly as he makes Samson lament his, that in any case his loss was gradual, in a sense chosen, not inflicted by gloating opponents, and at first mitigated by public respect, affluence, leisure, and the like. The telling fact remains that Milton could conceive modes of existence in which blindness, and later defeat, deprivation, even imprisonment, were not decisive arguments for preferring to life death in triumph over enemies.

The Samson we hear long for death through scene after scene can resolve his *agon* only with death for himself as well as his enemies. It is entirely understandable, entirely in character, entirely terror-and-pity-moving; it is not the mark of the saint. A martyr loses himself wholly in a purpose beyond himself, and neither desires, nor hastens, nor relishes his death. Samson does all three. After the scene with Harapha, he is still saying:

> But come what will; my deadliest foe will prove
> My speediest friend, by death to rid me hence;
> The worst that he can give to me the best. (ll. 1262–1264)

That feeling has apparently not vanished when he forewarns the Chorus of his change of mind about the Philistines' summons:

> I begin to feel
> Some rousing motions in me, which dispose
> To something extraordinary my thoughts. . . .
> If there be aught of presage in the mind,
> This day will be remarkable in my life
> By some great act, or of my days the last. (ll. 1381–1399)

Nor has it vanished when he bids them farewell with his final words on stage: "The last of me or no I cannot warrant" (l. 1426).

Doubtless Samson in his last day of life comes nearer to wisdom than ever in his earlier successes. He can recognize the hubris he was guilty of when "like a petty God / [He] walked about admired of all

and dreaded" (ll. 529–530). He can name the error that brought him
to disaster: "shameful garrulity" (l. 491). But that he wants to be admired and dreaded still, everything he says and does bears witness to.
That he is garrulous still, even a theater-going audience inured to Beckett and Albee must grant. He easily outtalks the Chorus (their lyrical
passages, of course, excepted). He similarly outtalks Manoa, though
old age is generally reckoned garrulous. He answers all but one of
Dalila's speeches (if we except her parting speech, which he has no
chance to answer) with speeches yet longer, though he makes the common accusation against female long-windedness (ll. 905–906). After
some initially laconic replies, he reduces even the windbag Harapha to
relative silence. His ratio of lines with the Officer, though he aims at
taciturnity, is in the first round 24 to 14, and even in the second round,
though the Philistines' message constitutes six-and-one-half of the Officer's lines, 11 to 11. True, he keeps his final decision to himself, though
even then he cannot refrain from riddling it to his countrymen before
he leaves and to the Philistines before he smites them.

The riddling announcement to the Danites has more than a touch
of hubris still: they may expect to hear of him

> Nothing dishonorable, impure, unworthy
> Our God, our law, my nation or myself;
> The last of me or no I cannot warrant. (ll. 1424–1426)

The order of that penultimate line in Samson's final words on stage is
revealing in its shift from "our" to "my" and in its climactic progress:
our God, *our* Law, *my* Nation or *myself*. It is still something of a mono-
maniac who speaks, and the mania is still egomania—a not uncommon
flaw in tragic agents. His final conviction and concern is that "This day
will be remarkable in [his] life."

The flaw has tainted Samson's speeches throughout. As even his
doting father recognized earlier, to choose "death as [his] due, *self*-
rigorous . . . argues . . . *self*-displeased / For *self*-offense, more than for
God offended." And Samson proves Manoa right when he answers, "His
pardon I implore; but as for life / To what end should I seek it?" That,
of course, was Samson before the discovery in his mind, with its attendant reversal, that there is indeed something he can yet do— with his life
and his renewed strength, with the very command of his Philistine masters: he can deal death.

He has gained in wit when he speaks his ironically intended words
to the Officer, agreeing finally to perform as gladiator-jester for the

Philistines and their fish-god Dagon: "And for a life who will not change his purpose?" He has grown subtle in warnings when he leaves the Chorus behind: "your company along / I will not wish." He has not grown beyond equating the fulfillment of divine purpose with Samson's violent defeat of his enemies and with Samson's glory-in-death. Providence so arranges it that the arched roof brought down in his final act smites only responsible Philistine heads:

> Lords, Ladies, Captains, Counsellors, or Priests,
> Their choice nobility and flower. (ll. 1653–1654)

There is no evidence that Samson cares who his victims among the Philistines may be. What the Messenger tells is that, once placed between the pillars, Samson

> stood as one who prayed
> Or some great matter in his mind revolved—(ll. 1637–1638)

then spoke:

> Hitherto, Lords, what your commands imposed
> I have performed. . . .
> Now of my own accord such other trial
> I mean to show you of my strength, yet greater;
> As with amaze shall strike all who behold. (ll. 1640–1645)

The riddling Samson relishes his death riddle—a shade too like Satan gloating in ambiguous words over the destruction he intends for the Edenic pair or for the loyal angels on the battlefield. Samson's deep need is still that his strength *amaze* and *strike*. And we must comment on the whole final sequence with a meaning far other than his father's: "Samson hath—indeed—quit himself like Samson."

The catastrophe uses up *all* that we have seen of him onstage: his steady conviction that God is just, but also his death wish, his impulse to violence—renewed in the scenes with Dalila and Harapha, his concern with *his* "race of glory" and *his* "race of shame." The catastrophe does not substitute another different Samson offstage. Oedipus at Colonus we witness onstage markedly changed from his erring self before we learn of his mysterious transfiguration offstage. Adam and Eve we witness in Book X earning partial forgiveness before Book XI informs us that grace was granted them in order that they might earn it. To sup-

ply such grace and transfiguration offstage for the only Samson we have
seen and heard is to substitute our guesses for what the poet gives.

On stage self-concern has dominated. His very love-and-hate of
Dalila—patently disproportionate to her temperament—exceeds its
mark. Her importance is the extension of his: she was, after all, his wife.
And the blindness with which he still overestimates her shows the measure by which he measures everything and everyone. Poor Dalila is
sincere enough—indeed we might subtitle her scene "Dalila, or the inade-
quacy of mere sincerity." She had little in her head but that she would
have liked him to be more "normal"—more like other men, not constantly
embroiled and off on dangerous exploits, setting her at odds with her
people; she does now want to "make it up to him" by revolving her life
about him in a domestic way. She never was aware that a nation's freedom was at stake, and the disparity between a higher and a lower civilization. Like Ophelia she only supposed that she was doing the best for
everyone. She still cannot see that X and anti-X are incompatible. Her
arguments cancel each other out not because she is an accomplished
hypocrite—a hypocrite would do better than that—but because she lacks
minimal logic. The first thing we learn at her appearance tells her story.
Dressed to the nines, she comes to visit a blind man, imprisoned because of her betrayal: she has not grasped that he will not see her gay
attire, or that if he could, it would not move him, except perhaps to
surmise that this is what she used her traitress' payment for. Presumably the gay attire gives her courage to come, just as her parting thrust
—born not of malice, but of her need for some small remnant of self-
esteem—enables her to get offstage head up. Dalila is surely the most
bird-brained woman ever to have gotten herself involved in major tragedy. And at this *femme* merely *moyenne sensuelle* Samson hurls invec-
tive, as though he were Antony reviling Cleopatra. But she is hardly
Cleopatra, though he is more Antony than Caesar, and more Caesar than
saint. In her own nature, without radical change she is a fit target
rather for Meredith's Comic Spirit than for "out, out hyena"—of the company, say, of James' Contessa Gemini or Jane Austen's Mrs. Elton. (We
can almost hear her muttering about her "inner resources" as she leaves
the scene.) That she moves Samson to violence ("Let her not come near
me"—"Not for thy life") as formerly she moved him to betray his trust—
that alone makes her appropriate in tragedy. For Samson drew this "ship
of Tarsus" into very deep waters indeed, way beyond her depth. Little
wonder that he drove himself off course to shipwreck.

In context, of course, Dalila is not comic. Her betrayal, however
secondary to Samson's of himself, did lead to his capture, blinding, im-

prisonment, and his whole present misery. But her motive in coming is far from obscure: she wants Samson's forgiveness, wants "in some part to recompense" him for her betrayal, had not expected the Philistines who suborned her to blind and imprison her husband, does now hope to gain their favorable ear so that she may fetch him home to her love and care, is attached enough to him so that she desires to approach and at least touch his hand. Even if she fatuously expects her touch to move his relentance, as her pleas have not, why should she want his forgiveness at all if she does not, in her admittedly empty-headed way, love him? Tending that wrecked hulk of a man would hardly be the dream of a sensual enchantress or deliberate villainess.

Yet Samson in his strenuously maintained delusion can declare that he loved her, not she him:

> I, before all the daughters of my tribe
> And of my nation, chose thee from among
> My enemies, loved thee, as too well thou knewest—
> Too well. (ll. 876–879)

Charles Dunster noted the inconsistency here with Samson's earlier assertion:

> Here he professes a violent affection for Dalila, as the sole motive of his marrying her; whereas he had before asserted that he was in a certain degree determined to it by hopes of finding occasions thereby to oppress the Philistines. . . . Manoah likewise says, that Samson pleaded "divine compulsion." . . . But Milton may be understood to have imagined Samson in his marriage with Dalila acting merely from inclination, and (as people, who do so, are apt to reason falsely in their own vindication) *falsely* attributing and ascribing it to divine impulse.[9]

At any rate, if Samson chose Dalila for wife as occasion to injure Philistines, he did not marry her because he loved her; if love made him choose her, he might have observed that love also made her choose him above the sons of her tribe and nation—and still makes her choose him, the now broken enemy of her people. But the inconsistency Dunster notes and resolves surely stems from Samson's habitual confusion of his own impulse with "divine compulsion." It is at best a chilling defense of a marriage choice that his argument from God's intent offers; probably Dunster is right to dismiss it as self-vindication, though we may go beyond Dunster in questioning the self that thinks such an argument from opportunity to "oppress Israel's oppressors" (ll. 233–234) a vindication.

Given a Samson self-deluded earlier about his divinely inspired impulse to marry Dalila, his final impulse may be as little divine in its inspiration. True, the Chorus and Manoa take his last deed as proving God's renewed favor. And if we could credit them with wholly reliable views, with speaking for the author, their testimony would annul any construction other than theirs of the catastrophe. In fact the Chorus and Manoa have consistently been out of their depth with Samson, missing his point at every turn. And if in their dialogue with him, when he is there onstage, they do not fully understand him, and so speak not Milton's but only their own limited vision, their final verdict on what happens offstage cannot speak Milton's. Manoa asserts:

> Nothing is here for tears, nothing to wail
> Or knock the breast . . . ,
>   nothing but well and fair,
> And what may quiet us in a death so noble. (ll. 1721–1724)

And surely old Manoa may be allowed such comfort as he can wrest from his son's catastrophe. But when there is in fact nothing for tears, we do not say so.

The Chorus too may be allowed their self-comforting words. But to allow them sudden illumination would make this a miracle play indeed. We are left with "calm of mind, all passion spent" in a sense other than theirs. The whole due tragic economy of the decidedly better than average, indeed eminently noble, man bringing himself to destruction through his shortcomings exhausts our capacity for sympathetic experience of horror and pity. Where the end of a Socrates, a Saint Joan, even of a Lear or an Oedipus, suggests exaltation, the end of Samson leaves every beholder *spent*. And "the new acquist of true experience" that the Chorus feel they have gained from "this great event" has a different meaning for us, who see the whole as they cannot. Doubtless Providence has managed it that Samson's strength preserves the Israelites; but the drama concerns Samson Agonistes not Jerusalem Delivered.

The one speaker who witnessed the catastrophe feels what he describes as unmitigated horror. The gloating over the destroyed Philistines that Manoa and, still more, the Chorus speak hardly corresponds to Milton's habit. And Samson's own ironic gloating as he pulls down the roof corresponds even less: he can see only the way of violence in both his *agon* and its resolution. As with tragic agents generally, his is the way of multiple mistakes. It leads to that final death-dealing, as he conceives a way out that is right for tragedy, where a fit audience, seeing the cost, may be healed, but not by rejoicing in sacrifices heaped up, nor by assuming that such bloody sacrifices prove anyone redeemed. Tragedy offers its healing with no shallow comforts and assurance, only if we endure to recognize the full horror, the full pity of the mistakes and the sufferings it imitates. It speaks to our rational understanding of human affairs and of human nature. And we must credit Milton with similarly rational understanding of human nature in Samson, Manoa, the Chorus, Dalila, and the Philistines.

If we take Samson as protagonist of the tragedy, but not our sole concern, allowing the other agents to matter too, and not only as they provide Samson's occasions, if we concentrate on the entire action rather than exclusively on divine prediction, we see a more meaningful and moving tragedy that shows a far more profound grasp of how humanity in its mixtures of wisdom and folly behaves. At least we may reconsider what Milton wrote. For if he thought the label "Philistine" enough to signify "properly doomed to extinction by the properly vengeful God of Israel," he wrote some inconsistencies into his play. The Philistine Officer could be much worse—rude, arrogant, with the self-importance of the petty underling doing the behests of power. He is, in fact, rather kindlier than his office requires: "By this compliance thou wilt win the lords / To favour, and perhaps to set thee free" (ll. 1411–1412). Harapha too could be made worse—less the comic *miles gloriosus*, more the deliberately sadistic tormentor. He is hardly even responsible for the Philistines' immediate summons; his parting threat remains as unfulfilled as all his other boasts; his role in the plot is to stir Samson's rage for another round of physical violence in "mortal fight" so that when the wider opportunity for death-dealing comes soon afterward, Samson will be ready to seize it.

And that death-dealing will include the two Philistines who have been threatened with violence on stage. For presumably Dalila and Harapha go off to honored seats in the temple of Dagon. They are the only two we have seen of the "Lords, Ladies, Captains, Counsellors, or Priests" on whose heads Samson will pull down destruction. And while they are trivial souls both, we hardly rejoice at their death: they are too hollow to seem worth destroying. They are, of course, not the worst of the Philistines, those who bribed the wife to betray her husband and, not content to sheer him of dangerous strength, blinded him, put him to slave labor, and now call for him, their broken captive, to make them

sport. Even so, we have to observe that the most profoundly evil of the
Philistine lords did not kill their murderous enemy when they could
have. We need argue no greater compassion in them than in Cornwall
blinding Gloucester to recognize that Samson was a deadly threat to
them and fulfilled the threat.

Or is that too an observation that Milton forbids us to make? It is
a fact in his play. And Milton manages to suggest decidedly varied types
of Philistine just before the catastrophe, when Manoa reports on the responses he met in the course of pleading to ransom his son:

> Some much averse I found and wondrous harsh,
> Contemptuous, proud, set on revenge and spite;
> That part most reverenced Dagon and his priests;
> Others more moderate seeming, but their aim
> Private reward, for which both God and State
> They easily would set to sale; a third
> More generous far and civil, who confessed
> They had enough revenged, having reduced
> Their foe to misery beneath their fears,
> The rest was magnanimity to remit,
> If some convenient ransom were proposed. (ll. 1461–1471)

Since Manoa has good hope of success, the venal and the generously
civil evidently outnumbered the spitefully vengeful. It is just at this
point that we begin to learn of Samson's final vengeance: the Chorus
rightly guesses "that outcry / From slaughter of one foe could not as-
cend" (ll. 1517–1518). To any fine ear the magnanimity of the third sort
of Philistine contrasts with the "plain heroic magnitude of mind" the
Chorus has earlier praised in Samson (l. 1279) and now rejoices at his
having shown (ll. 1660–1707). If Milton intended us to rejoice with
them he wrote *Samson Agonistes* out of motives largely unlike those
of his other known works. So too if he intended us to accept their view
of the final inspiration of God's champion. In *A Treatise of Civil Power*
he argued: "divine illumination . . . no man can know at all times to be
in himself, much less to be at any time for certain in any other" (Columbia ed., VI, 6). The passage concerns the impropriety of using force in
matters of conscience, something of a favorite theme with Milton, and
not only when he wrote against kings and bishops: in the *Treatise* he
was addressing those of his own political faction.

Indeed, the burden of proof ought to be on those who ask us to take
Milton's Samson as a model of divinely illumined conduct. Samson's
announced vocation was to deliver Israel, not to slay Philistines. Ask

for that great deliverer at the end, and find him dead in Philistia among his "slaughtered foes in number more / Than all [his] life had slain before" (ll. 1667–1668). The Chorus may equate that with deliverance —"living or dying thou hast fulfilled / The work for which thou wast foretold" (ll.1661–1662)—but even Manoa hesitates to call the Israelites quite liberated: "let but them / Find courage to lay hold on this occasion" (ll. 1714–1715). We need only read past Chapter 16 in the Book of Judges to learn how much deliverance Israel gained.

The biblical Samson can have various meanings, some of which Milton used in other works. He can be an emblem for the dependence of strength on wisdom (as in *Eikonoklastes*), more simply the strong man "shorn of his strength" by the harlot (as in *PL* IX.1059–1062), a figure of the tyrant-queller (as in the *First Defense*). The Samson of the tragedy has all these meanings. Closer to his total meaning is the prolonged simile in *The Reason of Church-Government* likening the king among the prelates to Samson among the Philistines and ending with the ominous words: "till he, knowing this prelatical rasor to have bereft him of his wonted might, nourish again his puissant hair, the golden beams of law and right; and they sternly shook, thunder with ruin upon the heads of those his evil counsellors, *but not without great affliction to himself*" (Columbia ed., III, 276). The tone of the phrase I have italicized, with its implied threat to the king who foolishly lets the harlot prelates divest him of law and just prerogatives, shows that, here at least, Milton regarded Samson's last act as disastrous to himself as well as to the Philistine tyrants.

But his other references, even in their sum, do not encompass enough of what Milton put into *Samson Agonistes* to tell us how to read it. A rather different use of the Samson figure appears in Andrew Marvell's verses on *Paradise Lost*:

> the Argument
> Held me a while misdoubting his Intent,
> That he would ruin (for I saw him strong)
> The sacred Truths to Fable and old Song
> (So Sampson grop'd the Temple's Posts in spite)
> The World o'erwhelming to revenge his sight.[10]

Marvell's words sanction our finding Samson not entirely the redeemed champion of God for every seventeenth-century Protestant.

And a further impression remains from Milton's tragedy. His Samson among the Philistines and Danites alike is something of a Gulliver among Lilliputians, not only in his superior stature, but in his coming partly to accept, in spite of himself, the Lilliputian scale of values. To be willing "By combat to decide whose god is God" (l. 1176) in duel with Harapha, even to allow that "All the contest is now / 'Twixt God and Dagon" (ll. 461–462) is to reduce God to the Philistine scale of tribal deity, however superior in miracle-working might. No word of Samson's, for all his invoking of God in the course of his tragedy, remits that diminution.

Of course, Samson's gropings toward clarity about himself, his vocation, and God's purposes raise him above even the best of what the Chorus or Manoa say. And of course the Philistines are cruel tyrants to him and his people. We do want tyrants put down and their captives released from their power. Only, we want much more than that in *Samson Agonistes*, and in the way of tragedy we get something that defies our wish but by defying it assures us that our wish is right. Because Samson is so much better than those among whom we find him, we want him to be better still—to win through to some total comprehension, to be redeemed by his intolerable suffering, to recognize the sheer futility of a Dalila, a Harapha, to rise above his own brute strength and learn what deliverance means. And like tragic agents generally, he is too deeply enmeshed in snares of his own and others' weaving to break wholly free.

More like Hamlet and Othello than like Lear or even the ultimate Oedipus, he cannot rise to Lear's "No, no, no, no! Come let's away to prison . . . / And take upon's the mystery of things, / As if we were God's spies" or even to such final words of healing as Oedipus speaks. He can at best wish fame among his countrymen, like Hamlet, and prepare for his final deed with riddling words, like Othello.

But the tragedy to which *Samson Agonistes* has the most obvious parallels is *Antony and Cleopatra*, and not merely because both involve in gross terms a like subject: the man of power who falls from eminence through passion for a treacherous woman. In finer terms too, they share common themes—not, admittedly, the major theme in either: the man of power stands high in a superior civilization whose success or failure is important to the entire civilizable world; the treacherous woman, his passion for whom causes his downfall, belongs to a civilization corrupt and corrupting—self-indulgent, loose-tongued, greedy of glitter, superstitious, callous to the rights and pains of others. The downfall comes in part by corruption, in part by treachery; both falls end with the man of power dead yet somehow magnified. The unlikenesses are, of course, enormous: Rome, the higher civilization, dominates the world of *Antony and Cleopatra* both at the outset and at the end; Philistia, corrupt and corrupting, is brought low only in the catastrophe. Antony's passion makes him prefer Egypt, not only in its royal embodiment Cleopatra, but as home; Samson's never interfered with his adherence to the superior culture of Israel. The importance of Rome's victory to the world is as nothing compared to the importance of Israel's survival; the personal clash between Caesar and Antony for dominion gives victory to the more thorough Roman but leaves the victor—as it found him—the smaller, meaner, shallower of the pair, where the more impersonal clash of Samson with all Philistia gives victory to the more admirable Samson. The reality of Antony's love for Cleopatra—however much he strains against it—enlarges even as it corrupts him, as the reality of Cleopatra's for Antony—however readily at crisis after crisis she betrays him—gives her too finally a dignity almost equal to her variety and subtlety; the impossibility of Samson and Dalila's ever remotely comprehending each other precludes between them any love that could capture the imagination of either. *Antony and Cleopatra* is the tale of a man and a world torn apart for love, *Samson Agonistes* the tale of a vocation betrayed at the insistence of a light-headed woman and the consequence of that betrayal. And the list of major divergences could easily be extended.

Yet something of Shakespeare's tragedy echoes in Milton's—most clearly as the defeated strong man, struggling against the horrors his defeat entails, welcomes death as release. Antony's "The long day's task is done, / And we must sleep" (IV.xiv.45–46) has its counterpart in Samson's "My race of glory run, and race of shame, / And I shall shortly be with them that rest" (ll. 597–598). Again, the alternative of a private life that cannot be thought dangerous to the foe, which Antony fatuously suggests through his emissary and Caesar denies him (III.xii.14 ff.), Samson rejects when proposed by his father as well as by Dalila. The intolerable shame at defeat sprung from a dishonorable deed tears Antony for a time (III.xi.1–26, 51–75) as it tears Samson almost to the end. What makes the defeat still more intolerable is the contrast with past eminence (III.xiii.174–179; *SA* 19 ff.) and the sense in the defeated man of how he doomed himself. Caught thus in the toils of shame, self-disgust, dishonor, each at one point makes the wholly futile gesture of a challenge to single combat (Antony to Caesar, III.xiii.30–33; Samson to Harapha). Each looks back with dismay on his past arrogance in error, Antony generalizing on how the gods "make us / Adore our errors, laugh at's while we strut / To our confusion (III.xiii.140–142), Samson berating himself for having, "Fearless of danger, like a petty God, / . . . walked about admired of all and dreaded" until "swollen with pride" he fell into the snare (ll. 528–530).

Some minor resemblances cause minor echoes. The dotage that is all Rome ever sees in Antony's entanglement with Cleopatra is all the blind Samson admits in his former entanglement; the fetters that Antony at first calls his love Samson literally wears as a result of his. The politically useful marriage, which Antony hopes will reunite him with Caesar, turns out to divide them; the marriage to a Philistian woman, which Samson expected to further his defeat of Israel's enemies, has led to his own defeat. Perhaps the involvement of the sea and ships in Antony's fate suggested the extraordinary number of sea-and-ship images in *Samson.*

But these are minor matters. Still, even if to compare Milton's tragedy with Shakespeare's chiefly clarifies the disparity between their centers of concern, it helps to read Milton with his greatest English compeer in mind. However much he preferred the tragedies of Aeschylus, Sophocles, and Euripides, he too was an Englishman of the Renaissance, fed by all the traditions, Hellenic, biblical, Italian, native, that produced the era. And he paid a tribute to Shakespeare incomparably higher than to any other poet:

> What needs my Shakespeare for his honored bones
> The labor of an age in piled stones? . . .
>
> Dear son of memory, great heir of Fame,
> What needest thou such weak witness of thy name?
> Thou in our wonder and astonishment
> Hast built thyself a livelong monument. . . .
>
>   . . . each heart
> Hath from the leaves of thy unvalued book
> Those Delphic lines with deep impression took. . . .

What somehow gets between Milton and readers is an assumption that he is less poet than polemicist, doctrinaire rather than doctrinal, rigidified by his Christian convictions into inhumanity rather than illumined to a clearer reading of the human condition. It is understandable that Dr. Johnson preferred to read Milton as narrowly partisan and bigoted. It is less understandable that Milton's professed admirers so consistently diminish his whole human awareness. Yet facts pertinent to the reading of *Samson* are not hard to find. In all of *Christian Doc-*

trine, where biblical phrase and Old Testament figure repeatedly supply evidence for his theology and ethics, Milton never once refers to the delusive paragon of the Chorus, "That heroic, that renowned, / Irresistible Samson"—and Milton's views on heroics, on renown, and on victories through violence tell why. His Samson, like other tragic agents, along with virtues has a *hamartia* so deep in his ethos that he snares himself in folds of dire necessity more subtly woven even than those in which Clytemnestra netted Agamemnon. Agamemnon too, we may remember, identified with his own preeminence divine decree and the victory due his people. The pattern is appropriate in tragedy.

NOTES

1. I have throughout modernized Milton's spelling and punctuation in quoting the poems from the edition of Merritt Y. Hughes (New York, 1957) and the prose from the Columbia edition, ed. Frank Allen Patterson et al. (New York, 1931–1938), except where otherwise noted.

2. "Tragic Effect in *Samson Agonistes*," *University of Toronto Quarterly*, XXVIII (1959), 205–222.

3. The translation of *Christian Doctrine* is that of Bishop Sumner as printed in *The Student's Milton*, ed. F. A. Patterson (New York, 1933).

4. Although *agonistes* among its meanings includes "actor" and "saint," Milton did not tend to use recondite meanings of Greek words. The point of "A book was writ of late called *Tetrachordon*" is that a normally literate reader should have recognized the "four notes" of the title, just as a normally literate reader is expected to recognize "things pertaining to the Areopagus" in *Areopagitica* and the "image-breaker" in *Eikonoklastes*.

5. The translation of Aristotle's *Poetics* is that of Lane Cooper, *Aristotle on the Art of Poetry* (New York, 1913). The passages quoted are from Chapter 13.

6. Even in *Comus*, the distinctive Miltonic preference for the ethic of free will appears in the condition-contrary-to-fact of the closing lines: "Or *if* Virtue feeble *were*, / Heaven itself *would stoop* to her."

7. "Samson and Christ," *From Shadowy Types to Truth* (New Haven, 1968), pp. 181–202.

8. I take the phrase from Cumberland, as quoted by Henry John Todd, *The Poetical Works of John Milton*, 5th ed. (London, 1852), III, 220. Cumberland (*Observer*, Vol. IV, No. 111; Todd, III, 218–221) was apparently the first commentator to take this line as a way of answering Dr. Johnson.

9. Quoted by Todd in his note on line 878, III, 275–276. Dunster's remark on line 1645 is also worth citing: "It too much resembles the language of the evil angels in the sixth book of *Paradise Lost*, on producing their artillery and witnessing the successful effect of it" (Todd, III, 315).

10. The relevance of Marvell's verses to my argument was suggested by James Holly Hanford at the MLA meeting in 1965, where I read a brief version of this paper.

Melancholy Against Melancholy: *Samson Agonistes* as Renaissance Tragedy

RAYMOND B. WADDINGTON
UNIVERSITY OF WISCONSIN

Start with what we can agree upon. The problem of Dr. Johnson's middle has been reduced with almost universal recognition that the process of Samson's spiritual regeneration constitutes the action preceding the catastrophe. The dilemma about the "spirit" of the drama has come to seem more properly a concern for Arnold scholars as, increasingly and not surprisingly, Miltonists discover its intellectual context to be seventeenth-century Protestant Christianity. The indignation that followed upon Krouse's—to some readers—blasphemous suggestions has been succeeded largely by a grudging awareness that, while Samson is *not* an allegory of Christ, he *is*, in the technical sense, a type of Christ—that is, both like and unlike him in important ways. This view has been reinforced by recent examinations of the Chorus, laying stress upon the limitations of their responses within the dramatic context, while the same responses heighten reader comprehension on a different level. With Johnson posthumously confounded, the consideration of Milton's theoretical orthodoxy, or lack of it, has taken the form of a close scrutiny of the preface to *Samson*. The results indicate that, whether Milton took his Aristotle neat or mixed, he drank from a cup molded by Renaissance commentators.[1]

Since *Samson Agonistes* is a tragedy "wov'n close, both matter, form and style," in the present essay I shall touch upon these several strands in an effort to show the relatedness of matter and form which leads to comprehension of structure and meaning.

259

I

William Madsen's argument that Milton was at pains to preserve
the integrity of Samson as an Old Testament type has an inherent plau-
sibility, although Madsen was anticipated by Arthur Barker's more flex-
ible formulation:

> A type is significant both for its contrast with and its likeness to
> what it types, by being itself according to the decorum of the
> circumstances of its dispensation in time and an indication of
> what the process of time moves towards. . . . In his way and time,
> Samson is the type of what the Christian may be the type of in
> his way and time, fulfilling the letter of the type by bringing into
> appropriate action the gifts of the Spirit.[2]

Yet, even strict obedience to the rules of biblical typology and to the
decorum of Old and New Dispensations does not disbar, in a dramatic
poem, the presence of literary typology; and, in this sense, Milton's
use of typology seems more subtle and implicational than Madsen's
strictures would allow.[3]

Krouse also made accessible the tradition which treats Samson and
Hercules as parallel figures and, indeed, frequently made Hercules a
Greek theft from the Book of Judges. While Krouse himself saw no
evidence of the parallels intersecting in *Samson Agonistes*, other readers
have discerned differently: J. C. Maxwell points to a possible adaptation from Sophocles' *Trachiniae*; Barker posits an audience "which
rightly sees Samson as a Hebraic Hercules"; Roger Wilkenfeld notes a
similarity in the Phoenix simile, which figuratively projects a Samson
who "dies in flames, like Hercules"; and long ago Merritt Hughes suggested the possibilities of Hercules allusions at line 150 and lines 1038–
1039.[4] The likelihood of other borrowings and echoes seems strong. In
The Trachiniae Hercules describes his suffering as a plague and addresses Hyllus, the igniter of the funeral pyre, as the healer of his sufferings and only physician of his pain (l. 1209), perhaps contributing
to Milton's conception of the far more extensive disease imagery in
Samson. And Samson's darkness-at-noon lament (ll. 80–82) may owe
more to the account of Hercules' madness in Seneca, "medium diem
cinxere tenebrae" (*Hercules Furens*, ll. 939–940) than to Luke's account
of the Crucifixion. But far more important than any specific point of
influence is the cumulative effect of a tragic vision, shared by Sophocles,
Euripides, and Seneca, exploiting the contrast between the invincible

physical heroism of the past and the dramatic present of, as Eugene
Waith has phrased it, "a man almost broken by suffering, who nevertheless finds strength to endure."[5]

Milton surely knew as well as Bishop Patrick the etymology which
derived the names of both Samson and Hercules from *sun*, thereby
making them fit comparisons to the Sun of Righteousness; and in both
the *Nativity Ode* and *Paradise Regained* he alludes to Hercules as a type
of Christ.[6] In his one direct linkage of Samson with Hercules, however, he shows his awareness that both Adams are met in the Hercules myth by recalling, implicitly, the "effeminate slackness" of the
Omphale episode. The wakening of Adam from his sexual fall is described: "So rose the *Danite* strong / *Herculean Samson* from the Harlot-
lap / Of *Philistean Dalilah*, and wak'd / Shorn of his strength" (*PL*
IX.1059–1062).[7] Adam and Eve, of course, create the archetype of luxurious folly of which Hercules and Omphale or Samson and Dalila
necessarily are the derived types of human behavior.

Another conventional association, which Milton very likely knew
and which, I think, had a shaping influence upon the tragedy, was the
tradition, originating with the pseudo-Aristotelian *Problemata* and revived in the Renaissance by the Florentine Neoplatonists, that viewed
Hercules' madness as an excess of melancholy. Rolf Soellner has traced
for us the history of the melancholy Hercules and shown its theatrical
implementation by Heywood, Marston, and Shakespeare.[8] The stage
convention of a mad Hercules is itself suggestive not only in view of the
generic choice which makes Samson protagonist in a tragic action,
but also through the play-within-a-play connotations of the imagery
which depicts Samson as player in a "spacious Theater," whose final act
evokes *admiratio*.[9]

D. C. Allen's thesis, that *Samson* is Milton's fullest analysis of the
problem of Christian despair and that regeneration from this despair
constitutes the middle of the tragedy, has influenced a generation of
Miltonists.[10] I would only refine it by a further discrimination: Herculean Samson's despair is inspired by the pervasive religious melancholy which besets him at the opening of the tragedy. Manoa believes
that Samson's morbid thoughts proceed "From anguish of the mind and
humors black" (l. 600), a fairly standard description of the combination of factors, the temperamental imbalance of black bile and the
mental activity, believed to eventuate in religious melancholy.[11] Burton
eloquently anatomizes the Devil's technique of effecting despair through
melancholy:

His ordinary engine by which he produceth this effect
is the melancholy humor itself, which is *balneum Diaboli*, the
Devil's bath; and as in Saul, those evil spirits get in, as it were,
and take possession of us. Black choler is a shoeing horn, a bait
to allure them, insomuch that many writers make melancholy an
ordinary cause and a symptom of despair for that such men are
most apt, by reason of their ill disposed temper, to distrust, fear,
grief, mistake, and amplify whatsoever they preposterously conceive or falsely apprehend. *Conscientia scrupulosa nascitur ex
vitio naturali, complexione melancholica,* saith Navarrus. (*Anatomy of Melancholy* III.IV.ii.3)[12]

Loneliness, intense meditation of spiritual questions, especially anxiety
over salvation, and the nagging of conscience are the secondary causes
most likely to transform the melancholy into despair:

The main matter which terrifies and torments most that are troubled in mind is the enormity of their offenses, the intolerable
burthen of their sins, God's heavy wrath and displeasure so deeply apprehended that they account themselves reprobates, quite
forsaken by God, already damned, past all hope of grace, unca-
pable of mercy, *Diaboli mancipia*, slaves of sin, and their offenses
so great they cannot be forgiven. (*Anatomy* III.IV.iii.6)[13]

This state of mind (despair in theological terms means the individual's
loss of hope for salvation) brings about the external symptoms docu-
mented so thoroughly by Burton: unquiet sleep, weariness with life,
perpetual anxiety and restlessness, pessimism, impatience, questioning
of God's ways.[14]

It is instructive to consider *Samson* with details of the melancholy
tradition in mind. His wretched garments (ll. 122–123), for instance,
are conventional attributes of melancholy; but his posture—"With
languish't head unprop, / As one past hope, abandon'd" (ll. 119–120)
—plays off against conventional expectation. The iconographic representation of the melancholic supporting his head by resting the cheek
on one hand was so commonplace that "unpropt" seems a deliberate
violation of that expectation.[15] The inference would seem to be the one
which the Chorus draws: this is worse than an ordinary case of melancholy; Samson has already lapsed into despair—"by himself given
over." We are expected to remember the image and mark the difference
when, in the temple, Samson first "inclines" his head in prayer, then announces his final feat to the Philistines "with head erect" (ll. 1636–

1639). Samson's simile for the "restless thoughts" that plague him "like a deadly swarm / Of Hornets" possibly has a basis in the iconography of melancholy,[16] as does Manoa's embittered description of God's gifts drawing "a Scorpion's tail behind" (l. 360). The image of the scorpion doubtless primarily summons associations of deceit and cruelty; however, it may also allude to the belief that the terminus of the sign of Scorpio belonged to Saturn and engendered melancholics.[17] Even the striking moment at which Samson violently spurns Dalila's appeal, "Let me approach at least, and touch thy hand" (l. 951), has prosaic forebears in the melancholic's contempt for sexual passion.[18]

Burton's accounts of the difficulty of distinguishing pathological melancholy from the melancholy inspired by a genuine sense of sin, the melancholy delusions of visions, miraculous powers, and special marks of God's favor, as well as the dispute over whether melancholics have genuine prophetic powers, would all seem relevant context for some of the careful ambivalences of *Samson*.[19] Indeed, the description of setting in Samson's opening monologue should be compared to the advice of Du Laurens and Burton that light and cheerful surroundings with warm, moist air be a part of the treatment.[20] Samson feels "amends" here (l. 9) because the therapeutic process has begun. Similarly, since it is the Chorus who diagnose Samson's condition and define their own role as supplying healing "Counsel or Consolation" (ll. 183–186), perhaps some of their obtuseness and digressiveness should be seen as deliberate, in accordance with the mental diversion and distraction which Burton advocates as curative.[21]

Is, then, the initial diagnosis of the Chorus accurate? Allen and Woodhouse believe that Samson exposes his despair in the opening monologue;[22] but Stein, concentrating upon the discrepancy between the monologue and the Chorus' visual assessment of self-abandonment, argues to the contrary: "The moral gestures toward responsibility and Providence indicated a stage well this side of despair. . . . He is no more abandoned than he is resigned. His grief is fresh enough to hurt. The anger and self-contempt are too powerfully felt and expressed to represent despair; so is the exacerbated sensitivity to insult. . . ."[23] Several things need to be remarked. First, the descriptions of Samson by the Chorus and other speakers have to be accurate, since they are all we have, though we do *not* have to accept their evaluations of the descriptions. The image of Samson is that of a man suffering extremely from melancholia. Next there are degrees of despair, just as there are degrees of melancholy, and Samson vacillates. Allen comments that "there is a fluctuation throughout the early part of the tragedy in Samson's attitude towards himself, a fluctuation arising from the contention between his sense of sin and the fear that he has been abandoned by God."[24] Huntley, in a close analysis of the monologue, finds that the "moral gestures" are immediately undercut by the questioning of God's will and ways, concluding "he is actually blind to the discrepancy between his verbal acceptance and emotional rejection of responsibility." Thus the speech reveals "a man protecting himself from unbearable guilt and despair" and projecting "onto God the guilt he cannot assimilate."[25] Stein perhaps errs through an overly static concept of despair. For Milton it encompasses more than resignation and the Slough of Despond. Loss of hope for the fallen angels of *Paradise Lost* is epitomized by ceaseless mental torment—"where peace / And rest can never dwell"—and Samson's condition is best characterized as a profound disease of mind (ll. 14–22). Though his release from the mill momentarily "amends" his spirits, the effect, ironically, is to give full release to his "restless thoughts"; and the climax of thought and dominating tone is established with "O dark, dark, dark," which denotes the modulation from melancholy to despair—"total Eclipse / Without all hope of day!" —in the transformational image of his Herculean progenitor. The furor of the tormented god lends both a frame of allusion and a gauge of Samson's anguish.

Allen's observation that *Samson* "includes in its circular scope all of the theological dicta on the genesis and cure of despair" receives important corroboration through the implications of the general study done by Susan Snyder. Like Allen, Miss Snyder details the symbiotic relationship of pride and despair (significant in the monologue for Samson's humiliation at his abasement, chagrin at appearing a fool), the association of despair with sloth, and the popular conviction that despair ends in suicide.[26] More than this, however, her analysis of the significance of despair in Protestant theology serves to strengthen the bridge between Allen's thesis and those of scholars such as Patrides, who locates the well of Milton's inspiration in Geneva, or Steadman, for whom *De Doctrina Christiana* is the best guide to the movements of the drama. Her discriminations between the positions of Luther and Calvin, when compared to *De Doctrina* II.3, would place Milton's notion of despair more firmly in the camp of the latter. Moreover, Miss Snyder's discussion of despair in relation to Law and Grace helps make clear the essential consonance between the despair reading and Barker's conviction that "Christian liberty" is what the later poems, including

Samson, are really about.[27] Her account of the commonplace belief that despair is the "special temptation of God's elect," be they saints or sinners with special endowments, reminds one both of Samson's Nazarite role and of the tradition of commentary which makes Samson an honorary Christian saint. Although the Chorus declares that patience is the "exercise / Of Saints" (ll. 1287–1288) and Harris has traced the opposition of patience to despair in the tradition of the cardinal virtues, Miss Snyder tells us that hope is the usual opposite of despair (as it is in *De Doctrina* II.3).[28] Milton would seem to have incorporated both antidotes by having his hero attain first patient endurance and then renewed hope.

For its literary consequences in application to *Samson*, however, the most suggestive part of Miss Snyder's study is her discernment of two complexes of imagery habitually used in theological and literary accounts of despair. The first of these involves "helpless imprisonment and danger":

> The Bernardine parable of the prodigal son has despair as a prison, another recurring metaphor. Chrysostom uses terms of slavery and servitude—an iron collar, a millstone. Related to this group are the images of storm and shipwreck in Augustine's commentary on Psalm ci and Gregory's *Moralia*. Augustine and others identify the "profundum marum" of Psalm lxvii.23 with despair. In the *Epistola optima contra desperacionem* the despairing soul is a swimmer overcome by storm-waves.[29]

The other complex embraces imagery which is "anti-life, anti-health, anti-fertility": barrenness, lack of fertility, withered vegetation, fruitless trees, sterile earth, chilling cold, and winter are images of despair employed by Gregory, Bernard, Thomas, Bonaventure, and others. Despair is the dark night of the soul (Walter Hilton), a living death (Augustine), or a living hell (Gregory and Isadore).[30]

It would seem a belaboring of the obvious to dwell at length upon how strikingly apposite these two groups, and most of the particular examples, are to a consideration of the imagery in *Samson*. The dominant image patterns of the tragedy convey the thematic paradoxes of blindness and sight, freedom and imprisonment, disease and health. As Stein has observed, the major themes are introduced at the very outset of Samson's monologue, extend to a nexus of related images, and operate on several levels of reference.[31] Thus, the blindness and sight pattern includes darkness and light (and, since blindness is an impairment of

health, implicitly relates to the disease and health imagery) and applies
not only to Samson, but to the Philistines, who are "with blindness internal struck" (l. 1686), and to Manoa and the Chorus, whose blindness to
the meaning of Samson's agony is alleviated by a degree of illumination. The problem of attaining freedom from bondage exists for Samson in particular and for Israel in general; the two are inextricably connected by the prophesied role of Samson as Israel's deliverer, although
both Samson and the Chorus must come to understand the difference between deliverance by act and by example. As Samson again becomes
God's servant the change is marked with the replacement of his "slavish
habit" by the raiment of a "public servant"; that Samson's audience does
profit from his example may be inferred from Manoa's conclusion: Samson "To *Israel* / Honor hath left, and freedom, let but them / Find courage to lay hold on this occasion" (ll. 1714–1716), seemingly confirmed
by the Chorus' final designation of themselves as "God's servants." The
complex of disease and health imagery, which I shall consider further
in the following sections, includes medicines and cures: "healing words,"
rest, "cooling herbs," cleansing water, purifying fire, "The breath of
Heav'n."

    With each of the major patterns a paradoxical reversal or transcen-
dence—from physical to spiritual, literal to figurative—should be observed: Samson's physical blindness ceases to image his spiritual blindness as he is "With inward eyes illuminated"; he comes to understand
that "These rags, this grinding, is not yet so base / As was my former
servitude . . . / True slavery, and that blindness worse than this" (ll. 415–
416, 418); and the disease of mind may be seen, retrospectively, as a
part of the curative process, which, however painful, is preferable to the
deceptive tranquillity of Samson's previous state.

    Of the secondary image patterns, perhaps the most significant is the
shipwreck and storm complex, which is used by Samson in reference to
himself (ll. 198–200), by Dalila in reference to Samson (ll. 960–964), the
Chorus in reference to Samson, Dalila, and Harapha (ll. 1044–1045, 710–
719, 1061, 1068–1070), and by the Messenger in reference to Samson
(ll. 1646–1652).[32] Samson chooses the image of living death to define the
consequences of blindness and enslavement to his enemies, "Myself
my Sepulcher, a moving Grave" (l. 102), and his thought finds confirmation with the Chorus: "Thou art become (O worst imprisonment!) / The
Dungeon of thyself" (ll. 155–156). Possibly because of the association
suggested by the account in the Book of Judges of the circumstances of
Samson's birth, "I pray'd for Children, and thought barrenness / In wed-

lock a reproach" (ll. 352–353; cf. Judg. 12:2–3), Milton consistently assigns the imagery of infertility to Manoa, who nurtured Samson "as . . . a Plant" (l. 362), which he now sees blighted. His analogy,

> But God who caus'd a fountain at thy prayer
> From the dry ground to spring, thy thirst to allay
> After the brunt of battle, can as easy
> Cause light again within thy eyes to spring, (ll. 581–584)

casts Samson as the sterile earth forsaken, for whatever period of time, by God. And Manoa responds to the tragic frustration of his ransom scheme in these terms:

> What windy joy this day had I conceiv'd
> Hopeful of his Delivery, which now proves
> Abortive as the first-born bloom of spring
> Nipt with the lagging rear of winter's frost. (ll. 1574–1577)

The imagistic structure, which I have briefly sketched here, will not be new to any careful reader of *Samson*. The points to be emphasized, however, are these: only a portion of this imagery could be considered inherent in the Samson story (and the Book of Judges does not amplify upon the imaginative potential in barrenness, blindness, and imprisonment); the three major and several secondary patterns discussed contribute significantly to the reader's comprehension of *Samson's* meaning; the unlikelihood that this particular confluence of imagery could derive from a tradition or context other than the literature of despair attests to the centrality of this theme.

II

If Weinberg's *History* stands as a *summa critica* for the Renaissance misunderstanding of Aristotle, the burgeoning literature upon the preface to *Samson Agonistes* has come to resemble a late-Scholastic footnote. But, while it may be tempting to suggest that the most valuable function of Milton's theory of catharsis is to draw off the excess humors of a sequence of Causabons, the concentrated and sometimes cryptic statements in the preface nevertheless do have an important bearing on the poetic drama which they accompany. According to Mueller, "Milton's concept of catharsis is characterized by three features: a) the

combination of purgation with the Aristotelian mean; b) the homeopathic analogy; and c) a rather complex relationship of imitation, purgation, and pleasure."[33] As the most distinctive of these features, the
homeopathic analogy has attracted particular comment: Mueller follows
the leads offered by Spingarn and Gilbert in positing Minturno and
Guarini as possible sources for Milton's usage, but also nominates Lorenzo Giacomini to the slate; Arthos calls attention to Girolamo Bartolommei's espousement of homeopathic purgation; Sellin, while minimiz-
ing the significance of the homeopathic element, insists upon Heinsius
as *the* source, despite Heinsius' admitted indebtedness to the Italians;
Steadman sees the recourse to medical imagery as a conventional element in commentaries upon Aristotle.[34]

Even so deceptively small a point as Milton's decision to render the
Aristotelian *katharsis* as *lustratio* in the Latin epigram, before descending to the solid English of the preface's "purge," has teased the commentators out of thought. Scott-Craig, stressing the religious and ceremon-
ial connotations of the Latin term, found its primary meaning to be a
theological "loosing"; and more recently Sellin has argued that by his
use of *lustrationem* Milton intends to convey the idea of a milder purgation than tragic catharsis.[35] But Hughes makes perhaps the most relevant contribution, telling us that in Renaissance dictionaries "the first
meaning given for *lusis* is the medical one of release from pain or passion," and I would fully agree that "it is the medical meaning of the
term that Milton clearly has in mind when he goes on in the first sentence
of his preface to say that Aristotle regarded the nature of tragedy as
consisting in its 'power by raising pity and fear, or terror, to purge the
mind of those and such like passions. . . .' "[36] The homeopathic analogy,
"Nor is Nature wanting in her own effects to make good his assertion:
for so in Physic things of melancholic hue and quality are us'd against
melancholy, sour against sour, salt to remove salt humors," unmistak-
ably, I believe, was included to help the reader gloss the concept of
catharsis operative in the tragedy which the preface accompanies. With
a side glance at the disease imagery, Hughes notes, "If we force [Mil-
ton's] meaning only a little here by laying stress on *Nature*, it is possible
to look at the whole process of Samson's regeneration in a medical
light" and to see it as illuminating "key passages."[37]

More than this, I wish to maintain, the statement, as it qualifies
the formulation of tragic catharsis, acts as a significant clue to the structure of the tragic action. Milton describes his preface as serving a
function similar to the classical "Epistle," employed "in case of self defence, or explanation." While the preface is not by any means a fully

articulated treatise on the nature of tragedy, it is more than a conventional rhetorical apologia; the preface is, rather, an "explanation" of those elements of Milton's tragic theory most immediately relevant to the comprehension of *Samson Agonistes*. As such it implies that the structural pattern of the tragedy is not the "trial by what is contrary" pattern of *Areopagitica* and *The Reason of Church-Government*;[38] instead, the pattern is that of like curing like.

The sequence of melancholy "against melancholy, sour against sour, salt to remove salt humors," in a sense, offers three ways of looking at a black mood, for salt and sour humors were simply variant descriptions of melancholia.[39] Milton knew the conventional treatments for melancholy and from them selected music as the symbolic cure in *L'Allegro* and *Il Penseroso*;[40] but for "Herculean Samson" he evidently concluded that neutralizing the poison by poison best suited his dramatic conception. A number of readers have commented on the ways in which Dalila and Harapha present Samson with images of his own past weaknesses and echo his own thoughts. Barker alone has perceived deliberate parody in all three encounters, although a thematic rather than a character parody, deriving from the nature of Samson's previous actions which all "have been perverse and inadequate parodies of the significance of his calling": "Each of Samson's temptations is itself a parody related to the Law and containing distorted elements of the truth of what is really demanded under the Law. They reminiscentially underline, ironically, the increasingly parodic quality of Samson's own earlier acts, chiefly motivated by the impercipient preoccupation with his function as national hero and his own natural strength which made him his own idol."[41] It will be the burden of the following section to argue that all three encounters involve thematic and character parody; that Samson successively is presented with images of himself; that the process of repudiating these images, the melancholy of Manoa, the sour of Dalila, the salt of Harapha, is the therapeutic action by which Samson reduces to just measure "such like passions" in his own mind. The parodic encounters, through which Samson finds it possible to recognize and control the excesses of his own passions, are, in fine, the dramatic enactment of the like-cures-like purgation to which the preface alerts us.

III

The entrance of the Chorus "revives" Samson, even though he denies the efficaciousness of their "apt words" as "Balm to fester'd wounds" (ll. 184–186), assuaging by their very presence the critical despair of his soliloquy. His explanations of his weakness and marital folly, his denial of responsibility for the fact that "*Israel* still serves with all his Sons" (l. 240), trace an ascending emotional spiral, a new (to the play, old to the man) confident mood that must fragment in the presence of Manoa. The emotional import of this episode is analogous to the flower passage in *Lycidas*, an interposition of "a little ease," a dallying with "false surmise," a perhaps half-consciously false respite before visiting the emotional bottom of his own monstrous world.

Arnold Stein, ever a responsive reader, describes for us the intrusion of Manoa's voice into the drama: "The first effect is different and shocking, partly because of the quality of the new voice, which is recklessly willing to articulate attitudes not yet articulated; but partly also because that new voice repeats what has already been said, but turns it peremptorily into the special expression of a new and forceful dramatic position."[42] This quality of repeating what Samson knows or has said, but saying it in another voice, without Samson's own hedge of equivocation, and so sharpening the articulation, crystallizing it, defines Manoa's function: "That is Manoa's office, to name the names, and to let Samson face his feelings as a proposal from without."[43] Manoa thus exteriorizes Samson's attitudes and the structure of the episode becomes a dialectic between Samson and Samson as he evaluates, qualifies, and corrects the stances in his soliloquy and assertions to the Chorus.

Manoa's first words, "O miserable change!" (l. 340), confirm frontally and brutally the Chorus' first view of Samson; yet the immediate parallel may be misleading, for the important affinities of the speech are with Samson's monologue (ll. 23–64), rather than with the words of the Chorus. As Samson there contemplated his birth and ordained role "As of a person separate to God, / Design'd for great exploits" (ll. 31–32), lamented the failure of strength, and flirted with complaint against God's justice (ll. 52–64), so Manoa here recounts the miraculous birth and prophesied career (ll. 352–367), decries "ever failing trust / In mortal strength" (ll. 348–349), and reproaches God overtly (ll. 368–372). The tormented tentativeness of Samson's speech is gone; the doubt, verging upon blasphemy, is direct. Moreover, the bitter description of prayer as worthless and treacherous (ll. 350–360) has the effect of undercutting any positive value in Manoa's subsequent advice, "to avert / [God's] further ire, with prayers and vows renew'd" (ll. 519–520).

Samson's response is threefold. First, he affirms his conviction that God is just, this time without the previous emotional foot-dragging. As Stein remarks, "The announcement is not new but the quality of the statement is."[44] With this step, awareness that he has "profan'd / The mystery of God giv'n me under pledge / Of vow" (ll. 377–379) allows the beginning of comprehension that he has degraded *both* "Honor and Religion" (l. 412), an advance upon the monologue's exclusive preoccupation with personal debasement and humiliation. Finally, in self-answer to the "loss of sight" complaint (ll. 66–109), which culminated in "Myself my Sepulcher, a moving Grave," Samson attains the realization that

> The base degree to which I now am fall'n
> These rags, this grinding, is not yet so base
> As was my former servitude, ignoble,
> Unmanly, ignominious, infamous,
> True slavery, and that blindness worse than this,
> That saw not how degenerately I serv'd. (ll. 414–419)

With this first movement toward figurative understanding of the paradoxes of his predicament, Samson grasps where he had never reached.

The pattern in the following Manoa-Samson exchanges does not differ markedly from this first. Manoa's next thrust, "A worse thing yet remains," exploits the opening afforded by Samson's brief acknowledgment that he has profaned his religion. Dagon shall be magnified and God "Disglorified, blasphemed," the most shameful of Samson's offenses. The frank acknowledgment that he has

> . . . brought scandal
> To *Israel*, diffidence of God, and doubt
> In feeble hearts, propense enough before
> To waver, or fall off and join with Idols:
> Which is my chief affliction, shame and sorrow,
> The anguish of my Soul . . . (ll. 453–458)

implies a recantation of his earlier denial of responsibility for Israel's continued servitude: "That fault I take not on me, but transfer / On *Israel's* Governors" (ll. 241–276). Although that denial has been read as a salutary sign of recovery,[45] in fact it would seem to be a narrowly legalistic formulation of his role, a definition of what it means to be a Nazarite in accordance with the letter rather than the spirit. This negative reading of the denial may be confirmed by the parodic (and sanctimonious) quality of Samson's condemnation:

> But what more oft in Nations grown corrupt,
> And by thir vices brought to servitude,

Than to love Bondage more than Liberty,
Bondage with ease than strenuous liberty. (ll. 268–271)

Here Samson unwittingly describes his own corruption under the name
Israel (which cannot be free without a free leader), though of course
until the Manoa encounter he is incapable of recognizing it.

Samson's avowal of faith that God will vanquish Dagon with himself out of the lists now refines our perception of the despair with which
he is afflicted. Aquinas and Bonaventure both discriminate between loss
of faith in general and the retention of faith while despairing in particular of hope for oneself.[46] The latter is Samson's predicament. During
the Manoa encounter he makes great advances in self-awareness; yet
paradoxically this advancement serves immediately to renew and intensify his despair, for, as Miss Snyder comments, "self-knowledge is the
beginning of salvation, but without a corollary knowledge of God it
will bring only despair."[47] Samson comes part way toward spiritual enlightenment in this episode, but he must still learn the nature of God's
mercy, that he is himself still in the contest.

With devastatingly impeccable logic Manoa continues his cate-
chism. He has made Samson acknowledge his sinfulness to be so unfor-
givable that he is alienate from God; Manoa now asks, "But for thee
what shall be done?" (l. 478) and advances his ransom scheme. I take
Barker's cryptic reference to "Manoa's well-intentioned but senile offer of
juvenile ransom" as "a parody related to the Law" to allude to the ironic
interplay between Manoa's material and literal ransom plan, his eventual figurative (but still limited) comprehension of ransom by death
(ll. 1572–1573) and the conception of the Atonement as a "ransom."[48]
Samson knows that he cannot be ransomed in Manoa's coin: his "let me
here, / As I deserve, pay on my punishment; / And expiate, if possible,
my crime" (ll. 488–490) elicits Manoa's advice to observe the letter of
repentance, give lip service to it, while avoiding the spirit. A skilled advocate of the devil's casuistry, Manoa knows that "physical debilitation,
added to deep melancholy, naturally leads to a distaste for life,"[49] and,
still thinking in terms of physical punishment and death, offers the ultimate in unnecessary advice: "By warning Samson against suicide, he
puts the thought in his mind."[50]

Milton's adaptation of convention is brilliant. Manoa figures Despair as surely as do the giants of that name created by Spenser and
Bunyan, and he speaks their language as well. While he proffers no
knife, rope, or poison, his insinuation of the idea presents a true temptation to seek death. The process by which he reaches this point, though

he forebears quoting Scripture, is the same pseudo-pious, relentlessly rational application of the Law, leading to conviction of unrighteousness, which causes Redcrosse to accept the knife and which even the amateur theologian might recognize as "the devil's syllogism." It is not overt, but the syllogistic progression from sinfulness to damnation to despair and death lends a traditional structure to the movement of the dialogue.[51] The essential difference between the giants Despair and Milton's well-intentioned Manoa is one of complexity and subtlety. Or perhaps one should say, more simply, a difference of mode: Spenser and Bunyan present allegorical figures; Manoa is symbolic. The despair which he images is in Samson's own mind. Nor does Samson have Hopeful as companion and a Key called Promise in his bosom, a Una to remind him of heavenly mercies; all of these must generate from within his own mind as did the despair.

Manoa nearly succeeds. Samson, half in love with easeful death, will not take his own life, but neither will he seek to preserve it. The Chorus' interjection directs Samson's attention to his intemperance, relevantly, since the Aristotelian-Thomist notion of moderating the passions, as well as the Ciceronian concept of virtue as proper ordering of the emotions,[52] augments the despair tradition and, as Milton employs it, couples with the cathartic principle of moderation or reduction, rather than extirpation, of excess passion. The patient, however, cannot distinguish the discomfort of the purge from the pain of the sickness. To Samson

> My griefs not only pain me
> As a ling'ring disease,
> But finding no redress, ferment and rage,
> Nor less than wounds immedicable
> Rankle, and fester, and gangrene,
> To black mortification. (ll. 617–622)

Through the motif of blindness and darkness the theme of Samson's "disease" has hovered throughout on the verge of the reader's consciousness, but nowhere has the direct use of disease and medicine imagery been so pervasive as it is when Samson's new self-awareness leads him to this emotional cul-de-sac, given over "To death's benumbing Opium as my only cure. / Thence faintings, swoonings of despair, / And sense of Heav'n's desertion" (ll. 630–632).

Why does Samson not succumb? The question ultimately cannot be answered, because if "some source of consolation from above" does uphold his "fainting spirits" (ll. 663–666), the process is felt "within" and, like the moment when Samson stands silent between the pillars, remains uncommunicated. For a proximate answer we can turn only to the "God of our Fathers" choral ode, about which there are varying estimates. That Samson's despair has infected the Chorus seems beyond dispute. The general role of the Chorus is both complex and variable, for, if they are sometimes unreliable and obtuse commentators upon the action and must themselves undergo a spiritual renewal parallel to Samson's, they are not always unreliable or irrelevant. At this point the extension of Samson's despair to the "community" universalizes and emphasizes his condition; it also externalizes once again his earlier thoughts about the nature of God's justice.

If the reasoning of the Chorus is specious and deluded,[53] it is because they mimic, lagging as always a bit behind, what they have heard, their poison thus helping, too, to expel his. And their prayer might be understood as a departure from this delusion, as a verbal simulation of a non-articulated process within Samson's mind: "Having said the worst, the Chorus, like Samson, suffers through to a kind of resolution."[54] Luther taught that only by recognizing himself as damned under the Law could the sinner properly comprehend his total dependence upon God and move to knowledge of God's mercy through the Gospel.[55] The Chorus' final recourse to prayer suggests this progression, which again is the one Stein intuits in Samson's own mind: "There is no place further to go. Having reached the end, and named it, he is thrown back on the beginning, on God."[56]

About the principal function of the Dalila episode, that it gives Samson, first Adam and second Adam both, the opportunity to expunge his previous uxorious weakness by passing the test he once failed, there has been large agreement. Recognition of the parodic elements, as well, has been substantial, perhaps because of Dalila's own commentary upon her action: "Let weakness then with weakness come to parle / So near related, or the same of kind" (ll. 785–786). Stein describes her mirroring of Samson's preoccupation with self-justice ("It is a version that illuminates, with a marvelous intricacy of reflection and shadow, Samson's image of self-justice") and his narcissism ("the vanity of the warrior-athlete, his beauty of strength"). Wilkenfeld speaks of Samson's forced endurance of "Dalila's (perhaps unconsciously) cruel parody of his assumed position: 'I was a fool too rash and quite mistaken.'" Barker sees the precipitous sacrifice of Samson's secret to Dalila as "a parody of another kind of sacrifice, which he might, even in domestic relations with an unbeliever, have better imitated," and notes her "apologetic

parody of deeds answerable to a loyalty higher than the merely patri-
otic."[57]

The unconscious parody commences with her initial manner, ap-
proaching "with head declin'd / Like a fair flower surcharg'd with dew"
(ll. 727–728), a feminization of Samson's melancholy posture. Her declaration of "faith"—"My penance hath not slack'n'd, though my pardon / No way assur'd" (ll. 738–739)—mocks Samson's recent resolution;
but he perceives her behavior to be his own, as scripted by Manoa:

> To break all faith, all vows, deceive, betray,
> Then as repentant to submit, beseech,
> And reconcilement move with feign'd remorse,
> Confess, and promise wonders in her change. (ll. 750–753)

Samson refuses her appeal in the same fashion that he imagines God refusing his, by invoking a standard of legalistic absolutism (ll. 757–765).
Dalila responds by seeking forgiveness beyond the Law, appealing to
"Love's law," a kind of corrupt *caritas*, which "always pity or pardon
hath obtain'd" (l. 814), only to be thwarted by Samson's distinction between love and lust. Ostensibly dropping the theme of the New Dispensation, Dalila presents her first parody of Samson's role: "Adjur'd by all
the bonds of civil Duty / And of Religion" (ll. 853–854); but Samson,
charging "feign'd Religion," lectures on absolution from lesser laws by
higher laws and the way in which even religious laws can be tran-
scended. The formulation here is less direct; yet it is still a working
toward the realization of his own role.

As if recoiling from Samson's unexpected mental rigor, Dalila shifts
again to the projection of his own melancholy. Both Manoa and Dalila
exploit the despairing melancholic's well-known tendency toward physical lassitude; but, whereas Manoa worked upon the affinity between
despair and *acedia*, Dalila couches her temptation in terms of the link
between despair and *luxuria*.[58] Each offer constitutes a form of idolatry
to which, with the aid of the evolving self-realization, Samson now is
impervious; he is, as he recognizes (ll. 944–950), more genuinely at liberty in the Philistine jail than he could be in his father's house or his
wife's arms. Samson's refusal to permit Dalila to touch his hand underscores the distinction between the lover's melancholy with which she
hoped he was afflicted and the religious melancholy which actually
scourges his soul (cf. ll. 1354–1358). His action, further, focuses attention upon the stage of recovery yet remaining to be accomplished in the
Harapha episode—knowledge of God and the correlative understand-

ing that God has not withheld his mercy. Rather as he might imagine his God replying to him, Samson tells Dalila, "At distance I forgive thee, go with that" (l. 954). She has left only her pathetic imitation of Samson's old-time role as national hero and then departs, unwittingly having served her purpose in the mental dialectic.[59]

With Harapha and the modulation, if not quite from contemplative to active, at least from rejection to assertion (it is Samson who challenges Harapha), Samson meets the least subtle of his visitors and the least complex of his self-images. Harapha is, A. B. Chambers observes, "an image of the unreal heroism earlier embodied in Samson."[60] The Chorus epitomizes his character, "his look / Haughty as is his pile high-built and proud" (ll. 1068–1069), and Samson can visualize in his mind's eye his opponent in telling detail (ll. 1119–1122). This familiarity is possible because he knows the type of man all too well:

> . . . like a petty God
> I walk'd about admir'd of all and dreaded
> On hostile ground, none daring my affront.
> Then swoll'n with pride into the snare I fell. (ll. 529–532)

Martin Mueller has commented: "Samson's increasing self-awareness is seen in his changing attitude towards his strength. At the beginning of the play he is inclined to think of it as something physical, almost a magic charm hung in his hair. Harapha, who is like the unregenerate Samson in so many other ways, follows him in this too."[61] Therefore Samson's initial description of his strength (ll. 58–59) finds an echo from Harapha: ". . . some Magician's Art / Arm'd thee or charm'd thee strong, which thou from Heaven / Feign'd'st at thy birth was giv'n thee in thy hair" (ll. 1133–1135). Thrust back into the state of mind of his early soliloquy, Samson rebuts the charge:

> My trust is in the living God who gave me
> At my Nativity this strength, diffus'd
> No less through all my sinews, joints and bones,
> Than thine . . . (ll. 1140–1143),

using language that not only recalls the idea of strength hung in his hair but sweeps away the adjacent complaint that sight was not "through all parts diffus'd" (l. 96).

Proceeding from the distrust of God, Harapha's recollections of things past linger once more on the theme of despair: his speech beginning "Presume not on thy God" (ll. 1156–1167) assesses Samson's situation and has the greater familiarity for recapitulating the beliefs of the two previous visitors as well as saying what Samson had said.[62] Samson's impressive denial of this confluence of doubters deserves quotation in full:

> All these indignities, for such they are
> From thine, these evils I deserve and more,
> Acknowledge them from God inflicted on me
> Justly, yet despair not of his final pardon
> Whose ear is ever open; and his eye
> Gracious to re-admit the suppliant;
> In confidence whereof I once again
> Defy thee to the trial of mortal fight,
> By combat to decide whose god is God,
> Thine or whom I with *Israel's* Sons adore. (ll. 1168–1177)

The significance of the speech lies not only in the firmness with which Samson admits the justice of his punishment, the progression to "despair not," and the entrance into the lists as God's champion, but in the fact that the verbal echoes this time take us beyond the refractions of Samson's thought to an entirely external (though still Miltonic) perspective: "To Prayer, repentance, and obedience due, / Though but endeavor'd with sincere intent, / Mine ear shall not be slow, mine eye not shut" (*PL* III.191–193). Harapha tries to shake Samson's faith by insistence on punishment under Law (ll. 1178–1180, 1182–1191, 1224–1225), but fails and departs.

The three visitors have, each in his own way, tempered Samson's spiritual malady by opposing it with their imitations. To Samson his condition was "remediless"; they, however, have functioned as the medicine to alleviate that condition, as Harapha's very name possibly suggests.[63] In each encounter there has been a cyclical pattern as Samson resists the destructive image with which he is presented, rises to a height of new illumination and resolution, then in reaction falls back into a depressed state. The regenerative progression, nevertheless, is a line of steady ascent. His relapse following Dalila's departure ("God sent her to debase me," l. 999) is less severe than the despair at Manoa's exit; though Harapha's departure leaves Samson wishing for a speedy death (ll. 1262–1264), the Chorus correctly denotes his "reviving" spirit as the salient point. The visitors have simulated different aspects of Samson's self-image, ranging from present to past with Manoa mirroring Sam-

son's immediate misery, Dalila the weakness of his recent past, and
Harapha the vainglory of a more remote past. But, as Barker has argued,
a common theme unites the episodes, the theme of allegiance to and
dispensation from the Law.

There is no element of parody in the final visitor, the Philistine
Officer. The time has come for Samson to act upon the understanding
and self-control which he has attained. By acting in accordance with
the Law and refusing the Officer's command ("Our Law forbids at thir
Religious Rites / My presence; for that cause I cannot come," ll. 1320–
1321), Samson establishes his obedience to God and reinstitutes his role
as Nazarite. Yet, as both he and the Chorus understand, God "made
our Laws to bind us, not himself" (l. 309), and may dispense with the
Law whenever he has reason (ll. 1377–1379). At the second command
Samson responds to the "rousing motions" of God's will acting upon him
and accompanies the Officer to the temple; by so doing, as his treble
assurances indicate (ll. 1384–1386, 1408–1409, 1423–1425), not violating or dishonoring the Law and his Nazarite's vow but transcending it.[64]
For the first time Samson does not confuse the impulses of his own
libido with the will of God; instead, he truly becomes God's champion,
having progressed from self-knowledge to God-knowledge and comprehension of the mercy accessible to him.

IV

Milton's decision to display Samson's spiritual recovery as a catharsis effected by means of like-against-like exposes a certain predilection
for medical unorthodoxy. In the tradition of Galenic medicine, humoral
physiology and psychology demanded therapy on the principle that
contraries cure—a fever is tempered by the application of cold agents,
and so on. The homeopathic principle that the remedy for the disease
lies in its source gained currency in the Renaissance through vigorous
advocacy by the anti-Galenist and great medical innovator Paracelsus.[65]
The man whose very name, according to Donne, made Lucifer tremble
"as if it were a new *Exorcisme*," added to the classical system of the
four elements his own triad of chemical principles, mercury, sulphur,
and salt.[66] In conjunction with Milton's invocation of homeopathic catharsis and his appeal to the "effects" of "Nature" (which, conceivably,
suggests the prime matter or *Mysterium Magnum* underlying the Paracelsian conception of creation), it is tempting to see the entire analogy
in a Paracelsian light: melancholy, sour, and salt as corresponding to

mercury, sulphur, and salt; the principles of spirit, soul, and body ordering and shaping the thematic emphases in the homeopathic encounters
with Manoa, Dalila, and Harapha.[67]

There is a distinct appropriateness in Milton's grounding the medical analogy upon Paracelsian theory; for, if to Milton tragic purgation
means a process of spiritual regeneration, Paracelsian medicine also is
religious in import, acting, as Carl Jung perceived, as a kind of metaphor
for spiritual transmutation.[68] The philosophic bases of Paracelsian
thought lie in the context of Renaissance Neoplatonism, Pythagoreanism,
and Hermeticism, the popularity of which provided the impetus for
much of the magical science of this period.[69] It is doubly appropriate,
therefore, that Ficino and the Florentine Neoplatonists, fusing the Problemata's observation upon the coincidence of melancholy and genius
in the figure of Hercules with Plato's concept of the poetic furor, should
have originated the interpretation of the melancholic Hercules as a symbol of religious ecstasy and prophetic inspiration.[70] Samson Agonistes
commenced with its protagonist locked in the "brooding darkness" of
"loathed Melancholy" and progressed to the transformation of his humor to "divinest Melancholy." After the preparatory sequence of false,
mistaken, or unintended (but ironically true) prophecies by Samson
(ll. 465–471), Manoa (ll. 581–586), and the Chorus (ll. 682–686), Samson's return to God's service is marked by a genuine prophetic strain
(ll. 1388–1389). He has become one with his God in spirit, an ecstasy
which shortly will prove enduring as his soul literally departs from his
body.

The amazement which Samson promises will strike the Philistines
upon witnessing his final feat of strength was a central concept in Renaissance poetics, and, Eugene Waith asserts, of all heroes Hercules most
evokes that response.[71] Lee Cox has discerned imagistic parallels between the Messenger's account of Samson's pulling down the pillars of
the temple and the earlier description of Samson, bearing the gates to
the city, "Like whom the Gentiles feign to bear up Heav'n" (l. 150).[72]
The Herculean stance given to his final action would seem deliberate,
as would the latent parallel between Hercules' funeral pyre and the
"Holocaust" of the Phoenix simile. The frame of reference offered by
Ficino's spiritualized, transcendent Hercules implies very much the same
apotheosis for Samson as does the imagery of the semichoral ode—
release, inward illumination, purification by fire, rebirth into life through
death. Or as does the sequence of comparisons which cast Samson as
fiery, solar flying creature—dragon, eagle, Phoenix—which by the con-

ventions of allegorized metamorphosis all imply the same thing: spiritual ascent and transcendence beyond the merely human.[73]

Milton's Phoenix passage is one of those provoking much commentary, the infinite variety of which custom cannot stale. Unnecessary confusion has arisen through failure to grasp the validity of a dual response. Milton has the Chorus voice an image which his Christian audience must recognize as a conventional symbol of their Savior, even as the Chorus misinterprets it by emphasizing that last infirmity of noble mind, the element of worldly fame. One of the most subtle techniques which Milton exploits in adapting the tragic form as a vehicle for biblical narrative and Christian doctrine is the use of dramatic irony to convey the difference in perspective between his Old Testament characters, operating under the order of Law, and his audience, temporally under the order of Grace. I wish here simply to trace a few of the reticular associations of the Christ/Phoenix symbol as they especially relate to the matters discussed in this paper.

This choral ode is not Milton's only conjunction of eagle and Phoenix. In Book V of *Paradise Lost* God sends Raphael to advise and warn Adam of his impending danger; as Raphael descends, "within soar / Of Tow'ring Eagles, to all the Fowls he seems / A *Phoenix*, gaz'd by all" (ll. 270–272). This "glorious shape," to Adam "seems another Morn / Ris'n on mid-noon" (ll. 310–311), reminding us that at the temple "noon grew high and Sacrifice / Had fill'd their [the Philistines'] hearts with mirth" (ll. 1612–1613) and even of the Chorus' complaint that at "height of noon" God changes his countenance and hand toward his elect (ll. 682–686). The narrator's comparison of Raphael to a Phoenix intensifies the suggestions that the angel is a precursor of Christ: like the Son of God, he descends to earth to aid man; he is further described as "Like *Maia's* son" (V.285), paralleling the mortal-mother/divine-father parentage of Christ; finally, his name means "medicine of God,"[74] clearly anticipating Christ's function.

John Donne knew well the physician-of-the-soul metaphor, as witness his *Devotions*,[75] but the figure particularly is common in the context of Paracelsian medicine and alchemy. At the nadir of his despair Samson described his evils as "remediless" and saw in death "The close of all my miseries, and the balm" (l. 651), statements which are wrong and right, respectively. The healing balm or balsamum of Paracelsian theory, too, lent itself easily to metaphoric extension. Donne sermonized upon it: "Something that hath some proportion and analogy to this balsamum of the body, There is in the soul of man too."[76] This balsam originates in the same "*Arabian* woods that are the haunt of the Phoenix," as Milton tells us in *Epitaphium Damonis*,

> In medio rubri maris unda, et odoriferum ver,
> Littora longa Arabum, et sudantes balsama silvae;
> Has inter Phoenix, divina avis, unica terris,
> Caeruleum fulgens diversicoloribus alis,
> Auroram vitreis surgentem respicit undis (ll. 185–189),

and as he associatively projects to Raphael, passing "through Groves of Myrrh, / And flow'ring Odors, Cassia, Nard, and Balm; / A Wilderness of Sweets" (V.292–294).[77]

Paracelsus understood this concatenation of images, and in his description of preparing the "Tincture" or "Philosopher's Stone" we find eagle, Phoenix, and balm suggestively connected with fire and blindness:

> This work, the Tincture of the Alchemists, need not be one of nine months; but quickly and without any delay you may go on by the Spagyric Art of the Alchemists, and in the space of forty days, you can fix this alchemic substance, exalt it, putrefy it, ferment it, coagulate it into a stone, and produce the Alchemical Phoenix. But it should be noted well that the Sulphur of Cinnabar becomes the Flying Eagle, whose wings fly away without wind, and carry the body of the Phoenix to the nest of the parent, where it is nourished by the element of fire, and the young ones dig out its eyes: from whence there emerges a whiteness, divided in its sphere, into a sphere and life out of its own heart, by the balsam of its inward parts. . . .[78]

Here the Phoenix symbolizes the philosopher's stone, which, like the alchemists' tincture, the Great Elixir, the spiritual balm, is Christ himself.[79] The object of Paracelsian alchemy and medicine alike was transmutation, purification, the achievement of that elemental balance which changes the base metal to gold. To Donne the alchemical language was so patently the clay of poetry that Elizabeth Drury became the Elixir, "purifying / All by a true religious Alchymie," and the chemical resurrection of gold could function as the metaphor for Christ's "Resurrection, imperfect."

Although the homeopathic agents of Manoa, Dalila, and Harapha are the instrumental causes of Samson's cure, the final cause is Christ, the Medicine of God. Milton writes in *De Doctrina Christiana*:

it ought not to appear wonderful if many, both Jews and others, who lived before Christ, and many also who have lived since his time, but to whom he has never been revealed, should be saved by faith in God alone: still however through the sole merits of Christ, inasmuch as he was given and slain from the beginning of the world, even for those to whom he was not known, provided they believed in God the Father. (I.XX)[80]

But Paracelsian homeopathy presupposes sympathetic correspondence between microcosm and macrocosm,[81] a conception which helps to suggest the way in which both the tragic theory and structure of *Samson Agonistes* work finally as metaphors in the relationship of dramatic poem to audience or reader. The purpose of Milton's poetry is "to allay the perturbations of the mind and set the affections in right tune"; and, if the like-cures-like process serves to "temper and reduce" Samson's passions to "just measure," so his example is designed to initiate an analogous process in our minds "with a kind of delight, stirr'd up by reading or seeing passions well imitated" and dismiss us with "calm of mind, all passion spent." Christ heals us all.[82]

NOTES

1. It would be superfluous to document acceptance of the "spiritual regeneration" theme. For a statement of *Samson Agonistes* as "a classical tragedy with a Christian theme and outlook," see A. S. P. Woodhouse, "Tragic Effect in *Samson Agonistes*," reprinted in *Milton: Modern Essays in Criticism*, ed. A. E. Barker (New York, 1965), pp. 447–466; and, among others, J. M. Steadman, " 'Faithful Champion': The Theological Basis of Milton's Hero of Faith," reprinted in the Barker collection, pp. 467–483, and in Steadman's *Milton's Epic Characters: Image and Idol* (Chapel Hill, 1968), pp. 44–57; Barker, "Structural and Doctrinal Pattern in Milton's Later Poems," in *Essays in English Literature . . . Presented to A. S. P. Woodhouse*, ed. M. MacLure and F. W. Watt (Toronto, 1964), pp. 169–179; Ann M. Gossman, "Samson, Job, and 'the Exercise of Saints,' " *English Studies*, XLV (1964), 212–224.

F. M. Krouse, *Milton's Samson and the Christian Tradition* (Princeton, 1949), elucidated the traditions which made Samson into a saint and identified him with Christ. Krouse concluded, "Samson's story, paralleling as it does the story of *Christus Victor*, reveals him as *Homo Victor*, a palpable exemplification of the meaning to Man of his Redemption" (p. 133). For the current state of opinion, see Barker, pp. 178–179; and W. G. Madsen, "From Shadowy Types to Truth," in *The Lyric and Dramatic Milton: Selected Papers from the English Institute*, ed. J. H. Summers (New York, 1965), pp. 95–114, and reprinted in Madsen's *From Shadowy Types to Truth* (New Haven, 1968), pp. 181–202.

The unreliability of the Chorus is argued most forcefully by John Huntley, "A Revaluation of the Chorus' Role in Milton's *Samson Agonistes*," *Modern Philology*,

LXIV (1966), 132–145; and F. R. Baruch, "Time, Body, and Spirit at the Close of *Samson Agonistes*," *ELH*, XXXVI (1969), 319–339.

On the preface, see P. R. Sellin, "Sources of Milton's Catharsis: A Reconsideration," *Journal of English and Germanic Philology*, LX (1961), 712–730; "Milton and Heinsius: Theoretical Homogeneity," in *Medieval Epic to the "Epic Theater" of Brecht*, ed. R. P. Armato and J. M. Spalek (Los Angeles, 1968), pp. 125–134; Martin Mueller, "Sixteenth-Century Italian Criticism and Milton's Theory of Catharsis," *Studies in English Literature*, VI (1966), 139–150; John Arthos, *Milton and the Italian Cities* (New York, 1968); and J. M. Steadman, " 'Passions Well Imitated': Rhetoric and Poetics in the Preface to *Samson Agonistes*," this volume, pp. 175–207. Also relevant is Mueller, "*Pathos* and *Katharsis* in *Samson Agonistes*," *ELH*, XXXI (1964), 156–174.

2. Barker, "Milton's Later Poems," p. 179.

3. I object not to Madsen's thesis, but to the narrow and excessively literal reading of the drama to which he thinks it commits him. For instance, his response to the imagery:

> In *Samson Agonistes* there is no such metaphoric activity; at the most, stones are turned into bread, but physical hunger is not transmuted into spiritual hunger. The two major motives of blindness and delivery from bondage receive only a limited metaphorical extension that falls far short of Christ's achievement in *Paradise Regained*. (*From Shadowy Types to Truth*, p. 195)

For contrary reactions to the language and imagery, see, e.g., R. B. Wilkenfeld, "Act and Emblem: The Conclusion of *Samson Agonistes*," *ELH*, XXXII (1965), 160–168; Lee S. Cox, "Natural Science and Figurative Design in *Samson Agonistes*," *ELH*, XXXV (1968), 51–74; Anne D. Ferry, *Milton and the Miltonic Dryden* (Cambridge, Mass., 1968), pp. 127–177.

4. Krouse, pp. 44–45, 78, 111, 130; Maxwell, "Milton's Samson and Sophocles' Heracles," *Philological Quarterly*, XXXIII (1954), 90–91; Barker, "Milton's Later Poems," p. 177; Wilkenfeld, "Act and Emblem," p. 167; Hughes, *Paradise Regained, The Minor Poems, and Samson Agonistes* (New York, 1937), pp. 429, 587n.

5. Waith, *The Herculean Hero in Marlowe, Chapman, Shakespeare and Dryden* (New York, 1962), p. 26.

6. Patrick's *Commentary upon . . . Judges* is quoted by Krouse, p. 78. Kenneth Fell surveys the elements of solar mythology in the Judges Samson. See "From Myth to Martyrdom: Towards a View of Milton's *Samson Agonistes*," *English Studies*, XXXIV (1953), 146–147. Barbara H. Carson, "Milton's Samson as *Parvus Sol*," *English Language Notes*, V (1968), 171–176, argues that Milton employs Samson's solar associations as a basis for the light and dark imagery as well as the time scheme. I refer of course to *Nativity Ode*, ll. 227–228, and *PR* IV.563–568. A prominent locus for the Hercules-sun parallel is Macrobius, *Saturnalia* l.xx.6–12.

7. All Milton quotations, unless otherwise indicated, are from *John Milton: Complete Poems and Major Prose*, ed. Merritt Y. Hughes (New York, 1957).

8. "The Madness of Hercules and the Elizabethans," *Comparative Literature*, X (1958), 309–324. The relevant passages of *Problemata* XXX are quoted in Raymond Klibansky, Erwin Panofsky, and Fritz Saxl, *Saturn and Melancholy* (New York, 1964), pp. 18–19; see also p. 287 for graphic representations of the melancholy Hercules.

9. See Mueller, "*Pathos* and *Katharsis*," p. 170, n. 4; also Sellin, "Milton's Epithet *Agonistes*," *Studies in English Literature*, IV (1964), 137–162.

10. *The Harmonious Vision* (Baltimore, 1954), pp. 71–94. The importance of despair figures in the readings of Woodhouse, Steadman, and Gossman. See also

Arnold Stein, *Heroic Knowledge* (1957; Hamden, Conn., 1965), p. 210; W. O. Harris, "Despair and 'Patience as the Truest Fortitude' in *Samson Agonistes*," *ELH*, XXX (1963), 107–120; Huntley, "A Revaluation of the Chorus' Role," p. 134.

11. See Lawrence Babb, *The Elizabethan Malady: A Study of Melancholia in English Literature from 1580 to 1642* (East Lansing, 1951), pp. 47–54, 114, 117. That the translation of Hercules' melancholy to despair was effected well before Milton wrote is indicated by Gervase Markham: ". . . yet, I pray thee beware of this *Hercules*, despaire, least in the end hee make our ruine his conquest" (*The second and last part of the first booke of the English Arcadia* [London, 1613], fol. 17v). I owe this quotation to Professor Helen C. Gilde.

12. *Robert Burton: The Anatomy of Melancholy (A Selection)*, ed. Babb (East Lansing, 1965), p. 358. This text is based upon the 6th edition of 1651. The influence of Burton upon Milton (and Milton himself as melancholic) has been argued by G. W. Whiting, *Milton's Literary Milieu* (Chapel Hill, 1939), pp. 129–176. Milton's literary use of melancholy has been most discussed in relation to *L'Allegro* and *Il Penseroso*. See especially Rosemond Tuve, *Images and Themes in Five Poems by Milton* (1957; Cambridge, Mass., 1962), pp. 25–36. Whether or not Milton was actually melancholy in temperament, it was an important feature of his poet-prophet *persona*.

13. *Robert Burton: The Anatomy of Melancholy*, p. 370.

14. *Anatomy*, III.IV.ii.4. See also Susan Snyder, "The Left Hand of God: Despair in Medieval and Renaissance Tradition," *Studies in the Renaissance*, XII (1965), 38–39.

15. *Saturn and Melancholy*, pp. 286–289 and plates; see also André Chastel, "Melancholia in the Sonnets of Lorenzo de' Medici," *Journal of the Warburg and Courtauld Institutes*, VIII (1945), 61–67.

16. See *Saturn and Melancholy*, p. 302, n. 75, for an account of a graphic representation of melancholy with mental delusions symbolized as swarming insects.

17. See *Saturn and Melancholy*, p. 147, n. 68. Kester Svendsen, *Milton and Science* (Cambridge, Mass., 1956), pp. 149–150, gives non-melancholy scorpion lore.

18. See *Saturn and Melancholy*, p. 298 and plate 84. Jacques and Hamlet exemplify the attitude on stage.

19. See Babb, *Elizabethan Malady*, pp. 49–50, 52–53.

20. Babb, p. 39.

21. *Anatomy*, II.II.vi.2: "Help from Friends by Counsel, Comfort, Fair and Foul Means, Witty Devices, Satisfaction, Alteration of His Course of Life, Removing Objects, Etc."

22. Allen, p. 84; Woodhouse, pp. 449–450.

23. Stein, p. 143.

24. Allen, p. 84.

25. Huntley, pp. 133–134.

26. Allen, quotation, p. 83; pride, pp. 73–75; sloth, pp. 75–77; suicide, pp. 78–81. Snyder, pp. 18–59; for pride, see pp. 32, 46–47; sloth, pp. 43–46; suicide, pp. 50–57.

27. "Protestant theology": Snyder, pp. 23–24; C. A. Patrides, *Milton and the Christian Tradition* (Oxford, 1966); Steadman, *Milton's Epic Characters*, pp. 44–57. Luther and Calvin: Snyder, pp. 24–29. "Law and Grace": Snyder, pp. 24, 30–33; Barker, "Milton's Later Poems," pp. 172–173.

28. "Special temptation": Snyder, pp. 25–26. Patience: Harris, pp. 109–115; Snyder, p. 56.

29. Snyder, p. 58.

30. Snyder, pp. 58–59.

31. Stein, pp. 138–140. Most suggestive for the major image complexes are Wilkenfeld, Cox, and Mueller, "*Pathos* and *Katharsis*."

32. See Barbara K. Lewalski, "The Ship-Tempest Imagery in *Samson Agonistes*," *Notes & Queries*, N.S., VI (1959), 372–373. I believe that, beyond the despair associations, there may be some resonances from an important contemporary political metaphor. See J. M. Wallace, "Marvell's 'Lusty Mate' and the Ship of the Commonwealth," *Modern Language Notes*, LXXVI (1961), 106–110. Any such resonances of contemporary events are, of course, subordinated to a providential view of history.

33. Mueller, "Milton's Theory of Catharsis," p. 143.

34. Mueller, "Milton's Theory of Catharsis," pp. 146–148; Arthos, *Milton and the Italian Cities*, pp. 146–154; Sellin, "Sources of Milton's Catharsis," p. 716; Steadman, " 'Passions Well Imitated,' " pp. 175–207, this volume.

35. T. S. K. Scott-Craig, "Concerning Milton's *Samson*," *Renaissance News*, V (1952), 48; Sellin, "Sources of Milton's Catharsis," p. 725.

36. Hughes, p. 543.

37. Hughes, p. 543.

38. This suggestion has been made by Cox, "Natural Science," pp. 51–52, and Steadman, *Milton's Epic Characters*, p. 48.

39. See Babb, *The Elizabethan Malady*, p. 22.

40. On music as cure for melancholy, see Babb, pp. 39–40; *Anatomy*, II.II.vi.3; and Gretchen L. Finney, "Music, Mirth, and Galenic Tradition in England," *Reason and the Imagination*, ed. J. A. Mazzeo (New York, 1962), pp. 143–154. For the relevant intellectual background, see D. P. Walker, *Spiritual and Demonic Magic from Ficino to Campanella* (London, 1958), pp. 3–29.

41. Barker, "Milton's Later Poems," pp. 177–178.

42. Stein, p. 148.

43. Stein, p. 154.

44. Stein, p. 150.

45. E.g., by Stein, p. 146, and Huntley, pp. 137–138. Nearer to my view is that of Northrop Frye, *Five Essays on Milton's Epics* (London, 1966), p. 114.

46. See Snyder, p. 49.

47. Snyder, p. 22.

48. Barker, pp. 147–148. For the idea of the atonement as ransom, see C. A. Patrides, "Milton and the Protestant Theory of the Atonement," *PMLA*, LXXIV (1959), 7–13. Ann M. Gossman has written on classical analogues: "Ransom in *Samson Agonistes*," *Renaissance News*, XIII (1960), 11–15.

49. Snyder, p. 53; see the entire discussion of despair and suicide, pp. 50–57.

50. Allen, p. 86.

51. On rationality and the "devil's syllogism," see Snyder, pp. 30–32.

52. See Snyder, pp. 37–38.

53. As Huntley argues, p. 139.

54. Stein, p. 166.

55. See Snyder, p. 24.

56. Stein, p. 163.

57. Barker, pp. 177–178; Wilkenfeld, p. 163; Stein, pp. 170–177.

58. For *acedia*, see Snyder, pp. 43–46; for *luxuria*, p. 47.

59. The similarity between Dalila's description of her tomb (ll. 986–987) and Manoa's description of Samson's (ll. 1741–1742) cuts two ways: it points up Dalila's parodic function and it reveals the limitations of Manoa's understanding of Samson's role.

60. Chambers, "Wisdom and Fortitude in *Samson Agonistes*," *PMLA*, LXXVIII (1963), 319.

61. Mueller, "*Pathos* and *Katharsis*," p. 163.

62. For comment upon this speech, see Woodhouse, p. 454; Allen, p. 92; Stein, p. 181.

63. W. R. Parker, *Times Literary Supplement*, January 2, 1937, p. 12, quotes Edward Phillips' *The New World of Words*: "*Haraphah* (*Hebr.*) a Medicine, a *Philistim* whose sons being gyants were slain, by *David* and his servants." See also Jacob Leveen, *Times Literary Supplement*, January 23, 1937, p. 60; Steadman, *Milton's Epic Characters*, pp. 185–193. Samson seemingly puns upon the meaning of the name: "nothing from thy hand / Fear I incurable" (ll. 1233–1234).

64. Cf. Mueller, "*Pathos* and *Katharsis*," p. 165, and Barker, p. 176.

65. See Walter Pagel, *Paracelsus: An Introduction to Philosophical Medicine in the Era of the Renaissance* (Basel and New York, 1958), pp. 141–148, on homeopathy; also Allen G. Debus, *The English Paracelsians* (London, 1965), pp. 32–35.

66. Pagel, pp. 100–104, and Debus, pp. 26–29. That Milton should have combined the humoral conception of melancholy with homeopathy, despite Paracelsus' own rejection of the humors explanation of disease, is not particularly surprising. Paracelsus never satisfactorily explained the relationship of the four elements to his three principles, and his writings are confusing and inconsistent on the subject. Debus traces the influence of Paracelsus in England, ca. 1570–1640, and shows the development of an "Elizabethan compromise" in which aspects of Paracelsian therapy are adapted to Galenic medicine. See especially the conflation of Galenic and Paracelsian theory in the humoral systems of Joseph Duchesne (p. 67) and Robert Fludd (p. 120). Interestingly, in *The Anatomy of Melancholy*, while the particular discussions of cures are thoroughly eclectic, the total concept of the work is presented as homeopathic. "I write of melancholy by being busy to avoid melancholy," says Democritus, Jr.:

> Besides I might not well refrain, for *ubi dolor, ibi digitus*, one must needs scratch where it itches. I was not a little offended with this malady—shall I say my mistress Melancholy, my Egeria, or my *malus genius?*—and for that cause, as he that is stung with a scorpion, I would expel *clavum clavo*, comfort one sorrow with another, idleness with idleness, *ut ex vipera theriacum*, make an antidote out of that which was the prime cause of my disease (*Robert Burton: The Anatomy*, p. 10).

See also Donne's verse epistle to Wotton, "Sir, more than kisses, letters mingle Soules," ll. 59–62.

67. On the *Mysterium Magnum*, see Pagel, p. 93, and Debus, pp. 25–26; the spirit-soul-body analogy is Paracelsian commonplace (see Debus, pp. 93, 104). Edward Jorden describes sulphur as a "sowre iuyce" (quoted by Debus, p. 163); mercury may be associated with melancholy via Hermes Trismegistus and the tradition of intellectual melancholy. See *Il Penseroso* and Frances A. Yates, *Giordano Bruno and the Hermetic Tradition* (Chicago, 1964).

68. Jung, *Psychology and Alchemy* (London, 1953).

69. Debus, pp. 41–42; see also Frances A. Yates, "The Hermetic Tradition in Renaissance Science," in *Art, Science, and History in the Renaissance*, ed. C. S. Singleton (Baltimore, 1967), pp. 255–274.

70. See Soellner, pp. 314–315; also *Saturn and Melancholy*, pp. 241–274, especially pp. 258–260.

71. *The Herculean Hero*, pp. 38, 49–59; on *admiratio* see also J. V. Cunningham, *Woe or Wonder: The Emotional Effect of Shakespearean Tragedy*, reprinted in his *Tradition and Poetic Structure* (Denver, 1960).

72. "Natural Science," pp. 72–73. Hughes has suggested that line 150 alludes to Hercules assuming Atlas' burden. See n. 4 above.

73. I accept the reading by Lee S. Cox, "The 'Ev'ning Dragon' in *Samson Agonistes*: A Reappraisal," *Modern Language Notes*, LXXVI (1961), 577–584; the dragon is a winged dragon, whose name etymologically means "the seeing one." The most pertinent gloss upon eagle as sighted and solar bird is the *Areopagitica*: "Methinks I see her as an eagle muing her mighty youth, and kindling her undazzled eyes at the full midday beam; purging and unscaling her long-abused sight at the fountain itself of heavenly radiance" (Hughes, p. 745). Miss Cox touches on the implication of spiritual metamorphosis in "Natural Science," pp. 73–74.

74. On Raphael's name, see Hughes' note to *PL* V.221; and Svendsen, *Milton and Science*, p. 148.

75. See especially *Devotions* VIII, XIV, XIX, and XX. In "Meditation XXII" he uses the Phoenix myth to symbolize recovery of health.

76. Quoted by J. A. Mazzeo, "Notes on John Donne's Alchemical Imagery," reprinted in his *Renaissance and Seventeenth-Century Studies* (New York, 1964), pp. 68–69; see his entire discussion of balsamum, pp. 68–71. Martin Ruland, *A Lexicon of Alchemy (1612)*, trans. A. E. Waite (London, 1964), may be consulted on Paracelsian terminology.

77. See Geoffrey Hartman, "Adam on the Grass with Balsamum," *ELH*, XXXVI (1969), 183; pp. 181–184, on Raphael as Phoenix, and pp. 187–192 on "balm," particularly, are germane to the concerns of my argument. See also Svendsen, pp. 146–149, on the Phoenix.

78. *The Hermetic and Alchemic Writings of Paracelsus*, ed. A. E. Waite (London, 1894), I, 40; quoted by E. H. Duncan, "Donne's Alchemical Figures," *ELH*, IX (1942), 270.

79. See, e.g., F. Sherwood Taylor, *The Alchemists* (New York, 1949), pp. 222–223; Jung, *Psychology and Alchemy*, pp. 343–411.

80. *The Prose Works of John Milton* (London, 1861), IV, 340–341, trans. C. R. Sumner. See also Steadman, *Milton's Epic Characters*, pp. 46–47.

81. See Debus, pp. 29–32; and Mazzeo, pp. 65–67.

82. Since the completion of this essay, the direction of my argument regarding homeopathic purgation as the tragic structure has received corroboration from two other readers: Sherman H. Hawkins, "Samson's Catharsis," *Milton Studies*, ed. J. D. Simmonds (Pittsburgh, 1970), II, 211–230; and Georgia Christopher, "Homeopathic Physic and Natural Renovation in *Samson Agonistes*," *ELH*, XXXVII (1970), 361–373. Our essays differ considerably, however, in approach, emphasis, and detail. Miss Christopher would extend the homeopathic process even to Samson's death (p. 371).

Irony as Tragic Effect: *Samson Agonistes* and the Tragedy of Hope

JOHN T. SHAWCROSS

STATEN ISLAND COMMUNITY COLLEGE

Among the critical controversies which emerge periodically over Milton's *Samson Agonistes* is that of Samson's alleged regeneration. For, the often unstated yet underlying argument contends, there can be no tragedy if Samson is regenerated.[1] The question is: Can there be a Christian tragedy if "Christian" implies that God's providence has made the outcome possible and has turned that which is evil or negative into that which is good or positive, and if "tragedy" implies that the hero or his action is wasted, particularly through his *hamartia*? If Samson is regenerated, the argument goes, then the course of the headlong fall resulting from his *hamartia* has been altered and his "flaw" must have been overcome. Under such conditions there is no tragedy, for a good—whether Samson's regeneration or his act of destroying the Philistines—has arisen out of evil.

Samson Agonistes seems to run counter in certain ways to both older and modern concepts of tragedy. The fall-of-princes formula used by Boccaccio or Lydgate or *The Mirror for Magistrates* does not allow for Samson's regeneration, although his fall in the past has intensified the bondage of his people and thus a sense of this formula applies. Nor does it accord with Samson's position as Great Deliverer rather than as one of noble estate. The Chorus, expressing the significant difference, laments:

> O mirror of our fickle state
> Since man on earth unparallel'd!

> The rarer thy example stands,
> By how much from the top of wondrous glory,
> Strongest of mortal men,
> To lowest pitch of abject fortune thou art fall'n.
> For him I reckon not in high estate
> Whom long descent of birth
> Or the sphear of fortune raises;
> But thee whose strength, while vertue was her mate,
> Might have subdu'd the Earth,
> Universally crown'd with highest praises. (ll. 164–175)[2]

The drama lies somewhere between and apart from the common distinction of tragic and comic repeatedly enunciated during the Renaissance:

> There grewe at last to be a greater diuersitye betweene Tragedy wryters and Comedy wryters, the one expressing onely sorrowfull and lamentable Hystories, bringing in the persons of Gods and Goddesses, Kynges and Queenes, and great states, whose parts were cheefely to expresse most miserable calamities and dreadfull chaunces, which increased worse and worse, tyll they came to the most wofull plight that might be deuised.
>
> The Comedies on the other side, were directed to a contrary ende, which beginning doubtfully, drewe to some trouble or turmoyle, and by some lucky chaunce alwayes ended to the ioy and appeasement of all parties.[3]

Again, it is Samson's regeneration that gets in the way of the tragic label, while "joy and appeasement" in no way identify the ending of Milton's work. The didactic view of Dryden or Collier, typical of the Restoration and Augustan world, is not that which we encounter in this play:

> . . . not only pity and terrour are to be moved, as the only means to bring us to virtue, but generally love to virtue, and hatred to vice, by shewing the rewards of one, and punishments of the other; at least, by rendering virtue always amiable, though it be shewn unfortunate, and vice detestable, though it be shewn triumphant.[4]

Nor does Samson show the "greatness of mind well expressed" that Saint-Évremond assigned as an aim of tragedy any more than he meets Krutch's modern requirement that he exemplify the greatness of man.[5]

In Kenneth Burke's emphasis on *mathemata* (learning) as the result of *poiemata* (the act) and *pathemata* (suffering)[6] there is meaning for the reader of *Samson Agonistes*: Samson's regeneration points, first, to the treatment of God's agents in this world and, second, to the need for faith in God. But Samson has not understood his ensuing act at his moment of tragic vision (ll. 1381–1389, 1399–1409, 1413–1426). Indeed, his act of pulling down Dagon's temple on the Philistines is, for him, simply that. It does not have for him the metaphoric meaning that even the challenge of Harapha presented: "Whose God is strongest, thine or mine" (l. 1155). The Messenger tells us that he stood with his eyes fixed fast, "as one who pray'd, / Or some great matter in his mind revolv'd" (ll. 1637–1638). He then spoke, shouting that the assemblage would now see another trial of strength, yet greater. That this act would henceforth be interpreted as God's means of showing his power, as the Chorus unwittingly comments (ll. 1427–1430, 1660–1668), does not alter the realization that for Samson his act is what Manoa and the Chorus say it is: revenge. Obviously Samson's prayers have been answered: he has his strength returned; and obviously to his mind has come the way to use that strength. Samson's action attests to God's mysterious and inscrutable ways, though he, Manoa, and the Chorus do not fully understand what is pronounced in the final passage as a kind of summary of the lesson to be learned. Samson should be viewed ironically as one who, acting entirely out of his faith, commits an act whose meaning and consequences he does not understand—an act that achieves what he desired and what he would have done consciously had he been able. Samson's regeneration is equivalent to his learning to have faith in God, but he has nonetheless not learned what the reader has. What the Chorus has "learned" (though inadequately) is only hope: "Oft he seems to hide his face, / But unexpectedly returns" (ll. 1749–1750). It does not recognize in the simile of Samson "as an Eagle" who has "His cloudless thunder bolted on thir heads" (ll. 1695–1696) an allusion to God (that is, to the Son) employing his powers through all time[7]—at the beginning of man's time, in the midst of man's time as typically in the Samson story, at the end of time with the Judgment—to defeat Satan and his cohorts. The full meaning of Providence is clearly not understood by the Chorus or by Manoa. The meaning that the audience can derive does not come from any of the characters; it does not lie unavoidably there on the surface of the narrative.

Aristotelian concepts of tragedy have most frequently been employed to explain Milton's prefatory statement (since he cites Aristotle) and to discuss the tragic elements of the play: "Tragedy, then, is an imitation of an action that is serious, complete, and of a certain magnitude . . . through pity and fear effecting the proper purgation of these emotions."[8] The related matter of the tragic hero and his *hamartia* (excess of some quality of personality, and thus a "flaw" or "shortcoming"), which leads to his fall, underlies any discussion of Greek tragic mode. And these concepts will weave in and out of the ensuing discussion, which must first attend to the opposition created by regeneration.

The evidence for Samson's regeneration lies in the "rouzing motions" (l. 1382) which he feels and his illumination with "inward eyes" (l. 1689), both of which occur after he has rejected the temptations of necessity, fraud, and violence represented by Manoa, Dalila, and Harapha.[9] He has been forged into a champion of God, and this is made clear by his rejection of the vainglorious and yet servile aspects of the Officer's message from the Philistines. He places himself in God's hands, manifesting his returned faith, and as God's champion he will exalt God's name by bringing defeat upon the false god Dagon through some act against the Philistines. As *agonistes* he is one engaged in a struggle—to be interpreted both as a struggle against external forces (the temptation motif) and against internal forces (his despair, his plea for ease and rest, and the potential return of pride). As *agonistes*, also, he is one engaged in a play, an actor playing a part. The act toward which the "narrative" moves is symbolic: it is a kind of miracle, for who otherwise by his brute strength could bring down such a portico, or metaphorically, so destroy a nation? The act implies God's miraculous presence; it employs the great gift of strength allotted to Samson; and it culminates with Samson's overcoming of *tristitia*, with his development of patience, and with his returned faith in God. The regeneration of Samson seems certain, so viewed, as does God's part in the resulting act of that regeneration. This regeneration for some critics is a good in itself, and so regeneration becomes the theme of the play for them.[10] *Samson Agonistes* is thus a play whose aim it is to teach all men by example the need for repentance and faith.

Yet we end the play with a feeling of the tragic. In tragic formulas a catharsis such as Milton mentions in the foreword should take place, and it does take place if "calm of mind, all passion [i.e., suffering] spent" is a valid line. We may think of the way in which Samson's pride has caused him woe in the past; we may note his uxoriousness in what would have been the middle play, had a typical Greek trilogy on Samson been Milton's intention; we may cast the extant last drama in such a trilogy as the extirpation of the devils that have beset the hero and as his atonement in one great act of retribution. This angle of tragic vision suggests that the tragedy lies in the past, in Samson's wasting of time and nearly complete perversion of his God-given virtue, in the loss of more direct action had such regeneration not first been necessary. The theme of regeneration in this view is not by itself significant. We cannot infer that that circumstance which creates a regenerated soul is good since its result is desirable. The question of Christian tragedy is perhaps just this: Is the theme regeneration and the thesis that adversity will produce repentance in the good? If the answer is affirmative, we do not have tragedy, but a mode which moves through tragedy to Christian comedy.[11] Or, is the theme the wastage of good and the thesis that adversity must be overcome despite grave loss? Here we do have tragedy even though the overcoming of adversity involves renewal, for the renewal will still not replace the good that has been wasted. It is this realization that precludes calling *King Lear* anything but a tragedy, despite the Christian overtones that have been heard.

Nonetheless, the foregoing does not really account for the reader's reaction at the end of *Samson Agonistes*. This reaction, I believe, is due in large part to a vague identification with the hero and becomes the key to what I suggest is the tragedy which the play exposes. The substance of tragedy has been molded in various ways. At the base is the effect which the audience (or readers) feel when the final curtain falls, but effect is difficult to define or describe. As I read the final lines of *Samson Agonistes* I am crushed—perhaps typically—by a sense of waste, a sense of What is good?, a sense of frustration. Oh, Samson has triumphed and his faith in God has been shown, and the "evil" Philistines have been punished—but at such a cost? And have indeed the Philistines been punished? It is this sense of frustration which dominates. We are calmed by having experienced a serious imitation of our own sense of pity and our own fears of life, but we recognize that Samson's story is constantly played through time and that we are part of another recurrence. The pity we feel is both self-pity and compassion for others caught in the trials of life. The fears we experience concern both our personal conquering of temptation and the pernicious motives that surround us everywhere. What sets *Samson Agonistes* apart from much Elizabethan tragedy is that we do not feel simply a contest between virtue and vice with everything neatly colored white or black. We are not, in this single play, shown the road to ruin: the road already has been walked. We are not shown the way of all flesh: the flesh has previously succumbed. And we are not even shown the wages of sin: for through past sin has come the present means to achieve salvation.

What I imply is that the tragic hero is not simply Samson, but that he is all of us; that Samson's action is not simply his revenge on the Philistines or even only a metaphor for the Danites to follow to free themselves from bondage, but that it is a metaphor of the uselessness of such action if to be "useful" an action must have immediate, widespread, and lasting effect. What such action evokes from the Chorus is hope, for suddenly they remember that "if Vertue feeble were, / Heav'n it self would stoop to her" (*A Mask*, ll. 1022–1023). But what such action screams out to the reader who takes full perspective of the narrative is that only Samson achieves salvation. If we as fallen men, regardless of the reasons for our fall, can regenerate through regained faith in God—faith implying love and obedience—we too can hope for salvation. Yet constantly is it an individual experience, lived over and over again. Samson's story may bring catharsis for us, but it is quite different from the effect we feel, say, in *Oedipus Rex* or the *Eumenides*. Oedipus or Orestes is only through an abstracted analogy ourselves: the man who pursues disastrous truth, the man who atones for an evil in this world. Samson is all of us. Samson is man fallen, man tempted, man regenerated, man saved. Samson *agonistes* is a player on the stage of the world in the endless drama of life which goes on and on in successive acts.

    Samson Agonistes can thus be viewed as a tragedy in terms of the tragic hero Samson whose story exemplifies the wastage of good and the overcoming of adversity despite the loss of being. His story is an imitation of a serious action of life, and it effects in its readers a purgation of pity and fear. We the readers join the Chorus as servants of God who are dismissed

> with new acquist
> Of true experience from this great event
> With peace and consolation . . .
> And calm of mind all passion spent. (ll. 1755–1758)

With the Chorus we can also conclude that

> All is best, though we oft doubt,
> What th'unsearchable dispose
> Of highest wisdom brings about,
> And ever best found in the close. (ll. 1745-1748)

This is a belief Milton expresses over and over again in his works; he sees God and man joining together to achieve, whether in Sonnet VII, *A Mask*, or *Paradise Lost*. But the position of the Chorus (and us the readers) in these last lines is localized, circumscribed. The Chorus does not understand Samson's story as anything more than Samson's story.

It reminds them of God's mysterious ways, and it counsels them with hope that God will always unexpectedly return to his faithful champion. But it does not change their views of themselves or, we can infer, their future action; it does not radiate outward for them as a symbolic action should. Nor does it, on this level, for us. This level of tragedy is a presentation of the tragedy of a hero who is the focus of our concern; as Parker remarked, "Our sympathies and our attention—thanks to the poet's skill —are centred in Samson himself."[12] Milton, I feel certain, knew what he was presenting here, and I believe he knew that his readers would fall into the trap of joining the Chorus in its shortsightedness and its rationalization that "All is best," for this is how man repeatedly thinks. Unfortunately critics have fallen into the same trap, and so the arguments on Samson have persisted from Samuel Johnson to the very present. My own argument is that there are two versions of tragedy in Samson Agonistes: one, already discussed, is the tragedy of the self, the individual man subject to temptation, to waste, and to blindness in his lack of understanding of self and life.

The foregoing paragraph generally meshes well, I think, with Parker's view of emphasis in the play in his rebuttal to Sir Richard Jebb, though I ultimately take issue with his view as limited. Parker writes: "I have no doubt that Milton attempted to justify God's ways to men. I am equally confident that he sought to do this by showing that injustice to the individual is ultimately justice to mankind. But which is the greater impression left upon the reader, the sense of the blind hero's misery, or the sense of God's goodness? The matter is, of course, one of emphasis."[13] Parker sees emphasis on Samson's misery: "Milton's drama, despite the final chorus, is one in which human passions, human wrongs, seem more real than the divine scheme into which they fit."[14] "[W]e must not overlook the fact," he cautions, "that Samson advanced to death and victory with no more foresight, no more understanding of the future, than the Philistines had when they advanced to death and defeat."[15] Perhaps because his concern was to refute Jebb's Hebraic point of view (expressed in such positive statements as "This is the issue of the drama—Jehovah has prevailed over Dagon; Israel is avenged on Philistia"[16]) Parker failed to focus on what I consider the second level of tragedy in the work. For in a later statement he remarks, "Samson lived and died in vain, whatever heroic qualities he displayed in either action."[17] Certainly part of the dramatic irony is more than just our knowledge that Samson will pull down the pillars and avenge himself on the Philistines, while yet destroying himself. Certainly part of it is our knowledge that Samson's action seems to have no meaning in history. Samson is one of a long line of Judges, none of whom liberates Israel from bondage: he is not quite Moses. He is the Great Deliverer who in his first "marriage" to an infidel believes himself thereby beginning "*Israel's* Deliverance, / The work to which [he] was divinely call'd" (ll. 225–226). But the end of the play finds that "*Israel* still serves with all his Sons" (l. 240). Whatever advances have been made in the past, they are not quite sufficient to remove bondage.

The second version of tragedy which *Samson Agonistes* exposes, and Greek and Elizabethan tragedy do not, is the tragedy of hope which repeatedly dogs man, blinding him to realities, to full recognition of self, and to lasting achievement. The hero in such a tragedy should exhibit hope, in the present or in the past, in the meaningfulness of action, and the ending of such a tragedy should suggest to those who remain that things will be righted in the future after the drama is completed, and that evil will be exposed and defeated again. But the "hope" of the hero and the others will be dashed unless replaced by true hope, and the lesson afforded will not be learned. Here lies the philosophic meaning of the play, which is expressed on three levels: surface meaning, its ironic opposite, and its essential deeper meaning.

Unlike *Samson Agonistes, Hamlet,* decidedly not a tragedy of hope, projects for the future only Horatio's telling Hamlet's story, which will thus answer the false view otherwise forced on Denmark, and Fortinbras' just and peaceful rule. We have no concern beyond this somewhat "happy" ending; our concerns are totally with the single level of tragedy presented by the story of Hamlet. "Hope" is simply not part of the play. In contrast we might look at James Joyce's *A Portrait of the Artist as a Young Man.* Not that the novel partakes of either tragic or comic mode. But it does strongly project us into the future as Stephen Dedalus, all sure-fired of achievement in the world lying all before him, takes his solitary way. We recognize Man emerging from his mother's womb into the wide world of men, in which he must choose his place of rest. And we know with dramatic irony that Stephen is going to fall flat on his face. He will return, defeated; he will eventually awaken to the world around him and accept it with love and charity. He will find it the source for achievement only when he accepts it fully and without self-righteousness; but in the novel itself—a condition which persists beyond the closing page—he has not accepted the world. He rebels against it, or attempts to change it in his own ineffectual ways. The novel ends in hope of forging the conscience of the race, and the reader cannot overlook the projection into the future, or its immediate actuality. This is the tragedy of hope common to the young.

Not far from *A Portrait* but entirely different in its total view is *Paradise Lost*, for the future that lies before Adam and Eve (Man as he emerges from his mother's womb, the *hortus conclusus* which is the Garden) may become a tragedy for some but a comedy for others. The fact that we see the future with Adam in Books XI and XII emphasizes the dialectic of life: the tragedy which Man's Hope (Malraux's novel is a case in point) necessitates can be reversed only by acknowledgment of self and by love, which alone fulfills the Law (*PL* XII.403–404). *Samson Agonistes*, though dominated by one character who, like Hamlet, concerns us in the play but not beyond, also projects the future beyond the last line through the almost allegorical nature of the work and through frequent reminders of the Chosen People's bondage.

The allegorical nature of *Samson Agonistes* plunges through the fabric of the poem in three specific ways. The "plot" presents us with Manoa tempting Samson with a life of ease (necessity), with Dalila tempting him through fraud (*concupiscentia ocularum* appearing as her driving force), and with Harapha tempting him through violence to show his proudfulness. The temptations of this world besetting Samson, though plausible for him as presented, can nonetheless not be taken only literally. Here we have a "plot" of all men's lives, much more adroitly handled than in *A Mask*, though not antitypally, of course, as in *Paradise Regain'd*. The characters of at least Dalila and Harapha stand for types; their trappings, their speech, the humor attached to each bear this out. Harapha, indeed, becomes almost a caricature. And the ironic language, for example, Manoa's play on "Fathers house" (that is, both his home and God's heaven) in lines 447, 1717, and 1733, as well as line 518, indicates that something more than the literal is going on. This specific *double entendre* is employed also in *A Mask*. Obviously such allegorical relationships do not allow the drama to remain only the story of Samson, a person who conquered self and regained glory.

Samson constantly reminds us, as do the Chorus and Manoa, that the hopes of his people lie in him to free them from bondage. He is the Great Deliverer, and the people wait for him to deliver them. (Do we think perhaps of Samuel Beckett's *Waiting for Godot*?) We identify with him in our hope for future achievement. But the tragedy is that we, Samson as well as "the people," do not realize that deliverance comes only of the individual self. As Samson first appears, his hopes have all been dashed by his blinding and imprisonment. What is wrong is that he has not experienced real hope and he still views the fulfillment of his false hope through self-glory and aggrandizement.

The context is set forth almost immediately in the *prologos*. "Here leave me to respire," he tells his "guiding hand" in line 11 (is the number of the line significant?). Ostensibly he means "let me get my breath," "let me become again enlivened with 'the breath of Heav'n,'" but also, in its ultimate etymology, "let me be again filled with the anima of God: let me again hope." In lines 81–82 he comments that his is a "total Eclipse / Without all hope of day!" meaning many things: without (his former kind of) hope; without hope of sight; without hope of understanding; with only Satan as driving spirit; without hope of God's presence. The ironies of meaning, since we know the outcome of the play before us, are obvious. In its following *parados* the Chorus makes a similar observation of Samson: "As one past hope, abandon'd, / And by himself giv'n over" (ll. 120–121). A little later, however, we see that things are changing. In the midst of the second episode, the first temptation section, Samson is able to remark, "This only hope relieves me, that the strife / With me hath end" (ll. 460–461). A step toward regeneration has been taken, for he now puts God in the focal position as the deliverer of his people: "all the contest is now / 'Twixt God and *Dagon*" (ll. 461–462). To which Manoa, in his commonplace, human, and false hope, replies, "With cause this hope relieves thee" (l. 472). Ironically it is a prophecy of what is to come, but Manoa's assignment of man's hope to only God's action when and how He wills is unconscionable. The falsity of the "cause" he talks of and his self-indulgent nature (witness his appeal to Samson of a life of ease) are made clear when he adds:

> for God,
> Nothing more certain, will not long defer
> To vindicate the glory of his name
> Against all competition, nor will long
> Endure it, doubtful whether God be Lord,
> Or *Dagon*. (ll. 473–478)

Like Satan in *Paradise Lost* Manoa has assigned to God nefarious motives which are true of himself.

In the same episode the kind of hope that Samson was victim of in the past is emphasized:

when in strength
All mortals I excell'd, and great in hopes
With youthful courage and magnanimous thoughts
Of birth from Heav'n foretold and high exploits . . . (ll. 523–525)

But such hopes are now—thankfully, we should realize—"all flat" (l. 595). "Nor am I in the list of them that hope," Samson acknowledges as the episode ends. He sees his evils (of the past) hopeless of change—which implies a kind of hope in the thought they might be changed, and this inverse hope underlies his "one prayer" of "speedy death" (ll. 647–651). In sharp contrast in this episode is Manoa's constant "hopefulness" that he will free his son through bribery and lead him to a life of ease, ironically that which the guiding hand in the first few lines of the play is supposed to do.[18]

The remainder of the drama plays upon Samson's rejection of the false hope of the past and the rising, though specifically unstated, hope which culminates with his regeneration.[19] He seems to move to the denouement without hope, for he does not understand what he will achieve and does achieve. But what he has is true hope, for he now has implicit faith in God. He has no outward hope now in meaningfulness of action: all he can say is that his countrymen will "hear / Nothing dishonourable, impure, unworthy / Our God, our Law, my Nation, or my self" (ll. 1423–1425). But in reality he has hope, for hope is faith in God. Not understood, of course, any action seems useless; it becomes a metaphor for the uselessness of action to those who find use only if immediate changes result. Ironically, though, only this kind of "meaningless" action is true action in God's world.

The word "hope" is employed six times further in the *exodos* by the Chorus and Manoa. The attitude which is developed throws a clear light on the tragedy of hope, for the hope expressed is based on false concepts. The action is viewed as being meaningful in that it seems to right things and it seems to defeat evil, but the Chorus' and Manoa's remarks are specious. First, Manoa's hope is for his success in bribery (ll. 1452–1454), and the Chorus subscribes to it (ll. 1455, 1504–1505). Second, Manoa's hope involves a denial of what seems fact, a romanticizing that the desired end will nevertheless come about, and a succumbing to temptation ("tempts Belief," l. 1535). Third, this hope just cited is defeated by news of Samson's death (ll. 1571, 1575), the surest evidence of the falsity of Manoa's hope and his lack of faith in God. What follows now moves to "hopefulness"—ostensibly—but the ironies of the drama manifest how specious are the Chorus' and Manoa's rationalizations. The Chorus' earlier line, "Thy hopes are not ill founded" (l. 1504), had really clued us to the reversing images on which the main effects of the play are built.

The ironies of *Samson Agonistes* have been discussed at length by Parker,[20] and recently Anthony Low has argued for an additional ironic pattern: "This irony is characterized by a hypothetical choice, posited by one of the characters: either this is true or that, or more usually, either this will happen or that; but in the working out, both choices eventuate, even though they had been thought to be mutually exclusive."[21] The first irony that I see cast over the play as a tragedy of hope is that the action of Samson's revenge on the Philistines does bring hope to the Chorus and Manoa:

> O dearly-bought revenge, yet glorious!
> Living or dying thou hast fulfill'd
> The work for which thou wast foretold
> To *Israel* . . . (ll. 1660–1663)

>   *Samson* hath quit himself
> Like *Samson*, and heroicly hath finish'd
> A life Heroic, on his Enemies
> Fully reveng'd, hath left them years of mourning,
> And lamentation to the Sons of *Caphtor*
> Through all *Philistian* bounds. To *Israel*
> Honour hath left, and freedom . . . (ll. 1709–1715)

But the work is not done and freedom has not been achieved. In their blindness to the real situation the Chorus and Manoa fall into the conventional rationalization that God will bring things off rightly by himself. This kind of hope leads to inaction and to the critical trap of believing that anything smacking of regeneration is, by definition, nontragic. Second is the hope, so typical of man, that arises when things are not going well. Note the following colloquy just before the entry of the Messenger:

> *Chorus.* What if his eye-sight (for to *Israels* God
> Nothing is hard) by miracle restor'd,
> He now be dealing dole among his foes,
> And over heaps of slaughter'd walk his way?
>   *Manoa.* That were a joy presumptuous to be thought.
>   *Chorus.* Yet God hath wrought things as incredible

> For his people of old; what hinders now?
> *Manoa.* He can I know, but doubt to think he will;
> Yet Hope would fain subscribe, and tempts Belief.
>
> (ll. 1527–1535)

Manoa does not have real hope, because his belief (his "knowledge" of the situation, his "logic") denies what the Chorus speculates. It is this kind of "hope" that pervades the poem: a hope which runs counter to what one sees as logical but which arises from one's need to envision a good. Faith in God, which should be the basis of hope, falters because Manoa sees Samson as undeserving of God's help and God as vindictive. Ironically, hope, which should be positive, exists because of man's despair.[22] Manoa does not really concede that "All is best." Against knowledge of the situation and logic, hope finds sustenance in the deaths of the Philistine lords, however, as an example of God's omnipotence. If God must constantly reinforce man's faith by miracle, there is no real faith, little real hope.

Third, the hope of the future for the Chorus and Manoa lies exclusively in the province of God to work his miracles, if he will, *through* his champion. The need for related action between God and his champion is overlooked; the Chorus and Manoa are blind to it. As corollary we have Manoa's limited, mundane view of glory—typical of man. He promises to build Samson a monument, thereby to inflame the valiant youth "To matchless valour, and adventures high" (l. 1740). A sense of God's presence in the achievement of glory and matchless valor is notably missing. God simply allows things to happen. The Chorus' farewell to Samson pinpoints the fourth irony which this tragedy of hope predicates:

> Go, and the Holy One
> Of *Israel* be thy guide
> To what may serve his glory best, and spread his name
> Great among the Heathen round. (ll. 1427–1430)

The guiding hand that has led Samson on the stage has conducted him off; it has allowed him to go a little further on and to choose either sun or shade; it has, in a sense, assumed a joust with Dagon, and thus God's glory has been advanced. But such glory is short-lived and ineffectual for the Chosen People, for men do not follow Samson's lead, they simply wait for God to act. Samson is "sung and proverb'd for a Fool / In every street" (ll. 203–204); his prodigious strength is well known; but he did not become the symbol to after-ages of what action they should take to achieve honor and freedom. The Chosen People have not found the courage to lay hold on this occasion (ll. 1715–1716). Similar to the irony of alternatives which Low sees operating throughout the play, God's glory is served and his name potentially spread, but it all has very little meaning: it occurs and it might just as well not have. The final irony of the play is that it can be the story only of an individual, not really of his nation and not really of God's omnipotence. Like the Arabian bird, Samson's body dies and his fame survives, but it is hardly through his completion of divine prediction.

In these ironies of hope and man's attitude toward it we have the surface meaning of the "philosophy" of the play and its opposite. What Milton is driving at on this second level of tragedy is man's constant blindness to reality, to the meaninglessness of his reactions to "saints," and to the eternal disparities between his so-called hopes and his achievements. Much of the difficulty lies in man's concept of hope. Thwarting the meaning of action and action itself are man, like Samson, victim of temptation and pride, and his fellow men, unthinking and inactive, envious and evil. Samson overcomes temptation and pride, achieves action and thus meaning in such action (the first level of this tragedy), but his fellow men do not. And what makes this particularly tragic is that hope persists in man regardless of its hidden face: man does not learn that hope implies full faith in God and joint action between God and man. For Samson of the past, hope is self-doing and advancement of self-glory; for the Chorus and Manoa, hope is waiting for God to act (the second level of this tragedy).

Ironically Samson's story has symbolic meaning, but man does not pay heed to that meaning. Each man must conquer temptation himself and forge his own conscience. Each is a potential champion of God, but this requires full love of God, and Samson's example shows the way to make that potentiality a reality. Samson is the Great Deliverer in a sense unrealized by his countrymen and apparently by many of our modern critics: he is the Great Deliverer of man from the bondage of self, if his example be followed. He is—not only as sun god—a *figura* of the Son, and Milton (like others) acknowledged this through his narrative. Perhaps it is ultimately the critics' belief in the reality of the Christ myth that gets in the way of their understanding typology, particularly as used by the artist.

But beyond this there is also Samson the predicted Great Deliverer of his people. Though we can view the story allegorically as the deliverance of man from the clutches of Satan through the conquering of temptation on an individual basis, it also takes on larger proportions as the deliverance of the Chosen People from the Philistines, who represent Satan and his cohorts, just as Moses delivered Israel from Pharaoh's hand. I remarked earlier that Samson's action *seems* to have no meaning in history and that he is not quite Moses. In a recent paper on *Paradise Lost* and the theme of exodus I have proposed that a basic mythic structure exists in man's thinking and thus in literature quite apart from the cyclic myth of return: the myth of exodus.[23] This myth involves stages in history, moving through history though it is not completed in history. It is a constant moving forward through trial and purgation, the race proceeding onward into new "promised" lands until Judgment Day. The Great Deliverers of men from the bondage which their secured lives have created (allegorized by man's succumbing to the triple temptation of the flesh, the world, and the devil, as Samson did before the play begins) do not enjoy the new stage of history—witness Moses. But they take their places in the roll of the saints. The antitype of such deliverance I find in the temptation in the wilderness, a backdrop for Samson's movement toward regeneration.

Samson functions as a Moses figure whose action points the way to liberation, but the people do not follow. Part of the fault is Samson himself, since he does not understand what it is he is doing. He is the symbol of all bondage and the means of freedom from bondage. He has succumbed to temptation in the past and becomes literally imprisoned and literally blind. Now, in the play, he overcomes temptation's second assault by truth (recognition of his failures) and by faith. But besides this, he has shown in the past that he has had "the heart of the Fool" (l. 298). The Geneva Bible gloss to Psalm 14:1 is: "He [the psalmist] sheweth that the cause of all wickedness is to forget God," and Samson has forgotten God in his pride (cf. ll. 528–534), no matter how he with hindsight protests his thought of doing God's work. As the Chorus continues, no man is doctor to rid the fool of his denial of God except the man himself. The drama of *Samson Agonistes* is Samson's refinding of the God he has forgotten. The Chosen People, fallen into bondage by having forgotten God too, must tread the path Samson followed to achieve freedom and move to the next stage in history—or the next act in life's drama. But all they experience is hope, a false hope based on misconception and not on full faith in God. The tragedy of hope is that hope replaces truth and action in most people's lives. Samson's action seems to have no meaning in history, not because of him and his action, but because of man. Samson's action, as Milton presents it, becomes a metaphor of the uselessness of such action in terms of immediate influence and of lasting influence. The action itself is not useless: it is just that fit audiences are few. It comes to be of use, ironically, only to individual man. The irony—again similar to the irony of alternatives—is crushing, for what value inheres in action such as Samson's is not realized and what value is expected does not exist.

Milton, like George Bernard Shaw's Saint Joan, is really asking, "O God that madest this beautiful earth, when will it be ready to receive Thy saints? How long, O Lord, how long?" The saints of this world are persecuted, unheeded, destroyed. Yes, this is often so through their own failings, as in Samson's case, but the people—the ignorant, uncourageous, sycophantic people—continue to solace themselves with hope. Milton's drama is, I feel sure, a reflection of the evil which hope becomes in man, and a realization that it is the individual who must succeed in his own little world, in his own little way. The tragic effect we feel as we end the play results from a sense of waste, of the meaninglessness of good, and from frustration, from the ironies that abound. But dwelling upon this theme brings at least answers in terms of one's self. Someday, Milton might have thought, there will perhaps come another exodus of the Chosen from the grips of the Antichrist through a Paradise within developed in all men, whereby all are Great Deliverers from the bondage of Satan, but the Chorus and Manoa show that the time is not yet.

NOTES

1.   Typical is the comment of David Daiches in *Milton* (London, 1957): "From one point of view, a Christian tragedy is a contradiction in terms: nothing to a Christian can be tragic if seen in its proper perspective. . . . where God, all-just, all-powerful and merciful, is in control, no injustice and disproportion can exist" (p. 247).

2.   All quotations are from my edition of *The Complete English Poetry of John Milton* (Garden City, N.Y., 1963).

3.   William Webbe, *A Discourse of English Poetry* (London, 1586), quoted from *English Reprints*, ed. Edward Arber (London, 1870), p. 39.

4.   John Dryden, *Heads of an Answer to Rymer* (London, 1693), quoted from *The Critical and Miscellaneous Prose Works of John Dryden*, ed. Edmond Malone (London, 1800), Vol. I, Part II, p. 309. Compare Dryden's statement in the "Preface" to *Troilus and Cressida* (London, 1679), reprinted in *Essays of John Dryden*, ed. W. P. Ker (New York, 1961), I, 209–211. See also Jeremy Collier's comment in *A Short View of the Immorality and Profaneness of the English Stage* (London, 1698): "The business of *Plays* is to recommend Virtue, and discountenance Vice; To

shew the Uncertainty of Humane Greatness, the suddain Turns of Fate, and the Unhappy Conclusions of Violence and Injustice: 'Tis to expose the Singularities of Pride and Fancy, to make Folly and Falsehood contemptible, and to bring every Thing that is Ill Under Infamy, and Neglect" (p. 1).

5. See Saint-Évremond, *Of Ancient and Modern Tragedy* (London, 1672), and Joseph Wood Krutch, *The Modern Temper* (New York, 1929), esp. p. 127.

6. See "Dialectic of Tragedy," in *A Grammar of Motives* (New York, 1945), pp. 38–41.

7. Compare *Paradise Lost* VI.762–764:

> [Hee] Ascended, at his right hand Victorie
> Sate Eagle-wing'd, beside him hung his Bow
> And Quiver with three-bolted Thunder stor'd . . .

8. *Poetics*, Chapter VI, 1449b.

9. There have been steps in his regeneration, of course, such as his protest that "Nothing of all these evils hath befall'n me / But justly; I my self have brought them on, / Sole Author I, sole cause" (ll. 374–376), but the inflectional point (the *peripeteia*) occurs with lines 1381–1383. It should also be noted that the gloss in the Geneva Bible for Judges 16:22 says, "Yet had he not his strength againe, til he had called vpon God, and reconcild him selfe." I use the facsimile edition by Lloyd E. Berry (Madison, 1969).

10. The major argument for Samson's regeneration will be found in William Riley Parker's *Milton's Debt to Greek Tragedy in Samson Agonistes* (Baltimore, 1937). Professor Parker concluded: "The theme of *Samson Agonistes*, then, is the hero's recovery and its result. In other words, it is regeneration and reward" (p. 237). However, he also argued that the drama is tragic (see later), and it is his views that have primarily caused the controversy over Samson's regeneration. A review of some of the controversy will be found in French Fogle's "The Action of *Samson Agonistes*," in *Essays in American and English Literature Presented to Bruce Robert McElderry, Jr.*, ed. Max F. Schultz (Athens, 1967), pp. 177–196. Professor Fogle examines regeneration in terms of Milton's views on the subject in *De Doctrina Christiana*.

11. This is, of course, why I cannot consider *Paradise Lost* a tragedy: the theme of love in that epic implies regeneration of spirit, and its thesis of asserting Eternal Providence requires the constant possibility of God's miraculous act to save the worthy, whether he be Israel as in Psalm 114 or the Lady in *A Mask*.

12. Parker, p. 231.

13. Parker, p. 230. See Jebb's "*Samson Agonistes* and the Hellenic Drama," *Proceedings of the British Academy*, III (1907–1908), 341–348.

14. Parker, p. 233.

15. Parker, pp. 235–236.

16. Jebb, p. 344.

17. *Milton: A Biography* (Oxford, 1968), II, 909. Parker comments further: "This biographer believes, moreover, that readers will some day agree with him that the poem is intensely, almost unbearably pessimistic, with Samson's 'victory' a final irony, since—in the perspective of Biblical history—Samson dies in vain, as Milton very well knew, and with no promise of immortality, as Milton's silences more than remind us" (p. 937).

18. Manoa as false adviser to his son is like Saul as false adviser to his son Jonathan. Only by his partaking of the honey are Jonathan's eyes enlightened. Milton is most aware that right reason involves denial of seeming good and of false employ-

ment of God's commandments. The honey is bitter but it will be sweet in the mouth, as St. John assures us in Revelation.

19.   He uses the word "hope" once more in the Dalila episode: "Love seeks to have Love; / My love how couldst thou hope, who tookst the way / To raise in me inexpiable hate" (ll. 837–839). Is not Samson talking of man and his relationship with God? But like God, Samson forgives.

20.   *Milton's Debt to Greek Tragedy,* pp. 157–167.

21.   "Action and Suffering: *Samson Agonistes* and the Irony of Alternatives," *PMLA,* LXXXIV (1969), 514.

22.   Satan deceives himself with a pertinent statement: "So farwell Hope, and with Hope farwell Fear, / Farwell Remorse" (*PL* IV.108–109).

23.   See *Milton Studies,* II (1970), 3–26.

Appendices

by
Joseph Anthony Wittreich, Jr.

Illustrators of *Paradise Regained* and Their Subjects (1713–1816)

THE ILLUSTRATORS

This catalogue was prepared after examining the editions of *Paradise Regained* in the following libraries: Beinecke Library (Yale University), Henry E. Huntington Library and Art Gallery, Houghton Library (Harvard University), Lilly Library (Indiana University, Bloomington), Newberry Library (Chicago), New York Public Library, Pierpont Morgan Library (New York), Princeton University Library, Sterling Library (Yale University), University of California Research Library (Los Angeles), University of Illinois Library (Urbana), University of Wisconsin Library (Madison), Widener Library (Harvard University), and the William Andrews Clark Memorial Library (Los Angeles). In this catalogue, I have attempted to include those artists who illustrated *Paradise Regained* but whose illustrations never accompanied an edition of the poem. Some of these artists have doubtless eluded me. Moreover, although I have probably not missed an illustrator of the poem, I may have overlooked a rare edition in which those illustrations are reproduced. In the catalogue itself, I have identified, however briefly, each designer and listed the various engravers. The first entry for each illustrator enumerates the designs. Thereafter, I have been content with listing the editions in which those illustrations are reproduced, and only when information is different from that provided in the first entry (e.g., signatures, number of illustrations, etc.) do I specify. Since this catalogue is intended to provide a context for Blake's illustrations to *Paradise Regained*, I have terminated my survey with the editions of the poem published in 1816. Milton's poem, of course, provided subjects for illustrations after that time.

Bibliography: Joseph Strutt, *A Biographical Dictionary; Containing an Historical Account of All the Engravers, from the Earliest Period of the Art of Engraving to the Present Time; and a Short List of Their Most Esteemed Works* (2 vols.; London, 1785); Mantle Fielding, *American Engravers Upon Copper and Steel* (Philadelphia, 1917); *Bryan's Dictionary of Painters and Engravers*, ed. George C. Williamson, rev. ed. (5 vols.; London, 1925–1927); Emmanuel Bénézit, *Dictionnaire critique et documentaire des peintres, sculpteurs, dessinateurs et graveurs* (8 vols.; France, 1948–1955).

Pigné's Designs, 1713

NICHOLAS PIGNÉ (1690–?). Born at Chalons, Pigné became a student of Bernard Picart and later went to England. An engraver of portraits and an illustrator of religious subjects, Pigné is best known for his portrait of Richard Fiddes (1718) and his depiction *The Virgin with the Infant Christ*. Pigné's illustrations to *Paradise Regained*—a frontispiece and four illustrations, one prefacing each book of Milton's poem—were engraved at different times by Pierre Fourdrinier, David Coster, John Lightbody, and S. Wheatley. These designs appeared first in: Paradise Regain'd. / A / Poem. / In Four Books. / To which is added / Samson Agonistes. / And / Poems upon several Occasions. / With a Tractate of Education. / The Author / John Milton. / The Fifth Edition. Adorn'd with Cuts. / London: Printed for J. Tonson, at Shake- / spear's Head, over-against Catherine- / Street in the Strand. 1713.

Frontispiece: [Christ's Triumph over Satan]. Lower right corner below engraving: Title [barely visible]. See *PR* I.1–7, 150–160.

Illustration to Book I: [The Baptism of Jesus]. Signature, barely legible, in lower right corner of engraving: Pigné. In lower right corner below engraving: p. 1. [Carries ll. 1–17] See *PR* I.29–32, 280–282.

Illustration to Book II: [Jesus in the Temple]. Lower right corner below engraving: p. 19. [Carries ll. 1–18] See *PR* I.255–258, II. 96–101.

Illustration to Book III: [Jesus Discoursing with Satan]. Lower right corner below engraving: p. 36. [Carries ll. 1–18] See *PR* III.1–250.

Illustration to Book IV: [The Angels with Jesus, Singing of His Victory]. Lower right corner below engraving: p. 52. [Carries ll. 1–18] See *PR* IV.586–587.

Other appearances of Pigné's designs:

1721. Paradise Regain'd. / A / Poem. / In Four Books. / To which is added. / Samson Agonistes. / And / Poems upon several Occasions. / With a Tractate of Education. / The Author / John Milton. / The Fifth Edition. Adorn'd with Cuts. / London: Printed, and are to be Sold by / W. Taylor, at the Ship and Black- / Swan, in Pater-Noster-Row. 1721. The frontispiece of the 1713 edition is used as a fifth illustration opposite p. 72.

1725. Paradise Regain'd: / A / Poem. / In Four Books. / To which is added / Samson Agonistes. / And / Poems upon several Occasions. / With a Tractate of Education. / The Author / John Milton. / The Sixth Edition, Corrected. / London: / Printed for J. Tonson, at Shakespear's Head, over- / against Catherine Street in the Strand; and for M. / Poulson. M.DCC.XXV. [The Baptism of Jesus] is the only design used in this edition, where it serves as a frontispiece.

1727. Paradise Regain'd: / A / Poem. / In Four Books. / To which is added / Samson Agonistes; / And / Poems upon several Occasions. / With a Tractate of Education. / The Author / John Milton. / The Seventh Edition, Corrected. / London: / Printed for Jacob Tonson in the Strand. / MDCCXXVII. [The Baptism of Jesus] is the only design used in this edition. Lower left corner below engraving: P. Fourdrinier scul.

1730. Paradise Regain'd: / A / Poem. / In Four Books. / To which is added / Samson Agonistes; / And / Poems upon several Occasions. / With a Tractate of Education. / The Author / John Milton. / The Seventh Edition, Corrected. / London: / Printed for J. Tonson, at Shakespear's Head, over- / against Catherine Street in the Strand; and for Ri- / chard, James, and Bethel Welling- / ton. M.DCC.XXX. [The Baptism of Jesus] is the only design used in this edition; it is also engraved by Fourdrinier.

1731. The / Poetical Works / of / John Milton: / Vol. II. / Containing, Paradise Regained, / Samson Agonistes, / and His / Poems On Several / Occasions, &c. / A new Edition carefully corrected. / London, / Printed in the Year / M. DCC. XXXI. [Two-volume set] There are no illustrations to the second volume, but [The Baptism of Jesus] is used as a frontispiece to the first volume. The engraver is D. Coster.

1738. Paradise Regain'd: / A / Poem. / In Four Books. / To which is added, / Samson Agonistes; / And / Poems upon several Occasions. / With a Tractate of Education. / The Author / John Milton. / The Seventh Edition Corrected. / London: / Printed for James Hodges, at the Looking-Glass, / on London-Bridge, 1738. [The Baptism of Jesus], engraved by Fourdrinier, is the only design used in this edition.

1739. Paradise Regain'd: / A Poem. / In Four Books. / To which is added / Samson Agonistes; / And / Poems upon several Occasions. / With a Tractate of Education. / John Milton / The Author. / London: / Printed for a Company of Stationers; / MDCCXXXIX. Pigné's four illustrations, but not his frontispiece, are included in this edition. Illustrations to Books I, II, and IV are signed in lower right corner below engraving: I°. Lightbody sculp^t.; the illustration to Book III is signed: I: Lightbody Sculpt. In the left corner above each engraving the book number is given: e.g., Book I., Book II., etc. All engravings are in reverse.

1742. Paradise Regain'd: / A / Poem. / In Four Books. / To which is added / Samson Agonistes; / And / Poems upon several Occasions. / With a Tractate of Education. / The Author / John Milton. / The Eighth Edition Corrected. / London: / Printed for J. and R. Tonson in the Strand. / MDCCXLII. This edition carries [The Baptism of Jesus], engraved by Fourdrinier.

1743. Paradise Regain'd. / A Poem, / in Four Books. / To which is added / Samson Agonistes; / and / Poems upon several Occasions, / With a Tractate of Education. / The Author / John Milton. / The Eighth Edition. / London: / Printed for J. and R. Tonson, R. Ware, J. Hodges, R. Wellington, R. Chandler, J. Brindley, / R. Caldwell, and J. New. / MDCCXLIII. This edition carries [The Baptism of Jesus], engraved by Fourdrinier.

1747. Paradise Regain'd. / A / Poem, / In / Four Books. / To which is added / Samson Agonistes; / And / Poems upon several Occasions. / With a Tractate of Education. / The Author / John Milton. / London: / Printed for J. and R. Tonson and S. Draper, [etc.] / M DCC XLVII. [Volume I of two-volume set] This edition carries [The Baptism of Jesus], engraved by Fourdrinier.

1748. Paradise Regain'd. / A / Poem, / In / Four Books. / To which is added, / Samson Agonistes; / And / Poems upon several Occasions. / With a Tractate of Education. / The Author / John Milton. / The Ninth Edition. / Dublin: / Printed on Irish Paper, / For G. Risk, G. and A.

Ewing, and W. Smith, / Booksellers in Dame-Street. / M,DCC,XLVIII. This edition includes [The Baptism of Jesus]. Lower left corner below engraving: Frontispiece. Lower right corner: S. Wheatley Sculp^t.

Note. In *Milton & English Art* (Manchester, 1970), Marcia Pointon attributes this set of illustrations to John Baptist Medina, the first illustrator of *Paradise Lost.* In doing so, she does not take notice of the barely legible signature to the second design (1713). Moreover, what she calls "conclusive evidence" (p. 16) is unconvincing: iconographic details, as Pointon's book amply demonstrates, are often transferred from one eighteenth-century artist to another. See also pp. 2, 10–11.

Chéron's Designs, 1720

LOUIS CHÉRON (1655–1725). Painter and engraver, the brother of Elizabeth Sophie Chéron Le Hay, Chéron was born in Paris. A Calvinist sympathizer, he left France for England in 1695. In London, Chéron did numerous designs for the publishers Bowyer, Tonson, and Watts. His illustrations to *Paradise Regained*—a title-page design and twelve illustrations—were engraved by Gerald Vander Gucht and Samuel Gribelin, Jr. They appeared in: The Poetical / Works / Of / Mr. John Milton. / Volume The Second. / [Title-page design] / London: / Printed for Jacob Tonson, at Shakespear's Head in the Strand. / MDCCXX. [Two-volume set]

Title-page design: [The Baptism of Jesus]. See *PR* I.29–32, 280–282.

Head-piece to Book I, p. [1]: [The First Temptation]. Lower left corner below engraving: L. Cheron Inv. Lower right corner: G. Vander Gucht Sculp. See *PR* I.310–351.

Letter-design to Book I, p. [1]: [The Nativity]. See *PR* I.238–254, II.69–75.

Tail-piece to Book I, p. 24: [Satan Departing from Jesus]. Lower left diagonal: L. Cheron Inv. Lower right diagonal: G. Vander Gucht Sculp. See *PR* I.497–502.

Head-piece to Book II, p. [25]: [The Banquet Temptation]. Lower left corner below engraving: Lud. Cheron inv. Lower right corner: Saml. Gribelin Junr. Sculp. See *PR* II.338–367.

Letter-design to Book II, p. [25]: [Satan Bearing the Fruits of the Earth].

Tail-piece to Book II, p. 48: [Temptation to Wealth and Riches]. Lower left corner below engraving: Lud. Cheron inv. Lower right corner: Sam¹. Gribelin Junʳ. Sculp. See *PR* II.426–486.

Head-piece to Book III, p. [49]: [The Temptation of Parthia]. Lower left corner below engraving: L. Cheron Inv. Lower right corner: G. Vᵈʳ Gucht Scul. See *PR* III.302–346.

Letter-design to Book III, p. [49]: [Crowns, Sceptre, Wealth, and Riches].

Tail-piece to Book III, p. 70: [The Temptation of Rome]. Lower left corner below engraving: L. Cheron inv. Lower right corner: G. Vᵈʳ. Gucht Sculp. *PR* IV.44–108.

Head-piece to Book IV, p. [71]: [The Tempter Inspiring Jesus' Ugly Dreams]. Lower left corner below engraving: L. Cheron Inv. Lower right corner: G. Vᵈʳ. Gucht Sculp. See *PR* IV.401–425.

Letter-design to Book IV, p. [71]: [Crown of Thorns].

Tail-piece to Book IV, p. 101: [The Temptation on the Pinnacle]. Lower left corner of design: L. Cheron Inv. Lower right corner: G. Vᵈʳ. Gucht Sculp. See *PR* IV.561–562.

Hayman's Design, 1752

FRANCIS HAYMAN (1708–1776). A historical painter and book designer, Hayman exhibited his work at the Royal Academy, where he was librarian from 1769 to 1772. His best-known illustrations are to Milton, Pope, and Cervantes. The illustration to *Paradise Regained*—a frontispiece—was engraved at different times by Johann Sebastian Müller [or Miller], Charles Grignion, and John Dixon. It appeared first in: Paradise Regain'd. / A / Poem, / In / Four Books. / To which is added / Samson Agonistes: / And / Poems upon Several Occasions. / The Author / John Milton. / A New Edition, / With Notes of various Authors, / By Thomas Newton, D. D. / London: / Printed for J. and R. Tonson and S. Draper in the Strand. / M DCC LII.

Frontispiece: [The First Temptation]. Lower left corner below engraving: F. Hayman inv: et del:. Lower right corner: J. S. Müller Sculp:. Below designer's signature: Paradise Regain'd. See *PR* I.310–351.

Other appearances of Hayman's design:

1753. Paradise Regain'd. / A / Poem, / In / Four Books. / To which is added / Samson Agonistes: / And / Poems upon Several Occasions. / The Author / John Milton. / The Second Edition, / With Notes of various Authors, / By Thomas Newton, D. D. / Volume the Second. / London: / Printed for J. and R. Tonson and S. Draper [etc.] / M DCC LIII. [Two-volume set] Lower left corner below engraving: F. Hayman inv. Lower right corner: C. Grignion Sculp. Upper right corner above engraving: Vol. 1. page 1.

1754. Paradise Regain'd. / A / Poem, / In / Four Books. / To which is added / Samson Agonistes: / And / Poems upon Several Occasions. / The Author / John Milton. / A New Edition; / With Notes of various Authors, / By Thomas Newton, D. D. / Volume the First. [Portrait of Milton] / Dublin: / Printed for John Exshaw, at the Bible in Dame-Street. / MDCCLIV. [Two-volume set] Hayman's design is in reverse. Lower left corner below engraving: J. Dixon Sculp. Upper right corner above engraving: Vol: I. P. 3.

1760. Paradise Regain'd. / A / Poem, / In / Four Books. / To which is added / Samson Agonistes: / And / Poems upon Several Occasions. / The Author / John Milton. / The Third Edition, / With Notes of various Authors, / By Thomas Newton, D. D. / Volume the First. / London: Printed for C. Hitch and L. Hawes [etc.]. / MDCCLX. [Two-volume set] The design is engraved by Grignion.

1761. The / Poetical / Works / Of / John Milton. / With Notes of various Authors, / By Thomas Newton, D. D. / In Three Volumes. / Volume The Third. / London: / Printed for J. and R. Tonson in the Strand. / M DCC LXI. The design is engraved by Müller.

1766. Paradise Regain'd. / A / Poem, / In / Four Books. / To which is added / Samson Agonistes: / And / Poems upon Several Occasions. / The Author / John Milton. / With Notes of various Authors, / By Thomas Newton, D. D. / Volume the First. / London: Printed for J. and R. Tonson [etc.]. / MDCCLXVI. [Two-volume set] The design is engraved by Grignion.

1773. Paradise Regain'd. / A / Poem, / In / Four Books. / To which is added / Samson Agonistes: / And / Poems upon Several Occasions. / The Author / John Milton. / A New Edition, / With Notes of various Authors, / By Thomas Newton, D. D. / Now Lord Bishop of Bristol. / Volume the Second. / London: / Printed for J. Beecroft, W. Strahan [etc.]. / MDCCLXXIII. [Two-volume set] The design is engraved by Grignion.

1777. Paradise Regain'd. / A / Poem, / In / Four Books. / To Which Is Added / Samson Agonistes: / And / Poems upon Several Occasions. / The Author / John Milton. / A New Edition, / With Notes of various Authors, / By Thomas Newton, D. D. / Now Lord Bishop of Bristol. / London: / Printed for W. Strahan, J. F. and C. Rivington [etc.] / M DCC LXXVII. The design is engraved by Müller.

1785. Paradise Regain'd. / A / Poem, / In / Four Books. / To which is added / Samson Agonistes: / And / Poems upon Several Occasions. / The Author / John Milton. / A New Edition. / With Notes of various Authors, / By Thomas Newton, D. D. / Now Lord Bishop of Bristol. / Volume the First. / London: / Printed for W. Strahan, J. F. and C. Rivington [etc.] / MDCCLXXXV. [Two-volume set] The design is engraved by Grignion.

Note. The Houghton Library has a volume which carries on its spine the title *Drawings By Hogarth, Gravelot, Hayman, Wales & c.* and which contains five large drawings by Francis Hayman (nos. 55–59)— his illustrations to *Paradise Regained, L'Allegro* and *Il Penseroso, Samson Agonistes,* and *Comus* respectively (see Houghton Catalogue No. MS Typ 487). And see below, *Müller [or Miller]-Hayman Designs, 1756.*

Müller [or Miller]-Hayman Designs, 1756

JOHANN SEBASTIAN MÜLLER [OR MILLER] (ca. 1720–?). A German engraver, born at Nuremberg, Miller came to England with his brother where besides doing many engravings after Hayman he did several plates for Boydell. The conception for Miller's design clearly derives from Pigné's [Christ's Triumph over Satan] of which it is an inept and grotesque adaptation.

FRANCIS HAYMAN (1708–1776). See *Hayman's Designs, 1752.*

Miller's frontispiece first appeared with Hayman's illustration in: Paradise Regain'd. / A / Poem, / In / Four Books. / To which is added / Samson Agonistes; / And / Poems upon Several Occasions; / With a Tractate of Education. / The Author / John Milton. / London: / Printed for J. and R. Tonson; / And for C. Hitch [etc.]. / MDCCLVI.

Frontispiece: [Christ's Triumph over Satan]. Lower left corner under engraving: J. Miller del: et Sc:. See *PR* I.1–7, 150–160.

Illustration to Book I: [The First Temptation]. Upper left corner above engraving: N°. 2. Upper right corner: faceing pa: 1. Lower left corner below engraving: F. Hayman inv: et del:. Lower right corner: J. M. sc. See *PR* I.310–351.

Other appearances of the Miller-Hayman designs:

1760. Paradise Regain'd. / A / Poem, / In Four Books. / To which is added / Samson Agonistes; / And / Poems upon Several Occasions: / With a Tractate of Education. / The Author / John Milton. / London: / Printed for C. Hitch and L. Hawes [etc.]. / MDCCLX. Centered below signatures: Paradise Regain'd.

1765. Paradise Regain'd. / A / Poem, / In / Four Books. / To which is added / Samson Agonistes; / And / Poems upon Several Occasions: / With a Tractate of Education. / The Author / John Milton. / London: / Printed for J. and R. Tonson [etc.] / M DCC LXV.

1772. Paradise Regain'd. / A / Poem, / In / Four Books. / To which is added / Samson Agonistes; / And / Poems upon Several Occasions: / With a Tractate of Education. / The Author / John Milton. / London: / Printed for J. Beecroft, W. Strahan [etc.] / M DCC LXXII. This edition carries only Miller's frontispiece.

1785. Paradise Regain'd. / A / Poem, / In / Four Books. / To which is added / Samson Agonistes; / And / Poems upon Several Occasions: / With a Tractate of Education. / The Author / John Milton. / London: / Printed for W. Strahan, J. F. and C. Rivington [etc.] / M.DCC. LXXXV.

Anonymous Design, 1777

Designed anonymously, this illustration appears in: Paradise Regain'd. / A Poem. In Four Books. / Samson Agonistes. / A Dramatick Poem. / Comus. A Mask: / With / Poems on Several Occasions / And / A Tractate of Education. / The Author / John Milton. / London: / Sold by J. Banners, W. Slackman, F. Ren- / nington, W. Jones, & D. Newton. / MDCCLXXVII.

Illustration to Book I: [The First Temptation]. See *PR* I.310–351.

Anonymous Design, 1779

This unsigned illustration appears in: Paradise Regain'd. / A / Poem, / In / Four Books. / The Author / John Milton. / London: / Printed for Toplis and Bunney, in Holborn; / and J. Mozley, Gainsbrough. / M,DCC,LXXIX.

Frontispiece: [Christ's Triumph]. See *PR* I.1–7.

Another appearance of this anonymous design:

1786. Paradise Regain'd. / A / Poem, / In / Four Books. / The Author / John Milton. / London: / Printed For W. Osborne And J. Griffin, In / St. Paul's Church-Yard; And J. Mozley, / Gainsbrough. / MDCC. LXXXVI.

Malpas' Design, 1780

Malpas' frontispiece appeared in: The / Poetical / Works / Of / Mr. John Milton. / Vol. III. / London: / Printed for A. Millar, and J. Hodges. / MDCCLXXX. [Four-volume set]

Frontispiece: [Christ's Resurrection from the Tomb]. Upper right corner above engraving: N. 4. Lower right corner below engraving: Malpas del. et Sc. The following lines are printed under the illustration: ————————In his blest life / I see the path, & in his death, the price / And in his great ascent, the proof supreme / Of Immortality————And did he rise? / Hear O ye nations! hear it O ye dead! / He rose! He rose! He burst the bars of Death.

Westall's Designs, 1795

RICHARD WESTALL (1765–1836). An extremely popular illustrator, Westall attended the Royal Academy, where in 1792 he was elected an associate and in 1794 made an academician. Employed by Boydell to illustrate Milton and to paint five subjects for the Shakespeare Gallery, Westall also illustrated Crabbe, Moore, and Gray and in 1808 published a volume of poems, *A Day in Spring*, accompanied by plates engraved after his own designs. Westall's four illustrations to *Paradise Regained*, one to each book of the poem, were engraved by Moses Haughton,

Benjamin Smith, and William S. Leney. They appeared in: The /
Poetical Works / Of / John Milton. / With / A Life Of The Author, /
By / William Hayley. / Vol. II. / London: / Printed By W. Bulmer And
Co. / Shakspeare Printing-Office, / For John And Josiah Boydell, And
George Nicol; / From the Types of W. Martin. / 1795. [Three-volume
set]

Illustration to Book I, opp. II, 217: [Jesus Hungering among the Wild
Beasts]. Lower left corner below engraving: R. Westall R. Adell. Lower
right corner: M. Haughton Sculp[.] Centered below signatures: Paradise Regain'd. Below title: B. 1. L. 310. Bottom of plate: Publish'd June
4. 1795, by J. & J. Boydell, & C. Nicol, Shakspeare Gallery, Pall-Mall;
& Nº. 90, Cheapside.

Illustration to Book II, opp. II, 229: [Mary Meditating]. Lower left
corner below engraving: R. Westall R. A. del^t. Lower right corner:
B. Smith Sculp^t. Centered below signatures: Paradise Regain'd. Below
title: B. 2. L. 66. Bottom of plate: same as above.

Illustration to Book III, opp. II, 250: [Jesus Rejecting the Temptation
to Glory]. Lower left corner below engraving: R. Westall R. A. del.
Lower right corner: W. Leney Sculp. Centered below signatures:
Paradise Regain'd. Below title: B. 3. L. 106. Bottom of plate: same as
above, but no comma between "90" and "Cheapside."

Illustration to Book IV, opp. II, 283: [The Temptation on the Pinnacle].
Lower left corner below engraving: R. Westall R. A. del^t. Lower right
corner: B. Smith Sculp^t. Centered below signatures: Paradise Regain'd.
Below title: B. 4. L. 560. Bottom of plate: same as line below illustrations to Books I and II.

Note. The New York Public Library has an extra-illustrated copy of
Hayley's edition in eight volumes; the sixth volume, copiously illus-
trated, carries *Paradise Regained* with the following title page: The /
Poetical Works / Of / John Milton. / With / A Life of the Author, /
By / William Hayley. / Vol. VI. / Paradise Regained. Books I.–IV. /
London: / Printed By W. Bulmer And Co. / Shakespeare Printing≈
Office, / For John and Josiah Boydell, And George Nicol; / From Types
of W. Martin. / 1794. Although this and the other seven volumes carry
the same date (1794), the edition was obviously put together during
the last half of the nineteenth century; for the *Paradise Lost* volumes
carry designs by Gustave Doré (1833–1883). Of the many designs used
to illustrate *Paradise Regained*, only those by Westall were done with

the poem in mind; the others are chiefly biblical illustrations which the compiler has set within the context of *Paradise Regained*. This extra-illustrated edition also conveniently assembles many of the illustrations to *Paradise Lost*, most notably the *very rare* ones by Thomas Stothard in both black and white and color. See below, *Westall's Designs, 1816*.

Anonymous Design, ca. 1795

This contemporary design, probably done about the time of publication, is on the fore-edge of: Paradise Regained, / A / Poem, / In / Four Books, / By / John Milton. / A New Edition, / With Notes Of Various Authors, / By Charles Dunster, M. A. / [Epigraph from Plato] / London: / Printed for T. Cadell, Jun. And W. Davies, (Successors To Mr. Cadell,) / In the Strand. / 1795. This fore-edge painting, somewhat faded though the coloring was probably not originally any more brilliant, appears on a presentation copy for Dr. W. Falconer from the editor. The copy is in the Lilly Library.

Fore-edge painting: [Great and Glorious Rome]. See *PR* IV.45.

Burney's Design, 1796

EDWARD FRANCIS BURNEY (1760–1848). Relative of Dr. Burney and friend of Sir Joshua Reynolds, Burney was born at Worcester and in 1780 exhibited three designs for *Evelina*. He is well known for a portrait of Fanny Burney engraved as a frontispiece for her works. Burney's frontispiece to *Paradise Regained* was engraved by James Fittler and first appeared in: Milton's / Paradise Regained; / With / Select Notes Subjoined: / To Which Is Added / A Complete Collection / Of His / Miscellaneous Poems, / Both / English and Latin. / London: / Printed by T. Bensley; / For T. Longman [etc.]. / 1796.

Frontispiece: [The Baptism of Jesus]. Centered above engraving: FRONTISPIECE. Lower left corner below engraving: E. F. Burney del. Lower right corner: J. Fittler sculp. Below signatures: Published 21 May 1796, for C. Dilly in the Poultry, & the rest of the Proprietors. See *PR* I.29–32, 280–282.

Note. Burney's frontispiece did not appear again until 1817.

Rosa's Design, 1800

SALVATORE ROSA (1615–1673). Born at Renella, Rosa, an impetuous youth, left home at the age of eighteen. The painter of many subjects from classical mythology and the Bible, Rosa was commissioned to paint the portico and the loggia of the palace of Cardinal Brancaccia. However, it was his painting *Prometheus* that brought him his greatest reputation as an artist. Engraved by Thomas Phillips, who is best known for his portraits—especially the one of Blake—Rosa's frontispiece is thought by Dunster to be a source for Milton's poem; says Dunster, "In the first scene of the Temptation, the poet [Milton] has availed himself of it" (p. iv). The frontispiece appears in: Paradise Regained / A Poem / By / John Milton, / with Notes of various Authors, / By / Charles Dunster, M. A. / [Title-page design] / London / Printed by Geo. Stafford, Crane Court Fleet Street; and Sold by R. H. Evans [etc.]. / [1800]

Frontispiece: [The First Temptation]. Lower left corner below engraving: S. Rosa Design^t. Lower right corner: T. Phillips fecit. See *PR* I.310–351.

Rigaud's Designs, 1801

STEPHEN FRANCIS D. RIGAUD (1777–1861). An English watercolor painter, Rigaud attended the Royal Academy, where his work was first exhibited in 1797. Four years later, he received a gold medal for his *Clytemnestra and Agamemnon*. In 1804, Rigaud became an original member of the Water-Colour Society, exhibiting there until 1813 at which time he, Chalon, and a few others seceded. As late as 1851, Rigaud was showing his work at the Society of British Arts. Besides illustrating *Paradise Regained*, Rigaud did two illustrations to *Paradise Lost*: *Satan in the Bower of Adam and Eve* (1805) and *Sin and Death* (1807). The illustrations to *Paradise Regained*, one to each of the four books of Milton's poem, were engraved by William Bernard Cooke, Anker Smith, and James Stow. The designs appeared first in: The / Poetical Works / Of / John Milton, / From / The Text Of Dr. Newton: / With / A Critical Essay. / By J. Aikin, M. D. / Vol. III. / London: / Printed For J. Johnson, G. G. And J. Robinson [etc.] / By H. Baldwin and Son, New Bridge-street, Blackfriars. / 1801. [Four-volume set]

Illustration to Book I: [Jesus Meditating]. Upper right corner above engraving: Vol. 3 Page 13. [Carries *PR* I.224–246] Lower left corner below engraving: S. Rigaud del. Lower right corner: W. Cooke sculp. Centered below signatures: quotation of *PR* I.229–233. Below quotation: Paradise Regaind. Book I. Bottom of plate: Published Jany. 1st. 1801, by Cadell & Davies, Strand.

Illustration to Book II: [Jesus Walking Alone into the Desert]. Upper right corner above engraving: Vol. 3 Page 34. [Carries *PR* II.109–131] Lower left corner below engraving: S. Rigaud del^t. Lower right corner: Anker Smith sculp. Centered below signatures: quotation of *PR* II.109–114. Below quotation: Paradise Regaind. Book II. Bottom of plate: same as above, but no comma between "Davies" and "Strand."

Illustration to Book III: [Jesus Rejects the Temptation to Glory]. Upper right corner above engraving: Vol. 3 Page 59. [Carries *PR* III.131–153] Lower left corner below engraving: S. Rigaud del. Lower right corner: Stow sculp. Centered below signatures: Paradise Lost. Book III [.] Bottom of plate: same as above but *with* the comma.

Illustration to Book IV: [The Angels Receiving Jesus in the Air]. Upper right corner above engraving: Vol 3, Page 100. [Carries *PR* IV.568–590] Lower left corner below engraving: S. Rigaud del^t. Centered below the signature: quotation of *PR* IV.581–585. Below quotation: Paradise Regaind. Book IV. Bottom of plate: same as above.

Another appearance of Rigaud's designs:

1808. The / Poetical Works / Of / John Milton, / From The Text Of / The Rev. Henry John Todd, M. A. / With / A Critical Essay, / By J. Aikin, M. D. / Vol. III. / London: / Printed For J. Johnson, W. J. And J. Richardson [etc.]. / 1808. [Four-volume set]

Craig's Design, 1805

WILLIAM MARSHALL CRAIG (1788–1828). Having spent his early years in Manchester, Craig settled in London about 1791. Especially adept as a draughtsman on wood and as a book-illustrator, he exhibited his work at the Royal Academy and the British Institute. In 1821, his *Lectures on Drawing, Painting, and Engraving* were published. Craig's illustration to *Paradise Regained*, engraved by John Pye, appeared in: Poetical Works / Of / John Milton. / Paradise Lost * Paradise Regain'd / The Mask of Comus, / L'Allegro and Il Penseroso / [Portrait of Milton] / London. / Publish'd by W. Suttaby, Stationers Court, Ludgate Street; / and C. Corrall, Charing Cross. / 1805.

Illustration to Book I, opp. p. 3: [The Baptism]. Lower left corner below engraving: Craig del. Lower right corner: Pye sculp. Centered below signatures: Paradise Regained. Below this identification: *PR* I.79–83 is printed. Below that: Pub^d. by W. Suttaby Stationers Court. March 1, 1805.

Note. See below, *Craig's Designs, 1806*.

Anonymous Design, 1805

Though designed anonymously, this frontispiece was engraved by Samuel Harris (1783-1810), who is known primarily for his certificates, calling cards, and bookplates. The design first appeared in: The / Works / Of The / English Poets. / With / Prefaces, / Biographical and Critical. / By / Samuel Johnson, LL.D. / Re-edited, / With New Biographical And Critical Matter, / By J. Aikin, M. D. / Vol. XIII. / [Three volumes devoted to Milton: XII–XIV] / London: / Printed For J. Heath, Russel-Place, / Fitzroy-Square; / And G. Kearsley, Fleet-Street. / 1805.

Frontispiece: [Jesus Walking Alone into the Desert]. Lower right corner below engraving: S. Harris Sc. Below signature: Paradise Regain'd. Book II. 109.

Another appearance of this anonymous design:

1805. The / Poetical Works / of / John Milton, / from / The Text Of Dr. Newton: / with / A Critical Essay. / By J. Aikin, M. D. / Vol. II. / Charlestown: / Printed and Published / By S. Etheridge & C. Stebbins. / 1805. [Two-volume set]

Craig's Designs, 1806

WILLIAM MARSHALL CRAIG (1788–1828). See *Craig's Design, 1805*. These new illustrations by Craig, engraved by M. Macki[nville?], appeared in: Paradise Regain'd; / A Poem: / In Four Books. / To Which Is Added, / Samson Agonistes. / By John Milton. / A New Edition: /

With An Abridgment Of The Copious And Learned Notes / Collected
By / Bishop Newton. / Illustrated By Engravings. / Albion Press: /
Printed And Published / By James Cundee, Ivy-Lane, / Paternoster-
Row. / 1806. [Volume III of three-volume set] Illustrations in the other
volumes carry signatures that are barely legible. The first two illustrations to *Paradise Regained* look as if the names of the designer and engraver have been erased; however, there are no traces of signatures on
the third and fourth illustrations.

Frontispiece: [The First Temptation]. Arched over the illustration in
ornate lettering: Paradise Regained. Centered below title: Book. I.
Centered below illustration: quotation of *PR* I.342–343. Far right be-
low quotation: p. 19. [Carries *PR* I.338–358] Bottom of plate: Pub. by
James Cundee, Albion Press, London.
Illustration to Book II, opp. III, 26: [The Banquet Temptation]. Arched
over the illustration in ornate lettering: Paradise Regained. Centered
below title: Book. II. Centered below illustration: quotation of *PR*
II.368–370. Far right below quotation: p. 48. [Carries *PR* II.357–374]
Bottom of plate: Pub. by James Cundee, Albion Press, London.
Illustration to Book III, opp. III, 56: [Jesus on the Mountain with
Satan]. Arched over the illustration in ornate lettering: Paradise Re-
gained. Centered below title: Book. III. Centered below illustration:
quotation of *PR* III.265–266. Far right below quotation: p. 71. [Carries
PR III.254–269] Bottom of plate: Pub. by James Cundee, Albion Press,
London.
Illustration to Book IV, opp. III, 84: [The Angels Receiving Jesus in the
Air]. Arched over the illustration in ornate lettering: Paradise Re-
gained. Centered below title: Book.IV. Centered below illustration:
quotation of *PR* IV.581–584. Far right below quotation: p. 114. [Carries
PR IV.572–591] Bottom of plate: Pub. by James Cundee, Albion Press,
London.

Thurston's Design, 1806

JOHN THURSTON (1774–1822). Born at Scarborough, Thurston's principal employment was as a book illustrator. In 1806, he became an associate of the Water-Colour Society. Thurston's illustration to *Paradise
Regained*, engraved by Charles Heath, appeared first in: The / Poetical
Works / Of / John Milton. / With A / Preface, / Biographical And

Critical, / By / Samuel Johnson, LL. D. / Re-edited, / With New Biographical And Critical Matter, / By J. Aikin, M. D. / Vol. II. / London: / Printed For G. Kearsley, Fleet-Street. / 1806. [Three-volume set]

Illustration to Book I: [The First Temptation]. Upper left corner above engraving: Vol. II. p. 237. [Carries *PR* I.294–323] Lower left corner below engraving: Thurston del. Lower right corner: Heath sculp.

Another appearance of Thurston's design:

ca. 1806. The / Poetical Works / Of / John Milton. / In Three Volumes. / With A / Preface, Biographical and Critical, / By J. Aiken, M. D. / Vol. II. [London, ca. 1806] In this edition, the information around the engraving is the same as above; however, the illustration appears opposite p. 231 rather than p. 237. Centered below the illustration are the following lines from *Paradise Regained*: I.314–317.

Uwins' Design, 1811

THOMAS UWINS (1782–1857). Born in London, Uwins led a stunning career. At the age of twelve, he became a student at the Royal Academy. In 1809, he was elected an associate of the Water-Colour Society and in 1810 a full member. Three years later he became secretary to the Society, from which he resigned in 1818. Uwins went to Italy for seven years in 1824 but returned to England, whereupon he abandoned watercolor painting for oil. In 1833, he became an associate of the Royal Academy and five years later a full member. By 1844 he was appointed librarian of the Academy. The next year he became Surveyor of the Queen's Pictures and in 1847 Keeper of the National Gallery. Uwins' illustration to *Paradise Regained*, engraved by Richard Rhodes, appeared in: The / Poetical Works / of / John Milton. / [Title-page design] / London / Published by J. Walker, Paternoster Row, & J. Harris, / S^t. Paul's Church Yard. [London, 1811]

Title-page design: [The Nativity]. Lower left corner below engraving: T. Uwins del. Lower right corner: Rhodes sc. Centered below signatures: quotation of *PR* II.72–74. Below quotation: Paradise Regain'd. Book 2.

Westall's Design, 1816

RICHARD WESTALL (1765–1836). See *Westall's Designs, 1794–1797*. This new illustration was engraved by William Finden and appeared in: Paradise Regained / Etc. / The Author / John Milton. / [Title-page design] / London; / Printed for John Sharpe, Piccadilly, / 1816. [Volume II of three-volume set] Lower right corner of title page: Proofs. The Westall designs and new title page are bound in the 1859 Baskerville edition of *Paradise Regained*, etc.

Title-page design (a new title page to *PR* is inserted before the old Baskerville title page): [Jesus' Dream]. Below illustration: quotation of *PR* II.266–268. Below quotation: Line 267, Book 2. Below citation: Paradise Regained. Bottom of plate: Drawn By Richard Westall R. A. Engraved By William Finden; / Published By John Sharpe, Piccadilly. / Aug. 24. 1816.

Note. Westall's design appeared again in 1817 and often thereafter.

Designs by Fuseli, Romney, Flaxman, and Stothard

Besides the aforementioned illustrations to *Paradise Regained*, all of which appeared in editions of the poem, four artists known to Blake made designs for Milton's brief epic. Sometime between May, 1794, and August, 1796, Henry Fuseli painted for his Milton Gallery [The Temptation on the Pinnacle, *PR* IV.549–560]. The design is now lost, but see Gert Schiff, *Johann Heinrich Füsslis Milton-Galerie* (Zurich and Stuttgart, 1963), p. 152; John Knowles, *The Life and Writings of Henry Fuseli, Esq.* (3 vols.; London, 1831), I, 204; and Paul Ganz, *The Drawings of Henry Fuseli*, trans. F. B. Aikin-Sneath (New York, 1949), p. 35. Inspired by a suggestion from William Hayley, George Romney began in 1795, but never completed, a depiction of Christ's ugly dream [The Temptation of Christ, *PR* IV.422–425]. This design is also lost, but see William Hayley, *The Life of George Romney, Esq.* (Chichester, 1809), pp. 229–230; John Romney, *Memoirs of the Life and Works of George Romney . . .* (London, 1830), p. 245; and Humphrey Ward and W. Roberts, *Romney: A Biographical and Critical Essay with a Catalogue Raisonné of His Works* (2 vols.; London and New York, 1904), II, 197. John Flaxman's design [Christ's Triumph, *PR* I.1–7] was done about 1802 and published as part of a frontispiece design in William Cowper's *Latin and Italian Poems of Milton* . . . (London, 1808). The original design is in the Henry E. Huntington Art Gallery. Thomas Stothard, whom Blake accused of stealing his idea for the Canterbury Pilgrims, also illustrated Jesus standing on the pinnacle, a design that may have been completed before 1816 but which made its first appearance in an edition of *Paradise Lost* and *Paradise Regained* published by Tegg in 1823. See A. C. Coxhead, *Thomas Stothard, R.A.: An Illustrated Monograph* (London, 1906).

Blake's Designs, ca. 1816

WILLIAM BLAKE (1757–1827). See this volume, pp. 93–132.

Illustration to Book I, ll. 29–39: [The Baptism of Jesus].

Illustration to Book I, ll. 337–345: [The First Temptation].

Illustration to Book II, ll. 18–24: [Andrew and Simon Peter].

Illustration to Book II, ll. 60–65: [Mary Watched by Two Angels].

Illustration to Book II, ll. 115–120: [Satan in Council].

Illustration to Book II, ll. 337–367: [The Banquet Temptation].

Illustration to Book III, ll. 251–266: [The Second Temptation].

Illustration to Book IV, ll. 401–425: [The Tempter Inspiring Jesus' Ugly Dreams].

Illustration to Book IV, ll. 426–438: [Morning Chasing Away the Spectres of the Night].

Illustration to Book IV, ll. 541–561: [The Third Temptation].

Illustration to Book IV, ll. 581–585: [Jesus Ministered to by Angels].

Illustration to Book IV, ll. 636–639: [Jesus Returning to Mary].

Note. Blake's illustrations to *Paradise Regained* are reproduced in this volume between pp. 102 and 103.

SUBJECTS ILLUSTRATED

Book I

ll. 1–7, 150–155: [Christ's Triumph over Satan, Sin, and Death]. Pigné, Miller, anon. (1779), Malpas, Flaxman.

Note. In *Paradise Regained*, Milton underplays the Passion, Crucifixion, and Resurrection of Christ; Pigné, Miller, and Malpas bring these events into focus. Flaxman's design, though it depicts a female figure rather than Christ himself, is a variation on the subject of Christ's Triumph: the female figure has subdued the serpent.

ll. 29–32: [The Baptism of Jesus]. Pigné, Chéron, Burney, Craig, BLAKE.

ll. 229–233: [Jesus Meditating]. Rigaud.

ll. 238–254: [The Nativity]. Chéron, Uwins.

ll. 310–351: [The First Temptation]. Chéron, Hayman, anon. 1777, Westall, Rosa, Craig, Thurston, BLAKE.

ll. 497–502: [Jesus Departing from Satan]. Chéron.

Book II

[Satan Bearing the Fruits of the Earth]. Chéron.

ll. 6–24: [Andrew and Simon Peter]. BLAKE.

ll. 60–66: [Mary Meditating]. Westall, BLAKE.

ll. 96–101: [Jesus in the Temple]. Pigné.

ll. 109–114: [Jesus Walking Alone into the Desert]. Rigaud, anon. (1805).

ll. 115–145: [Satan in Council]. BLAKE.

ll. 263–265: [Jesus' Dream]. Westall.

ll. 338–367: [The Banquet Temptation]. Chéron, Craig, BLAKE.

ll. 426–486: [The Temptation to Wealth and Riches]. Chéron.

Book III

[Crowns, Sceptres, and Gold]. Chéron.

ll. 1–250: [Jesus Discoursing with Satan]. Pigné.

ll. 106–149: [Jesus Rejecting the Temptation to Glory]. Westall, Rigaud.

ll. 251–266: [Jesus on the Mountain with Satan]. Craig.

ll. 302–346: [The Temptation of Parthia]. Chéron.

ll. 302–IV.393: [The Second Temptation]. BLAKE.

Book IV

[Crown of Thorns]. Chéron.

ll. 44–108: [Temptation of Rome]. Chéron, anon. (1795).

ll. 401–425: [The Tempter Inspiring Jesus' Ugly Dreams]. Chéron, Romney, BLAKE.

ll. 426–431: [Morning Chasing Away the Spectres of the Night]. BLAKE.

ll. 561–562: [The Temptation on the Pinnacle]. Chéron, Westall, Stothard, Fuseli, BLAKE.

ll. 581–585: [Jesus Ministered to by Angels]. Pigné, Rigaud, Craig, BLAKE.

ll. 638–639: [Jesus Returning to Mary]. BLAKE.

A Catalogue of Blake's Illustrations to Milton

The only previous attempt to catalogue Blake's illustrations to Milton's poems was made by Thomas Wright in *The Life of William Blake* (Olney, 1929), II, 167–170. That catalogue, though useful, requires both correction and expansion. In it Wright distinguishes ten groups of illustrations: the various sets of illustrations to Milton's poems, plus "Early Designs" and "Separate Designs." In this new catalogue, I have reduced the number of groupings to three: Engravings After Others' Designs, Separate Designs, and Sets of Designs. The main problem one confronts in preparing such a list is that Blake, besides illustrating Milton, illustrated the Bible. Many of those designs, however, are as involved with Milton's poetry as with scriptural text. A case in point is "The Third Temptation," a design that Keynes reproduces as one of Blake's illustrations to the Bible and associates with Matthew 4:11. But whereas Matthew says only that "the devil leaveth him," Milton says that "Satan smitten with amazement fell" (*PR* IV.562). Clearly Blake has Milton's passage in mind and perhaps even Westall's design to Book IV (see Appendix A). But even if such considerations make a definitive catalogue impossible, the list that follows at least suggests more completely than any existing source the number and variety of subjects Blake derived from Milton. It provides yet another piece of evidence to support the view that no poet exerted a greater influence on Blake's art—an influence that extended over Blake's entire career as poet and painter. (Since my completion of this catalogue, Marcia Pointon has published one as Appendix E to *Milton & English Art* [Manchester, 1970], pp. 261–263. Where I have missed an item, I have included a reference to Pointon's catalogue. Even so, my own catalogue contains a *significant* amount of material not included in Pointon's.)

The sets of designs for Milton's poems are available in the following sources: *Illustrations of Milton's Comus*, reproduced by William Griggs (London: Bernard Quaritch, 1890)—the Boston set in color; *On the Morning of Christ's Nativity*: *Milton's Hymn with Illustrations by William Blake and a Note by Geoffrey Keynes* (Cambridge: At the University Press, 1923)—the Whitworth set; Darrell Figgis, *The Paintings of William Blake* (London: Ernest Benn, Limited, 1925)—the Boston set of illustrations to *Paradise Lost* and the illustrations to *Paradise Regained*, nos. 2, 8, and 11 in color; *Twenty-seven Drawings by William Blake; Being Illustrations for Paradise Lost, Comus and the Bible* (McPherson, Kans.: C. J. Smolley, [ca. 1925])—the Boston sets of illustrations for *Paradise Lost* and *Comus*; *John Milton, Poems in English with Illustrations by William Blake* (2 vols.; London: Nonesuch Press, 1926)—Vol. 1: the Huntington sets of illustrations for the *Nativity Ode* and *Comus*, the illustrations to *L'Allegro, Il Penseroso*, and *Paradise Regained*; Vol. II: fifteen subjects from *Paradise Lost*, including the Boston set; *Comus: A Mask by John Milton* (London: Julian Edition, 1926)—the Boston set; *An Exhibition of William Blake's Watercolor Drawings of Milton's "Paradise Lost," May 12–July 31, 1936* (San Marino, Calif., [ca. 1936])—the Huntington set; *Catalogue of William Blake's Drawings and Paintings in the Huntington Library*, comp. C. H. Collins Baker (San Marino, Calif., 1938)—the Huntington sets of illustrations to *Paradise Lost*, the *Nativity Ode*, and *Comus*; *Paradise Lost by John Milton, with the Illustrations by William Blake* (New York: Heritage Press, 1940)—the Boston set in color; [John Milton], *Paradise Lost* (New York and London: Studio Publications, 1947)— the Boston set in color; Adrian Van Sinderen, *Blake The Mystic Genius* (Syracuse: Syracuse University Press, 1949)—illustrations to *L'Allegro* and *Il Penseroso* in color; *John Milton, L'Allegro and Il Penseroso, with the Paintings by William Blake, Together with a Note upon the Poems by W. P. Trent* (New York, Heritage Press, 1954)—illustrations to *L'Allegro* and *Il Penseroso*; *Catalogue of William Blake's Drawings and Paintings in the Huntington Library*, comp. C. H. Collins Baker, rev. R. R. Wark (San Marino, Calif., 1957)—the Huntington sets of illustrations to *Paradise Lost*, the *Nativity Ode*, and *Comus*; *William Blake, Water-Color Designs*, comp. Helen D. Willard (Boston, 1957)— the Boston sets of illustrations to *Paradise Lost* and *Comus*; *Hartford*

Studies in Literature, II (1970), 41–52—illustrations to *L'Allegro* and *Il Penseroso* and to *Paradise Lost* (the Huntington set). Blake's engravings after others' designs and his separate illustrations have been reproduced less frequently, but the most important sources for them are indicated with each entry in Parts I and II below.

In this catalogue, I have used the following abbreviations:

BI   *William Blake's Illustrations to the Bible*, comp. Geoffrey Keynes (London: Trianon Press, 1957).

Binyon   Laurence Binyon, *The Drawings and Engravings of William Blake* (London, 1927).

Blake   *Blake (1757-1827)*, comp. Geoffrey Keynes (London: Faber Gallery, 1946).

Butlin   *William Blake (1757-1827): A Catalogue of the Works of William Blake in the Tate Gallery*, comp. Martin Butlin (London, 1957).

CB&W   *Catalogue of William Blake's Drawings and Paintings in the Huntington Library*, comp. C. H. Collins Baker, rev. R. R. Wark (San Marino, Calif., 1957).

Figgis   Darrell Figgis, *The Paintings of William Blake* (London, 1925).

Gilchrist   Alexander Gilchrist, *Life of William Blake With Selections From His Poems And Other Writings*, 2nd ed. (2 vols.; London, 1880).

KE   *Engravings by William Blake, the Separate Plates, A Catalogue Raisonée*, comp. Geoffrey Keynes (Dublin, 1956).

Keynes   *The Complete Writings of William Blake with Variant Readings*, ed. Geoffrey Keynes (London, 1966).

PD¹   *Pencil Drawings by William Blake*, ed. Geoffrey Keynes (London: Nonesuch Press, 1927).

PD²   *Blake's Pencil Drawings, Second Series*, ed. Geoffrey Keynes (London: Nonesuch Press, 1956).

RM   *The Notebook of William Blake Called the Rossetti Manuscript*, ed. Geoffrey Keynes (London: Nonesuch Press, 1935).

Russell   A. G. B. Russell, *The Engravings of William Blake*
(London, 1912).

I: *Engravings After Others' Designs*

ca. 1779.   Stothard's Satan.
See Russell, pp. 142–143, no. 52.

ca. 1790.   Fuseli's Head of Satan.
See Russell, p. 155, and KE, p. 76, plate 42.

II: *Separate Designs*

ca. 1788.   God Creating the Universe (pencil).
See PD², plate 34.

early 1790's.   The House of Death (drawing).
See Butlin, no. 19, plate 8.

ca. 1793.   Adam Lying Prostrate.
See RM, p. 27.

Figures Dancing in the Air (*Comus*).
See RM, p. 30.

A Woman Holding a Child (*On the Death of a Fair
Infant*).
See RM, p. 73.

Satan's Mighty Stature.
See RM, p. 91.

Satan Exulting over Eve.
See RM, p. 112, and PD¹, plate 18.

Note. Other pencil drawings done by Blake about
this time are listed among the variants to the *Paradise Lost* illustrations. See below.

1794.   The Ancient of Days (relief etching).
See Russell, pp. 70–71, and KE, pp. 25–27, plate 16.

Note. There are numerous examples of this design,
which was done separately (six copies) and as a
frontispiece to Blake's *Europe* (fifteen copies, three
of them in proof state). The most famous and per-

haps the finest is the one Blake painted on his death-
bed for Tatham. A copy of the design, now in the
British Museum, is said by Basil De Selincourt to
carry lines 225–231 from Book VII of *PL* written
by "Blake himself" (*William Blake* [London and
New York, 1909], p. 206). But Binyon later corrects
him, saying that the British Museum copy carries
the lines from *PL*, but they are written "not by
Blake himself but possibly . . . by Tatham" (p. 107).

1795.	The House of Death (color print).

See Binyon, plate 31; Figgis, plate 26; Blake, plate
5; and Butlin, no. 20, plate 9.

Note. Rossetti says he has seen only two copies
(Gilchrist, II, 209), but Keynes knows of four copies
(see Blake, plate 5).

Satan Exulting over Eve (color print).
See Binyon, plate 38; Figgis, plate 26; and BI,
plate 9a.

ca. 1796.	The Warring Angels (pencil).

See PD[1], plate 32; and for a related version, dated
ca. 1810, see Keynes, *Drawings of William Blake:
92 Pencil Studies* (New York, 1970), plate 52.

1799–1800.	The Nativity (tempera).

See Binyon, plate 14, and BI, plate 91. Compare to
"The Descent of Peace" (*Nativity Ode* illustration). See below.

The Baptism of Christ (tempera).
See BI, plates 109a and 109b. Compare to "The
Baptism of Christ" (*Paradise Regained* illustra-
tion). See below.

1800.	Head of Milton (tempera).

See Thomas Wright, *The Heads of the Poets*
(Olney, 1925), plate [12].

Note. Blake writes to Hayley that he is "absorbed
by the poets Milton, Homer, Camoens, Ercilla,
Ariosto, and Spenser" (Keynes, p. 806 and n. 2).

ca. 1800.	Christ with a Bow, Trampling upon Satan (color print and sepia drawing). See Russell, p. 118; KE, pp. 34–35, plates 20 and 21; and BI, plate 169. *Note.* Russell suggests that the design is for *PL* VI.763; Keynes, on the other hand, argues that this citation is not relevant to Blake's design. His conclusion is that the design is for the Book of Revelation rather than for Milton's poem. What Keynes' conclusion ignores is that Blake's illustrations are not always literal renderings of a single passage. Often Blake's designs conflate passages and thereby punctuate the typological significance of a scene. Thus certain details of the design suggest Book VI, but in subject the design looks forward to the final books of *PL*; see esp. X.181, 191, 498, 1031; XI.155; XII.149, 233, 383, 385, 391, 430, 433.
ca. 1800–1805.	Satan in His Original Glory (watercolor). See Butlin, no. 29, plate 18, and BI, plate 82. The Third Temptation (watercolor). See Binyon, plate 75, and BI, plate 110. Compare to "The Second Temptation" and "The Third Temptation" (*Paradise Regained* illustrations). See below.
1804–1808.	The Spiritual Form of Milton. See the Trianon ed. of Blake's *Milton*, esp. plates 1, 16, and 18.
ca. 1805.	Michael and Satan (watercolor). See Figgis, plate 10. Adam and Eve (pencil and watercolor). See PD², plate 13, and BI, no. 7. *Note.* Other designs completed by Blake about this time are listed as variants to the illustrations to *Paradise Lost.* See below.
n. d.	Death Shaking the Dart. See Gilchrist, II, 268.

Death (pencil).

See Gilchrist, II, 276.

Satan.

Gilchrist, II, 263.

Note. See also Wright, II, 170, Group 10, nos. 2, 4, 9, 11, 15.

III: Sets of Designs

1801.

Eight Illustrations to *Comus* now in the Henry E. Huntington Library and Art Gallery.

Comus with His Revellers

Comus Disguised

The Brothers Plucking Grapes

The Two Brothers in the Wood

Comus with the Lady Spellbound

The Brothers Driving Out Comus

Sabrina Disenchanting the Lady

The Lady Restored to Her Parents

Note. See Blake's letter to Flaxman, dated October 19, 1801, in Keynes, p. 810.

1805–1810.

Eight Illustrations to *Comus* now in the Museum of Fine Arts, Boston.

The subjects are the same as those in the Huntington set. See above.

1807.

Twelve Illustrations to *Paradise Lost*, and one variant, now in the Henry E. Huntington Library and Art Gallery.

Satan Calling His Legions. (CB&W list three related versions.)

Satan Comes to the Gates of Hell. (CB&W list one variant, the Huntington has another. For a related pencil drawing, see PD^2, plate 14.)

Christ Offers to Redeem Man. (CB&W list the Boston version and two related pencil drawings.)

Satan's and Raphael's Entries into Paradise.

Satan Watches Adam and Eve. (CB&W list the Boston and Melbourne versions, one variant, and two related pencil drawings.)

Raphael Warns Adam and Eve. (CB&W list the Boston version.)

Rout of the Rebel Angels. (CB&W list the Boston version and one variant design but not the related pencil drawing; see Butlin, no. 77, plate 20.)

Creation of Eve. (CB&W list the Boston and Melbourne versions, as well as one related design and one pencil sketch.)

Temptation and Fall of Eve. (CB&W list the Boston version, two related designs, and a pencil sketch.)

Judgment of Adam and Eve. (CB&W do not list a related design, which is in the Director's Office at the Houghton Library, Harvard University.)

Michael Foretells the Crucifixion. (CB&W list the Boston version and the one in the Fitzwilliam Museum previously in the collection of Mrs. J. H. Riches.)

The Expulsion. (CB&W list the Boston version; for another version, see Keynes, *Drawings of William Blake: 92 Pencil Studies* [New York, 1970], plate 45.)

Note. Blake describes the first design in this series as an "experiment Picture"; see Keynes, p. 582. For designs related to Illustrations 6, 7, and 10, but not noted by CB&W, see Marcia Pointon, *Milton & English Art* (Manchester, 1970), pp. 262–263.

1808.

Nine Illustrations to *Paradise Lost* now in the Museum of Fine Arts, Boston.

Christ Offers to Redeem Man.
Satan Watching Adam and Eve.
Adam and Eve Sleeping. (a new subject)
Raphael Warns Adam and Eve.
Rout of the Rebel Angels.

The Creation of Eve.
Temptation and Fall of Eve.
Michael Foretells the Crucifixion.
The Expulsion from Eden.

Note. For a drawing related to the third illustration
in the set, see Marcia Pointon, *Milton & English Art*
(Manchester, 1970), p. 262.

1809.　　Two Sets of Six Illustrations to the *Nativity Ode*,
one in the Whitworth Institute Gallery, Manches-
ter, the other in the Henry E. Huntington Library
and Art Gallery.
The Descent of Peace.
The Night of Peace.
Shepherds and the Heavenly Choir.
The Old Dragon Underground.
The Overthrow of Apollo.
The Flight of Moloch.

Note. See Blake's letter to Butts, dated July 6, 1803,
in Keynes, pp. 823–824.

1816.　　Twelve Illustrations to *L'Allegro* and *Il Penseroso*
now in the Pierpont Morgan Library.
Mirth and Her Companions.
Night Startled by the Lark.
The Great Sun.
The Sunshine Holiday.
The Stories of Corydon and Thyrsis.
The Young Poet's Dream.
Melancholy and Her Companions.
Milton's Vision of the Moon.
Milton and the Spirit of Plato.
Milton Led by Melancholy.
Milton's Dream.
The Peaceful Hermitage.

Note. For Blake's descriptions of these illustrations,
see Keynes, pp. 617–619. For related versions of the
first design, see Binyon, plate 86; KE, pp. 53–55,
plates 35 and 36; Russell, no. 27, plate 14; and PD²,
plate 19.

ca. 1816.   Twelve Illustrations to *Paradise Regained* now in
                   the Fitzwilliam Museum, Cambridge.

                   The Baptism of Jesus.
                   The First Temptation.
                   Andrew and Simon Peter.
                   Mary Watched by Two Angels.
                   Satan in Council.
                   The Banquet Temptation.
                   The Second Temptation.
                   The Tempter Inspiring Jesus' Ugly Dreams.
                   Morning Chasing Away the Spectres of the Night.
                   The Third Temptation.
                   Jesus Ministered to by Angels.
                   Jesus Returning to Mary.

                   Note. Blake's illustrations to *Paradise Regained* are
                   reproduced in this volume between pp. 102 and 103.
                   The fact that Blake knew about and may even have
                   seen Romney's depiction of Christ's ugly dream (see
                   Keynes, p. 831) suggests a possible source for
                   Blake's design, though since the illustration by Rom-
                   ney is lost no definite comparisons can be made.
                   Hayley takes credit for providing Romney with the
                   idea for the design (see *The Life of George Romney,
                   Esq.* [Chichester, 1809], p. 230), which is described
                   by John Romney in *Memoirs of the Life and Works
                   of George Romney* (London, 1830). According to
                   John Romney, if the design had ever been complete-
                   ly finished, it would have ranked his father with
                   Michelangelo: "It was equal in original conception
                   and wild fancy to any thing ever produced by any
                   artist. When one looked at Christ, silent passiveness
                   was the idea which presented itself to the Specta-
                   tor; when at the fiends that assailed him, vociferat-
                   ing noise and boisterous insult. These visionary
                   beings were the human passions and appetites per-
                   sonified. To aid the malevolent purpose, the illusive
                   representations, or ghosts of Eve and Noah, were
                   called forth. And the arch-fiend, the Miltonic satan,
                   grand as the human mind can conceive him, viewed

from the upper corner of the picture, with malignant satisfaction, the ready obedience of his imps" (p. 245). The head of Christ from Romney's design is reproduced in Hayley's *Life*, opp. p. 231, and there are a number of examples of Romney's Satan in the Folger Library and in the Fitzwilliam Museum.

The First Temptation.

Note. Catalogued by Rossetti as "Christian beset by Demons . . . ," this design is "mistakenly included" in the series of illustrations to Bunyan's *Pilgrim's Progress* now in the Frick Museum, New York. In *Blake Studies* (London, 1949), Geoffrey Keynes observes that "the supposed figure of Christian exactly resembles Blake's representation of Christ Himself in other designs. The naked apparition raising a stone from the ground is clearly Satan, and the whole scene undoubtedly depicts The First Temptation, with the Spirits of Hunger crowded about Satan's feet. It is, in fact, a rejected design for *Paradise Regained*—rejected because another quite different version which agreed more closely with the text was eventually included in that series" (p. 184). This illustration, marked as no. XXIX and discussed on pp. xxviii and xxxi, is reproduced on p. xxix of the Limited Editions Club edition of *Pilgrim's Progress* (New York, 1941); it is also on different paper from those in the Bunyan series.

See also *Separate Designs*: The Baptism of Christ, The Third Temptation.

1822.   Three Illustrations to *Paradise Lost* from an unfinished set.
  The Creation of Eve. (National Gallery, Melbourne)
  Satan Watching the Endearments of Adam and Eve. (National Gallery, Melbourne)
  Michael Foretelling the Crucifixion. (Fitzwilliam Museum)

Note. Though these designs resemble the corresponding subjects in the Boston set, there are significant alterations in detail. See Gilchrist, II, 223. Anne T. Kostelanetz says there are two, not three, sets of illustrations to *Paradise Lost* (see "Review: Romantic Art in Britain," *Blake Newsletter*, II [1968], 5); but Martin Butlin properly corrects her, reminding us that Blake began a third set for Linnell but never finished it (see "Note," *Blake Newsletter*, II [1968], 34).

FEB 29 '72

LAKE ARAL

Sogdiana

SCYTHIA

Bactriana

MARGIANA

Baetra

Parthia

Artaxata

Araxas R.

Abus M.

ATROPATIA

R. Gozan

Habor

Caucasus

Heeatompylos

Ecbatana

Ariana

HYRCANIA

CANDAOR

ARACHOSIA

I

A

M E D I A

P E R S I A

Seleucia
Ctesiphon

Susa

Choaspes R.

Susiana

Persepolis

Balsara
Teredon

Persian Gulph or Bay
Balsaras haven

Drouth
or Desert

A R A B I A

S

Indus R.

I

N

D

A R A B I A N   G U L F

65°   70°   75°   80°   85°